American Boarding Schools

Directory of U.S. Boarding Schools
for International Students

Edited by
Celeste Heiter

Published by ThingsAsian Press   www.thingsasian.com

American Boarding Schools
Edited by Celeste Heiter

ThingsAsian Press
3230 Scott Street
San Francisco, California 94123 USA
info@thingsasian.com

Cover photo used with permission of Phillips Academy Andover.

Printed in Hong Kong.

ISBN 0-9715940-4-X

This book is dedicated to the teacher in all of us.

Acknowledgements

For their special contributions to American Boarding Schools, the publisher and editor would like to thank Leo Marshall, Director of Admissions, The Webb School; Rist Bonnefond, Headmaster, Kents Hill School; J. William LaBelle, The Winchendon School; Aimee Gruber Bellemore; Leigh Hallett, Maine Central Institute; Dawn Skilbred, Chatham Hall's International Student Coordinator; Stewart Miller, Assistant Director, The Greenwood School, Putney, Vermont; Joshua D. Clark, Admissions & Financial Aid, Gould Academy; Shuochieh Lee, Subiaco Academy; Noah Brenner, Crested Butte Academy; Brandon Reid, Crested Butte Academy; Duncan Tonatiuh Smith Hernández, Buxton School; Abdulla Bucheeri, Tabor Academy; Max May, Tabor Academy; Robynn Yip, Tabor Academy; and Gordon Kim, Subiaco Academy.

Contents

Getting In

Common sense advice and good research can enhance an international student's admission opportunities at a boarding school.

By Leo Marshall

Every year, U.S. and Canadian boarding schools enjoy an enormous number of requests for applications from international students, particularly from Asia.   No doubt, it is the remarkable diversity of our student bodies; wonderful array of academic and co-curricular opportunities; and exceptional college placement record that attracts the overseas candidates.   While we value beyond measure the international students we admit, I have become increasingly concerned for these families. In short, many just do not understand how the admission process works or how to find a school that may be suitable for their child. Many are simply receiving poor advice from family friends and consultants. Thus, these families are hopelessly at a disadvantage when applying to our schools, particularly the most selective schools.

A few hints from an old timer in this business might help:

Don't play the "numbers" game.

During a recent interview of an international candidate, I noted that her list of preferred schools included virtually every one of the most selective schools in the U.S. It was apparent to us that she did not know our institutions but, instead, was simply shopping for a placement in a school that her family thought would provide the ticket to the best university. In a similar case, after we expressed our concern that the candidate in question was not competent in English, her father's response was, "No problem. She's independent. How many Ivy League schools do your graduates attend?" Neither candidate was admitted.

Regardless of the relative strength of our college placement record, we are all completely different. If we were not there would be no reason for our individual institutions to exist. Our schools are looking for students who are a right match for the school, not those who see us as simply a way-station to college. In fact, admission to a university or college is the by-product of a student being well-matched at his or her boarding school.

For our part, we are all looking for students who are going to contribute significantly to the school community; students who want to take intellectual risk; students who will brighten the classroom and dormitories with their personality. We want students who will appear on stage, play in the orchestra, or participate in athletics. That requires us only to consider those applicants, regardless of nationality, who truly understand our individual missions and have demonstrated talents and strength of character that will make us a better school.

When choosing an educational consultant, choose carefully.

During the fall, my office is inundated with requests from a myriad of international consulting firms requesting information from our school or touting one of their candidates. Few seem to know anything about our school except that we have a strong academic reputation. In one major Asian city where U.S. boarding schools yearly host a large fair, one local organization stands outside the convention hall handing out flyers that imply in order for a family to apply to our schools, they must use that firm 's services. Nothing is farther from the truth.

Before selecting a consultant, the candidate's family should be clear about their expectations and the firm should be clear about what they will offer. No firm can guarantee admission to our schools. No firm can guarantee a winning SSAT or TOEFL score. There are reputable firms with whom some of us will enter into contractual agreements but they are few and far between. Since most of us have far more applications from countries like Korea and Taiwan, we are unlikely to enter into any agreements with firms in those countries.

Instead, we prefer to work with consultants with whom we have developed a relationship and who know our schools intimately. One measure for selecting such firms is to determine if they are associated with such organizations as the Secondary Schools Admission Test Board (SSATB) or the Independent Educational Consultants Association (IECA). Both organizations have specific requirements for membership and it is often at those organizations' national conferences where we admission officers meet consultants. Certainly, the international consultant who visits our schools; tours our campus; and meets with the director of admission will have an advantage when recommending candidates. Conversely, introducing the firm via email or letter, increasingly common, virtually gets no attention.

While there is more to admissions than a test, test results do matter when we are trying to assess students where English is their second language.

We are all looking for students who will contribute significantly to our schools. We all need the musician, the artist, the athlete, the academically talented and the leader. However, our international students must have a strong foundation in the English language to compete in the classroom. For those of us who do not offer English as a Second Language (ESL), it is important that students have admission test scores that predict relative success in our classrooms. Without sufficient training in English, no amount of test preparation is going to make a dramatic difference in their test scores. No one should be encouraged to take the entrance exam three or four times in the same year in the hope that scores will improve significantly. In fact, a red flag goes up in our office when we see students taking the test repeatedly. A low verbal and reading score in the Secondary

Schools Admission Test (SSAT), the preferred admission test for most of us who do not offer ESL, will not improve significantly within one year.

Therefore, students should be realistic when applying to a boarding school and taking the time to carefully research a school will increase the applicant's chance of finding the right match. Most of us list our minimum requirements for the admission of international students in our admission literature and on our websites. Some of us will accept the Test of English as a Foreign Language (TOEFL) but most will require the SSAT, in addition to the TOEFL. Such tests tell us that the student matches relative to students who have gone before him or her. Of course, grades in school and recommendations matter but if we have limited knowledge of the rigor or breadth of the program at an international school, we then tend to lean heavily on the test scores. While I personally do not like to suggest a minimum score, it is fair to say that I have an idea what scores clearly do not predict success at my school and as an admission director I am happy to review test results with an applicant's family before they apply.

Here are a few other quick tips:

All families should expect courtesy, clear communication, and specific details about costs and services. The good boarding school admission office understands that this is all about children and their parents' aspirations for their future. Therefore, our schools must treat every applicant as if they are the only child in the pool and the family must receive the appropriate guidance from that office to make the right choice.

Having a friend of a friend call us for an application when that person has no information about the candidate is not going to advance a student's chances. Such inquirers should have all the information, i.e. name, address, current school, grade applying for, phone number/email and entry year. We always prefer to talk with the candidate's parents directly, if possible.

These wonderful candidates are so motivated to apply to our schools that we often get a myriad of certificates of achievement, artwork, primary grade transcripts, and even CDs with PowerPoint presentations. While appreciated, unless they are recent and have real significance to the student's qualifications, we do not have time to review them in committee meetings and they will be eliminated from a student's file. Yes, the gifted musician should send a tape and it is always helpful if an athlete who has performed at an advanced level send us times, rankings, and lists of achievements from recent years. In short, tell us what is truly unique about the candidate and his or her accomplishments. When we have just a few seats for international students, it could make a huge difference.

Phone interviews do not work to a candidate's advantage under any circumstance. In a selective pool, these candidates are the last considered. Meeting a candidate face-to-face on campus will allow us to learn more about personality, sense of humor, special interests and interest in our school. In addition, it allows the student the opportunity to meet our students and see our campus. No one wants to be surprised on the first day of school. Campus interviews should be scheduled well in advance of the application deadline.

For international students, junior year (grade 11) is a very difficult year to enter our schools. That is not to say some schools won't consider such a candidate but most schools do not see this applicant as a priority candidate regardless of background - unless that applicant is extraordinary. This is the year when academics move to the most advanced level and when the social adjustment is the toughest. Therefore, we all prefer candidates who are applying to the lower divisions (grades 9 or 10).

The Association of Boarding Schools (TABS) hosts boarding school fairs every year in a range of Asian cities and SSATB hosts a fair in Hong Kong, specifically. These two organizations along with the National Association of Independent Schools (NAIS) are the primary organizations in the U.S. to which all our schools are members.

They have highly qualified staffs; are most knowledgeable about our schools; and have websites that can direct a family to an appropriate school. More importantly, they have our highest confidence. We always encourage our international applicants and families to attend one of these fairs to learn about the remarkable diversity and breadth of U.S. and Canadian boarding schools. In many cases, schools will agree to interview candidates in conjunction with the fairs or host receptions for interested families. For information about boarding school fairs in 2004-05 visit www.schools.com (TABS) or www.ssat.org (SSATB).

Careful planning, research and common sense can greatly enhance an international applicant's opportunities for admission to a U.S. or Canadian boarding school. There are no secrets to the process. Every one of us is looking for that great candidate who will change our school as have so many of our current and past students. There is no one criteria for success, no sure bet. No one consultant, relative, or family member has a lock on wisdom in this business. The best information comes directly from the schools themselves and their professional staff. When in doubt, simply call us. We in this profession are ultimately here because we love kids and understand that this can be a stressful process for any family.

Leo Marshall - lmarshall@webb.org - is currently the Director of Admission and Financial Aid at The Webb Schools in Claremont, CA. A veteran of 26 years in U.S. independent schools, he has led admission offices at schools in Hawaii, Seattle, Connecticut and, now California.

Choosing the Right Boarding School

By Rist Bonnefond

Finding the right secondary school with your son or daughter can be a challenging process, whether you are exploring opportunities close to home, or half a world away. Choosing the right school for you and your family takes time, persistence, and a thoughtful examination of not only your child's needs and interests, but also of a prospective school's mission, philosophy, goals and culture.

Why Boarding School?

Boarding schools – independent, collge-preparatory, residential communities offer compelling opportunity for students and families. They are mission-driven, not-for-profit educational organizations that are known for academic excellence, small classes, engaged faculty, individual attention, and value-based, character building education. In addition, they offer opportunities to, and often require active participation from their students in a wide variety of athletic, artistic, and extracurricular activities.

According to the National Association of Independent Schools, NAIS students:

Do twice as much homework as their counterparts

Watch only two-thirds as much television

Are significantly more likely to participate in varsity or intramural sports

Are more likely to agree that students and teachers get along well, discipline is fair, and teaching is good.

As the world becomes remarkably intertwined and increasingly unsettled, families are looking to boarding schools in the United States as partners in the education of their teenage sons and daughters.

Families that are concerned about personal safety and urban social pressures, which often force children to grow up too fast, find that boarding schools have remarkable opportunities academically, artistically, socially, and athletically.

American boarding schools provide the academic rigor to prepare students for college and teach personal responsibility, time management, independence, leadership and enduring moral values.

There are many fine secondary schools, each with its own distinctive strengths and personality. In time it will become apparent which ones are the best fit for your son or daughter and offer the programs that you want.

But where do you start?
Researching Schools Using the Internet

The Internet offers innumerable opportunities to lunch your search. On-profit trade associations such as The Association of Boarding Schools (www.schools.com) and the National Association of Independent Schools (www.nais.org) allow you to search for schools by type, location, and even course and program offerings. Commercial enterprises such as Peterson's and Vincent Curtis publish directories and also provide web-based search tools at www.ptersons.com and www.vincentcurtis.com.

Finally, educational consultants, hired by families to guide their searches, provide invaluable expertise and often decades of experience to help winnow hundreds of choices into a select few that best meet your child's needs and favor your family's philosophy of education. Visit the Independent Educational Consultants Association, the professional association of full-time, experienced educational consultants, at www.edeucationlconsulting.org.

Asking the Right Questions

As you begin to identify and gather information about the myriad of choices, consider the following questions suggested by NAIS for families conducting a school search:

Is the school accredited and by whom?

What is the school's mission and does its philosophy appeal to you?

Does the school have a special or particular educational focus?

Are academics rigorous?

Is the environment competitive? Nurturing? Structured?

Does the school met your child's needs?

How large is the school and its student body?

Where is the school located and what are your transportation options?

What variety of learning experiences are available at the school – in class, on the playing field, in extracurricular activities, and in community service? Are extracurricular activities obligatory?

Does the school have a diverse student body?

What are the graduation requirements?

What percentage of students enters colleges and what kind of colleges do they attend?

What is the tuition and how flexible are the school's financing options?

What is the school's application process?

Are deadlines drawing near?

Evaluating Schools and Fit

As you begin your search, you may feel inundated by the sheer number of opportunities and options. Take your time and keep asking questions until you discover which schools offer truly engaging academics and the right atmosphere for our son or daughter.

Most schools publish a course prospectus and faculty listing with the various academic offerings and the credentials of the faculty members who will be teaching your son or daughter. Course descriptions give thumbnail sketches of the classes taught, while graduation requirements will also speak to the rigor of the college preparatory curriculum offered. Advanced Placement courses and college placement are good indicators of top performing students, while the availability of and access to special learning needs and support may help younger students find classroom success more quickly. Ask about the average class size and student-faculty ratios. Talk with current families, teachers, coaches, and alumni. Hire a consultant to best evaluate your child's needs and options. Visit the schools of your choice.

Conclusion

Investing in our children's educations and futures is one of the most important and rewarding choices we can make as parents and families. It can mean the difference between the untapped potential of a frustrated scholar or artist, and the confident, purposeful growth of a responsible young man or woman of principle. If you are patient and thorough in your search, you and your child will be successful.

Rist Bonnefond is the headmaster of Kents Hill School (www.kentshill.org). Founded in 1824, Kents Hill School is a coeducational, college preparatory school of 225 in grades 9 through 12, and post-graduate. More than 100 courses are offered with AP and Honors classes in each department and outstanding performing and visual arts.

Choosing The Right Boarding School

Unique program offerings on the 600-acre, New England campus include the Waters Learning, Alfond Athletics, O'Connor Alpine Training, and Meadow View Equestrian Centers.

The American Boarding School Experience

By J. William LaBelle

In recent years, Asian families have become increasingly interested in sending their children to American schools. There are many obvious advantages. English is the language of choice for international business. The American market is important to all countries. An understanding of the American economy, culture and customs is an asset to anyone who plans to access the American marketplace.

American college preparatory boarding schools have become more receptive to accepting international students and many have developed appropriate programs, particularly in the teaching of English as a Second Language (ESL) and related subjects. However, the programs and experiences in American boarding schools vary considerably. Independent schools stress their independence, thus their differences. The missions of independent schools are extremely diverse as are the ways the schools carry out their mission. To a very large degree, the way an American boarding school operates is a reflection of the philosophy of the Headmaster and to a certain degree, the faculty and the Board of Trustees. Some American college preparatory boarding schools are very highly competitive, serving those students who are already great academic competitors. Other schools are meant more for students who need a great deal of support and nurturing in order to fulfill their academic potential. All schools are designed to fit somewhere on the continuum. Some schools fulfill their mission by conducting teacher-centered classes with lectures being the predominant method of teaching. Others use a more student-centered approach with a more "workshop" type of class that relies heavily on student participation and activity. Some schools assume that good study skills and study habits are already in place in their students and therefore they emphasize the "content" rather than the process of learning. Others make the teaching of study skills and the development of study habits a priority and therefore do not cover as much "content."

The degree of English proficiency required in different schools varies greatly. Some expect that international students will be able to fit into "regular" courses in all subjects. Others offer courses tailored for international students in all academic disciplines, while still others offer courses for international students in certain departments such as English or history, but expect that international students will be able to do "regular" courses in less language oriented areas such as mathematics, computer science, chemistry, physics or art. A careful reading of the course offerings is required in order to determine the school's position. In addition to knowing the mission and pedagogy of a school, parents and candidates should also have a sense of the lifestyle on a campus as that, too, can vary widely. Schools can hav a religious affiliation that impacts on the daily life. There are military schools with a high degree of structure, while others can b extremely liberal in approach. Where a school is on this "liberal to conservative" scale makes a great deal of difference in regard to the school's general environment and rules.

Extracurricular activities are an important part of boarding school life. Different schools put different emphasis on athletics, visual arts, performing arts, outdoor education and weekend activities.

Other factors that candidates should consider are factors such as whether the school is coeducational or single sex, the location in terms of area of the country and whether the setting is rural or urban. The climate from region to region in the United States varies tremendously. The location of the school has a great deal to do with activities and with general security and safety, both on the campus and in the surrounding vicinity.

Much can be learned about a school from the materials it sends in its admissions packet. Parents should request a packet from the admissions office of each school being considered. They and their child should review the materials carefully to get a complete sense of the overall program and lifestyle and then communicate with the schools with specific questions. It is important to understand that America boarding schools are probably more dissimilar than alike. Finding the right "match" or "fit" is very important and is well worth the time and effort taken to become well informed.

J. William LaBelle is the Headmaster at The Winchendon School in Winchendon, Massachusetts. He has been a teacher and administrator in boarding schools for 45 years. Mr. LaBelle would be happy to answer your general or specific questions about American borading schools. You may contact him at:

Phone: (508) 297-1223
E-mail: administration@winchndon.org
Fax: (508) 297-0911
Mail: The Winchendon School, 172 Ash Street, Winchendon, MA 01475.

Considering a North American Boarding School

By Aimee Gruber Bellemore

With U.S. university admission more competitive than ever, American boarding schools have a distinct advantage in helping Asian students gain entrance into top American universities.

TABS member schools offer small class size, individual attention and intense English language instruction. They also offer first-rate university preparatory courses, including the Advanced Placement courses now sought by most top universities. Boarding schools also have extraordinary extra-curricular programs that allow students to pursue in depth their special interests in the arts, athletics, sciences and social services.

American boarding schools have committed and dedicated teachers, many of whom hold advanced degrees. Most of the teachers actually live on campus and are available in the evenings or during weekends to offer students advice and extra help.

Most important, American boarding schools offer unparalled university guidance programs. University counselors work full time with small numbers of students so that the students get the individual attention that will help them gain admission to their university of choice.

There are many different kinds of boarding schools looking for different kinds of students. Some seek only the most serious and advanced students while others specialize in taking students who have not yet reached their full potential. These schools offer students a second chance, a chance not available in many Asian countries.

Every year, The Association of Boarding Schools (TABS) brings admission directors from many boarding schools to Asia. This year TABS will be holding Boarding School Fairs for families in Singapore; Bangkok, Thailand; Taipei, Taiwan; Tokyo, Japan; and Seoul, Korea.

The Asia Travel Program helps schools increase their visibility in Asia by providing direct access to families and educational professionals. Entering its ninth year, this successful program has built an extensive network of knowledgeable professionals whose collective experience identifies markets with the greatest potential. Participants in the program will receive comprehensive packets of information and resources including fair invitations, suggested contacts, country information, and detailed packing and planning lists. Fair logistics are managed by TABS' Hong Kong-based Asian advisor Frank Tracy who, along with associate director Aimee Gruber Bellemore, travels with the group to oversee the events in each city. In addition, participants find that traveling with colleagues from other schools offers support, camaraderie, and provides a unique opportunity for collaboration.

To learn more about the TABS Asia Fairs, please contact Aimee Gruber Bellemore.

Surviving in a New Culture

By Leigh Hallett

Moving to a new country requires a lot of courage and personal motivation. Making the decision about where to study, saying goodbye to friends and family, and traveling to your new home are all major accomplishments. Once you arrive and get settled in, however, there are many small steps you can take to make the transition into a new culture a wonderful experience.

For the first few days you'll be busy settling in, unpacking, and generally getting oriented to your immediate surroundings. (This is one of the best times to make new friends, since often there are many other newcomers around as well.) Be sure to take advantage of every opportunity when you first arrive. There may be campus tours, coffee houses, special outings, etc... Even if you feel stressed or jet-lagged, say "yes!" to every offer, since you will learn and see things which will help you to feel more comfortable right away. Plus, you will make many new friends.

Once you have found your way to the absolute essential places you need, don't relax in your explorations. It's easy to feel like you know everything you need to know about your new community, when really there are many more exciting places to discover. Walk, take buses, and ride along with other people. You never know where you might find the perfect, out-of-the-way coffee shop to share with your friends, or perhaps a tranquil little park. Don't let a fear of getting lost hold you back – people always love to help and are usually especially pleased to share information about their hometown. This is another great way to meet people.

While exploring your new location, be sure to talk to everyone. You needn't discuss important world events, of course. Asking questions is a good way to start a conversation. If the other person is a native of your new community, take advantage of their knowledge, and ask for advice about where to go and what to do. Smile and compliment people when you're waiting in line at the grocery store or bank. Make conversation with the assistants around campus who help you, and the cafeteria or restaurant people you meet. Not only is this a very good way to become comfortable with the local lingo, it's also a good way to impress people with your friendliness, and often to find out some useful information at the same time! Talk, talk, talk, in a friendly, upbeat way, and you are sure to make friends, even if you are naturally shy, or a little insecure about your conversation skills.

When you are not talking, read! Local newspapers are especially helpful for getting to know a new culture. Even if you can't really follow the stories in the papers, scanning them will start familiarizing you with the people, places, and issues which are important in your new community. You will learn what is interesting to your neighbors, who will usually be very happy to explain stories you don't understand, and very pleased that you are taking the time to read their local news. Newspapers are also excellent resources to find out about community events and activities. You'll notice movie listings, free public lectures, dances, museum exhibits, etc… to which you can invite your new friends!

When you are looking for things to do, don't forget to check out all of the local stores, not just the grocery store. Of course, you will find yourself in grocery stores often. When you do, don't just grab the familiar products you have used many times. If you really want to get to know the unfamiliar culture around you, there are few better places to start than the grocery store! You'll find local fruits and vegetables to try, as well as hundreds of other exotic foods to sample throughout the store. If you see someone buying a food you aren't familiar with, ask about it. Read the packages, and explore a new part of the store each time you visit. You might even want to set a goal of trying at least one new food each time you visit the grocery store!

As you learn your way around your new community, meeting new people, finding your own special spots, and trying new activities and foods, you will find yourself becoming more and more comfortable. By observing the behavior of the local people, you will quickly learn how you should act in order to fit in when you are unsure of yourself. Before you know it, you will be an expert on the culture around you, and feel totally at home!

Leigh Hallett, Maine Central Institute.

How to Deal with Homesickness

By Dawn Skilbred

Many students feel homesick when they attend boarding school in another country. The student may temporarily lose sight of the reasons she has come to study in America. Don't worry! You are not alone, and there are many ways to feel better about being away from home. Here are some tips that have helped students at Chatham Hall overcome homesickness:

Keep busy! The more your daily schedule is filled with activities, the less time you will have to sit in your room and think about what you miss about home. Join clubs and other extracurricular activities that interest you. Take horseback riding lessons or learn another sport. Become a member of Art Club. Take piano lessons.

Build relationships with others at your school. Although no one can take the place of your family, you may find that your friends at boarding school are a good substitute. Remember that everyone who is living at your school is also away from home and probably is missing family, too.

Share your culture with others. Students at your school will be eager to learn about you and your country 's customs and traditions, just as you will be anxious to learn about theirs. By sharing your culture, you may actually feel closer to home. You have a lot to bring to your school: cook traditional foods from your country, or invite friends to watch your favorite movie.

Keep in touch with friends and family from home. When you feel homesick, communicating with your friends or family may help. E-mail, instant messaging, and telephone calls are great ways to communicate. However, do not sit in your room and spend too much time doing this! Instead, limit yourself to a few minutes each day that you spend communicating with home. You should spend more time outside your room making new friends.

Stay healthy! Get plenty of sleep! When a person is sleep-deprived, it's easier to get upset and miss home and family. In addition, eating healthy foods and exercising will help you have the energy you need to survive the difficult times at school. Healthy habits will also help you avoid illness and emotional depression.

Spend time with others from your country or other international students. If there are other students from your country at your boarding school or in the surrounding area, spend some time with them. Talking in your native language or communicating about familiar things may help ease some homesickness. Be careful, however, not to separate yourself from American students, and try to avoid speaking your native language in front of others who do not understand it.

Make your room comfortable. This is the place where you will live for nine months! By making your boarding school more than just a school, you will start to create a second home for yourself. Little things in your room (such as pictures of friends, posters of movie stars or favorite music groups) will be fun reminders of your home.

Find someone who understands how you feel. Sometimes it is helpful to talk with a student who experienced homesickness in the past but now has adjusted to living far away from home. Ask how she overcame her feelings. Someone who has been through a similar experience is much more likely to understand!

Try to study but don't study all of the time! A good education probably will be your number one goal. Studying can help you keep busy and curb homesickness. However, if you spend all of your time with your books, you will miss valuable opportunities to make friends and have fun. Also remember that practicing your conversational English is important!

Have fun! When you think about home, you will probably miss the good times you had with friends and family. Try to make new, happy memories with your new friends at boarding school. It's important not to give up the fun experiences that make life worthwhile!

Dawn Skilbred is the International Student Coordinator at Chatham Hall.

Maximizing Potential

Educational Options for Students Who Learn Differently

By Stewart Miller

Is your child struggling in school, or has he or she been diagnosed with a learning difference? While initially this may be difficult to accept, it is imperative that as a parent, you reach an understanding of your child's academic needs.   This will help you ensure that the current school is offering your son or daughter the best opportunity for success. However, should you begin to question the current school's ability to help your child reach his or her true potential, it may be time to consider other alternatives.

With so many different options available, identifying the best educational environment for a student who learns differently can be a daunting task. Thorough testing that assesses cognitive potential and achievement in skill areas is an invaluable tool that will clarify an individual's distinct learning needs and style while specifying accommodations he or she will need to be successful. Once the student's strengths and weaknesses are delineated, there are many resources available (see resource list) to help parents find a school that will best meet their child's unique needs. While it is valuable to research many programs, one option that should be carefully considered is a school that works exclusively with students who learn differently.

Schools that focus on a LD population have many benefits. By offering integrated programs that consistently meet students' specific needs, and creating an environment where weaknesses do not overshadow strengths, these schools empower students to realize their potential. Probably the greatest gift specialized schools give students is a rediscovery of the correlation between effort and success; that is to say that students quickly realize that "If I put forth effort, I will be successful." Because all students in these schools learn differently, there is not a negative stigma associated with specialized instruction— everyone is taught in a way that strategically targets individual learning needs. These programs address academic strengths and weaknesses while giving students access to the arts, athletics, and other areas in which they might excel. Once in a true peer group, students quickly feel comfortable taking risks and participating in areas that they might not have before. As strengths are developed and weaknesses are remediated, self-esteem and confidence skyrocket.

Academically, schools that have programs specifically tailored to students who learn differently offer unparalleled opportunity. Challenging concepts are introduced and taught by using multisensory approaches, experiential learning, manipulatives, multimedia— anything, in short, to engage all the senses and encourage students to be actively involved in the learning process. This ensures that students are appropriately challenged and can enjoy success. Furthermore, the child does not have to fit into a particular program; because every teacher has expertise and specialized training, they have the flexibility to offer instruction that is most appropriate to each individual. For example, when remediating reading, teachers must have the knowledge and skills to design and implement a truly individualized reading program: this is what is referred to as diagnostic prescriptive teaching.

Teachers at these schools are truly specialists. Whether it is a science class, a math class, or a history class, these teachers have a thorough understanding of and sensitivity to students who learn differently. This compassion and knowledge is not limited to the "learning center" or "resource room," nor is it limited to the classroom. Adults who are in contact with students throughout the day— on the athletic field, in the art studio, or in a dormitory—all share this expertise and specialization. The result is that students are understood, their strengths are appreciated, their needs are consistently met, and they are not misperceived or mislabeled as being "lazy," "unmotivated," or "stupid."

It is also very important to note the difference between "support" and "remediation." Schools that offer academic support help students keep up with what is happening in the classroom. For example, if a student has a deficit in reading comprehension, academic support might help that student keep up with readings in history class, but support services do not directly address the student's reading comprehension deficit. Therefore, support services can be seen as a "band aide" approach to learning, where students simply get by. Conversely, remedial instruction is structured to explicitly and directly develop skills while teaching students important strategies to compensate for their weaknesses. Remedial instruction is evidenced by a separate and distinct curriculum that is individualized to students' learning needs.

It is important to understand that while no school can "cure" a student's learning problem, specialized schools offer effective, research-based instruction that will ensure your child has the best possible opportunity to make significant academic gains. Furthermore, by meeting the needs of the whole child, comprehensive programs help their students gain confidence, develop self-advocacy skills, appreciate their talents, and discover their potential.

Reasonable Expectations

Obviously, the best way to learn about a school is to visit. By visiting a school, you can see beyond the glossy marketing materials, and really get a sense of the school's culture. You can discover if the students are happy, and witness, firsthand, the interactions between the teachers and students. It is also strongly recommended that you visit more than one school so that there is a basis for comparison— and always visit when school is in session. While there are many important things to inquire about during a school visit, the following topics for discussion are specific to schools that work with students who learn differently:

It is very appropriate to inquire how the admissions staff determines if the school is a good match for your son or daughter. The admissions officer should be able to clearly communicate how the school's program will remediate weaknesses while giving your child an opportunity to develop his or her strengths. Remember you are interviewing the school as much as the school is interviewing your child.

Considering the spectrum of learning differences, the admissions officer should explain what population the school does and does not work with in the areas of cognitive potential, achievement in skill areas (i.e. reading, written language, math, etc.) social development, and behavior.

It is important to have an understanding of the level of structure and support the school offers and the minimum expectations the school has of its students.

Ensure you fully understand the school's mission (every school should have a mission statement).

Ask how the school measures student progress. There should always be an objective, standardized measure of progress.

Inquire about how the teachers (not just learning center teachers) are trained and what specific programs are utilized. It is always wise to observe a class and to see if these philosophies are practiced; it is crucial that schools do what they say they do.

It is important that the school offer professional development opportunities to ensure that teachers are using the most effective, research-based instructional strategies.

Consider what technology is available and incorporated into the program. Note: Technology is important, but it should not be the principal instrument for instruction.

Inquire about and assess how individualized the program is.

Examine how the school ensures that students reach a deeper understanding of how they learn, understand compensatory strategies they can use, and develop self-advocacy skills.

Attempt to gain the perspective of a current student.

Take the time to familiarize yourself with the school's Student & Parent Handbook. This document outlines different school policies, procedures, and rules.

Ask to contact a current parent; having the benefit of a current parent's perspective of and experience with the school is invaluable.

If possible, meet with the Head of School. This is the individual that is ultimately responsible for the educational program, the teachers, the school community, and, most importantly, for your child.

It is necessary to recognize that what these schools can offer is opportunity. The most significant variable is the extent to which your child engages in the program and puts forth effort. While this publication offers many suggestions, it is important to understand that choosing a school is not an exact, scientific process. It has to feel right, and you have to trust your gut instinct. People are the heart and spirit of a school. When visiting, pay close attention to the intangible human factor— the extent to which the community of teachers, students, and staff enjoy each other and create a culture of caring, mutual respect, and possibility.

Resources
International Dyslexia Association, interdys.org. Contact local chapter

Learning Disabilities Association, www.ldanatl.org. Contact local chapter

Independent Educational Consultants Association, 703-591-4850, www.IECAonline.com

National Center for Learning Disabilities, www.ncld.org

Children and Adults with Attention Deficit Disorder, 800-233-4050, www.chadd.com. Contact local chapter

Peterson's, 1-800-338-3282, www.petersons.com

The Association of Boarding Schools (TABS), 202-966-8705, www.schools.com

Reprinted with permission by The New York Branch of the International Dyslexia Association

Stewart Miller is the Assistant Director of The Greenwood School, Putney, VT.

The Importance of Immersion

by Joshua D. Clark

International students attend US boarding schools for two reasons, first to become familiar with the US educational system to eventually attend a US university, and second to experience American culture and become globally educated. However, it is not easy for anyone to attend a school in another country where the language and culture is different. It requires students to go beyond their level of comfort. Once here you may be tempted to keep things as comfortable as possible by seeking out students who speak the same language, not play in any extracurricular sports or activities, or do the minimum amount of participation in the classroom. By following this strategy you will not be able to take full advantage of your experience and will not fulfill your goals here in the US. Immersing yourself at your boarding school does not mean you have to lose your own identity or culture, it only means that you know why you are here in the US and then embrace every opportunity that allows you to do better in the US educational system and American culture.

First, the educational system in the US emphasizes a combination of creative thinking and active participation. At home, some students may be used to only taking notes without speaking in class, and memorizing facts for exams. In the US, students are expected to think creatively. While students still must take notes during lecture as well as memorize information for exams, they are also asked to speak in class and share their own thoughts about the information.

Do they agree? Do they disagree? Many exams require students to analyze information (a story, an historical event, or a scientific problem) and provide their own solutions. Teachers will ask students questions during class and expect them to discuss a topic and even sometimes to disagree and propose an alternate solution to a question. This style of learning requires you to think beyond the facts and create your own solutions. If you immerse yourself in class, begin to ask questions and volunteer your thoughts during discussion, you will be more successful.

Second, American culture is extremely diverse. While you can learn a lot about American culture by observing what others do, it is far more effective to participate in the culture as much as possible. Find some American friends. Join a sports team or an after school activity that you have never done before. Speak as much English as possible, in class, out of class, in the dorms, and during meals. The more you speak English the more you will become familiar with the colloquialisms that make up the English language and will better prepare you for the TOEFL exam. Finally, take advantage of every opportunity for a leadership role at the school.

It is healthy to maintain friendships with other students from your own country. It allows you to keep in touch with your own language and culture. However, this is only beneficial if you also have American friends and are speaking English much more during the day than your native language. If you are able to maintain a balance than you will begin to see drastic improvement in your English skills, your grades, and your experiences.

Joshua D. Clark, Admissions & Financial Aid, Gould Academy

Advantages of Studying Abroad

By Shuochieh Lee

America is the country we often refer to as the "melting pot." I fully explored the meaning of the "melting pot" by spending the past four years at Subiaco Academy living among people from different cultures all over the world. Going to school in America has helped me in a number of ways.

I have learned to become an independent thinker by going to school at Subiaco Academy. I do not hesitate to share my thoughts and my opinions with my classmates. I never thought that living with people from all over the world would increase my understanding of myself.

By living with students from different societies, I have had a chance to find my connection with my Chinese ancestry by understanding the cultures of others. Since I have had the experience about the culture diversities at Subiaco Academy, now I am prepared to go to college with people from all over the world.

I also learned how to be an independent adult by attending a boarding school for four years without assistance from my parents; I have to take care of everything by myself, which includes waking myself up every morning and doing my own laundry. Also, I have had to let myself know when it is time to study. I have become more responsible, and I am determined to prove that I deserve to be called a mature adult.

Attending Subiaco Academy has prepared me for college by making me an independent thinker, by showing me the cultural differences, and by making me an independent adult. Coming to school in the U.S. has helped me in a number of ways.

Shuochieh Lee is a Senior at Subiaco Academy.

A Day in the Life of a Boarding School Student

By Noah Brenner

In the morning, I wake up to my alarm clock going off at 6:30, but then I have the task of convincing myself to get out of bed to get to breakfast at 7:30. Unless I have something very important to do in the morning, I usually only manage to get up about ten minutes before that. I try to finish a few last-minute pieces of homework and go to class at 8:00.

I go to three classes, which are each 70 minutes long with 10 minute breaks in between. There are a few classes that are not quite my strong points, but they aren't too bad. The teachers are good, and we aren't separated from them; we call them by their first names. There are also a number of classes that are fascinating and are so much fun to go to, although there is often a lot of homework for these classes, but it's worth the trouble.

Lunch comes along at noon. Connor, my roommate tells everyone to "Be quiet for announcements." Once I finish lunch, I go downstairs to the kitchen for some exciting dishwashing. It can be fun, though, because of the people I'm working with. Next comes the athletic period, which lasts until the end of the school day. Most people go skiing or snowboarding, other work out in the gym. I practice my instruments and sometimes have music lessons.

Dinner comes along at 6:00, and then chores, again, to clean up in the kitchen, but we only have to work every fourth night. At 7:00 there is study hall until 9:00, but I often need a bit more time to do some of my work. Then we clean our rooms to the satisfaction of the dorm parent on duty, which actually isn't too bad unless they're feeling mean.

After that is time for socializing. I'm not exactly a party person, but there aren't exactly parties anyway. I'll go over to another dorm room and talk and listen to music. Every once in a while, I can convince my roommate, who plays the saxophone, to go play some music with me. On weekdays, upperclassmen have curfew at 11:00, so we have to be in our dorms and turn everything off but desk lamps, but we usually have to be reminded of this.

After another hour of talking and messing around, or sometimes homework, we have to turn off all of our lights and go to bed, hopefully remembering to set our alarm clocks again. By the time we get to sleep, it's usually a few minutes past midnight, so my roommate and I have a "tradition" of saying "Good morning" before we go to sleep.

Noah Brenner '04, Crested Butte Academy.

A Day in the Life of a Boarding School Student

By Brandon Reid

Seven o'clock in the morning rolls around, and I am awakened by a persistent squawking alarm clock. I push the snooze button as many times as I can afford. If I am late to breakfast at seven-thirty, it will cost me a tardy mark. I flop out of bed, dress myself and move out the door after decorating my hooves with sole. Typical breakfast at the Academy consists of pancakes, waffles, bacon, eggs, hash browns, and fresh fruit.

Depending on what day it is, my schedule follows two alternate course. On Mondays and Fridays, I attend three classes that are seventy minutes long in the morning. These classes are Pre-calculus, English, and Advanced Placement Biology. On Tuesdays, Wednesdays, and Thursdays, I begin my day by boarding a bus on the corner outside of the dormitory. This bus arrives at eight-thirty, and takes me on a ten-minute ride north to the Crested Butte Mountain. At the mountain, I adorn a snowboard, a plank about 5 feet tall and 11 inches wide, with straps designed to hold my feet securely. A snowboard is made to ride like a surfboard on the frozen water that accumulates on and around the pointed laccoliths from which our town is named. While snowboarding I am surrounded by great coaches, good friends, and beautiful scenery. The skiing and snowboarding in Crested Butte is comparable to the Alps in Europe, or so I have been told.

Following a morning of either classes or snowboarding, I eat lunch back at school around noon. Today we ate barbecue chicken, corn, and masked potatoes. Directly after lunch, I am required to complete my chores. This entails the maintenance of all the school vehicles. After chores, depending on what my schedule was that morning, I will either attend classes, or go snowboarding. Every day we have academics and athletics, the schedule just flip flops through out the week. In the afternoon, I typically hang out on campus with my friends or sign out and walk into town. Following my precious free time, I go to the dining hall for a scheduled dinner at six o'clock. Our chefs are excellent and our meals are usually delicious. If, however, you feel the urge to dine elsewhere, it is a simple matter of going to one of my fine restaurants only a short walk away.

After dinner we have a little more time to ourselves, up until study hall at seven o'clock. Study hall is a two-hour block of time reserved for quiet study and the completion of homework. After study hall we clean our rooms and socialize with one another until our curfews at eleven o'clock. Depending on my school work, I usually go to sleep any time between ten o'clock and one o'clock. For a brief interlude in my busy life, I sleep for a time, preparing my mind and body to repeat the same agenda at seven o'clock the next morning.

Brandon Reid '04, Crested Butte Academy.

According to Philosophers, Poets and Writers

By Duncan Tonatiuh Smith Hernández

According to some philosophers, poets and writers of the twentieth century, life is full of anxiety, solitude and despair. I agree because I feel defenseless in the face of time.

At Buxton I've been incredibly happy, full of desire to create, to paint, take pictures, do carpentry—desire to be involved in the community. Here I've felt peace and satisfaction and a desire to share it and to learn from others.

At Buxton I've also felt incredibly overcome by sadness and loneliness, with no desire or intention, merely floating through the days incapable of communicating. Unwilling to talk to anybody, I've lived and fed in that darkness, full of secrets and full of fear that the sadness will never go away.

I believe my experience here has affected me in the deepest ways. I've had an enormous growth and I've changed drastically and for the better the way I live my life. Leaving Mexico and coming to boarding school in the United States was a big step. It has opened many opportunities and has broadened my possibilities and perspective of the world. Buxton is a fascinating school. It is so much more than what I could conceive it to be many years ago when I came as a prospect to my interview. I'm thankful I came here. Buxton for me has been a journey of independence, of possibility but also somehow an acknowledgment of solitude.

I believe all that I've said. But it's hard for me to explain it; it's hard for me to make sense out of it. I wish I had more time to clear my thoughts and emotions. But life seems to be always on the go. Time goes by and you can't stop it. I feel defeated by time. Things go, things die, things end, it's sad. The past is gone and all that is left is that I'm leaving.

But I've influenced some people here in a good way, even if it is subtle. I know it's true because the people here that know me and love me the most have told me so.

Maybe it is not the end. I believe some of me will trickle its way into Buxton even after I'm gone. After all, I am a hero. I've been down and dirty, to then redeem myself. And I'm a myth, because I'm the kid who got suspended for writing and posting an awful, offensive letter about the girls at Buxton but eventually managed to learn and change.

Existentialists say humans live full of anxiety, solitude and despair. But they also say that when a human creates something, makes something possible, he makes it possible for all of humanity.

Duncan Tonatiuh Smith Hernández is a student at Buxton School.

Chapel Speech

By Abdulla Bucheeri

One of the hardest things in life is to be away from your family, your friends, the people you grew up, the ones whom have shared your laughs and cries, your smile and tears, your happiness and sadness, the ones whom have always been there for you when you needed them most, the ones whom have always supported you and stood by your side.

I never realized this truth till I was faced by it when I came to continue my studies in the US. I kept ignoring it as if it was something really far ahead. But as my departure date came closer and closer, it was a total disaster. I didn't know what I needed, I didn't know what I should take and what I should leave. I wondered, "How is my school going to be? Will I have a good roommate or will he be a crazy maniac? ".

At the moment that I left my friends and family, my whole life started flashing in front of my eyes, all the beautiful memories I had since I was a child till now. As it is said "We do not know the true value of our moments until they have undergone the test of memory." But what had to be done had to be done, so I boarded the plane and started my journey.

We were a group of four prep school students, all excited about our new life in our new boarding schools, yet nostalgic for the beautiful memories we had in our old schools. We arrived in the United States after a long, thirteen-hour trip, and started our journey dropping everyone at his school. The Hun School of Princeton was our first stop, where two students were going to go. Choate Rosemary hall was the other stop where we dropped one student. Then we headed for Tabor.

Since Tabor was our last stop I got the chance to see both of the other schools. To be frank both schools were amazingly beautiful, which made me worry whether Tabor would be as good as those schools or not, since I have never been to Tabor before.

When I reached Tabor I realized the truth. Tabor was not as good as those schools ... Tabor was even better. There was something about Tabor unlike any of the schools I have been to, something unique. The students, friends, faculty, teachers, the whole atmosphere made Tabor the beautiful place it is. Tabor possessed a special quality that made it exceptional for me.

My first day in Tabor was kind of weird. Everyone was wearing the blue "Tabor for all" t-shirts. At the beginning, I didn't quite realize what that phrase meant, but as time passed, the meaning began to get more and more clear to me:

Tabor for all ... the beautiful times you get to spend in this school.

Tabor for all ... the beautiful friendships you get to make.

Tabor for all ... for all the stressing classes and tests you get to take.

Tabor for all ... for all the memories you get to have and cherish for your whole life.

A friend of mine once told me, it doesn't matter which school you go to. What's important is what you make out of the school once you are there. That is my goal now, and I know that I have come to the right place to do it.

Abdulla Bucheeri, from Bahrain, is a student at Tabor Academy.

Chapel Speech

Chapel Speech

by Max May

Last year one morning at breakfast, I was asked if I had ever thought about studying abroad. My answer was, "Oh no Dad, I won't study abroad. There 's no way I will ever do that." He answered, "Just think about it…I am sure you'll change your opinion."

After some months of thinking and thinking, I finally realized that my father was right, that studying abroad would be one of the greatest chances I'll ever get in my life. I told a friend of mine at school about this. We had a long debate on this theme. He counted all the disadvantages of a year abroad. I only said, "Sure, there are disadvantages, but you cannot stay your whole life at the same place. You have to collect new experiences." He answered, "You are crazy." It seemed to be that he was a bit angry at me. Yes he was angry, because I would leave him and all my other friends. Sure, it was a difficult decision for me, but everyone has to look into the future.

The next step was to choose to go to a boarding school, or live with an American host family. I decided on a host family. But I was wrong again. I thought that a boarding school is like a prison. But I figured out that one of the most important advantages is that you can have a really good connection to the friends you'll make.

So I was ready to go. I applied to 4 boarding schools, one in Maine and 3 in Massachusetts. My mother told me that I have to do a phone call to all of these four schools. Tabor was the first one that I contacted. So I dialed the number of Tabor Academy. I was really nervous, but after I talked with Mrs Conway, I felt at ease. Soon, I received letters from all 4 schools. All 4 schools said "Yes." As you can imagine, I was very happy. But now I had to choose which school I would like to attend. I knew right away that I wanted Tabor Academy. I wasn't sure why, but I had the feeling that that would be the best choice – and I was right. It's a wonderful place to study. The faculty and the teachers are very nice and especially the students are great. It is a great chance for me, and I'm glad I changed my mind from that morning when there was nothing that could have persuaded me to study abroad.

Max May, from Germany, is a student at Tabor Academy.

Chapel Speech

By Robynn Yip

One morning three years ago, I walked up to my mother and said, "I think I want to go study in the States." It was a random statement that came out of nowhere, and it just sounded like I was just joking around. But surprisingly, my mother said, "OK" From then on, my life was no longer the same. At home, my school was only 20 minutes away, and I got back home at about 2 in the afternoon. Now each September I need to pack 2 or 3 suitcases to get ready for school. My trip to school takes 18 hours by plane and then 2 hours by car. And I only get to go home three times a year. Everything is so different from before.

When my parents and I first arrived in the States, they did not know any English whatsoever and I had to translate every single thing for them. We stayed in Boston for a couple of days to buy my school stuff. Once, we walked into a Verizon phone store because my mom wanted to get me a cell phone. I knew that Tabor didn't allow boarders to have cell phones, but my mom still wanted to get me one anyway, and we had a stupid argument because of that. Since I refused to speak to the saleslady for her, mom tried to speak English. She struggled hard to get her point across as best she could, but the saleslady didn't understand her. Afterwards, she yelled at me loudly in the shop for what seemed like forever, in front of everyone. She was just panicking and was so annoyed because she can't speak English. That was a stressful day, and I felt bad afterwards because I had been so mean to her.

When I first arrived at Tabor, my jaw dropped when I saw the beautiful campus. I knew I have made the right choice. I was so happy. When my parents left, I didn't feel sad at all. I was just so excited and felt so ready to have this wonderful change in my life. And on top of that, I wouldn't have to listen to my mom whining and scolding me. So I didn't feel homesick, and I didn't even have jetlag.

I still remember the first time walking into the dining hall with my tray, feeling lost because I didn't know where to sit. I remember meeting my roommate, feeling so scared that she would not be nice to me. But she was, and she's my roommate again this year. I remember my global partner, who was so nice to me, even though I had a tough time understanding her English with a Korean accent. But I loved her, she is a great person. Being an international student is tough, because you are not using your first language to learn, and everybody seems just so different from you. But I have to say that I'm pretty lucky, because I have made a lot of friends, both international and American, and I have had wonderful and understanding teachers and dorm parents. I enjoyed most of my time here, and I hope that it would stay this way for the remainder of my Tabor career.

Robynn Yip, from Hong Kong, is a student at Tabor Academy.

Subiaco Academy in the Land of Opportunity

By Gordon Kim

Being an international boarding school student in Subiaco has its good sides and bad sides. Subiaco has what the schools I went to in Korea didn't have. Extracurricular activities and sports are a few of them. Being in the United States also has advantages. But it can sometimes be difficult to cope with the hardships of being far away from home.

Compared to the schools I went to in Korea, Subiaco offers more extracurricular activities and sports programs. Unlike what I experienced in Korea, academics are not the only aspect of student life Subiaco focuses on. Music, art, drama and sports are some of the things students are encouraged to do. Music and sports programs give students a broader range of learning and help to relieve the stress from academics. I enjoyed taking drum classes because it gave me a chance to exercise my creativity and forget about my academic struggles.

Another advantage of being in Subiaco is the fact that it is located in Arkansas, USA. This has advantage and disadvantage at the same time. The people here are usually very nice and friendly. Unlike Korea, where everybody's ethnicity is Korean, people here are from different cultures and countries. I have friends who are from Mexico, Croatia, and Texas. Some of them are African-American and some of them are Hispanic. The diversity gives me an opportunity to learn about different cultures and share my culture with others. But the disadvantage of being in Arkansas is that its population is not very diverse compared to other states. The advantage of diversity may not be as big as in other states. Majority of the people are white. Arkansas is also very rural. The state has a beautiful rural environment with hills and lush forests but it can be a very boring environment for people who do not appreciate that. I personally prefer a more urban environment with cities and people.

Other downsides of being in Subiaco are the facts that international students are many miles always from their home and it is an all boys' school. I sometimes have to deal with homesickness and the lacking of girls. I miss my family, friends, and Korean food. There are not a lot of oriental restaurants in Arkansas. Also being in an all boys' school can be less fun than being in a coed institution.

Subiaco is a cool place. Teachers are eager to help you and you learn a lot from them. Extracurricular and athletic activities are plentiful. The environment is very pretty. If you are able to cope with the downsides of being in an all boys' school and being homesick, Subiaco is a good place to go to school.

Gordon Kim is a Junior at Subiaco Academy.

Schools in Alphabetical Order

Asheville

Avon Old Farms

Bement

Ben Lippen

Brehm

Buxton

Cambridge

Canterbury

Cate

Chaminade

Chapel Hill

Chatham

Cheshire

Christ School

Crested Butte

Dunn

Emma Willard

Episcopal High

Fay

Foxcroft

Gould

Governor Dummer

Gow

Grand River

Greenwood

Hackley

Happy Valley

Hargrave

High Mowing

Hillside

Houghton

Idyllwild

Indian Mountain

Indian Springs

Kents Hill

Kildonan

La Lumiere

Lawrence

Linden Hill

Madeira

Maine Central

Marianapolis

Marvelwood

Maur Hill

Middlesex

Millbrook

Miss Hall's

Miss Porter's

Northwest

Oak Grove

Oakwood Friends

Ojai Valley

Perkiomen

Phillips Andover

Rabun Gap

Southwestern

St. Andrews

St. Johnsbury

St. Stanislaus

St. Timothy's

Stevenson

Stoneleigh-Burnham

Storm King

Subiaco

Tabor

Thatcher

Vanguard

Virginia Episcopal

Wasatch Academy

Washington Academy

Webb

Webb Schools

Wilbraham & Monson

Williston

Winchendon

Note: All information contained in American Boarding Schools was obtained from school websites and promotional materials with permission from school administrators.

Asheville School

Location: Asheville, North Carolina (U.S. Mid-Atlantic East Coast)

360 Asheville School Road, Asheville, NC 28806
Phone: 828-254-6345, Fax: 828-252-8666
Website: www.ashevilleschool.org
Email: admission@asheville-school.org

Mr. Charles Baldecchi, Director of Admission
Phone: 828-254-6345, Fax: 828-252-8666
Email: admission@asheville-school.org

Mission Statement: Every action undertaken by faculty and staff at Asheville School supports our sacred mission. That mission is: To prepare our students for college and for life, and to provide an atmosphere in which all members of a diverse school community appreciate and strive for excellence - an atmosphere which nurtures character and fosters the development of mind, body, and spirit. Our School Motto, Vitae Excelsioris Limen translates to "Threshold for a Higher Life."

Admission Requirements for International Students: Since English is not taught as a second language, international applicants should have a good command of the English language. A TOEFL score is required.

Grade Level: 9-12.

Student Gender: Boys & Girls.

Enrollment: 218 Students, 107 boys, 111 girls, 173 boarders, 55 day.

Number of International Students: Asheville currently has 27 international students attending. At Asheville School we bring together students from a variety of geographical, ethnic, racial, religious, and socio-economic backgrounds. Each year, students more than a dozen foreign countries join our family. Roughly 15% of our students are students of color. Brought together into one coherent community, our students learn how to appreciate the fresh perspectives of their neighbors.

Accredited by: SACS

Head of School: Archibald R. Montgomery IV, University of Pennsylvania (B.A., 1975), Monterey Language School (Russian, 1976), University of Texas School of Law (J.D., 1982).

Faculty: The members of our faculty of 56 teachers are attracted by the opportunity to work with bright, motivated kids. We expect and teach for excellence. At the same time, with an overall student-faculty ratio of 4:1, a professionally staffed Learning Center, and roughly two-thirds of our faculty residing here on campus, students find the help and support they need.

Tuition: Tuition and Boarding for 2003-2004 is $26,750.

Class Size: 11 students, with a student/teacher ratio of 4:1.

Curriculum: Tradition and innovation. That's not an oxymoron at Asheville School. To support our commitment to excellence, we've created a rigorous curriculum organized around a core of classical disciples (Humanities, Mathematics, Foreign Language, Science, and Fine Arts). In addition, a remarkable number of Advanced Placement and Honors classes, as well as several electives, allow students to accelerate and tailor their learning. High standards guarantee that our students leave Asheville School with the problem-solving and creative thinking tools they'll need to succeed in college and in life. We're passionate about teaching and genuinely care about student life. In this environment, students receive an unparalleled liberal arts education as they develop a strong sense of self and a strong sense of community.

Average SAT Scores of Graduating Students: The middle 50% of the class of 2003 scored from 1110-1390 on the SAT.

College Placement: Recent Asheville graduates have been accepted to Brown, Clemson, Cornell, Davidson, Duke, Emory, Furman, Harvard, NYU, Oberlin, Princeton, Stanford, Swarthmore, Vanderbilt, Wake Forest, Washington and Lee, William and Mary, Williams, and the Universities of North Carolina (Chapel Hill), Pennsylvania, and Virginia.

Academic Requirements: To qualify for an Asheville School diploma, each student must earn a total of 17 credits: 4 credits of English, 3 credits of History, 3 credits of Math, 3 credits of Foreign Language, 3 credits of Science and 1 credit of Art.

Sports: Asheville School requires all students to participate in either athletics or arts as part of our afternoon activities program. Freshman and sophomores must play on one interscholastic team during the year. The upper grades have no specific interscholastic requirement. Yet, in any given year, more than 75% of our students choose to play at least one team sport.

The reason is simple: We offer an unbelievable number of sports for a school our size. With the help of a seasoned coaching staff, we can find an activity to suit the skill level and interest of every student. Above all, our program emphasizes good sportsmanship, both on and off the field. At the same time, we like to win and produce very competitive teams.

The Ashville curriculum includes baseball, basketball, cross country, field hockey, football, golf, mountaineering, soccer, swimming, tennis, track and field, volleyball and wrestling.

Extracurricular Activities: Asheville School offers an interesting array of afternoon programs to complement the academic schedule. Every student is required to take part in an afternoon activity for a minimum of 90 minutes Monday through Friday. Every freshman and sophomore is required to participate in one interscholastic sport each year. By participating in drama, art, music, or sports, students get to know one another better. They learn the value of teamwork. They also learn to take risks and try new things. This makes for a more well-rounded student and supports the School's mission to nurture students' "development of mind, body, and spirit." Activities include Chapel Choir, Chorus, Christian Fellowship, Fine Arts Society, Handbell Choir, Host Society, International Club, Debate Club, Service Club, and Student Council.

Campus: Set on a hilltop with magnificent views of the area peaks, our 300-acre campus boasts comfortable, recently renovated, single dorm rooms wired for internet access, fine athletic facilities, a complex including the Tyrer Student center, Sharp Hall (Dining) and Crawford Gallery (Art) and a outdoor center with an alpine tower and ropes course, a state-of-the-art library and conference center. We're in the process of improving our facilities even more. Current projects include a $7 million addition to Rodgers Athletic Center to be completed in early 2003, We will add 28,000 square feet to that facility, including a new fitness center, a multipurpose room, and a new Science, Arts, and Technology building to follow. Beauty has not been sacrificed for function. As a matter of fact, many of our buildings are listed with the National Register of Historic Places.

Dormitories: Most students have their own rooms. There are three dormitories with faculty apartments on each corridor, in Anderson Hall (1900), Lawrence Hall (1907), and Kehaya House (1990).

Nearest International Airport: Dulles International, Washington DC.

Avon Old Farms School

Location: Avon, Connecticut (U.S. East Coast, New England)

500 Old Farms Road, Avon, CT 06001
Phone: 860-404-4100; Fax: (860) 404-4138
Website: www.avonoldfarms.com
Email: admissions@avonoldfarms.com

Mrs. Terry Cutler, Director of Admission
Phone: 860-404-4100; Fax: 860-675-6051
Email: cutlert@avonoldfarms.com

Mission Statement: Avon Old Farms is first, and always, a boys' school. It offers a broad college-prep curriculum that challenges the most gifted students while providing support and extra assistance for those who need it. Avon is a community where boys grow into exceptional men.

We are a dynamic community of learning, which challenges boys to stretch themselves and to explore untapped potential in their journey to manhood. Mentored by a dedicated, talented faculty who offer successful models for our students to emulate, Avonians develop the self-confidence to cope with the anxieties of adolescence and to forge the critical foundations of adult identity.

Our School motto: "Aspirando et Perseverando," effectively communicates our expectations for students; in every aspect of a boy's life, we expect him to strive consistently for his best. Our core values of honesty, integrity, and service permeate life at Avon and remain with our graduates throughout their lives. Our magnificent campus, with its distinctive Cotswold architecture, accentuates the traditional approach to education which is so successful here.

As a boys' boarding school, our programs are designed specifically to help young men focus on their development at a time in life when distractions abound. Although numerous opportunities exist for our students to interact with girls from Miss Porter's, Ethel Walker's and other nearby schools, boys are free to live and learn in our structured, supportive environment.

In an all-boys context, our students embrace scholastic challenges and compete in the athletic arena while feeling safe exploring the arts, experimenting with poetry, expressing school spirit, and just being themselves.

Avon's academic program is anchored in the liberal arts and we require our students to explore fully the major disciplines in order to prepare for the intellectual rigor of college. The diversity of our student body is impressive, with students from some 30 states and over a dozen foreign countries. The rich array of cultures coexisting within our small community is charged with significant learning opportunities. The rapport that exists between faculty and students is exceptional, and the bonds developed among our students are lasting.

On our website you may read descriptions and view images that will better inform you about Avon Old Farms. However, only a visit to campus will truly illuminate the special characteristics that make us a unique school. We look forward to hosting you.

Grade Levels: 9-12.

Student Gender: Boys only.

Enrollment: 369 boys, 272 boarders, 97 day.

Accredited by: NEASC, CAIS/CT

Headmaster: Kenneth H. LaRocque, Harvard College, B.A., Harvard University, M.Ed. E-mail: larocquek@avonoldfarms.com

Faculty: 60 full-time, 5 part-time, with 53 faculty/administration members living on campus.

Tuition: For 2003-2004: $31,125 for boarding, $21,425 for day.

Financial Aid: 31% of the students were awarded scholarships totaling $1,963,885.

Endowment: $26.7 Million.

Class Size: 12 students, with a student-teacher ratio of 6:1.

Curriculum: At Avon, academic excellence consists of thorough instruction in the basic disciplines, the development of sound study habits, and the opportunity to be challenged by increasingly complex subject matter. Because of the quality and experience of the faculty and the careful organization of time set aside for personal instruction and guidance, we believe that a boy will find a superior academic program at Avon Old Farms.

With rare exceptions, all seniors go on to college. Thus, Avon's graduation requirements closely parallel the admission requirements of many colleges.

Each year a student pursues a program of studies consisting of at least five classes, including at least four "core" subjects chosen from the following disciplines: English, history, mathematics, science, and foreign language.

Departmental Honors courses are offered to all students who combine intellectual ability with the desire to study more demanding material. Honors and Advanced Placement courses are offered in every discipline. and there is an academic-enrichment hour four nights a week. Many of these courses prepare students directly for the Advanced Placement Examinations of the College Entrance Examination Board. Placement in these sections is by student request and teacher recommendation.

Advanced Placement: Avon offers Advanced Placement courses in Biology, Physics, Environmental Science, Calculus, Statistics, U.S.History, U.S. Government, English, French, Spanish, Studio Art, Computer Science and Economics.

Average SAT Scores of Graduating Students: 533 verbal, 565 math.

College Placement: Students from the Class of '03 have matriculated to colleges and universities such as University of Pennsylvania, U.S. Naval Academy, Boston College, Trinity College, Bates, Harvard, Dartmouth, Cornell, Middlebury and Williams.

Academic Requirements: Avon students are expected to complete the following studies: English - Four years; History - Three years (including U.S. History); Mathematics - Three years (Algebra 1,

Geometry, Algebra 2); Science - Three years with intensive laboratory work (including Biology); Foreign Language - Two years of the same language; Fine Arts - One course; Electives - Two years.

Sports: Avon believes deeply in the importance of athletics as an integral part of a total education of mind and body; each student is required to participate in a sport during each of the three seasons. Interscholastic sports include baseball, basketball, cross-country, football, golf, ice hockey, lacrosse, riflery, downhill skiing, soccer, squash, swimming, tennis, track and wrestling. Non-competitive sports include bicycling, conditioning, cross-country running, cross-country skiing, golf, jogging, scuba diving, swimming and tennis. There are 37 teacher-coaches and 2 full-time trainers.

Extracurricular Activities: Community service projects include Habitat for Humanity, Toys for Tots and an annual blood drive. Activities include the student council, yearbook, newspaper, The Riddlers choral group, jazz ensemble, chorale, computer club, rock and roll, history club, Nimrod club, social activities committee, rugby club, community service and international clubs. In addition, one musical and two dramatic productions are produced each year in coordination with students from Miss Porter's School.

Campus: The campus features the new Ordway Science and Technology Center, school-wide computer network, hockey rink, pool, new tennis complex, library, theatre, and fine arts building, all set on 1000 acres.

Dormitories: 7 dormitories with all rooms wired for computer use. Each of the boarding students lives in a single, double, or triple room and is assigned to a dormitory adviser who is also his personal and academic adviser.

Nearest International Airport: Bradley International Airport, Hartford, CT.

Nearby Lodgings: The Hartford/Farmington Marriott, 860-678-1000; Centennial Inn Suites, 860-677-4647; Avon Old Farms Hotel, 860-677-1651.

Bement School

Location: Deerfield, Massachusetts (U.S. East Coast, New England)

Main Street, Deerfield, MA 01342
Phone: 413-774-7061; Fax: 413-774-7863
Website: www.bement.org; Email: admit@bement.org

Mr. Matthew Evans, Director of Admission
Phone: 413-774-7061; Fax: 413-774-7863
Email: admit@bement.org

Mission Statement: What's most important at Bement is the community we strengthen each day. At Bement, the kind of person you become matters most, and we spend a fair amount of time tending to that development. In the midst of studying literature and history, we realize we're often studying relationships. Small classes enable students and teachers to know each other well. All teachers eat with students, which furthers the friendship adults and young people have at Bement. We speak to each other by name, and students never know what Bement faculty or staff member may appear in what role. The business manager is often seen riding with our mountain bikers, our assistant cook takes international boarders home with her over long weekends, and the head of school is an eighth grade English teacher. Older students are constant models for younger ones, and our formalized Reading Buddy program fosters meaningful and lasting friendships across the grades. No one at Bement believes, "That's not my job." There is a strong and pervasive belief that each of us contributes to the success of each day at Bement.

The affection we have for one another is evident in many ways. Each week we celebrate birthdays at our all-school meeting. We sing to each other and an original Bement bookmark is presented to commemorate each student's birthday. Morning meetings are also times when we recognize accomplishments big and small: a student qualifies for a New England cross country meet; a student carries an armload of projects to the fifth grade teacher's car. We're proud of both. The growth and nurturing of 230 children and 65 colleagues are at the heart of every Bement decision.

Grade Levels: Boarding Grades: 3-9, Day: K-9.

Student Gender: Boys & Girls.

Enrollment: 110 boys, 116 girls, 30 boarders, 196 day.

Accredited by: AISNE

Headmaster: Shelley Borror Jackson, B.A.English, Wheaton College M.A. English, Ohio State University Certificate of Advanced Studies in Education and Language Arts, University of Maine.

Faculty: The Bement School has 42 faculty members, 26 of whom hold master's degrees. 13 live on campus.

Tuition: Tuition and boarding for 2003-2004 is $30,955.

Class Size: 12 students, with a student/teacher ratio of 5:1.

Curriculum: The Bement School's academic program consists of core subjects including English/language arts, math, history/social studies, science and foreign language. All students are encouraged to explore creativity in solving problems, perseverance in completing tasks, and a love for seeing things in a new way.

Sports: Sports are an integral part of Bement's program. All students are involved in some form of sport or physical education throughout the school year.

Students are involved in programs suited to their skill levels. In addition to helping each student develop individual talents, coaches emphasize important concepts of teamwork and good sportsmanship. Students choose from a variety of competitive and non-competitive offerings each season.

Athletic Director Matt Palumb is a 1990 graduate of Syracuse University. While at Syracuse, Matt was a four-year letterman in lacrosse, and was the starting goalie on three consecutive national championship teams ('88-'90). Personal accolades include All-American status as well as MVP in the 1988 national championship game. More recently, Matt has stayed involved with lacrosse as an official at the collegiate and professional levels. He has officiated two national championship games at the college level, making him the only person to ever have both played and officiated an NCAA championship.

The Lower School program aims to develop coordination, game skills, sportsmanship, and a general awareness of the importance of physical fitness. Grades 4 and 5 concentrate on seasonal sports, playing intramural games and developing sport-specific skills that they will use in the upper school when interscholastic sports begin. All students in kindergarten through fifth grade participate in an instructional swimming program at the beginning of the spring term at the Deerfield Academy pool.

Extracurricular Activities: At Bement, students also participate in drama, art, writing, music, and outdoor skills. Students in grades 7–9 and their advisers participate for one term in an intergenerational community service program. Typical weekend activities include trips to points of local interest, sporting events, plays, and movies. Outdoor activities include hiking, bicycle trips, skiing and skating.

Campus: Bement is located on 12 acres in the historic Deerfield area near five area colleges which also provides additional educational opportunities. The Bement Upper School building houses classrooms, science labs, and locker rooms. The Upper School library is located in Snively House. The Drake School Building contains classrooms for grades 3–5, the Lower School library, and a computer lab with fifteen Macintosh terminals. Each classroom has Internet access. The fine arts facility features classrooms for art, music, and chorus, a darkroom, and a theatrical stage.

Dormitories: Bement's junior boarders, ages 9 through 15, live in restored colonial homes with dorm parents who commit themselves to monitoring closely each boarder's personal as well as academic growth.

Nearest International Airport: Logan International, Boston MA.

Ben Lippen School

Location: Columbia, South Carolina (U.S. Mid-Atlantic East Coast)

7401 Monticello Road, Columbia, SC 29203
Phone: 803-786-7200; Fax: 803-744-1387
Website: www.BenLippen.com
Email: blsadmissions@benlippen.com

Mr. Bobby Young, Admission
Phone: 803-786-7200; Fax: 803-744-1387
Email: blsadmissions@benlippen.com

Mission Statement: The mission of Ben Lippen School is to glorify God by assisting the family and church in equipping students spiritually, academically and socially under the Lordship of Jesus Christ. Our vision is to be a center of influence in the Christian school movement, and as a model school, to infuse into the movement three elements that are sometimes missing: Christian discipleship, high academic standards, and a world vision.

Admission Requirements for International Students: It is important that parents understand and support the philosophy and teaching of the school. Ben Lippen is primarily designated for families who accept the Bible as God's Word, confess Jesus Christ as their Savior and Lord and attend an evangelical church. Ben Lippen is unable to provide services for students with serious emotional, behavioral or academic problems. Applications may be filed as early as one year in advance. The application procedure includes the following: 1. A complete application form along with a (non-refundable) $50 application fee. 2. Parent and Student Questionnaire and references from the pastor, English teacher, and math teacher (see reference packets above). 3. A transcript from the previous school to include standardized test scores and grades. 4. A student entrance examination. 5. A student/parent interview with the appropriate principal. Initial inquiries are welcome throughout the year. Introductory sessions are set up periodically for those who would like to visit the school. Interviews are scheduled by the principals upon completion of the application procedure.

Grade Levels: Boarding Grades: 9-12.

Student Gender: Boys & Girls.

Enrollment: 466 boys, 430 girls, 46 boarders, 850 day.

Ben Lippen's current student body is composed of 337 elementary students, 192 middle school students and 348 high school students.

Accredited by: SACS /ACSI

Faculty: Ben Lippen has a faculty of 76 teachers, 33 of whom have advanced degrees and 2 reside on campus.

Tuition: With Room & Board, Grades 9-12: $20,960.

Faculty-student ratio: 1:15

Curriculum: Ben Lippen offers a college preparatory program with instruction in grades K-4 through 12.

Advanced Placement: Advance placement courses are offered in English, Biology, French, Calculus, Chemistry, Spanish, and U.S. History.

Average SAT Scores for Graduating Students: SAT verbal: 580, median SAT math: 540, median combined SAT: 1120. 34% scored over 600 on SAT verbal, 35% scored over 600 on SAT math, 27% scored over 1200 on combined SAT.

College Placement: Over 90% of our graduating seniors go on to higher education each year. Colleges attended by Ben Lippen students include: Air Force Academy, Cedarville University, Columbia College, Columbia International University, Covenant College, Clemson University, Eastern Nazarene College, Erskin College, Georgia Institute of Technology, Johns Hopkins University, Liberty University, Taylor University, The Citadel, University of South Carolina, U.S. Naval Academy, Wheaton College, Winthrop University.

Academic Requirements: Students are required to have at least 25 credits including Bible studies. English – 4 credits, Mathmatics- 4 credits, Lab Science – 3 credits, Social Sciences – 3 credits, Foreign Language – 2 credits, Physical Education/Health – 1 credit,

Computer Applications – 1 credit, Electives – 3 credits, Bible – 1-4 credits (1 for each year of attendance).

ESL Program: The boarding portion of our program is specifically designed for high school students from the United States and around the world. We currently have several international students and offer beginning, intermediate and advanced English as a Second Language (ESL) classes.

Sports: The Ben Lippen athletic program includes Baseball, Basketball, Cheerleading, Cross-country, Football, Golf, Soccer, Softball, Swimming, Tennis, Track & Field, Volleyball, and Wrestling.

Extracurricular Activities: Student Activities include Marching Band, Concert Band, Choir, Drama, Foreign Language Club, Literary Magazine, Math Team, National Honor Society, Student Council, Student Mission Fellowship, Super Fans Club, and Yearbook.

Leisure activities include basketball, softball, volleyball, jogging, fishing, weight lifting.

Campus: Ben Lippen is locaeted in a quiet suburban setting with 9 main buildings on a 100-acre campus.

Dormitories: Ben Lippen offers an alternative to typical dorm life in traditional boarding schools by creating a family atmosphere within contemporary-style houses. Up to 16 students live in each house with houseparents that seek to provide love and guidance.

Nearest International Airport: Columbia International Airport, Columbia SC.

Brehm Prepatory School

Location: Carbondale, Illinois (U.S. Midwest, Central)

1245 East Grand Avenue, Carbondale, IL 62901
Phone: 618-457-0371; Fax: 618-529-1248
Website: www.brehm.org; Email: brehm1@brehm.org

Ms. Donna Collins, Director of Admission
Phone: 618-457-0371; Fax: 618-549-2329
Email: admissionsinfo@brehm.org

Mission Statement: Brehm's mission is to empower students with complex learning disabilities to recognize and optimize their full potential. By fostering a family environment where educational, social, and emotional needs of each student are addressed in a focused, holistic program, through partnership among staff, students, parents, board, and the community.

To accomplish this mission, we place high value on student empowerment, integrity, strategies for interactive problem solving, ongoing open communication, staff development, continuous improvement in programs, and financial stability.

Brehm is a place of learning and growth for the student with learning differences. Brehm is a multi-faceted learning process; it's a continually evolving holistic process that integrates academic, emotional, social, and life skills. It is recognized that every interchange with a student is a learning moment. Our goal is to empower each student to become an advocate in his/her own learning process, capitalizing upon his/her unique gifts. A key outcome of the process is for each student to develop the capacity to be in control of his/her own destiny, to be motivated, and to be persistent in achieving his/her own goals along the way.

Brehm is an extended family of students and all the lives they touch, with each person communicating to foster and celebrate student successes and transitions, encouraging student independence with responsibility, and networking to support each other in dealing with the challenges of daily life.

Brehm provides a support system, allowing for the development of individual transition plans that encompass realistic options for higher education, career development, and independent living skills, leading each student to a productive, fulfilling life in his/her community.

As an expression of an environment, Brehm is a "State of Being," an energy and a spirit that once experienced, continually evokes in all of us the urge to grow and serve. It respects differences and honors uniqueness.

Admission Requirements for International Students: Brehm has a rolling admissions policy. Students are accepted throughout the year based on availability of space. Brehm School provides a nine and one-half month academic year program.

As a prerequisite to acceptance and enrollment, each prospective student must have a complete psycho-educational evaluation, and a primary diagnosis of a specific learning disability and/or A.D.D.. After a review of this information, the application, and other information pertinent to assessing the applicant's needs, an on-campus interview will be offered if it appears likely that Brehm Preparatory School would be an appropriate program.

Persons seeking admission to Brehm Preparatory School or the OPTIONS Program should submit the following information:

1) A completed application and $50.00 application fee
2) Current transcripts from high school and/or colleges (if applicable)
3) Current IEP and/or 504 Plan (if applicable)
4) Copies of earliest testing
5) Copies of current testing or additional evaluations that have been administered.

WISC III (Wechsler Intelligence Scale for Children – Third Edition, all subtest scores)

WAIS III (Wechsler Adult Intelligence Scale – Third Edition, all subtest scores)

The Woodcock-Johnson Psycho-Educational Battery III, Cognitive and Achievement, including Supplemental Battery (all summary scores)

CELF-3 (Clinical Evaluation of Language Fundamentals – Third Edition)

TOWL-3 (Test of Written Language – Third Edition, Spontaneous Writing sample only. Include copy of sample.)

Grade Level: 6-12

Student Gender: Boys & Girls

Enrollment: 62 boys, 24 girls, 80 boarders, 6 day, from 27 states and 4 foreign countries.

Accredited by: ISACS

Faculty: All faculty are certified in their content area as well as being LD certified and/or approved by the Illinois State Board of Education.

In addition, faculty members receive ongoing in-service training in multisensory teaching techniques. The majority of the faculty have Masters Degrees as well as years of professional experience, and several have Ph.D.s.

Brehm's faculty members are involved in studying and creating improved educational methodologies on an ongoing basis. Faculty members frequently present scholarly papers at national conferences.

Tuition: Tuition and boarding for 2003-2004 is $43,780.

Class Size: 8-10 students.

Curriculum: Brehm Preparatory School provides coursework in subjects required for junior high and senior high school graduation. A full range of coursework is offered in the areas of Laboratory

Sciences, Micro-computer Usage, Visual Arts, Mathematics, Physical Education, Social Sciences and the Humanities. A driver and traffic-safety education course is offered on a contractual basis to qualifying students.

Core content classes are limited to 8-10 students and instruction is integrated to meet the student's needs, while allowing him or her the opportunity to also function as part of a group.

Instructors in the classroom utilize multisensory teaching methods. Emphasis is placed on student strengths while providing compensatory strategies and remediation in deficit areas. Students are empowered to become independent learners and self-advocates.

On Monday through Friday of each week, students experience a full academic day. Students meet with their advisors each morning at 8:15 to prepare and organize for the school day.

A supervised study period is held each evening, Sunday through Thursday, from 7:00 p.m. until 9:00 p.m. Dorm parents and tutors monitor and provide assistance to the students during study hall time.

Study hall activities are organized through the use of a standardized Brehm assignment book consisting of learning strategies as well as homework assignments. The use of the assignment book enhances consistent communication between teachers, study hall tutors and dorm parents.

Campus Forum meets once a week under the direction of the Headmaster, Associate Headmaster or other administrative staff. The goal of Campus Forum is to create a positive school culture in which students can safely address adolescent issues. It is a direct instructional format where appropriate information is presented to students. Students then have the opportunity to respond and generate their thoughts related to issues. It is a problem solving format which leads to student empowerment. It prepares students to relate to real world issues by creating one informed set of strategies and allows students to set policy concerning these issues. Students discuss such topics as: peer relationships and cultures, harassment issues, date rape, drugs and alcohol, boy and girl relationships, friendships, and L.D./A.D.D.

Sports: Each day, one class period is devoted to physical education. Brehm's physical education director develops a program of exercises appropriate to each student's abilities and growth needs, the goal of which is personal fitness.

Extracurricular: On weekday afternoons the time between 3:30 and 5:00pm is the designated Recreation Period. Weekday activities vary widely and may include such things as: swimming, golf, hockey, jogging, photo journalism, aerobics, Historical Armed Combat Club, walking, fishing, and skating. Students also have the opportunity to develop their own personal recreation and leisure activities. Individual lessons include: horseback riding, yoga, pottery, music, dance, tennis, martial arts, and much more.

Students who have earned a high tier rating may choose an independent weekend recreation, which involves the student identifying an alternate activity (i.e. bike riding, movies, salon visits, etc.) and participating in the activity with another student after coordinating with the recreation supervisor. Students earning a high tier rating may also take part in special activities such as concerts and plays.

Weekends allow time for more extensive activities and longer trips. A number of alternate activities are scheduled for the same day. Some activities require a fee, but the recreation staff schedule several cost-free activities during each weekend. Activities in a typical month include: Comedy Show at SIUC, Miniature Golf/Go Kart Racing, On Campus Basketball, Paint a Saluki Puppy (Craft Project) at the Craft Shop, 5K Walk, SIUC vs. Murray Football Game Ultimate Gymnastics, Paintball, Teen Night Dance Party, Candle Making (Craft Project) at the Craft Shop, Haunted Hayride, Shopping in Nashville, Tennessee, Ice Skating, Bowling and Billiards, Underway Adventure High Ropes Course, Thrift Store Extravaganza, Hunan Lunch and a Movie, St. Louis Cardinal Baseball Game, Rope Courses, and Camping.

Campus: The Brehm campus consists of 80 acres with five dormitories, three classroom buildings and a student center.

Dormitories: Dormitory life is an integral part of the Brehm education. Brehm offers a family style living environment, designed to foster independence and responsibility. Students learn both the social skills for interacting with other people and the practical skills of independent living.

Each dorm is designed and built much the same as an apartment house, with bedrooms having one, two, or three occupants per room. This allows for a small group living arrangement of approximately 18 peers. Meals are prepared by the dorm parents and served in the dorm kitchen.

Two dorm parents, living within each dorm, supervise the students living in the dorm. In this supportive environment, emphasis is placed on group living; socialization and developing appropriate study behaviors.

Each student is responsible for the maintenance of his/her personal living space, along with the responsibility for a share of general dorm chores. Each student is also responsible for his/her own laundry.

Nearest International Airport: O'Hare International, Chicago IL.

Buxton School

Location: Williamstown, Massachusetts (U.S. East Coast, New England)

291 South Street, Williamstown, MA 01267
Phone: 413-458-3919; Fax: 413-458-9427
Website: www.BuxtonSchool.org
Email: Admissions@BuxtonSchool.org

Ms. Cheryl Deane, Director of Admissions
Phone: 413-458-5403; Fax: 413-458-9427
Email: Admissions@BuxtonSchool.org

Mission Statement: From its inception, Buxton has been known as an innovative school, one devoted to experimentation and change. Today, that devotion remains steadfast. Academic courses, activities, and community life are all vital parts of education at Buxton. Renewal and growth are fundamental. Underlying a student's academic and intellectual pursuits is the understanding that the same clear vision will be needed to understand, affect, and change the life that lies ahead. Social effectiveness leads beyond graduation, too, for the bridge to the larger world is the skilled, sensitive, informed, confident self that developed here during adolescence.

Admission Requirements for International Students: Students are admitted into grades 9 through 11, with the majority enrolling in the 9th and 10th grades. International students must possess some proficiency in English and can show academic success in their previous schools. English as a Second Language assistance is individually arranged, for which there is an additional fee. An on-campus interview is generally required, and formal applications are given to prospective students at that time. The campus visit affords the prospective student the opportunity to interact with students and faculty. However, when great distance and expensive travel are involved, an exception to this campus visit may be made. The aim of the admissions process is to help a student and his or her family determine if Buxton is the right school for them.

Grade Level: 9-12.

Student Gender: Boys & Girls.

Enrollment: 46 boys, 44 girls, 90 boarders.

Number of International Students: 5%

Accredited by: NEASC

Headmaster: C. William Bennett, Director (1969), B.A. Williams College,. E-mail: Director@BuxtonSchool.org

Faculty: There are approximately 20 faculty members working at Buxton, 13 of whom live on campus either in apartments in the dorms or with their families in houses on campus. The adults at Buxton are available and open to young people, concerned with their growth in academic disciplines and in every other respect as well. Along with teaching in the classroom, faculty members have leadership, administrative, and caretaking responsibilities.

Tuition: Tuition and boarding for 2003-2004 is $31,500.

Class Size: 7 students, with a teacher/student ratio of 5:1

Curriculum: The curriculum at Buxton is broad and demanding, offering a combination of traditional subjects, courses in the arts, and some studies rarely encountered before college. Courses, activities, and community life all contain vital potential for growth, so individual course programs allow for a mixture of academic and non-academic pursuits.

ESL Program: ESL instruction at Buxton is individually arranged for each international student.

College Placement: Colleges and universities attended by Buxton graduates in recent years include Amherst, Dartmouth, Macalaster, Mount Holyoke, Oberlin, Pitzer, Smith, Swarthmore, and Wesleyan.

Academic Requirements: Students are expected to complete the following studies: Sixteen credits are required for graduation, which include 4 years of English and a year of American history. Students are also counseled to complete a minimum of 3 years of mathematics, 2 years of social science, 2 years of laboratory science, and a minimum of 3 years of a foreign language. In addition, students are also strongly encouraged to pursue courses in the arts.

Sports: As with the other activities at Buxton, competitive and recreational sports are an integral part of life at the school. Competitive sports are not mandatory, but regular outdoor activity is expected of everyone.

In the fall, the school fields varsity and junior varsity soccer teams for boys and girls. In recent years, athletic competitors have included The Academy at Charlemont, Berkshire Country Day School, Darrow School, Deerfield Academy, Hoosac School, Northfield Mount Hermon School, The Putney School, and Bennington College.

During the winter months, students can choose from a variety of indoor and outdoor athletic activities such as varsity basketball, skiing, snowboarding, cross-country skiing, and ice-skating.

In the spring, biking, tennis, softball, soccer, volleyball, running, and swimming are offered.

The school's athletic resources include a weight room, two playing fields, an outdoor basketball court, and skating ponds. Additionally, Buxton is situated next to a thousand acres of undeveloped forest and meadow, providing easy access to trails for hiking and biking. Riding classes can be arranged.

Extracurricular: Each Friday evening an activity for the whole school is planned and organized by the Recreation Committee, a group of four student-elected individuals. It is expected that all students attend these creative activities. Dances, talent shows, relay races, skits, or games may be scheduled. More often, the evening is organized around a theme such as Ninja night, Wild West, or Beach night. Always, the evening requires the effort and goodwill of the entire community. In an age when so many are accustomed to the passive entertainment of TV, film, the Internet, and computer games, Rec Committee activities provide an opportunity to actively engage and direct one's own amusement.

All weekends, except for the two designated home weekends, are spent on campus. Saturday morning is reserved for Work Program, and in the afternoon and evening, students are free to go into Williamstown to do errands or attend a movie or cultural event. Saturday meals are planned and prepared by students. After Sunday brunch, the afternoon is available for academic work and recreation. The formal Sunday dinner is often followed by outside speakers or by student performances in the arts. Students wishing to do so attend religious services locally.

Campus: Buxton is located in a small historic New England town in the heart of the Berkshires. The campus itself, encompassing 150 acres of meadow and forest, is a backdrop for the enthusiasm and energy that unfolds at Buxton.

Dormitories: Student life at Buxton reflects a sense of family and community. All students attending Buxton live on campus. Girls live in the Main House and the Gate House; the Barn is home to the boys. Roommates are assigned at the beginning of the school year. Three times a year thereafter, students choose new roommates and change rooms. Room Change is an exciting time for all. This tradition gives students the experience of living closely with many different people while at Buxton.

There are many opportunities at Buxton for students to develop their leadership skills. Examples of such opportunities are serving as a dorm supervisor or head of a work crew. Each morning the entire student body attends to minor tasks within the dorms. These chores are organized and overseen by a small group of dedicated students, the dorm supervisors, who also serve as mentors and guides to the younger students as they navigate the complexities of dorm living.

Nearest International Airport: Albany International Airport

Nearby Lodgings: The Williams Inn, 413-458-9611; Maple Terrace Motel, 413-458-9677; Holiday Inn Berkshires, 413-663-650; The Porches Inn, 413-664-0400.

The Cambridge School of Weston

Location: Weston, Massachusetts (U.S. East Coast, New England)

Georgian Road, Weston, MA 02493
Phone: 781-642-8650; Fax: 781-398-8344
Website: www.csw.org; Email: admissions@csw.org

Ms. Trish Saunders, Director of Admission
Phone: 781-642-8650; Fax: 781-398-8344
Email: admissions@csw.org

Mission Statement: Welcome to the Cambridge School of Weston!
CSW is a community that is driven by its mission to attract intellectually and creatively talented students and faculty, and to provide
them with a stimulating and supportive environment in which to
thrive.

"Truthe and Gentil Dedes," the school motto, is a phrase that encap-
sulates our culture. I see it every day on a plaque that hangs in my
office from the original Cambridge School founded in 1886. These
words speak to the generosity of this school community; they
indicate how we each, as individuals, give to the whole. At CSW, we
define these actions as democracy at work.

To be a student at The Cambridge School of Weston means wanting
to be part of our mission, while enjoying participation in opportunities for leadership and social engagement. We will encourage you to
think for yourself, to take responsibility for your actions, and to live
within the framework of a caring, ethical, day and boarding school
community. We promise that you will find a way to be challenged.
You will also have fun, use your creativity, your intellect and your
personality. Come and visit The Cambridge School of Weston and
learn more about our program. We look forward to meeting you!

Admission Requirements for International Students: The application
process is designed as a way for both the applicant and the school to
assess the appropriateness of CSW as a next step. Interested students
and families are asked to schedule a visit of approximately two
hours on a school day. This visit typically includes a campus tour
with our students, class visits, and a chance to discuss school plans

and goals with an Admissions staff member. CSW's application deadline is February 1 for notification on March 10. Accepted students have until April 10 to notify us of their decision to enroll. Applications completed after February 1 are considered if space permits. International students should submit complete TOEFL or SLEP score reports.

Grade Level: 9-12.

Student Gender: Boys & Girls.

Enrollment: 310 students.

International Students: 12%, including students from Bahamas, Canada, Cote d'Ivoire, India, Japan, Korea, Spain, Switzerland, and Taiwan.

Accredited by: NEASC

Head of School: Jane Moulding

Faculty: On our faculty are published writers and poets, exhibiting artists, prominent choreographers, research mathematicians and scientists, and performing musicians. In selecting teachers, CSW looks for men and women who are committed to their students and their subjects and who convey their scholarly enthusiasm and curiosity to those they teach. Among our full-time faculty, 78% hold advanced degrees in their fields.

Tuition: Tuition and boarding for 2003-2004 is $32,600.

Class Size: 14 students with a student to teacher ratio of 8:1.

Curriculum: In 1972, the faculty of The Cambridge School of Weston designed the Module Plan, an educational program that permits intensive learning in two or three subjects at a time. CSW has employed this nationally-recognized program ever since.

Under the Module Plan, the year is divided into seven terms or "modules" (with an eighth module added in the summer of 2001), each lasting approximately four and one-half weeks. The school day consists of four blocks, either 75 or 90 minutes long. Students are in class for the first three academic blocks each day. Students are also involved in an activity (sports, theater, music, dance, student activities, etc.) during the fourth block for most of the year. Teachers write comments and give grades at the end of the each module so that families have frequent reports from the school.

We have developed a challenging program that is responsive to the needs of our students. Features include a diverse curriculum, the opportunity to concentrate on subjects of particular interest, and the close faculty-student relationships fostered by long daily classes together.

We do not have an honor roll. We acknowledge individual differences by combining different age groups in math, foreign language, some English and history classes, and the arts. Ninth graders take a few courses with older students; tenth graders take more. Eleventh and twelfth graders commonly work in classes together. Mixing students with other age groups as they get older is a conscious design to acknowledge developmental needs as well as different rates of academic and social growth. We offer over 300 courses; no two student schedules are alike. Each student is assigned an advisor who works with the student, the parents, and the Academic Office, in an effort to help students create a schedule that balances personal interests with college expectations and the school's requirements for grades nine through twelve and post-graduate.

The CSW Course Catalogue describes CSW's courses and requirements. The master schedule indicating when specific courses are taught during the year is published separately and can be obtained from academic advisors or from the Academic Office. Some of the courses in the catalogue may not be offered if there are changes in scheduling or teaching personnel. New courses may be added as the school year progresses.

ESL Program: Every course in the International Program grants credit towards graduation. The courses address the needs of incoming international students with a two-tiered focus: building each student's background knowledge and developing his or her academic English abilities. Early in the school year, incoming students fortify their English skills by focusing on grammar, writing, listening, and speaking within an academic context. As the year progresses, the curriculum shifts the focus from language skills to academic content. Students apply their English abilities to science, literature, and history courses. Unique to CSW's International Studies Program is its goal of balancing academics and language-learning course work with classes that allow students to use English imaginatively. International students should be fully prepared for mainstream classes by the end of the course sequence.

Average SAT Scores of Graduating Students: SAT I scores: Middle 50%: 570-680 Verbal, 550-680 Math. Percentage of 2003 Class students scoring SAT I over 700: 20% Verbal, 20% Math.

College Placement: Virtually all CSW graduates go on to four-year colleges and art schools. Art Institute of Chicago, Boston University, McGill University, New York University Northwestern University, Brown University, Sarah Lawrence College Smith College, Columbia University Tulane University, Cornell University, University of Chicago, Dartmouth College, and Vassar College.

Academic Requirements: Graduation requirements are the following: four years of English, three years of mathematics (at least through Algebra II), two and three-quarter years of history, three years of science, including at least eight blocks of lab science, a minimum of three years of foreign language, and a half years in the arts, one quarter year of an arts history, yearly school service, health education (9th or 10th grade), The Capstone Project (seniors), and three credits of athletics per year. Please refer to our Course Catalog for a detailed description of requirements per grade level.

Sports: Each academic year students are required to complete three athletic credits through participation in a competitive team sport or in a combination of various recreational physical education classes/activities, wilderness experiences, or dance courses. Team sports grant three credits; participation in recreational sports four days per week per module grants one credit, or two days per week for two modules grants one credit. Most dance courses grant athletic credit.

Athletic credit is available for: Soccer, Field Hockey, Basketball, Baseball, Ultimate Frisbee, Softball, Tennis, Fencing, Yoga, Weight Training, Conditioning for Dance and Sports, Volleyball, Cycling, Martial Arts: Tae Kwon Do, Ropes and Wilderness Trips.

Extracurricular: Students are expected to participate in a wide range of afternoon activities for most of the year. The program includes clubs, committees, school service work, academic or arts labs, Chorus, Percussion Ensemble, the Literary Magazine, the Yearbook Committee, and more.

Campus: Our 65 acre wooded campus is located 12 miles from Boston. The academic facilities surround a tree-shaded quadrangle and include nine buildings housing classrooms, the library, a computer center, five science laboratories, the computerized foreign language lab, the Mugar Center for the Performing Arts, and the Cohan Academic building. Each of the four dormitories houses 15 to 25 sutdents and two dorm parent families. Six other faculty members live on campus. Most students live in double rooms, but some singles are available.

Dormitories: CSW's boarding program offers a home-like environment, appropriate structures to support students' academic commitments, professional dorm parents, and an excellent weekend activities program which takes advantage of our proximity to Cambridge and Boston.

Nearest International Airport: Logan International Airport.

The Canterbury School

Location: New Milford, Connecticut (U.S. East Coast, New England)

105 Aspetuck Avenue, Box 5000, New Milford, CT 06776-1739
Phone: 860-210-3800; Fax: 860-350-4425
Website: www.cbury.org/index.html; Email: admissions@cbury.org

Mr. Keith Holton, Director of Admission
Phone: 860-210-3800 or 860-210-3832; Fax: 860-350-1120
Email: kholton@cbury.org

Mission Statement: Founded in 1915, Canterbury is a lay Catholic, coeducational college-preparatory school. While academics are paramount, our size encourages building wonderful relationships among students and faculty. Our program is designed to challenge, support and encourage each and every student to realize his or her full potential. At the core of our existence is our faith. As a Roman Catholic school, we nurture the spiritual development of our community as part of the overall education our students receive and foster an atmosphere where service to others plays a crucial part in our students' growth.

Whether you are interested in a specific academic program, the arts, athletics, drama, music or community service, you will have the opportunity to excel in a number of areas. A recently refurbished academic building, a new athletic center, and up to date technology enable our outstanding faculty to guide our students and enhance their experience at Canterbury.

We invite you to visit our campus and meet the faculty and students who make up Canterbury School. You will experience firsthand that sense of community and learning which have been hallmarks of a Canterbury education since the School's inception.

Admission Requirements for International Students: There are 3 steps in the admissions process at Canterbury School.

1. Inquiry - Contact the Admissions Office to receive an application package and viewbook or inquire on-line.
2. Interview - Schedule an on-campus visit which includes a tour

and interview.

3. Apply - Send in the application and arrange to have your transcript and teacher recommendations sent.

Grade Level: 9-12.

Student Gender: Boys & Girls.

Enrollment: 358 students, 219 boys, 139 girls, 218 boarders, 140 day.

Accredited by: CAIS/CT

International Students: Australia, England, Germany, Japan, Korea, Spain, Taiwan, Venezuela.

Headmaster: Thomas J. Sheehy, III, B.A. Bowdoin College, M.A. Pennsylvania State University. E-Mail: tsheehy@cbury.org

Faculty: Canterbury has a full-time faculty of 69 teachers, 48 of whom hold advanced degrees. Each faculty member advises a group of 6 to 8 students.

Tuition: Tuition and board for 2003-2004 is $32,000.

Financial Aid: Canterbury School offers grants to its students with proven financial need. Financial Aid applications will not affect Admission Applications decisions. They are considered separately. Financial aid is awarded only to students who have completed the Admissions Office application process and been officially accepted.

Class Size: 12 students, with a student/teacher ratio of 6:1.

Curriculum: Canterbury believes that all students should be challenged according to their level of proficiency. Students take five and one half courses each semester. The School has two marking periods of six weeks each during the first semester; three in the second semester. The Director of Studies works with students and their parents to prepare a slate of courses appropriate for that student.

Canterbury students are eager learners who pursue a college preparatory program, offering more than 100 courses and Advanced

Placement courses in 15 subjects. Teachers are keenly aware of each student's strengths and gifts. and balance the demands of intellectually demanding course work with the appropriate amount of personal support and extra help, in and out of class.

Advanced Placement: Advance placement courses are available in English Literature, Statistics, Calculus, American History, World History, Economics, Biology, Chemistry, Art, Music Theory, French Language, French Literature, Spanish Language and Spanish Literature.

ESL Program: Canterbury offers an English as a second language (ESL) program. Students are tested at the beginning of the school year and placed in an appropriate level of instruction with the opportunity for higher placement as English proficiency progresses, until academic mainstream proficiency is achieved.

College Placement: Recent graduates of Canterbury have been accepted to Boston College, Colby, Cornell, Dartmouth, Georgetown, Holy Cross, the U.S. Military Academy, and the Universities of Notre Dame and Pennsylvania.

Academic Requirements: Students are expected to complete the following studies: English - 4 credits, Math - 4 credits, Foreign Language - 3 credits in one language, History - 3 credits, Science - 2 credits, Fine Arts - 1 credit, Electives - 2 credits. Total – 20 credits.

Sports: Canterbury has a proud history of interscholastic athletics. We compete in the Western New England Athletic Association and in the New England Prep School Athletic Conference at the Division I and II levels. We believe that physical activity and athletics are an important part of a child's education, creating an invaluable arena for personal growth as well as providing a focus for school spirit. We stress sportsmanship, attitude, effort, skill development and cooperation. The team comes first and every member of the team is valuable. Each student is required to participate during the fall, winter and spring seasons. Canterbury sponsors 48 teams in 18 sports which compete interscholastically on different levels so that all students, regardless of ability, have the opportunity to participate. We compete primarily on Wednesdays and Saturdays with some varsity teams playing during vacations. Canterbury hosts five tournaments during the year. A state-of-the-art training room is staffed by two certified athletic trainers and a nurse is always on call. The Ade Family weight and fitness room is supervised by a certified personal trainer.

Extracurricular: Students help the Assistant Dean of Students program weekend activities. Activities include trips to a local eatery and movie theatre, trips to Danbury Fair Mall, excursions to Broadway or a professional sports event, dances on or off campus, movies in the lecture room, and outdoor concerts.

Campus: Canterbury is proud of its beautiful location. Set atop a hill in New Milford, the campus affords spectacular views to the west and east. It feeatures150 acres and 26 buildings. Recent changes to campus include a $6 million athletic center (which includes a new fitness room and five international size squash courts) a new music center, a renovated classroom building, wired dorms and classroom for computers. These developments have occurred while Canterbury has maintained its dedication to educating its students in a challenging and supportive atmosphere.

Dormitories: For each boarding student, the dormitory serves as a home away from home. Life in the dormitory is a richly rewarding experience. Each dormitory houses a wide variety of people with different needs: single and married faculty, faculty children, and students from diverse cultural, social, and economic backgrounds. These many personalities represent a wide range of personal preferences and interests. Boarding students live in seven dormitories on campus and are grouped according to gender and class. Most rooms are singles, but several accomodate two students. Evening study hall is conducted in each dorm by dormparents and proctors Sunday - Friday.

Nearest International Airport: Hartford International Airport.

Nearby Lodgings: Danbury Sheraton, 203-794-0600; Ethan Allen Inn, 203-744-1776; Holiday Inn, 203-792-4000; Ramada Inn, 203-792-3800.

Cate School

Location: Carpinteria, California (U.S. West Coast)

P.O. Box 5005, 1960 Cate Mesa Road, Carpinteria, CA 93013
Phone: 805-684-4127; Fax: 805-684-8940
Website: www.cate.org; Email: admission@cate.org

Mr. Peter Mack, Director of Admission
Phone: 805-684-4127 ext. 217; Fax: 805-684-2279
Email: admission@cate.org

Mission Statement: Cate inspires each student to seek self-fulfill-
ment and to serve others. Through a challenging program which
prepares adolescents to meet high expectations, Cate enables each
student to grow intellectually and emotionally, to act purposefully
and morally, and to lead an active, healthy life.

In Cate's beautiful setting, promising students and devoted teachers
are brought together to live, work, and play in an intimate community in which young people learn through experience that the best
development of self occurs among others, in relationships based on
respect, compassion, and hope.

Admission Requirements for International Students: Because Cate
does not offer English as a Second Language, all candidates must be
fluent in English. It is recommended that non-native English
speakers take the Test of English as a Foreign Language (TOEFL).

Grade Level: 9-12.

Student Gender: Boys & Girls.

Enrollment: 265 students, 220 boarders, and 45 day.

International Students: 12% of the student population calls a foreign
country home. 14 different countries are represented.

Accredited by: WASC

Headmaster: Benjamin Williams IV, B.A. American Studies Williams
College, M.A. American Civilization Brown University.

Faculty: The Cate School faculty is a distinctive group of 50 exceptional scholars. Our teachers have outstanding credentials - more than 70 percent have advanced degrees, many from such highly regarded institutions as Stanford, Columbia, and Princeton. They are professionals who are actively involved in their fields, enthusiastic and talented athletes, highly accomplished individuals with a wide range of interests. Cate faculty members assume multiple roles as teachers, dorm parents, coaches, advisors, mentors, and friends. Our teachers take pride in their singular devotion to their students. For students as well as faculty, this means positive interaction that extends well beyond the academic day and into the evening hours - sometimes late into the evening hours - and on weekends. Most of the faculty members and their families live on the campus, and all faculty members advise or coach an extracurricular student activity such as athletics, public service, outdoor program, student clubs, yearbook, and student newspaper.

Tuition: Tuition and boarding for 2003-2004 is $31,500.

Class Size: 10 - 12 students with a teacher-student ratio of 6 to 1.

Curriculum: Cate School's course of study is carefully designed to foster and build upon the developing skills and aptitudes of students as they progress from grades 9 and 10 through grades 11 and 12.

In both 9th and 10th grades, all students are required to take a course—sometimes a particular course—in each of seven academic departments. The number of class meetings in these programs is restricted so that students carry a reasonable course load. Because the School believes that academic specialization is inappropriate for 9th and 10th graders, they develop their skills and investigate their strengths and interests by studying a full range of disciplines. This coherent lower-school program also allows departments to coordinate the development of academic skills across the curriculum.

Prior education is taken into account for placement in mathematics, science, and foreign language courses. In some subjects, the most able and interested students are sometimes placed into honors sections. Having gained a firm foundation of broad skills and knowledge, students in 11th and 12th grades pursue elective offerings in all disciplines, including honors and Advanced Placement courses if capability warrants.

Throughout the School, classes are small, typically eight to fifteen students, and there are always opportunities for teachers and students to work together closely outside of class. Full-credit courses meet four or five times weekly, with three to four hours of homework per week. Enrichment courses and electives, which are intended to serve student interests and to complement the basic course of study, meet from one to three times each week.

The Cate academic program educates whole students. Our carefully designed curriculum enhances intellectual growth through solid college preparation and a number of distinctive offerings not often found at a school this small. We provide an in-depth education in mathematics and the natural sciences guided by faculty who have earned national recognition for their innovative teaching. We are also known for an integrated arts program that encompasses music, drama, and the fine and visual arts. Seniors can choose among numerous Advanced Placement (AP) courses (AP exams are course requirements in many departments), four languages, and courses in Multimedia Productcion. We offer a nationally recognized Asian Studies program and a nationally recognized Human Development program, which in addition to being a one-of-a-kind learning experience will help students adjust to life at a boarding school.

Advanced Placement: Advanced Placement preparation is offered in all disciplines.

ESL Program: The Cate School does not offer an ESL program.

SAT: The median SAT score of graduating seniors is 1300.

College Placement: 100% of Cate graduates attend four-year colleges including. UC Berkeley, USC, Columbia, Pomona, University of Colorado, Colorado College, Princeton, University of Pennsylvania, Vanderbilt and Cornell.

Academic Requirements: Graduation requirements are generally as follows:

Arts—Foundation Arts (a year-long course for 9th graders and those students entering Cate in 10th grade) plus two additional half-credit courses.

English—one year-long course each year (seniors take two semester-long courses; 9th grade students take Humanities - a combination of English and history).

Foreign Language—successful completion of a third-year course, or, for students entering with advanced standing, study through the sophomore year.

History—one course in each of the first two years (9th grade students take Humanities), and U.S. History in 11th or 12th grade.

Mathematics—one course each year through the junior year, with the final course determined by the initial Cate entry level; all students are expected to complete Algebra II.

Science—Conceptual Physics and Chemistry in grades 9 and 10; Biology or AP Environmental Science/Biology in grades 11 and 12.

Human Development—Freshman Seminar (two meetings per week) for all freshmen; Sophomore Seminar (two meetings per week) for all sophomores.

Sports: Cate's interscholastic athletic program is designed to offer students a wide variety of healthy competitive options. It is a program with a place for everyone—from the nationally-ranked athlete to the student with no experience at all. It is not uncommon for a student to start a sport during his or her freshman or sophomore year and eventually be a pivotal member of a varsity team as a senior.

Extracurricular: All Cate students participate in an afternoon program. Most play on an interscholastic team while others, depending on the athletic season, hike, bike, surf, kickbox, rock-climb or dance. Some take part in a weight-training program in the fitness center. Others head to the track and fields for "power training," a regimen that combines yoga stretches with a strenuous workout. Students may also elect to use their afternoon time tutoring local public school students through Cate's public service program.

Campus: Cate's understated Mission-style architecture and the village-like campus let students appreciate the School's magnificent setting. In fact, the quiet nature of the Mesa and Cate buildings in some ways belies the extraordinary facilities available to students.

The Cate Arts Center houses the 450-seat Hitchcock Theater, where students and faculty gather for assemblies, concerts and plays. There are also photography darkrooms, a multimedia lab, two recording studios and a sun-drenched art studio for student use. At the Bruno Art Gallery and Hooker Art Gallery, students can view work by fellow students and visiting artists. The ceramics barn is equipped with ten pottery wheels and three kilns. The Seeley G. Mudd Science Building is the school's center for scientific study and research. There are fully equipped labs, classrooms, preparation rooms, project rooms and a seminar room. The Keck Computer Lab accommodates individuals and classes through networked PC and Macintosh computers with word processing, spreadsheet, HyperCard, Pascal, C++, Java, Twin Bridge Japanese and Chinese software, as well as science, mathematics, history and art applications.

The Johnson and McBean Libraries house 25,000 volumes, 110 periodicals and a variety of audiovisual materials. Through the CD-ROM catalog students can access the Cate library collections as well as an additional 100,000 items in the Independent School Library Exchange of Southern California. At the Wiegand Community Center, students can gather informally to listen to music, watch a movie or catch up with friends. Cate's athletic and outdoor program facilities include two gyms, the Fleischmann Gymnasium with two squash courts and a basketball court and the Caryll M. and Norman F. Sprague, Jr. Gymnasium, with two regulation-size basketball courts, two volleyball courts and a fully equipped fitness center. For outdoor sports, there are four athletic fields, an all-weather composite track, baseball and softball diamonds, eight tennis courts and a heated swimming pool. The campus also boasts a dance studio, the Claire Andriveau Drake Memorial Ropes Course and a technical climbing tower.

Dormitories: Cate has nine dormitories, many with stunning views of the Santa Barbara Channel and Santa Ynez Mountains. Almost all students live in single rooms, most with balconies or patios. The Katharine Thayer Cate Memorial Chapel, with its stunning stained-glass windows, provides a beautiful setting for concerts, Tuesday Talks and contemplation.

Nearest International Airport: Los Angeles International Airport.

Nearby Lodgings: Best Western Carpinteria Inn, 805-684-0473; Comfort Suites, 805-566-9499; Four Seasons Biltmore Hotel, 805-969-2261; Radisson Hotel, 805-963-0744.

Chaminade College Preparatory School

Location: St. Louis, Missouri (U.S. Midwest, Central)

425 South Lindbergh Blvd., St. Louis, MO 63131-2799
Phone: 314-993-4400
Website: www.chaminademo.com; Email: email@chaminade-stl.com

Mr. Roger Hill, Director of Admissions
Phone: 314-993-4400 ext. 150; Fax: 314-993-5732
Email: rhill@chaminade-stl.com

Mission Statement: Chaminade College Preparatory School is an
independent Catholic school for young men in grades six through
twelve. The mission of Chaminade is to provide a holistic and high
caliber education, grounded in faith, that prepares its students for
success in college and in life. The school bears the name of Blessed
Father William Joseph Chaminade, a priest who lived during the era
of the French Revolution and who founded the religious order
known as the Society of Mary (Marianists). The school maintains an
active relationship with this Society through governance structures
and the employment of lay and Marianist religious committed to a
conscious effort to keep alive the Marianist charism in all aspects of
the institution's functioning. It is the school's Marianist roots that
cause it to emphasize growth in faith, the development of the whole
person, and the cultivation of moral values. Faithful to the tradition
of the Society of Mary, all of these take place in a warm, nurturing
family environment. These emphases shape the school as a true
community of learning where all members of the Chaminade Family
are encouraged to grow, develop, and contribute as fully as possible
to the school's mission of education.

The Chaminade Family encourages students to live by a system of
religious and moral values rooted in Catholic heritage and character-
istic of the Marianist tradition. These values include devotion to
Mary, community life, and demonstration of living the gospel in all
times and places. The role of Mary was central to Father
Chaminade's vision. He saw her as the one who received the word
of the Lord and pondered it in her heart; the woman who gave
Christ to the world; the Mother who forms all believers. His hope
was to gather all Christians - men and women, young and old, lay

and clerical - into a unique community of Christ's followers, unafraid to be known as such; committed to living and sharing their faith; and dedicated to supporting one another in living the Gospel to the fullest in their everyday life.

Much of the school's Christian and Marianist approach is summarized and presented to the students through the school's motto, "Esto Vir." This motto, which literally means "Be a man," is interpreted to be a challenge to maximize the potential of all the gifts and talents which God has placed in each person. Thus it becomes clear that education at Chaminade is much more than an academic undertaking; it is an endeavor that encompasses all aspects of the young man's being.

Admission Requirements for International Students: A Linguistics and Experience America Program (L.E.A.P.) is required of new international students,who have not previously attended school in the United States. L.E.A.P. begins three weeks prior to the beginning of the school year. This orientation program is designed to introduce students to dormitory life, the United States, St. Louis, Chaminade, and American culture.

Grade Level: 6-12.

Student Gender: Boys only.

Enrollment: 970 boys, 60 boarders, 910 day.

Accredited by: CAIS/CT

Faculty: True to Father Chaminade's vision, the faculty possess a strong commitment to the total education of their students. As educators, they dedicate themselves to helping their students learn to analyze and respond appropriately to the many forces and ideologies operating in the world around them. As educators in the Christian and Marianist tradition, they set for themselves the personal goal of modeling a sensitivity to humanity and responsible norms of conduct.

Faculty commitment to professional development and furthering its own education is strong as well. They recognize the importance of adapting methodology to fit the changing needs of student learning styles and to meet the demands of modern society.

The faculty is assisted in its mission by a wide variety of support staff who share the commitment to foster the development of each student. While not as directly involved in the process of education, these staff members likewise attempt to model the values which Chaminade stands for and to help create the familial atmosphere that is so much a part of the school.

Tuition: Tuition for 2003-2004 is $9,750. Room and board is $10,450.

Financial Aid: Chaminade wants to make it possible for all qualified students to attend. Chaminade's financial aid budget enables more than 200 students (including many from middle class families) who are not able to pay the full tuition to attend. Over $903,000 has been awarded to our students for the 2003-2004 school year. Many types of financial assistance are available:

Direct grants: These are awarded to students demonstrating financial need and do not have to be repaid. These awards range from $250 to $6,000.

Work / study grants: These are awarded to students demonstrating financial need. For every $300 in aid received, students work 50 hours.

Chaminade student loans: These loans are made through an agreement with Chaminade. The loan amount is $500 per school year, and interest is not charged until the student graduates from Chaminade. As an option, interest only can be payable for the first four years after graduation. Interest and principal will be payable over the following four years.

Curriculum: Chaminade College Preparatory School has an academic curriculum which promotes the Christian world and fulfillment of all members of the school family through knowledge, academic skills, analytical and critical thinking, a respectful attitude and a sense of aesthetics.

Chaminade students acquire knowledge of the world-past, present and future, through the study of natural and political history, the study and experience of multi-culturalism and languages of the world, geography, literature, philosophy, grammar, religious studies, social science, physical and biological sciences.

Chaminade students are taught skills which include computer science, practical arts and physical education. Chaminade students learn analytical and critical thinking through logic, math, science, history and economics. Chaminade students learn a respect for all forms of life through studying life sciences, learning about comparative religions, ethics and different lifestyles, and acquiring a sense of aesthetics through exposure to literature, music and the arts.

Chaminade students perform more than 30,000 service hours per year, giving of their time and talents to serve those who are less fortunate. Students in grades six through eleven work twenty hours per school year. Seniors are required to work ten hours plus complete a fifty hour service project. Service projects are coordinated through Campus Ministry and religious studies classes.

Academic Requirements: Students are expected to complete the following studies:

Sixth: Religious Studies, English, Social Studies, Math, Science, Physical Education, Fine Arts, and Practical Arts to total 8 class periods.

Seventh: Religious Studies, English, Social Studies, Math, Science, Introduction to Languages, Physical Education, Fine Arts and Practical Arts to total 8 class periods.

Eighth: Religious Studies, English, Social Studies, Math, Science, Classical/Modern Language, Physical Education and Fine Arts to total 8 class periods.

Freshman: Religious Studies, English, Social Studies, Math, Science, Classical/Modern Language, Physical Education, Fine Arts and Practical Arts to total a minimum of 7 1/2 units.

Sophomore: Religious Studies, Composition, Literature, Social

Studies, Math, Science, Classical/Modern Language, Physical Education and Fine Arts to total a minimum of 7 1/2 units.

Junior: Religious Studies, Composition, Literature, Social Studies, Math, Science, Physical Education and electives to total a minimum of 7 units.

Senior: Religious Studies, Composition, Literature, Social Studies, Physical Education and electives to total a minimum of 7 units.

Graduation Requirements: Religious Studies - 4, Classical/Modern Languages - 2, English - 4 1/2, Physical Education - 2, Social Studies - 4, Fine Arts - 1, Mathematics - 3, Practical Arts - 1, Science - 3, Electives - 4 1/2. Total: 29 Units (one unit equals one full year of a high school course.)

Sports: Athletics is a very important part of life at Chaminade. To the participants it offers a great opportunity to represent their school while learning how to work toward both individual and team goals. To the student body, parent, alumni and friends, it offers an opportunity to show their support for Chaminade.

An experienced quality coaching staff and superior athletic facilities offer the dedicated student athlete the chance to reach his personal goals. Membership in the prestigious Metro-Catholic Conference assures Chaminade strong athletic competition and recognition for its teams. All this adds up to success for the individual athlete and the teams wearing the Chaminade uniform.

Baseball, Basketball, Cross Country, Football, Golf, Hockey, Racquetball, Soccer, Swimming/Diving, Tennis, Track & Field, Volleyball, Water Polo, and Wrestling.

Extracurricular: When a day of classes comes to an end, the fun is just beginning at Chaminade. With all the after school activities offered, the campus is continuously buzzing with excitement. Involvement is an important part of any student's education, in and out of the classroom. That's why there's an activity for every Chaminade student, whatever his interest might be. He can choose from a host of sports programs plus a variety of clubs to cultivate his inherent talents and skills. Each activity is supervised by a qualified

Chaminade faculty member. These instructors are dedicated to developing a well-rounded student who will be prepared for college and life. Activities include: American Youth Foundation, Art Clubs, Bands, Biology Club, Chess Club, Computer Club, Mock Trial, NASCAR Club, National Honor Society, National Junior Honor Society, Newspaper, Photography Club, Drama, Robotics Club, Earth Club, Rocket Club, Focus St. Louis, Scholar Bowl, Future Business Leaders of America, High School Student Council, Student Ambassadors, Liturgical Choir, Table Tennis, Marianist Life Communities, Weatherization Club, Math Club, WCCP (filmmaking), Middle School Student Council, and Yearbook.

Chapel Hill-Chauncy Hall School

Location: Waltham, Massachusetts (U.S. East Coast, New England, 10 miles outside Boston)

785 Beaver Street, Waltham, MA 02452
Phone: 781-894-2644; Fax: 781-894-5205
Website: www.chch.org; Email: admissions@chch.org

Ms. Julia Jones, Director of Admission
Phone: 781-894-2644; Fax: 781-894-5205
Email: juliajones@chch.org

Mission Statement: Chapel Hill-Chauncy Hall is fortunate in being the union of three schools: Chapel Hill, Chauncy Hall, and the Huntington School. We are proud of our rich heritage and still preserve many of the important traditions established at these schools. We continue to maintain a small class size, celebrate the individual student, and provide a diverse and nurturing educational environment.

We believe students with a variety of learning styles are not only capable of success but have unlimited potential. Our size allows faculty, students, and staff to enjoy close relationships that foster learning. With the rich diversity of our distinctive learning community, we celebrate a multiplicity of peoples and cultures. We are fortunate to grow every day within the spacious grounds of a lovely 30 acre campus. These unmistakable characteristics not only identify us, but nourish our success. Come visit and see firsthand the exceptional learning process, the natural setting, and above all, the wonderful people that make Chapel Hill-Chauncy Hall such a remarkable place.

Admission Requirements for International Students: All international students must have an interview, which can be either a phone interview or they may come and visit the campus. Also International students must submit scores for SLEP or TOEFL. (SLEP is preferred.) SSAT scores are optional for international students.

Grade Level: 9-12,PG.

Student Gender: Boys & Girls.

Enrollment: 89 boys, 81 girl, 68 boarders, 102 day.

International Students: 12%

Accredited by: AISNE, NEASC

Head of School: Siri Akal Khalsa, B.A., Brooklyn College, M.F.A, Brandeis University, M.S., Baruch College, M.A., Columbia University, Ed.D., Columbia University. E-mail: siriakalkhalsa@chch.org

Faculty: 62 faculty and staff members, about 35% resident. 42% of our faculty and staff have Master degree or higher.

Tuition: Tuition and boarding for 2003-2004 is $33,400.

Class Size: 8-14 students, with a student/teacher ratio of 5:1.

Curriculum: In the belief that every part of the students' lives offers lessons and opportunities for personal development, Chapel Hill-Chauncy Hall provides many challenging programs in the classroom and beyond. The academic program is designed to support and challenge each student and to acknowledge that students learn in a variety of ways. The curriculum also incorporates programming in areas such as afternoon activities, athletics, physical fitness, health education, community service, student presentations, residential life, student clubs and organizations, and leadership training opportunities. The underlying goals of the curriculum are to provide students with the opportunity to develop self-confidence as learners and to achieve a greater degree of independence and maturity in thinking, making decisions, and taking actions. All students at Chapel Hill-Chauncy Hall are expected to pursue a program of study appropriate to their abilities, skills, and interests that will prepare them for further study after graduation.

Advanced Placement: Art and English, there are also advanced classes in the science for students who are looking to pursue a science major in college.

ESL Program: An ESL program is available for international students at an extra annual fee of $2360 for two classes per week, or $3540 for three classes per week.

College Placement: Students of Chapel Hill-Chauncey Hall have gone on to attend college and universities such as Boston University, Illinois Institute of Technology, New York University, Northeastern University, Rutgers University, Sarah Lawrence College, University of Massachusetts Amherst, University of Miami, Worcester Polytechnic Institute, and University of Pennsylvania.

Academic Requirements: 4 years of English; 4 years of History; 3 years of Math; 3 years of Science; 2 years of art; 2 years of a foreign language

Sports: We've never abandoned the old-fashioned ideal of a sound mind in a sound body at Chapel Hill-Chauncy Hall. But we also work very hard to keep competitiveness in proper perspective.

The thrust of our athletic programs is teamwork, variety, and building self-confidence and physical competence. We offer nontra-ditional athletes many opportunities to become involved in organ-ized league sports. If students are interested, all they have to do is speak with a head coach and generally they'll be welcomed on the team. Though we encourage students to join an athletic team that meets five days a week, it is not a requirement of the school. All students must, however, fulfill a physical activity requirement 2 days per week. This could include recreational sports such as racquetball, kick-boxing, and fitness.

Extracurricular: There are a plethora of exciting social activities to join on the weekends. Remember, Boston and all its celebrated attractions are only 10 miles away. You can cheer on the Red Sox, stroll through the Museum of Fine Arts, visit historic Fanueil Hall, or simply walk along the Charles River or through Copley Square.

Other weekend activities include going to the movies, taking a shuttle to Downtown Waltham, joining a whale watch, or going skiing, shopping, or out to dinner.

Other than league athletics and visual and performing arts, there are many other afternoon activities to choose from, including Cooking

Around the World, Kick-Boxing, Newspaper, Personal Fitness, Racquetball, and Yearbook.

Campus: Chapel Hill-Chauncy Hall's 37-acre campus is what typically comes to mind with "New England boarding school". It's quiet, safe, and peaceful, with big trees, lots of green lawn, bicycles and few cars, traditional buildings, and a history that goes back to 1860. The incredible part is that downtown Boston is only ten miles away. On weekends, students can join trips into Boston to see a play, or attend a sporting event, or simply walk its historic streets. They return to an extremely pleasant, homelike environment, where it's easy to concentrate and there's plenty of space to learn and grow.

Dormitories: Chapel Hill-Chauncy Hall boarding students are the heart of the school. Because campus is their home, they make it feel like home for everyone else too.

Whether you're from Tacoma or Taiwan, Haiti or Hartford, Springfield, Massachusetts or Springfield Illinois, boarding is a positive experience. Indeed, boarders are often a diverse group, so the boarding life offers students the rare chance to bridge cultures, races, countries, and social backgrounds.

Boarding life is close, with three to five houseparents in each dorm (along with their kids and dogs). Dorms also include proctors, who are integral to the operation of the dorms, as they support First Year Students and sophomores and assist in the communication between students and houseparents. Every night from 7:30 to 9:30 p.m. is supervised study hall. Convenient workstations were added in the dorms in 2001 with state-of-the-art programming and high-speed internet access. Nightly supervised study is balanced with free time to relax, check e-mail, or just chat with friends. Before long, students have made friendships that will last a lifetime. Staying on campus for the weekend can be just as enjoyable as visiting Boston. You can watch a DVD and eat pizza in the student union, play a pick-up game of basketball in the gym, or have a cookout.

There are two girls' dorms on campus, North Hall and South Hall. The top floors of North Hall contain girls' dorm rooms and faculty apartments. South Hall is located close to the duck pond and also houses the school bookstore. The boys' dormitory, Worcester Hall, is divided into two sections, one for Freshman and Sophomores, and the other for Juniors and Seniors. Worcester Hall also houses the wrestling room.

Nearest International Airport: Logan International Airport, Boston.

Nearby Lodgings: Doubletree Guest Suites Hotel, 781-890-6767; Four Points by Sheraton, 781-890-0100; Westin Hotel, 781-290-5600.

Chatham Hall

Location: Chatham, Virginia (U.S. Mid-Atlantic, East Coast)

800 Chatham Hall Circle, Chatham, VA 24531-3085
Phone: 434-432-2941; Fax: 434-432-2405
Website: www.chathamhall.org; Email: admission@chathamhall.org

Ms. Alexis Weiner, Director of Admission and Financial Aid
Phone: 434-432-2941; Fax: 434-432-2405
Email: aweiner@chathamhall.org

Mission Statement: Chatham Hall prepares young women for college and productive, fulfilled lives. We esteem equally the intellect and character of each student. A community of honor and trust, we value our Episcopal heritage and welcome students from diverse backgrounds. Our rigorous educational program encourages intellectual growth, creative development, and personal responsibility.

As an all-girls Episcopal boarding school, Chatham Hall invigorates students intellectually and provides a community of trust that teaches and nurtures each girl's sense of responsibility and respect for herself. Through its strong Honor Code, Chatham Hall instills in girls a high degree of integrity which guides their choices and actions. A challenging academic program, combined with rich co-curricular opportunities and a supportive faculty, promotes self-discipline, reflection, and the courage to try new experiences.

Girls learn that leadership cannot be separated from honor and service, and that every girl is a leader in the choices she makes and the responsibilities she assumes in and for her community. The unique essence of the school lies in its freedom from sham and pretense and its appreciation of individuality; as a community, Chatham Hall cherishes each girl for herself, and that self blossoms as a result.

Chatham Hall helps each girl find and develop her own unique voice. One way the school promotes this development is by bringing to the School powerful women's voices. Students have chances to meet and hear from visitors such as Nobel Peace Prize winner Shirin Ebadi, first woman president of Ireland and former U.N. High

Commissioner for Human Rights Mary Robinson, poet and activist Nikki Giovanni, social activist Sherialyn Byrdsong, and many others.

Admission Requirements for International Students: Contact admission@chathamhall.org for details.

Grade Level: 9-12.

Student Gender: Girls only.

Enrollment: 135 girls, 115 boarders, 20 day.

International Students: 19 students, from countries including Azerbaijan, Bahamas, Costa Rica, Germany, Japan, Korea, Scotland, and Taiwan.

Accredited by: VAIS

Headmaster: Dr. Gary Fountain B.A. Brown University, M.A. Yale Divinity School, Ph.D. English and American Literature, Boston University. E-mail: gfountain@chathamhall.org

Faculty: 50% of teaching faculty have advanced degrees; 21% with Ph.D.s or terminal degrees in their fields. More than half of faculty members live on campus; all teachers are available outside class periods to help students with academic or personal issues.

Chatham Hall teachers are in demand throughout the education world as authors and speakers on topics including art, history, science, communications, and many others. One current teacher is among the top 100 U.S. science educators recognized by Radio Shack; a history teacher has just returned from a Fulbright teaching exchange in Budapest, Hungary; the academic dean has just published his ninth book on history.

One parent described the quality of the faculty this way: "The faculty encourages independent thinking and ... will move mountains to provide each girl with whatever she needs in order to pursue individual interests."

Tuition: Tuition and boarding for 2003-2004 is $28,500.

Class Size: 8 students, with a student-faculty ratio of 4:1.

Curriculum: At Chatham Hall, we encourage the girls to help develop and run our entire program. Although our classes are challenging and our program is designed to help prepare girls for college, there are many more course choices here than in almost any comparably-sized school. Even with our strong core curriculum, girls are not locked into any fixed slate of classes in any one year; we encourage them to branch out and try different electives throughout their Chatham Hall years. We also believe strongly that the fine and performing arts are an integral part of education; that is why we include them as part of the daily academic schedule and don't ask students to fit them in only as after-school extracurriculars.

Student leadership and personal responsibility affect every part of life at Chatham Hall. Students take responsibility for managing their own academic programs with the support of faculty and grade-level advisors. Students also are in charge of developing and running the many on-campus clubs. The Student Council oversees the honor code and disciplinary system. They help run the dormitories and serve as advisors to other students. So many schools create student leadership positions which have few real duties; at Chatham Hall we depend on our student leaders on a daily basis to help us administer the school.

Advanced Placement: Advanced Placement courses are offered in English Literature, European History, Human Geography, U.S. History, Calculus, Biology, Chemistry, Physics, Latin, Literature, French Language, French Literature, Spanish Language, Music Theory, and Studio Art.

ESL Program: An English as a Second Language Program is available for international students for an annual fee of $2,500.

Average SAT Scores of Graduating Students: All students, including international: 75%ile Verbal 640, Math 620, 50%ile Verbal 560, Math 530, 25%ile Verbal 500, Math 500.

College Placement: Recent graduates have attended Princeton, UVA,

Bryn Mawr, and Duke.

Academic Requirements: To graduate from Chatham Hall, students must complete their senior year at the school and fulfill the following minimum requirements: Four (4) years of English, Three (3) years of mathematics, Three (3) years of history (1 of which must be U.S. History), Three (3) years of one foreign language or (2) years of two languages, Three (3) years of lab science including biology and chemistry, One (1) year of fine or performing arts, One (1) trimester of religion, One (1) trimester of ethics, In addition, students must participate in physical education and fitness each trimester. A minimum of 20 credits are required. The normal course load is (6) academic classes, and the minimum is (5).

Sports: Everyone participates in sports at Chatham Hall. From intramural competition, to physical education classes, to varsity teams, athletics are enjoyed at all levels. Chatham Hall fields eight interscholastic teams which compete in the Blue Ridge Conference. The school has won six Conference Championships in the last five years. Athletes compete interscholastically in volleyball, field hockey, cross-country, swimming, basketball (JV and Varsity), tennis, and soccer. The Purple and Gold teams fan the flame of school spirit with intramural events throughout the year that culminate in a banquet in May to celebrate the victorious team. Girls who are not on an interscholastic team take physical education classes, learning habits of lifelong fitness. Click below to see an athletic schedule for the current season and the results thus far.

Extracurricular: From the thrill of Virginia Boarding School Day at Kings Dominion amusement park to the excitement of a live band at the Woodberry Forest Mixer, weekend fun at Chatham Hall is non-stop! Students attend Christian fellowship retreats with other boarding schools, sporting events at UVA, Habitat for Humanity projects in Danville, and plays at the Mill Mountain Theater in Roanoke.

Students also hold leadership positions in the many clubs at Chatham Hall. For the literary student there is the yearbook, school newspaper, and literary magazine. Artistically talented girls may wish to join the drama club, the art club, choir, or the modern dance troupe Panache. French, Spanish, Latin, and International clubs all celebrate different cultures while the Menaboni club highlights the beautiful natural surroundings of Virginia.

Each member of the Chatham Hall community participates in the school's Service League. A long-standing tradition at Chatham Hall, the student-run Service League organizes service to Chatham Hall, St. Mary 's Chapel and to the larger community of Pittsylvania County. Each spring break a group of students also commits to the Appalachia Service Project in conjunction with Woodberry Forest School.

Campus: Pruden Hall, renovated in the summer of 1997, contains the entrance hall to our school, administrative offices and two floors of dormitory space. Dorm rooms in Pruden and Dabney Hall are wired with phone and modem ports.Dabney Hall, renovated in the summer of 1996, houses most of the classrooms and two floors of dormitory space. Yardley Hall contains the schools dining hall. Food service is provided by Meriwether-Godsey which focuses on healthful meals and attractive presentation. Most meals are served buffet-style. The Edmund J. and Lucy Lee Library contains approximately 30,000 volumes, an electronic card catalog and Internet access for students who do not have computers in their rooms. The Shaw Science and Technology Building opened in 2003, is a 16,000+ square-foot building that includes four fully-wired laboratory/classroom areas, a high-tech lecture hall, a greenhouse and offices for the science faculty. The Holt Language Building is the new home of Chatham Hall's language department as well as the location of faculty housing. St. Mary 's Chapel was built in 1939 and restored in 1994-1997. Chapel services are conducted on Tuesday and Friday mornings and Sunday evenings and are required.

The Whitner Art Studio contains two large rooms for the visual arts, including a gallery space, and a dance studio where the modern dance and ballet classes are conducted. The Commons is the gym, where basketball and volleyball are played. There are two locker rooms and a large balcony area for spectators. The riding facilities include the indoor, 125' x 250' Mars Riding Arena, 40 stalls, two practice rings, a show ring and a permanent hunter–jumper course. Willis Hall houses the advancement office and two large classrooms.

There are homes on campus for 18 faculty members. These include family dwellings as well and single faculty housing in duplexes. The Rectory is where the Rector lives and entertains alumnae, parents and other visitors.

Dormitories: Because over 80% of the girls at Chatham Hall are boarding students, dorm life is a focus of the school. In addition to the wide range of weekend activities offered, students often spend time in their dorm parent's apartment just talking, watching television, and working on homework. Each dorm parent teaches only part-time, allowing for plenty of time and energy to devote to the building of community. The Honor Code dramatically affects the quality of life on dorm where students can trust their neighbors and their roommate to respect them and to be considerate. Several Student Council members live on each hall and help girls get along with the roommates, manage their time, and get used to being away from home.

Nearest International Airport: Dulles International Airport, Washington DC.

Nearby Lodgings: Chatham Hall Guest House, 434–432–5612; The Columns, 434-432-6122; The Sims-Mitchell House, 434-432-0595; The Blacks' Guest House, 434-432-7721; Holiday Inn Express, 434-369-4070.

Cheshire Academy

Location: Cheshire, Connecticut (U.S. East Coast, New England)

10 Main Street, Cheshire, CT 06410-2496
Phone: 203-272-5396; Fax: 203-250-7209
Website: www.cheshireacademy.org
Email: admissions@cheshireacademy.org

Mr. Michael McCleery, Dean of Admission
Phone: 203-272-5396; Fax: 203-439-7601
Email: michael.mccleery@cheshireacademy.org

Mission Statement: Cheshire Academy is a college-preparatory school that is committed to the potential in each individual student, excellent teaching, and global diversity. As a college-preparatory boarding and day school, Cheshire Academy encourages high academic achievement through rigorous curricular demands for each student while facilitating intellectual, social, physical, and moral growth and responsibility in a culturally diverse, family environment. As a college-preparatory boarding and day school, Cheshire Academy encourages high academic achievement through rigorous curricular demands for each student, while facilitating intellectual, social, physical, and moral growth and responsibility in a culturally diverse, family environment.

Intellectually, we encourage students to strive for excellence in a traditional college preparatory curriculum designed to develop solid study, communication, computational, and critical thinking skills. Meeting challenges appropriate for their individual talents builds our students' self-confidence, making their experiences joyful, fulfilling, and meaningful.

Socially, we instill understanding, respect, and appreciation for cultural and personal differences by enrolling a diverse student body. Our students come from eighteen states and twenty-two countries around the world with 28% of the student body receiving financial assistance. Students are encouraged to share their traditions and customs with the community at community assemblies and special celebrations.

Physically, we promote the concept that physical fitness enhances mental acuity and encourage students to commit to a lifelong pursuit of good health through physical activity. We encourage student participation in team activities to provide opportunities for leadership, sportsmanship, teamwork, and the enjoyment of friendly competition.

Morally, we make character development a primary consideration in all aspects of community life through the Eight Pillars of Bowden Hall: Respect, Responsibility, Caring, Civility, Citizenship, Morality, Fairness, and Trustworthiness. These eight principles guide the students in the decisions they make each day and help them develop personal responsibility and accountability. As the Eight Pillars reinforce sound moral values, students develop community awareness and positive attitudes encouraging them to be thoughtful, responsible, and contributing members of the Academy.

Admission Requirements for International Students: International applicants must attend Cheshire Academy Summer School and enroll in an ESL program. To acquire knowledge and fluency of the English language should be the primary goal. If the student has already attained sufficient fluency to function well in the grade desired, Summer School may be waived. Keep in mind however that a cultural and social adjustment is one important benefit of the six-week program as well. The student and his or her family must understand that actual grade placement at the end of Summer School will depend upon the proficiency in reading, writing, speaking and listening skills of the English language attained during the ESL program. We also require results from either the TOEFL or SLEP standardized tests, as well as a $1000 International Student Fee (for the first year only).

Grade Level: 9-12.

Student Gender: Boys & Girls.

Enrollment: 142 girls, 240 boys, 183 boarders, 140 day.

International Students: 78 international students from 22 countries,

Cheshire Academy

including Aruba, Bermuda, Bhutan, Brazil, Canada, Czech. Rep., Fiji Islands, Germany, Hong Kong, Jamaica, Japan, Korea, Mali, Morocco, Nigeria, Panama, Russia, Singapore, Spain, Taiwan, Thailand, Venezuela, Yugoslavia. Approximately twenty percent of Cheshire 's students come to us from outside the United States.

Accredited by: NEASC

Headmaster: Gerald A. Larson, Ed.D.

Faculty: Cheshire Academy has a faculty of 93 teachers, 36 of whom have advanced degrees. 27 faculty members live on campus.

Tuition: Boarding tuition for 2003-2004 is $30,900.

Class Size: 12 students.

Curriculum: A student-centered school recognizes that students' needs are the driving force in the learning environment. At Cheshire Academy, this model is called Cheshire Academy Student-Centered Learning Environment or CASCLE. In this kind of learning community, education is not done to students, it happens within students, between students, and among students and teachers. Student-centered learning places the learner at the center of an integrated process. It encourages asking questions and trusting intuition through connections and risk-taking.

Students take responsibility for learning, rather than passively receiving it. Students use resources to construct their own knowledge, based on needs; this means students must participate in positively identifying their learning style and what they need to learn. Teachers provide students with clear expectations and desired outcomes before lessons begin. Students "learn how to learn" by developing problem-solving skills, critical thinking, and reflective thinking. Learning is considered in context of differences that account for, and adapt to, the various learning styles of students. Teachers guide and facilitate the learning process so that students encounter learning opportunities as they need them.
Teachers are responsible for their own knowledge of content and of the learning process.

Advanced Placement: American Government, Biology, Calculus I, Calculus II, Chemistry, English: Language and Composition, English: Literature and Composition, European History, French, Music Theory, Physics, Spanish, Studio Art, and US History.

ESL Program: International students have been an integral part of Cheshire Academy since 1817 and support our mission to foster intercultural understanding. While many international students arrive at Cheshire fluent in English, others take advantage of our English as a Second Language Program. The program is designed for students at the beginning, intermediate, and advanced levels of English acquisition. Because international students come with such varied levels of English proficiency, the sequence in which they follow the curriculum is individualized. Students entering at the beginning level are expected to complete the full four-year curriculum in order to acquire English at an academic level of proficiency. It is the expectation of the ESL department that the vast majority of students who go through this three- to four-year program will be able to gain admittance to an American university, commensurate with their cognitive abilities, without being handicapped by language difficulties. The fee for the ESL program is an additional $2,000 per year.

Sports: At Cheshire Academy, we provide the opportunity for all students to contribute to our Afternoon Program in a manner appropriate to their interests and ability level. From the elite athlete looking to compete on the collegiate level to the inexperienced first time participant, we provide a positive experience to all our students. We believe that students should participate as members of well-coached teams led by dynamic instructors, and that the experience of contributing to an interscholastic program is a valuable one that provides countless teachable moments.

We are proud that our Afternoon Program plays an integral role in lives of our students. Our coaches are teachers and dorm parents as well, providing students at Cheshire Academy the opportunity to create lasting relationships that extend outside the classroom. The Afternoon Program upholds the Eight Pillars of Bowden Hall, as our students learn the value of self-discipline, commitment, teamwork, and sportsmanship. While every student may not be a star on the field, we believe that there is an athlete in everyone.

Extracurricular: At Cheshire Academy, there are myriad programs that enhance the day-to-day life of the students. Some of the most prominent and easily recognized include athletics, drama and other after school activities, clubs and organizations, community service, weekend activities and trips, student government, the campus life curriculum, and the residential program. Other programs, like the Proctors, Peer-Listeners, and Citizenship Committee are less visible but equally fundamental to what we do. Still others, like our attention to emotional intelligence in our behavioral management process, our work with the 7 Habits of Highly Effective People, and our leadership training, are more related to how we do things, not just what we do. Each individual piece makes Cheshire Academy a more vibrant, authentic, and whole learning environment that supports and enhances Student Life. At a smaller school like Cheshire Academy, students are able to voice their opinions about the activities that interest them. Students are always invited to approach the Student Activities Director with ideas for new activities or clubs.

Dormitories: Our 105-acre, self-contained campus provides a secure residential setting for our boarders. Faculty house parents, many of whom have young children and pets, reside in every dormitory, creating a sense of family and a source of ongoing support. Within the dormitory, each floor is considered "a house," with its own house parent—an arrangement that encourages students to take the lead in organizing group activities and forging community spirit. Boarders appreciate the campus' convenient location. They need only walk a few blocks to buy supplies and snacks, or go out for dinner or pizza with friends.

Nearest International Airport: Bradley International Airport, Hartford, CT.

Christ School

Location: Arden, North Carolina (U.S. Mid-Atlantic East Coast)

500 Christ School Road, Arden, NC 28704
Phone: 800-422-3212; Fax: 828-684-2745
Website: www.christschool.org; Email: admission@christschool.org

Mr. Denis Stokes, Director of Admission
Phone: 828-684-6232 ext. 106; Fax: 828-684-4869
Email: admission@christschool.org

Mission Statement: Christ School is a college preparatory school affiliated with the Episcopal Church. Our mission is to produce educated men of good character, prepared for both scholastic achievement in college and productive citizenship in adult society. We achieve this mission through a fourfold process. First, and most important, we challenge and encourage each student, in the nurturing environment of a clos knit campus, to develop academically to his maximum potential. Second, through competitive sports, student self-governance and a variety of extracurricular activities, we help each to develop his physical fitness and leadership skills, and his respect for others regardless of their origins, cultures, or beliefs. Third, by involvement in the care of our campus home, civic duty is learned, along with a sense of the dignity of honest labor. Finally, through religious instruction and regular participation in chapel activities, each of our students learns the sustaining value of faith and spiritual growth throughout his life.

Grade Level: 8-12.

Student Gender: Boys only

Enrollment: 185 students, 155 boarders, 30 day.

Number of International Students: 17.

Accredited by: SACS

Headmaster: Paul Krieger

Faculty: Christ School has a faculty of 35 teachers, 21 of whom have advanced degrees.

Tuition: Tuition and board for 2003-2004 is $27,900.

Class Size: 8-12 students.

Curriculum: While Christ School prepares you for the most competitive colleges in the nation, our challenging curriculum also prepares you for adult life. For this reason, we provide individualized attention and an environment designed to help you learn. We offer small but demanding classes that help you develop critical thinking, research, analytical, and writing skills. We also offer 22 honors level and 13 Advanced Placement courses to give you an opportunity to perform at the highest possible level.

You might sometimes need extra help. We've got it. If you need more, we've got learning labs and tutorials. We offer enrichment courses‹short courses in architecture, ethnic cooking, music, and life skills that will enhance your self-discovery. And when you're ready to move on, our college guidance program will help you take your place in the institution of your choice.

Our mission is not just to educate you, but to help you discover who you really are. In our classrooms you'll find out how much you can discover about yourself by discovering the world around you.

Advanced Placement: Advance Placement courses are available in Biology, Calculus, Computer Science, English Language, English Literature, Environmental Science, French Literature, Latin, Physics, Spanish Language, Studio Art and U.S. History.

Average SAT Scores of Graduating Students: SAT I – Mid-50% range. Verbal 480-600, Math 510-640.

College Placement: Recent graduates of Christ School have been accepted to American University, Art Institute of Boston, Brown, Clemson, Duke, Furman, George Washington, Georgia Tech, Howard, Indiana University at Bloomington, Macalester College, Morehouse College, Northeastern, Presbyterian, Rensselaer Polytechnic Institute, Southern Methodist, the University of the

South, Wake Forest, Washington and Lee, Wheaton, Wofford, and the University of North Carolina at Chapel Hill.

Academic Requirements: To earn a Christ School diploma you will need 20 credits. English - 4 units. An English course is required each year. Science - 3 units. Credits are required in Biology, Chemistry, and a third lab science. A fourth year of science is strongly recommended. Mathematics - 3 units (4 units, beginning with the class of 2006). Credits are required in Algebra I, Geometry, and Algebra II and one additional math course. Foreign Language - 2-3 units. 2 credits are required in the same language. History - 3 units. Requirements include 1 credit each in Modern European History, U.S. History, and one other. Fine Arts - 1 unit. One-half credit must be in music. Computer Literacy – One-half unit. Religious Studies – One-half unit. New Testament or Old Testament is required. Electives - 2-3 units.

Sports: The athletic program strongly encourages each student to participate in two team sports out of the three seasons each year. Organized sport fosters a sense of commitment with the goal of instilling a positive attitude and sense of pride for the athlete. To meet this goal, the athletic department provides adequate team positions for all skill levels. The younger level teams help our athletes develop skills needed for varsity competition. The main focus is on helping boys learn to compete and gain a better understanding of what "team" means at Christ School. The varsity level commitment is to formulate and compete with the best team possible. Varsity selection is based on the student athlete's skills, commitment, and teamwork. Student athletes in junior varsity and other teams will earn the right to play through proper attendance, attitude, and work habits, while increasing your skill level in different sports.

All Christ School coaches and teams are required to conduct themselves in the spirit of good sportsmanship. The team goals are to develop a sense of school pride, to play with dignity, and to be accountable for their individual actions. This includes displaying a proper level of courtesy, respecting the decision of the officials within the spirit of competition, exercising self-control, and winning with humility.

Extracurricular: Life is busy at Christ School, but there will be time to kick back and have fun! The 8,600 square foot student center is the nucleus of daily student activity and entrertainment after the class day. It houses a 42 seat movie theatre, a barber shop, a fully stocked snack bar, pool tables, fireplaces, televisions, a ping pong table, and an air hockey table. This is the place where you can relax, eat a pizza, and enjoy time with your friends.

Weekends are a chance to try a variety of activities. Paintball, amusement parks, ski trips, professional or college sports, area festivals and concerts are just a few of the possibilities. Asheville is fortunate to have rich musical offerings and students have the chance to attend concerts on a weekly basis. Honor roll students can even attend the occasional concert mid-week.

Attending an all boys school does not mean there are no girls. Christ School has two sister schools in NC to share activities with. Dances, ski trips, rafting trips, rock concerts, and community service projects are just some of the opportunities to interact with girls.

Campus: On a boarding school campus there is always something going on and someone to do it with. With about 180 teenage boys from a broad spectrum of backgrounds attending Christ School, there is constant activity ...a lot of good work and a lot of hard play goes on here.

The village-like campus has several different activity centers. The student residences have their own house-centered activities and intramural sports teams, but the new Patrick Beaver Student Center is the heart of most communal activity. This is a place where you can relax, play air hockey, watch a movie, or eat a pizza with friends. When it is time for quiet reflection, there are places for that in the century-old chapel or the 500-acre wooded campus.

Dormitories: A program of regular evening meetings in the houses centers on life skills that are needed in a boarding school environment. It focuses on those issues that are related to community living, such as trust and honesty, diversity, stress, and other important topics related to young men. The curriculum also addresses issues that arise due to specific occurrences or events, such as September 11, or the war in Iraq. At least two faculty members and four senior leaders are assigned to each student residence. With the idea of building house unity and identity, individual housemasters have some autonomy in how their specific house will operate.

Nearest International Airport: Charlotte Douglas International Airport.

Crested Butte Academy

Location: Crested Butte, Colorado (U.S. Western Central, Rocky Mountains)

P.O. Box 1180, 505 Whiterock Avenue, Crested Butte, CO 81224
Phone: 970-349-1805; Fax: 970-349-0997
Website: www.crestedbutteacademy.com
Email: admissions@crestedbutteacademy.com

Ms. Karin Holmen, Director of Admission
Phone: 970-349-1805; Fax: 970-349-0997
Email: admissions@crestedbutteacademy.com

Mission Statement: At Crested Butte Academy, we believe that a liberal arts education leads to a more fulfilling life. As a boarding school, we also recognize that it is our duty to educate the whole person, and that is why we have strong programs in athletics, the arts, residential and student life, and leadership. In academics, we offer a fully documented core curriculum. In all subjects we emphasize fundamental and advanced skills, broad and deep cultural literacy, and historical knowledge. Our goal is to guide our students in such a way that they acquire the habits of independent thought, come to aspire to intellectual excellence, and develop a lasting commitment to free inquiry. To be a great educational institution a school must nourish creativity. At the Academy, we provide strong programs in drama, music, creative writing and dance, staffed by faculty with extensive professional experience. The lessons young people learn from athletics are also an inherent part of a good education. Our mountain sports programs, especially in winter sports, are among the best in the world. Every year several of our competitive skiers and snowboarders rank among the best juniors in America.

Life outside of the classroom is a crucial part of any boarding school. Our Residential Faculty not only teach and coach but also administer a fully documented Residential Life Curriculum that addresses issues from social life to nutrition, study habits how to deal with the myriad challenges young people face as they prepare for adulthood.

Our standards are high in all areas, and we are well-prepared to support students to reach ambitious goals. In the end, Academy students learn that what we care about most are ethical values such as integrity, self-discipline, inquisitiveness, tolerance, and leadership. These are strong and idealistic words, but we try to live up to them every day.

Grade Level: 9-12.

Student Gender: Boys & Girls.

Enrollment: 41 boys, 24 girls, 40 boarders, 25 day.

International Students: The number of international students varies from year to year. Recent students have come from Japan, Scotland, England, South Korea, Germany, and Serbia.

Accredited by: ACIS

Headmaster: David J. Rothman, Ph.D., A.B. in History and Literature, Harvard, Ph.D. in English, New York University.

Faculty: Crested Butte's faculty includes 9 full-time and 5 part-time teachers, many of whom hold advanced degrees.

Tuition: Boarding tuition for 2003-2004 is $25,000.

Curriculum: Crested Butte Academy offers a comprehensive program of core courses which enable the student to think independently, to write competently, to speak with clarity, and to appreciate the value and joy of learning. Students graduate from CBA self-confident and proud of their own talents, capable of attending their college of choice, and well prepared for a successful path through life. Through their partnership developed with the faculty, students can work towards their potential for growth and development.

Advanced Placement: Advanced Placement Offerings include English Literature, United States History, Biology, Calculus, and Spanish V.

College Placement: In the past five years, Crested Butte Academy graduates have been accepted to Cornell, Colorado College, Dartmouth, Denver University, New York University, Smith College, Stanford, University of Colorado, and University of Oregon.

Academic Requirements: Crested Butte Academy's Standard Curriculum:

Freshman Year - English Literature I (Novel I, Writing & Grammar, Poetry I, Short Story I), Ancient World History, Foreign Language I (Spanish, French, German), Biology, Algebra I or Geometry.

Sophomore Year - English Literature II (Dramamatic Literature I, Narrative Poetry II, Novel II), United States History, to 1865, Foreign Language II (Spanish, French, German), Chemistry, Geometry or Algebra II.

Junior Year - English Literature III (Short Story II, Essay, Lyric Poetry I), United States History, to 1865 to present Foreign Language III (Spanish, French, German), Physics, Algebra II or unctions/Statistics/Trigonometry.

Senior Year -English Literature IV (Novel III, Lyric Poetry II, Drama II), Twentieth Century World History, Foreign Language IV (Spanish, French, German), Advanced Biology, Functions/ Statistics/ Trigonometry or Calculus.

Enrichment Courses - Music Appreciation, Art History/Studio Art, SAT Preparation, Writing and Grammar, Geography, Computer Science.

Sports: The mission of the Crested Butte Academy Athletic Education Program is to be one of the best high school mountain sports programs in America. The Curriculum focuses on mountain biking, kayaking, rock climbing, skateboarding, wilderness education, mountaineering, snowboarding and skiing, and also provides opportunities for students to pursue team sports and a range of individual interests with other educational organizations in our community. In each sport, the Academy offers a rigorous fully documented curriculum in technical skills, along with a strong competitive option. In all areas standards and expectations are high. Beyond helping students to acquire the physical skill, coaches in the Athletic Education Program also teach self-discipline, good sportsmanship, courage, and commitment to excellence. The program's goal is to support all students as they strive to reach their personal athletic goals, and to give them the knowledge and skills to enjoy mountain sports for the rest of their lives.

Extracurricular: Crested Butte offers drama, music, photography, yearbook, literary magazine, newsletter, and more. Every weekend, there are planned trips, including wilderness backpacking, cultural trips to Denver and other cities, and trips to local resorts for skiing or snowboarding. Students also participate in community service programs.

Campus: Crested Butte Academy is located in a town of 1500 people, near Crested Butte Mountain in the Rocky Mountains at an altitude of 8,885 feet. The campus is a renovated hotel in the center of town. Crested Butte's academic facilities include small class-rooms, a computer lab, a science lab, a library, and a darkroom. The campus and surrounding landscape also offer the opportunity for outdoor studies, and a conveniently located bus stop provides students with public transportation to Crested Butte Mountain

Dormitories: Boarding students live on campus in separate facilities for boys and girls. Rooms are divided into suites with common living/study and areas separate bedrooms. Each suite houses 6 students with shared baths. Teachers and coaches also serve as dorm parents. The Student Commons includes a weight room. The purpose of the Residential Life Curriculum is to teach students self-respect, integrity, and social skills. We consider it a crucial part of our school's mission to involve each student in the social life of our school, and to create, sustain, and develop a safe and supportive boarding community for all students. All the programs in the Residential and Student Life Curriculum are designed to help students grow and mature toward adulthood. Like most intentional residential communities, we also have clear policies that must be consistently followed in order to maintain a clean, safe, and con-structive home for all our dorm community members. We offer several formal programs in the Residential Life Curriculum, but we also pursue its goals informally, by offering students support, guidance, and clear, appropriate boundaries. We have organized this curriculum guide to give a clear outline of the various programs we offer. The Life Discussions Program, the Prefect Program, the Weekend Activities Program, and the Student Activities Program are all designed, in conjunction with our Academic and Athletic Education Curricula, to create an exciting and educational year for all our students. The section on Daily Life in the Dorms outlines school policies the school has which are particularly important for boarding students, as well as graduated privileges given to upper-classmen in good standing. The follwong options will provide you with a more detailed explanation of student life.

Nearest International Airport: Denver International Airport.

Dunn School

Location: Los Olivos, California (U.S. West Coast, Southern California)

P.O. Box 98, 2555 Hwy. 154, Los Olivos, CA 93441
Phone: 805-688-6471; Fax: 805-686-2078
Website: www.dunnschool.org; Email: admissions@dunnschool.org

Ms. Ann Greenough-Coats, Director of Admission
Phone: 805-688-6471; Fax: 805-686-2078
Email: admissions@dunnschool.org

Mission Statement: As a college preparatory school with an essential focus on scholarship, leadership, teamwork, and compassion, Dunn School is committed to developing each individual's academic and personal potential, building self confidence and character, fostering individual and collective excellence, and empowering students for success in college and in life. Dunn offers a broad range of programs, including academics, athletics, arts, outdoor education, and community service within a diverse community of students, faculty, and staff. We believe that the depth and quality of the relationship between students and teachers is central to the process of education. One-to-one communication and rapport between a teacher and student best stimulates the desire to learn. Through our dedicated faculty we are committed to the guidance and support of the personal and academic growth of every person entrusted to our care.

Admission Requirements for International Students: Dunn School accepts into its full college preparatory program a limited number of students who do not speak English as their native language. Applicants for the program are evaluated for admission based on standard admission criteria: candidates must submit an independent evaluation of their proficiency in the English language, such as TOEFL.

Grade Level: 9-12.

Student Gender: Boys & Girls.

Enrollment: 100 boys, 74 girls, 106 boarders, 68 day.

Number of International Students: 30 students from 11 countries.

Accredited by: WASC, CAIS/CA

Headmaster: James Munger, M.Ed., Sierra University, B.A., Goddard College. Email: jmunger@dunnschool.org

Faculty: In addition to getting to know students in their classrooms, teachers are also coaches and dorm parents. Each teacher is also a faculty advisor to no more than six student advisees. Faculty members work on a daily basis with their advises to set goals, monitor coursework, and serve as a liaison between the school and the student's parents. This critical link between student, teacher and parent is key to facilitating the success of each Dunn student.

With most of Dunn's teachers living on campus, students enjoy in-depth personal relationships with their teachers. It is not uncommon for the French teacher to host her class at her home for a group prepared French feast, or for a Dunn student to attend the preschool graduation of his faculty advisor's four-year-old son. Students quickly learn that they are members of a caring, compassionate campus family.

Tuition: Tuition and boarding for 2003-2004 is $30,000.

Student/Teacher ratio: 6:1

Curriculum: At Dunn School, there are a variety of programs integrated into the curriculum, as well as extracurricular programs, that a student can participate in. The programs help define Dunn School as a whole and contribute greatly to the community of students, staff, and faculty.

Students who are identified by Department Heads, Advisors or classroom teachers as being able or promising scholars are invited to join the Academy. In the Academy, students and teachers alike investigate new material, share scholarly reactions to that material and generally become equals in the marketplace of ideas. Students in the Academy are required to maintain a normal course load and accumulate, with a high G.P.A., the necessary credits for graduation. Members of the Academy will be designated as such along with a printed explanation and illumination of the program so that university admissions' officers will have an understanding of the extraordinary length and breadth of an Academy education.

Advanced Placement: Advanced Placement courses are offered in English Language, English Literature, U.S. History, Calculus, Chemistry, Biology, Physics, Environmental Science, Spanish and Studio Art.

ESL Program: Dunn does not offer a specialized English as a Second Language (ESL) program, but offers modified curriculum, courses, and grading requirements for students whose academic achievement may be impacted by their lack of fluency in English.

College Placement: Colleges that have offered admission to our seniors in the last five years include Cal Poly, Cornell, Denver University, Lewis and Clark, Saint Mary 's College, Smith, UC Berkeley, UC San Diego, and Washington University.

Academic Requirements: A student in good standing shall be eligible for a Dunn School diploma upon successful completion of all courses. Under normal circumstances, a student's academic program will include the following requirements: English - Four Years, Foreign Language - Third Level, Mathematics - Four Years, Computer Science - One semester, History/Social Science - Three Years, Fine/Performing Arts - One Year, Science - three years of a laboratory science (one of which must be a physical science), and Outdoor Education.

Freshmen - English 9, Integrated Math 1 or 1 Honors, History 9, World Cultures, Conceptual Physics, Foreign Language, Introduction to Art.

Sophomores - English 10 or 10 Honors, Integrated Math 2 or Honors 2, History 10: European History or Honors, Chemistry, Foreign Language, Human Development (1 Semester), Elective.

Juniors - English 11 or AP English Language, Integrated Math 3 or 3 Honors, 20th Century US History or Honors US History, Biology or

Chemistry or Physics, Foreign Language, Elective

Seniors - English 12 or AP English Literature, Integrated Math 4 or AP Calculus, Senior Social Science Elective, Physics or AP Physics or AP Biology or Environmental Science or Anatomy & Physiology, Foreign Language, Elective.

Sports: Baseball has a long tradition at Dunn School. It is coached in the spring trimester as a varsity coed sport. Baseball is played on a newly built diamond that was donated in 1996. It is by far the finest field in the Condor league. Dunn School Basketball is offered to both men and women as a varsity sport in the winter trimester. The teams practice during the week, sharing gym hours with each other. Both men's and women's basketball are coached by faculty or staff. The programs highlight hard work through practice. Climbing/ Kayaking is offered to students who would like to participate in a non-competitive sport and who have talent for climbing and kayaking. Tryouts are held for the program. Participation is based on performance during the tryouts and the skills shown therein. Within the program, students use the 30 foot climbing wall located in the gym and the climbing "cave" for practice. Trips are made to local climbing spots. The pool is used regularly for kayaking practice to perfect essential skills for white-water excursions that are also made by the group. Dunn School Cross Country has long been a great pride of the Dunn School Athletics Department. For many years running, Dunn has placed in the top three seats of the Condor league. Coach Daves has been with the program for quite a few years now and always produces excellent athletes.

Extracurricular Activities: Understanding that rigorous academic work must be balanced with the opportunity to explore extracurricular and social activities, Dunn provides a variety of on- and off-campus activities in which students may participate.

Students work with the Activities Coordinator to create a schedule of events that appeals to the personal interests and talents of the student community. Weekend activities vary according to student input and interest. Activities include dorm competitions, interscholastic athletics, concerts, surfing, school dances, movies, rock climbing, dramatic/musical performances, museum trips, trips to

Santa Barbara, mountain biking, bowling, roller skating, U.C.S.B. special events trips, Disneyland/Knotts Berry Farm trips, beach trips, coffee houses, and driver education. Aspiring writers, journalists, and designers work on the publication of the yearbook, a bi-monthly newspaper, and the Bell View Literary Journal.

Dunn's geographical location is ideal for entertainment. The campus is bordered by the San Rafael wilderness, which is a hiking and biking paradise, and many Dunn students regularly surf at numerous nearby beaches. The local communities of Solvang, Los Olivos and Santa Ynez are within walking or biking distance. Cultural and athletic events are only thirty miles away in beautiful Santa Barbara, where students and faculty might se a movie, enjoy dinner at an ethnic restaurant, shop or just relax over coffee at a coffee house.

Campus: The 40-acre Dunn School campus houses many academic and extracurricular facilities. In addition to classrooms, science labs, a library, and up-to-date computer facilities, there are five dormitories and a wealth of sports facilities. These sports facilities include a full-size outdoor track with all necessary equipment to hold meets, a brand-new baseball diamond, six new tennis courts, a full-size gym, a cross-country course, two soccer fields, and a brand-new lacrosse field as well as a practice lacrosse field.

Dormitories: Students are housed in single-sex dormitories.

Nearest International Airport: Los Angeles International Airport.

Emma Willard

Location: Troy, New York (U.S. East Coast, New England)

285 Pawling Avenue, Troy, NY 12180
Phone: 518-833-1300; Fax: 518-833-1820
Website: www.emmawillard.org
Email: admissions@emmawillard.org

Mr. Kent Jones, Director of Enrollment and Public Relations
Phone: 518-833-1320; Fax: 518-833-1805
Email: kjones@emmawillard.org

Mission Statement: At Emma Willard, girls excel. Their ambitions
are as varied as their talents. Ever dynamic and exuberant, the
Emma Willard community encourages each girl's aspirations and
offers her opportunities for accomplishment every day. In and out of
the classroom, we promote leadership and celebrate citizenship. We
explore values and reward intellectual risk taking. We challenge girls
to take responsibility for developing their minds and their hearts to
the fullest and putting their talents to good purpose.

Since 1814, Emma Willard School has been one of the nation's
leading college- preparatory boarding and day schools for young
women. At Emma Willard, every possible resource is dedicated to
developing in its students the values and skills that form the foundation of a life of accomplishment, leadership, and fulfillment. These
include a love for the life of the mind, a commitment to service,
courage and confidence, grace and creativity, and collaboration and
friendship. Known for its rigor, the School promotes intellectual
curiosity and disciplined study habits through a challenging curriculum distinguished by a wide array of advanced placement courses
and electives. It also promotes active involvement in the life of the
campus and off-campus communities through a rich co-curricular
program. In all they do, students are both challenged and closely
supported by an outstanding faculty and staff. The School's extraordinary physical plant, listed on the National Register of Historic
Places, provides a breathtakingly beautiful, yet state-of-the-art,
setting for learning and living. Throughout its history, Emma
Willard has been committed to enrolling a diverse student body
from across the Capital Region, across the country, and around the

world.

Grade Level: 9-12.

Student Gender: Girls only.

Enrollment: 308 girls, 186 boarders, 122 day.

International Students: 49, from 14 foreign countries.

Accredited by: NYSAIS

Head of School: Trudy E. Hall, M.A.L.S. from Duke University, M.Ed. from Harvard Graduate School of Education, B.S. in psychology and sociology from St. Lawrence University.

Faculty: Ours is a talented and dedicated faculty who instills in students a lifelong love of learning and the skills to pursue it. The Emma Willard faculty is mindful that a teacher's influence can reach beyond the classroom and that this is both a responsibility and a privilege. In thoughtful lectures, in the dynamics of classroom give-and-take, in tutorials, in the introspective dialogue of the advisor/advisee relationship, the Emma Willard faculty epitomizes the satisfactions of an intellectual life, the energizing vigor of discovery and exchange, and the personal and professional rewards of learning as a lifelong process. Emma Willard faculty members live on or near campus, bringing to this community an accessibility and a generosity of spirit that know no bounds. Unlike some schools, Emma Willard does not require the teaching faculty to live in the residence halls; we believe a teacher's first obligation is to be an academic professional and mentor–a role model. Emma Willard 's faculty includes 55 full-time, 11 part-time; 75% female/25% male; 48 hold advanced degrees, including 5 doctorates and 43 master's.

Tuition: Tuition and boarding for 2003-2004 is $31,200.

Class Size: 11 students with a Student/Faculty Ratio of 5.3 to 1.

Curriculum: The Emma Willard curriculum develops those abilities and qualities of mind that are essential to the successful woman. The rigorous college-preparatory curriculum ensures a strong foundation in all major academic areas in addition to extensive exposure to the arts. Each student's faculty advisor helps her plan her courses in coordination with the college counselor and academic dean. Practicum, Emma Willard 's independent study program, provides opportunities to earn credit and test a career track through hands-on experience in many industries and professions. Annual trips are taken by students with faculty chaperones each year to countries such as Greece, France, the British Isles, Germany, Spain, and Russia.

Advanced Placement: Emma Willard offers AP preparation in English, Spanish, French, calculus, computer science, chemistry, biology, physics, U.S. government, U.S. history, European history, art history, and Latin.

ESL Program: A student for whom English is not her first language is required to demonstrate adequate English skills before she is allowed to enter certain regular academic courses. The English as a Second Language program is a one-year or a two-year program. Placement in ESL is determined by school-administered tests.

SAT: Average combined SAT I scores for the Class of 2003 was 1270.

College Placement: Seventy-three students in the Class of 2003 are attending 59 colleges and universities, including Bryn Mawr, Carnegie Mellon, Colgate, Colorado College, Columbia, Cornell, Denison, Dickinson, Duke, Grinnell, George Washington, Harvard, Lafayette, Lehigh, Macalester, Mount Holyoke, NYU, Northwestern, Princeton, RPI, RISD, Sarah Lawrence, Smith, Trinity, Tufts, University of Rochester, USC, and Washington & Lee.

Academic Requirements: Students are expected to complete the following studies:

Four years of English and literature courses. During 9th, 10th, and 11th grades a student must take yearlong English courses. In 12th grade she must choose one elective each semester from the English Division.

Mathematics sequence through the third level following the sequence: Algebra I, Geometry: Plane and Solid, and Algebra II and Trigonometry.

Foreign Language up to the third level of a single foreign language. This does not apply to students who enroll in English as a Second Language.

Two units of laboratory science: one year of biology and one year of chemistry.

Three yearlong courses in history and social science or their equivalents, including one year of United States history taken at the 11th- or 12th-grade level.

For entering 9th graders, successful completion of 2 units of arts electives; 1 of these units must be completed by the end of 10th grade; among the two units there must be some performing and some non-performing arts courses, but not necessarily in equal numbers. For entering 10th graders, successful completion of 1 unit of arts electives; among these courses there must be some performing and some non-performing arts courses, but not necessarily in equal numbers. For entering 11th graders, successful completion of 1 unit of arts courses with no distribution required among the arts.

By graduation every student needs to have completed the course Computer Science I, or to have demonstrated an equivalent competency to the Science Division.

All students must take physical education classes or their equivalent in team sports or dance during 9th, 10th, and 11th grade. 12th graders are required to take 10 weeks of physical education class or their equivalent.

Entering ninth-graders must complete six hours of community service at some time between September and May. The school's Practicum & Community Service Directory organizes several two- or three-hour weekend projects throughout the year. However, students can fulfill the requirement through participation in any event, at school or at home, that benefits a nonprofit organization. A letter from an adult supervisor confirming the hours and the type of work is required.

Sports: Every Emma Willard student benefits from a rigorous program of sports and fitness. Whether she plays on an interscholastic team, maintains personal fitness through organized exercise, or improves her skill at lifetime sports, each student learns cooperation while building character and strength, and she enjoys the feeling of well-being that comes from being physically fit. Varsity and JV sports include basketball, crew, cross country, field hockey, lacrosse, soccer, softball, swimming, tennis, and volleyball. Physical Education offerings include aerobics, fitness walking, outdoor skills/camping, running, self-defense, soccer, swimming, tennis, ultimate Frisbee, volleyball, weight conditioning, yoga, and more.

Extracurricular Activities: Extracurricular Activities include Activities Council, Black and Hispanic Awareness, Cartoon Club, Campus Players, Clock student newspaper, Current Events Club, Foreign and American Student Organization, Gargoyle yearbook, Gay-Straight Alliance, Junior Singing Group, Orchestra, Outing Club, Quiz Team, Science Club, Ski Club, Speech, Students Against Drunk Driving, , Tour Guides, Triangle art and literary magazine, Twelve Tones singing group, and The Women's Collective.

Campus: Emma Willard 's extraordinary 137-acre campus on Mount Ida above the City of Troy contains 30 buildings. The three oldest buildings, all of collegiate Tudor Gothic style, include a cathedral-like reading room, classrooms, offices, a main auditorium, a dance studio, a lab theater, three residence halls, two dining facilities, a student center, and a chapel. The art, music and library complex opened in 1967. The library holds more than 25,000 volumes and 108 periodical subscriptions. Microfilm and microfiche readers are available for student use. The collection also includes more than 1,500 records, a sizable art and architecture slide collection and the archives, which include nineteenth-century photographs and manuscripts and some medieval manuscripts. Athletic facilities include a gymnasium with two basketball/ volleyball/indoor tennis courts, full facilities for fitness training and aerobic dance, a weight room, an aquatics center housing a competition-size pool, three large playing fields and a 400 meter track. The three-story Hunter Science Center houses state of the art laboratories and teaching facilities for chemistry, biology, physics, and mathematics. The campus is famous not only for its gothic beauty but for its system of interconnecting underground tunnels. Approximately 50 percent of the faculty reside on campus in houses and apartments provided by the school.

Dormitories: Mutual respect and consideration are the essential elements of the residential experience at Emma Willard. Ten professional residence faculty members (some with families and/or pets) manage the dorm community and are committed to working with and supporting young women. The student to residence faculty ratio is 16 to 1. Each houseparent is responsible for specific halls within the dorms and acts as a resource for students about all aspects of life within and beyond the School. A team of 12th-grade proctors assists the residence faculty in leading, inspiring, and guiding students through the academic year. Ninth graders share a common hall, while upperclasswomen live on halls of mixed age groups. Dorm rooms are configured as singles, doubles, and suites. Each day student has a residence hall to which she belongs each year.

Nearest International Airport: Albany International Airport.

Nearby Lodgings: Best Western Rensselaer Inn, 518-274-3210; Franklin Inn & Suites, 518-274-8800; Courtyard at Marriott, 518-482-8800; Clarion Inn & Suites, 518-785-5891; Holiday Inn Express, 518-286-1011.

Episcopal High School

Location: Alexandria, Virginia (U.S. Mid-Atlantic East Coast)

1200 North Quaker Lane, Alexandria, VA 22302-3000
Phone: 703-933-3000; Fax: 703-933-3016
Website: www.episcopalhighschool.org
Email: admissions@episcopalhighschool.org

Contact: Director of Admission
Phone: 703-933-4062; Fax: 703-933-3016
Email: admissions@episcopalhighschool.org

Mission Statement: Episcopal High School is dedicated to the student's pursuit of excellence and to the joy of learning and self-discovery in a caring and supportive community. Enriched by the educational and cultural resources of the nation's capital, Episcopal's dynamic academic program encourages students to develop individual talents and prepares them to attend selective colleges and universities.

Students from diverse backgrounds live and learn together in a residential community based on a foundation of honor, spiritual growth, responsibility, and mutual respect. They develop enduring relationships at EHS and grow as discerning, self-reliant, creative, and compassionate individuals. The Episcopal High School community prepares young people to lead principled and fulfilling lives of leadership and service to others.

The 130-acre campus' pastoral setting is enhanced by access to all the resources of the Washington, D.C. area. The traditions of the School serve as a foundation for a progressive college preparatory learning environment with a spiritual foundation. Athletic development, community service, and creative pursuits come together to strengthen the whole student. These complementary opportunities make Episcopal one of a kind.

Admission Requirements for International Students: International students must take the SSAT, and may also submit the TOEFL in addition to the SSAT. We expect proficiency in English, though we admit students who still need English language improvement.

Grade Level: 9-12.

Student Gender: Boys & Girls.

Enrollment: 240 boys, 175 girls, 415 boarders.

International Students: from 10 countries.

Accredited by: VAIS, SACS

Headmaster: Rob Hershey, B.A. Williams College, M.Ed. University of Virginia. Email: frh@episcopalhighschool.org

Faculty: At Episcopal High School, teaching is a vocation that calls on the whole person to help students not only achieve a mastery of required subject matter but also develops skills for critical thinking. Episcopal's teachers foster lifelong enjoyment of learning, and inspire the confidence and desire to put this learning to use for the benefit of others. EHS faculty members provide a reservoir of knowledge and they readily share these personal qualities with students. Nearly 75% of EHS faculty members have advanced degrees, with 9% having earned their doctorates. Many graduated from the most prestigious and rigorous universities in the country – Columbia University Teachers College, Dartmouth, Duke, Georgetown, Harvard, Middlebury, New York University, Princeton, Stanford, University of North Carolina, University of Virginia, Washington and Lee, Yale, and Williams to name a few. Some also have experience teaching at the college level. In addition, many have exciting career experiences in their field of expertise and bring a wide range of interests to campus. Episcopal High School has a faculty of 79, of which 80% live on campus.

Tuition: $29,300 comprehensive fee.

Class Size: 12 students, most are between 9-14, with a student teacher ratio of 6:1.

Curriculum: Episcopal's course of study reflects a commitment to the liberal arts and sciences, and a dedication to prepare students for college and for life. Small classes, usually comprised of 10 to 12 students, encourage open and lively discussion. Forty AP and honors courses provide opportunities for advanced specialized study. The Episcopal curriculum is broad: students study everything from English, Foreign Languages, Science, Mathematics, and Social Studies to Drama, Visual Arts, Theology, and Music.

Advanced Placement: 40 Advanced Placement and honors courses, including Biology, Calculus, Chemistry, English Language and Composition, English Literature, Environmental Science, European History, French Language, Government & Politics, Human Geography, Macroeconomics, Microeconomics, Music Theory, Physics, Spanish Literature, Statistics, Studio Art, and U.S. History.

ESL Program: No.

SAT Scores of Graduating Students: ranges between 1250 and 1280.

College Placement: Students of Episcopal High School have been accepted to colleges such as American College, Boston College, Cornell, Dartmouth, Duke, Georgetown, Harvard, Princeton, John's Hopkins, Princeton, Smith, Stanford, Vanderbilt, Wellesley, Wake Forest, and Yale.

Academic Requirements: To earn a diploma from EHS, students must earn 23 credits and meet the following requirements: English – 4 credits, Mathematics- 3 credits, Social Studies – 2 credits, Foreign Language – 2 or 3 credits, Laboratory Science – 2 credits, Fine Arts – 1 credit, Theology – 1 credit, Physical Education - 2 credits.

Sports: Episcopal High School is dedicated to the student's pursuit of excellence and to the joy of learning and self-discovery in a caring and supportive community. Episcopal believes that physical exercise and conditioning are very important to the health of every teenage boy or girl and that habits and routines of exercise begun at a young age are important to lifelong health. In addition to exercise for the sake of health, EHS is also committed to the values taught by athletic competition. The values of sportsmanship, self-discipline, and perseverance are often learned through interscholastic sports. Most importantly, Episcopal's athletic teams provide an opportunity for students from diverse backgrounds to learn the value of teamwork, cooperation, and mutual respect. Sports Offerings include Aerobics, Lacrosse, Baseball, Outdoor Program (varies by season; could include kayaking, rock climbing), Basketball, Soccer, Crew, Softball, Cross Country, Squash, Dance, Tennis, Field Hockey, Track, Football, Volleyball, Golf, and Wrestling.

Extracurricular Activities: It's not ALL hard work at Episcopal. Having fun is a preeminent part of every teenager's life, and EHS has a wide variety of clubs and activities designed specifically for this purpose. Club and committee meetings typically occur in the evenings after dinner, but many other activities offered are a part of the Afternoon Program.

Students find that joining is a great way to get involved in campus life, pursue a personal interest and also have a good time. Extracurricular Activities include A Cappella Groups, Activities Committee, Bocce Club, Book Club, Bowling Club, Writing Club, Cheerleaders, Choir, Chronicle student newspaper, Daemon art and literary magazine, Discipline Committee, Dorm Council, Environmental Club, Global Affairs Club, Investment Club, It's Academic, Jazz Ensemble, Kayaking Club, Latin Club, Math Tutors, Military History Club, Orchestra, Outdoor Club, Peer Mentors, Robotics Club, Spanish Club, Spectrum, Stop AIDS for Everyone Club, Student-formed Rock Bands, Student Health Awareness Committee, Student Waiters, Tour Guides, Vestry, Web Publications, "Whispers" yearbook, Young Democrats, and Young Republicans.

Campus: While situated on 130 acres of pastoral terrain, Episcopal is in the midst of one of the most dynamic and historically significant areas in the country and only minutes from the nation's capital. Outings beyond the campus provide firsthand opportunities to regularly experience culture, explore history and current events and investigate breakthroughs in science and technology.

Episcopal's academic facilities include six buildings with 45 classrooms, all of which are wired for data, voice and video; a fully automated library with more than 30,000 books and videos; more than 2,000 music CDs, 150 periodicals, 12 newspapers, CD-ROMs covering every academic discipline; and access to DIALOG (an information retrieval service) and to a national inter-library loan network via OCLC.

Dormitories: Students at Episcopal High School live in dormitories with single, double, and triple rooms. Currently, there are four boys' and four girls' dormitories. One dorm for each gender is designated specifically for freshmen. Each contains commons rooms and laundry facilities.

Each dorm acts as a true "home" for students and promotes community. Dorms house faculty members and student Monitors, who help provide a comfortable place in which students can live and study. All new students are assigned roommates in the same grade. Students are responsible for cleaning and maintaining their own rooms. Blackford Hall serves as a student lounge, complete with a snack bar, student mailboxes, comfortable tables and booths, a juke box, and a big screen television where movies are shown on weekends. Additionally, students may spend their leisure time in the Robertson Commons, where they can watch movies or play pool and foosball.

Nearest International Airport: Dulles International Airport, Washington DC.

Nearby Lodgings: Embassy Suites Alexandria-Old Town, 703-684-5900; Holiday Inn Select, 703-549-6080; Hilton Alexandria, 703-837-0440; Radisson Old Town, 703-683-6000; Ritz-Carlton, 703-415-5000; Homewood Suites, 703-671-6500.

Fay School

Location: Southborough, Massachusetts (U.S. East Coast, New England)

48 Main Street, Southborough, MA 01772
Phone: 508-485-0100; Fax: 508-485-5381
Website: www.fayschool.org; Email: fayadmit@fayschool.org

Mr. Scott LeBrun, Assistant Director of Admission
Phone: 508-485-0100; Fax: 508-481-7872
Email: fayadmit@fayschool.org

Mission Statement: Fay School is committed to maintaining the diversity of its student body by making a fine education accessible to students from a variety of backgrounds, regardless of their families' financial resources. In meeting this objective, Fay helps its students to know and respect youngsters from all walks of life and from numerous states and countries. The School's programs rest on a well-tested and responsive structure in which challenging yet realistic expectations, combined with the teaching of moral principles, insistence on disciplined behavior, and the cultivation of responsible work habits help children develop the strengths and self-confidence necessary for success. Children at Fay feel they belong to something worthwhile, where they are valued for the unique personal qualities and perspectives each of them brings to the community. In such an atmosphere, valuable lessons in mutual respect, sportsmanship, and tolerance for different points of view become part of their everyday experience. Four components of this structure put success within the reach of all; limited class size, the effort system, the advisor system, and personalized, flexible scheduling.

Grade Level: 6-9.

Student Gender: Boys& Girls.

Enrollment: 209 boys, 173 girls, 112 boarders, 270 day.

International Students: Boys and girls from foreign countries comprise 15% of the student body. Recently they have beeen from the following countries: Aruba, Australia, Bahamas, Brazil, Canada,

China, Costa Rica, Dominican Republic, France, Hong Kong, Indonesia, Japan, Jordan, Korea, Malaysia, Mexico, Nigeria, Philippines, Russia, South Africa, Taiwan, Thailand, and Venezuela.

Accredited by: AISNE

Faculty: Children entering Fay School are welcomed into a family whose heart is the faculty. Faculty members are selected for their empathy and enthusiasm for working with students at the elementary and junior level, as well as for their expertise in a particular discipline. Students and teachers work, learn, play, and have meals together. In the boarding community they also spend weekends together, sharing many experiences both on and off campus. Among the 67 faculty members, one holds a doctorate as the terminal degree, 32 hold master's degrees, and 34 hold bachelor's degrees. Seventeen dorm parents are directly responsible for the welfare of the boarding students. Twenty-eight teachers reside on campus.

Advisors are teachers and administrators who form the nuclei of small groups of 6 or 7 students, both day and boarding. Advisory groups meet at least once a week. This peer support, combined with the guidance of a concerned and involved adult makes advisory groups an important source of nurturing for youngsters at Fay. A major responsibility for advisors is communicating with parents.

Tuition: Boarding - Non-U.S. Resident Mainstream - $34,175; Boarding - International with ESL Program- $38,430.

Average Class Size: 11 students

Curriculum: While Fay's primary focus in preparing its students for secondary schools is academic, the development of positive attitudes toward learning and living in the world beyond its campus is emphasized. Fay's small classes allow students to become active participants in their education and to develop a meaningful rapport with their teachers. Acceleration or specialization of coursework is encouraged in Fay's upper grades in cases where students display exceptional interest or proficiency. Over 200 class offerings, a flexible rotating schedule, and different ability levels in most subjects facilitate the designing of customized study programs.

Computer technology enhances coursework and pedagogy in all disciplines, and the library/media center is fully automated.

By limiting class size to an average of 11 students, Fay School enables children to become active participants in their education. Each student's specific needs and academic background are carefully considered when scheduling classes. A rotating schedule and more than 200 class offerings ensure maximum flexibility in designing study programs.

The School offers different levels in most subject areas. In the Lower School (grades 1-5), the program emphasizes individual growth and the development of sound learning skills. Courses of study in the Upper School (grades 6-9) provide sequential programs based on developing and strengthening basic practices in grades 6 and 7 and expand into advanced concepts and secondary school courses in grades 8 and 9. The development of study skills appropriate for each discipline, as well as research techniques where applicable, are stressed.

A full complement of courses within the five main disciplines of mathematics, English, history, science, and foreign language is offered in the Upper School. The School offers a comprehensive computer program to Lower School and Upper School students. The aim of the program is both to enable students to use the computer as a tool to enhance their academic performance and to gain a basic comprehension of how computer programs work. The program teaches the basics of keyboarding, programming, graphics, word processing, and resource management. All students must complete at least one term of art each year as well as a year-long course in music. A Learning Services Department provides specialized help for children who need support in following their regular course of study.

ESL Program: The International Student Program (ISP) serves students whose citizenship or residence is non-American. Students whose first language is not English are enrolled in ESL (English as a Second Language) classes. Four levels and small classes afford opportunities to tailor courses to individual needs. There are nineteen different ISP offerings and students are placed in classes appropriate to their level of English proficiency. As students' proficiency in English increases, they are integrated into core courses. Full participation in art, music, computer classes, and sports activities helps students adapt quickly to life in their new community. The ISP supports students in all aspects of their Fay experience, including travel arrangements, academic scheduling, secondary school placement, and communication with parents. There are also numerous special cultural events sponsored by ISP for the benefit of the Fay community, such as an International Dinner and an ISP Dance. Interaction between day students and international students is encouraged through vacation and weekend visits and homestays with local families.

Sports: Athletics plays an integral part of the Fay School mission to educate the whole child his/her fullest potential in preparation for a productive and fulfilled life. The fundamental purpose of Fay School athletics is to give each student the opportunity to become experienced, skilled, and confident in a variety of athletic areas. Developing health-related fitness, physical competence, and cognitive understanding about physical activity enables them to adopt healthy and physical active lifestyles.

Because of the value of sports, we provide as many opportunities for participation as possible to our students. We attempt to satisfy both the competitive needs as well as the recreational needs of every student. In order to accomplish this, we offer several different levels of competition in as many sports as possible. Participation in athletics is required during each of the three seasons for every student in grades five through nine. Students may tryout for competitive interscholastic teams or join an intramural team or activity. Fay's sports curriculum includes Soccer, Football, Basketball, Ice Hockey, Wrestling, Lacrosse, Baseball, Tennis, Field Hockey, Volleyball, Softball, Cross Country, Track, Golf, Riding, Dance, Fitness, Skiing, and Squash.

Fay's indoor athletic facilities include two full-sized basketball courts, volleyball / basketball / gymnastics room, wrestling room, weight room, training room, dance room, theater, darkroom, woodworking room, ski room, two coaches' rooms, two team rooms, two large equipment rooms, many large storage areas, and a small kitchen for hosting functions. Fay's outdoor athletic facilities include nine athletic fields, eight tennis courts, a swimming pool, an on-campus cross country course, and a trap-shooting facility. Our two hockey teams use the rinks at the New England Sports Center on weekdays and at St. Mark's School on Saturday mornings. Our golfers and squash players also use the facilities at St. Mark's, which is virtually across the street. Our skiers use Ski Ward in Shrewsbury.

Extracurricular Activities: Billiards, Boston Ballet & Symphony, Bowling, Concerts, Crafts Fairs, Dances, Eastern States Exposition, davill Railroad, Haunted Houses, Hiking, Horseback Riding, Ice Skating, International Celebrations, King Richard's Faire, Laser Light Shows, Laser Tag, Mall & Outlet Shopping, Movies, Museums, Mystery Tours, Mystic Seaport, New England Aquarium, OmiMAX Theater, On-Campus Activitis, Parades & Festivals, Pizza Parties, Plimoth Plantation, Quiet Time On Campus, Roller Blading, Seasonal & Holiday Events, Skiing, Special Occasion Dinners, Sports Events, Sturbridge Village, Theater Performances, Theme Parks, Whitewater Rafting, Water Parks and Whale Watches.

Campus: The Root Academic Center houses most Upper and Lower School classrooms, including the math and science wing with six state-of-the-art science labs, the Learning Center, the media lab, a writing lab, and a multimedia lab. The Reinke Building (1971) contains a large auditorium, a choral studio, the School Counselor's office, and the Summer and Special Programs office. The Picardi Art Center provides facilities for art classes, including a darkroom. The Harris Events Center is home to Fay's Performing Arts Program and includes five music practice rooms, two music classrooms, a band room, a dance studio, a multipurpose room, and a 400-seat theater. The School is completely networked, and the library contains 17,000 volumes.

Dormitories: Boarding boys are housed in the Steward Dorm, and girls dorms are located above the dining facilities in Webster House and in East House.

Nearest International Airport: Logan International Airport, Boston.

Foxcroft School

Location: Middlburg, Virginia (U.S. Mid-Atlantic, East Coast)

P.O. Box 5555, Middleburg, VA 20118-5555
Phone: 540-687-5555; Fax: 540-687-3675
Website: www.foxcroft.org; Email: admissions@foxcroft.org

Mrs. Rebecca Gilmore, Director of Admission
Phone: 540-687-5555; Fax: 540-687-3627
Email: admissions@foxcroft.org

Mission Statement: Foxcroft provides a residential learning experience for girls in which academic excellence, leadership, responsibility, and integrity are our highest values.

Grade Level: 9-12.

Student Gender: Girls Only.

Enrollment: 182 girls, 137 boarders, 45 day.

International Students: 13% non-U.S. citizens, from 12 countries.

Accredited by: VAIS

Head of School: Mary Lou Leipheimer was appointed Head of School in 1989. She is a recognized and respected leader in national independent school organizations and was awarded the coveted William B. Bretnall Award from the Secondary School Admission Test (SSAT) Board in 1999. She currently serves on the Board of the Virginia Association of Independent Schools (VAIS) and is a Director on the Board of The Association of Boarding Schools (TABS). She was affiliated with SSAT from 1990 to 2002, serving as Chair Emeritus from 1999 to 2002, as Chair from 1996 to 1999, a Board Director from 1992 to 2002, and on the Evaluation Committee from 1990 to 1993. She was a Founding Co-Chair of the National Coalition of Girls' Schools (NCGS), she has served on the Development Committee of the National Association of Independent Schools (NAIS), and she is a past Vice President of Region III of the National Association of Principals of Schools for Girls (NAPSG). In 1998, she was invited to be one of only 100 members of the prestigious Headmasters Association.

Faculty: Foxcroft has 30 full-time faculty and administrators who teach, 22 women and 8 men. Thirty-nine faculty and administrators live on campus, 19 with families. They hold 48 baccalaureate and 21 advanced degrees from such institutions as American University, Carnegie Mellon, Colgate, College of William and Mary, Columbia, Denison, Duke, Georgetown, Harvard, Pennsylvania State, Skidmore, Swarthmore, Wellesley, and the Universities of California (Berkleley), Massachusetts, New York Law, the South, Vermont, and Virginia. Two registered nurses staff the Health Center and a doctor is on call. Foxcroft capitalizes on the fact that 73% percent of the faculty and administrators live on campus. The faculty members and their families are the hub of a caring community. Each faculty member has a maximum of five student advisees.

Tuition: Tuition and boarding for 2003-2004 is $32,000.

Class Size: 10 students with a student / teacher ratio of 6:1.

Curriculum: Foxcroft offers a robust college preparatory academic program, which prepares young women for a future that demands intelligent responses, highly developed skills, and firmly rooted character. The central components of a Foxcroft education are intellectual; the academic curriculum is designed to challenge each student to develop analytical ability, critical thinking and communication skills, and rigorous independent thought. We educate each student to seek the confidence and character to meet her future with integrity, high purpose, and a sense of accomplishment.

We believe that our residential program provides an environment that is uniquely suited to meet those goals. Our student-faculty ratio of six-to-one and our maximum class size of 15 encourages academic leadership and utilizes the different learning styles of girls. The faculty uses collaborative learning techniques throughout the curriculum; students work in groups to develop skills, and formulate and analyze theories. Teachers regularly make interdisciplinary connections, and real-life lessons of the dormitories and the playing fields are frequently woven into the texture of the classes. Individual needs of students with varying interests and abilities are met by providing opportunities for independent study when appropriate.

Despite its small size, Foxcroft's curriculum includes approximately 70 courses each year in six academic disciplines. We participate in the College Board's Advanced Placement program, offering 14 AP courses in English, foreign language, history, mathematics, and science. The curriculum is further enriched by special school-wide programs such as Interim Term, the Goodyear Speaker Program, the Poetry Festival, and the Senior Thesis.

Throughout the curriculum, academic challenge is complemented by appropriate support and an emphasis on tolerance and mutual respect. Our two Learning Centers, Humanities and Mathematics, are places where both extra help and enrichment occur, and our Writing Lab is designed to provide cross-curricular support in all aspects of the writing process.

Advanced Placement: Courses available: English Language, English Literature, French Language, French Literature, Spanish Language, Spanish Literature, U.S. History, Macroeconomics, Algebra wih Trigonometry, Calculus, Biology, Chemistry, and Physics.

College Placement: Graduates of Foxcroft have been accepted at colleges such as American College, Boston University, Columbia Univeresiity, Emory University, Georgetown University, Johns Hopkins University, Loyola University, Oxford University, Princeton University, Rice University, Sarah Lawrence College, Stanford University, The Julliard School, Tulane University, University of Pennsylvania, Vassar College, and Wellesley College.

Academic Requirements: Students are expected to complete the following studies: English – 4 units; Foreign Language – 3 credits in a single language or 2 credits in one and two in another; History – 3 units – World Cultures, European, U.S. History; Mathematics – 3 units – Algebra I, Geometry and Algebra II; Science – 3 units- Biology, Physics and one additional unit; Fine Arts – 1.5 units – Introduction to the Arts and one additional unit in Dance, Drama, Music, Studio Art or Art history; Physical Education- 3 trimesters/year, Health – Sophomore Health Class.

Sports: Foxcroft's Athletic curriculum includes Basketball, Field Hockey, Lacrosse, Riding, Soccer, Softball, Tennis, Volleyball, Aerobics, Rock-Climbing, PE Conditioning, Strength Conditioning, Dance Technique: Ballet, Jazz and Tap, Sophomore Health Class, and Yoga.

Extracurricular Activities: Adopt-a-Grandparent, Middleburg Humane Foundation, Special Friends, Therapeutic Riding, Windy Hill Tutoring, Activities Committee, Art Club, Astronomy Club, Athletic Association, Bio Lab Assistant, Blue Planet Society, CAPs Tour Guides, Chimera Literary Magazine, Christmas Pageant Preparations, Coffee House, CEPED: Current Events / Philosophy / Ethics /Debate, Dance Company, Drama Club, Flag Float Committee, Fox/Hound Officers, Foxcroft Christian Fellowship, Foxcroft Reaching Out, Horse Show Club, Interim Committee, International Club, Lab Rats, Middleburg Humane Foundation, Old Girl / New Girl, Rhythm Nation, Riding Club, Riding Monitor, Singing Groups, Special Friends / Adopt a Grandparent, Spiritual Life Committee, Tally-Ho! Yearbook, Whippers In, and Windy Hill Tutoring. Various Washington, DC area events to increase awareness and fund research for AIDS, Breast Cancer, and Colon Cancer; to help out in soup kitchens; and to collect funds and food for needy families.

Campus: Foxcroft is located on 500 acres of land just north of Middleburg, Virginia. In addition to its natural beauty, the campus provides a wonderful setting for environmental studies, hiking, cross country, riding, and sledding when it snows.

The Schoolhouse has classrooms, a studio art wing, three music labs, an auditorium, photography darkrooms, and the Learning Center, along with the Math and Writing Labs. The Science Wing has three laboratory classrooms, lab preparation rooms, a plant and animal room, a science library, a computer-based laboratory, and facilities for permanent specimen collections.

The Currier Library, one of the largest independent school libraries in the country, offers nearly 50,000 print volumes as well as information in fourteen other formats, including electronic online access. The library serves as the academic and information hub for the campus. It is the location of Morning Meetings and houses two computer laboratories where students gain access to the internet and email, classrooms, seminar rooms, 85 study carrels, microfilm and audiovisual rooms, and the School archives.

The restored Brick House, dating from the 1700s, holds the Dining Room and kitchen facilities, reception rooms, the Development Office, and faculty and staff apartments.

The Engelhard Activities Building contains the gymnasium, a weight room, a student lounge and snack bar, and the dance studio. The outdoor swimming pool is open for recreational use in the early fall and late spring. Other athletic facilities include four playing fields (one with a softball diamond), eight tennis courts, three riding rings (one indoors), and three jump courses adjacent to the campus buildings. McConnell Stables and Indoor Ring allow riding throughout the school year and includes a 60-stall stable.

Other campus facilities include five dormitories, faculty housing, an observatory, a Guest House, the Head of School's home, a ropes and initiatives course, the Health Center, and a garden.

Dormitories: Students at Foxcroft live in five dormitories. Usually, two students share a room and a private bath, but there are also singles and quads. Each dormitory has a living room, sleeping areas, a kitchen, and free laundry facilities.

Nearest International Airport: Dulles International Airport, Washington DC.

Nearby Lodgings: Holiday Inn Carradoc Hall, 703-771-9200; Courtyard by Marriott - Dulles Airport, 703-709-7100; Dulles Holiday Inn, 703-471-7411; Dulles Hilton, 703-478-2900; Dulles Marriott, 703-471-9500; Hyatt Dulles, 703-713-1234.

Gould Academy

Location: Bethel, Maine (U.S. East Coast, New England)

P.O. Box 860, Bethel, ME 04217
Phone: 207-824-7777; Fax: 207-824-2926
Website: www.gouldacademy.org
Email: Admissions@gouldacademy.org

Mr. John Kerney, Director of Admission and External Affairs
Phone: 207-824-7777; Fax: 207-824-2926
Email: John.Kerney@gouldacademy.org

Mission Statement: Gould Academy is committed to the seven-day boarding school tradition that creates myriad opportunities for an incredibly diverse community of over 90 adults who intersect the lives of 220 students every single day. From a traditional and innovative curriculum that creates a rigorous academic experience, to the on-snow programs with training in alpine, snowboarding, freestyle and Nordic disciplines, our 167-year history provides a solid foundation as we encourage students to become responsible for, and excited about, their own learning. The White Mountain National Forest provides a tranquil yet vibrant setting in which we are allowed the time and space for reflection and growth, while our close proximity to Boston and Montreal reminds us that we are never far from the constant activity of an ever changing world.

Admission Requirements for International Students: International students are required to complete the regular application for admission to Gould Academy. We encourage international students to apply early since they will not be able to apply for an F-1 Student Visa until they have enrolled in school. The process to obtain an F-1 Student Visa may take time and the earlier the student begins the process the better.

Gould Academy provides English as a Second Language (ESL) instruction, as well as the Test of English as a Foreign Language (TOEFL) Preparatory program when necessary. International students must be able to succeed in an intermediate ESL course. Students are required to provide official English proficiency test scores during the application process. Acceptable exams are the

TOEFL or the Secondary School Admissions Test (SSAT). These standardized tests will aid the school in placing the student in an appropriate ESL course. There is no minimum score required for admission, however Gould has found that students with one of the following scores will be more successful at Gould Academy, TOEFL Paper-500, TOEFL Computer-173.

Grade Level: 9-12.

Student Gender: Boys & Girls.

Enrollment: 220 students, 135 boys, 95 girls, 180 boarders, 50 day.

International Students: 30 students, from countries such as Germany, Slovakia, Turkey, Australia, Japan and Korea. Gould Academy usually averages around 25-30 international students per year, making up around 15% of our total student population. Most of our international students are from Asia or Europe.

Accredited by: NEASC, ISACS

Head of School: Dan Kunkle, B..A., M.Ed., Brown University, Harvard University. Email: Daniel.Kunkle@gouldacademy.org

Faculty: Gould's first strength is its faculty – adults of substance and breadth of experience who have mad long-term commitments to developing self-confidence and independence in young people. To that effort Gould teachers bring both a fundamental affection for young people and the challenges of high academic standards. Each Gould teacher is the kind of individual whom we remember as the person who cared enough and had enough patience to thoughtfully challenge our thinking or show us the promise we could not see in ourselves at the time. Our teachers are athletic coaches, dorm parents, advisors, mentors and friends. They lead weekend expeditions. They share and foster students' enthusiasms for rock climbing, jazz, computer technology, poetry, skiing, and a myriad of other pastimes. The faculty's wide variety of academic and other interests enriches the curriculum and daily life. Students discover new passions and develop existing ones because of teachers' encouragement and contagious enthusiasm for their academic disciplines and life-long activities.

Tuition: Tuition and Boarding for 2003-2004 is $32,100.

Class Size: 10 students, with a student/teacher ratio of 6:1.

Curriculum: Given the constantly accelerating rate of growth in information in today's world, learning must truly be a lifelong process if one is to become an informed world citizen. With that in mind, the academic program at Gould Academy is designed to challenge students as they learn to become responsible for, and excited about, their own learning. The central focus of the academic program is reaching the highest levels of cognitive skill. Students develop problem-solving skills which will enable them to confront unanticipated problems in our evolving society.

Advanced Placement: Yes

ESL Program: Yes

Average SAT Scores of Graduating Students: 1165

College Placement: Recent graduates are attending Columbia, Dartmouth, Smith, Wesleyan, and Yale.

Academic Requirements: The following credits are needed to graduate from Gould Academy: English –4 credits, History – 3 credits, Mathematics – 3 credits, Science – 2 credits, Modern or Classical Language – 2 credits. Total- 18 credits.

Sports: Gould Academy's Athletic curriculum includes Soccer, Field Hockey, Cross Country, Golf, Basketball, Lacrosse, Softball, Tennis, Equestrian, Skateboarding, Rock Climbing, Mountain and Road Bike Racing, and Skiing.

Extracurricular Activities: Our students participate in a number of activities, events and off-campus trips. Some of these are organized, trimester programs such s drama, and the Herald yearbook. Others involve planning and execution of major events such as the annual Snow Ball dinner dance and the spirited competitions of Winter Carnival. Through Reachout, the school's service organization, students volunteer their time in the Bethel community and beyond.

There are always a number of activities scheduled each weekend and students are urged to help with sponsoring events and activities. The weekend planning meeting is held every Tuesday at lunchtime in Ordway Dining Hall.

Activities may include camping, canoeing and day hiking trips sponsored in all seasons by the Outing Club. Shopping trips to Portland or to Freeport, trips to movies in the area and trips to various concerts are offered on a regular basis as well. Athletic facilities are available during the weekend, and there are a number of other possibilities just waiting to take shape with student input and interest.

Campus: Amidst the spectacular setting of one of Maine's most picturesque resort villages, Gould offers a traditional liberal-arts curriculum. A nurturing community is central to the Gould experience, with a dedicated faculty providing an optimal balance between challenge and support. Facilities include a new, state-of-the-art, 22,000 square-foot science center, working farm, 500-seat theatre, MIDI lab, and extensive art studios. The competition center at nearby Sunday River ski resort supports on-site training for all levels of competitive alpine and freestyle skiers and snowboarders. Non-competitive skiers may pursue recreational skiing, ski instructing, or ski patrol programs. A traditional athletic program is complemented by such special offerings as rock climbing, equestrian, and mountain-bike racing.

Dormitories: Boarding students live in three large dormitories and two smaller faculty homes. In the large dormitories, faculty residents live on each floor and cultivate productive and enjoyable relationships with students living on those floors. The "dorm parents" and the elected student proctors, who also assume leadership roles on each floor, provide the kind of support most students need to adjust to living in a new community of friends. Dorm rooms are spacious and well maintained and each unit contains its own lounge, laundry, and areas for activities such as dances, television, quiet study, pool, or videos. All dorm rooms have telephone jacks for each student as well as data lines for Internet access and network ports for students' computers that connect up PCs with the school's main server. Dormitories become a "home away from home," and life in them becomes the bedrock of relationships that last for years.

Leadership of students by students is an important element of Gould. Each spring, students and faculty elect approximately 18 student proctors on the basis of dependability, initiative, fairness, and leadership.

These representatives, along with faculty members, help lead the new student fall orientation trips. They are a source of information and support for the new students as they settle into dorm life. Proctors also work with faculty to make the dorm and school environment cooperative and positive. Their involvement has ranged from organizing school dances to suggesting positive, school-wide policy changes to faculty.

Nearest International Airport: Portland, ME airport or Logan Airport, Boston.

Nearby Lodgings: Bethel Inn & Country Club, 800-654-0125; Norseman Inn & Motel, 207-824-2002; Sudbury Inn, 207-824-2174; The Victoria Inn, 207-824-8060.

Governor Dummer Academy

Location: Byfield, Massachusetts (U.S. East Coast, New England)

1 Elm Street, Byfield, MA 01922
Phone: 978-465-1763; Fax: 978-463-9896
Website: www.gda.org; Email: admissions@gda.org

Mr. Peter Bidstrup, Director of Admission
Phone: 978-499-3120; Fax: 978-462-1278
Email: admissions@gda.org

Mission Statement: Governor Dummer Academy expects and promotes the individual's active commitment to integrity, learning, academic excellence and the health of the community. Enriched by our unique tradition and beautiful surroundings, we are distinguished by our support of individual growth and achievement in academics, the arts and athletics in a diverse community that values teamwork, service and respect for others.

Grade Level: 9-12.

Student Gender: Boys & Girls.

Enrollment: 372 students, 92 boarding girls, 133 boarding boys, 80 day girls and 67 day boys.

International Students come from Australia, Canada, China, Czech Republic, Germany, Hong Kong, Indonesia, Korea, Iran, Japan, Thailand and Taiwan.

Accredited by: NEASC

Head of School: John M. Doggett, Jr., Williams College B.A. American Civilization, New York University M.A. History.

Faculty: GDA has a faculty of 75 teachers, 40 of whom hold advanced degrees. In addition to being classroom instructors, faculty members are dormitory parents, coaches, and advisers. 80 percent of the faculty members live on campus with their families. Each student at GDA has one faculty advisor.

Tuition: Tuition and Boarding for 2003-2004 is $31,800.

Average Class Size: 13 students

Curriculum: The Academy offers a challenging, thought-provoking and student-centered curriculum that inspires a passion for learning. By focusing on the learning process and the development of essential skills, GDA teaches students how to think critically, creatively and independently. We encourage students to acquire knowledge through hands-on activity, multi-disciplinary inquiry, analysis and reflection. Many structures—including the advising system, extra help sessions, and evening study hours supervised by dormitory parents—help students learn to study and manage their time well. Our goal is to teach young people to become actively accountable for their own learning and to grow by learning with others.

Longer class blocks are essential to the curriculum. Classes meet for 60- and 90-minute periods, affording students and teachers more opportunity to explore subject matter in depth, from different perspectives and with a variety of classroom activities. In addition to traditional assessments such as tests and papers, students debate, conduct hands-on laboratory and field experiments, make oral presentations, research in groups, use technology to create presentations, and design their own exhibits.

Students and faculty bring to GDA a richness of experience, perspective and diversity which adds immeasurably to the education of all. This is the spirit that inspires a community of learners.

Advanced Placement: Advanced Placement courses are available in English, Statistics, Calculus, U.S. History, French Language, Spanish Language and Literature, Physics, and Studio Art.

ESL Program: GDA offers both Intermediate and Advanced ESL courses. The focus of intermediate ESL is acclimation to American culture and the Governor Dummer community. Students are prepared to meet the academic and social expectations through extensive listening and speaking practice in class, and through reading, writing and reflecting on literature and their own first year experience. The focus of advanced ESL is to further develop the student's skills in all areas of academic English. Students are prepared to write research papers, make classroom presentations, and read and write with greater fluency.

Academic Requirements: Successful completion of 16 credits: English – 4 credits, Math- 3 credits, Social Studies – 2 credits, Science – 3 credits, Fine Arts – Introduction to Fin Arts in 9th grade, and one Fine Arts course thereafter, Foreign Languages – 3 credits. (ESL students are not required to complete the foreign language requirement with permission of the Academic Dean.)

Sports: Every student is required to be a part of the Afternoon Program for all three seasons. There are various requirements based on year in school. Sports offered are Baseball, Basektball, Cross Country, Field Hockey, Football, Golf, Hockey, Lacrosse, Soccer, Softball, Tennis, Track, Volleyball and Wrestling.

Extracurricular Activities: Many memorable moments and relationships happen outside the structures of the academic day and the Afternoon Program. There are lots of ways to be involved at GDA! We encourage our students to pursue interests to form their own organizations. For this reason, the clubs or organizations listed below may vary from year to year. Extracurricular programs include The Governor student newspaper, Chapel Committee, Gay/Straight Alliance, Environmental Club, Christian Fellowship, EPIC (Model UN), German Club, Governor Dummer Honor Society, Harvard Model, Congress, Health and Wellness Committee, Jewish Fellowship, The Milestone yearbook, The Fishing Club, Project Outreach, Poetry Society, P.R.I.D.E., Peer Advisors, Mansion House Proctors, The Spire literary magazine, Red Key, Tour Guides, and the Social Committee.

Campus: Situated on 450 acres 33 miles north of Boston and 4 miles from the Atlantic Ocean, GDA recently completed construction on a new math and science center and library. A new performing arts center opened in December 2001.

Dormitories: Nannie B, Eames, Ingham, Farmhouse, Moody, Perkins.... Students at GDA form fond attachments to their dorms. Living in singles or doubles with their classmates, ninth graders are housed in their own dorms, while all upperclassmen mix throughout the campus.

Members of the faculty reside in and supervise student life in our dormitories. These faculty members supervise study hours and share in creating a warm, social and family unit in the dorm. Dorm parents also serve as their students' advisors. With common areas complete with television, VCR, and comfy chairs, dorms are often the place that kids hang out in between study hours or other commitments. Quiet hours begin in all dorms at 7:00 p.m. to provide appropriate space for study hours. Male and female students may visit each other in the dormitory common rooms providing they follow parietal guidelines.

Members of the senior class are selected by the dorm parents to be dorm proctors. These students take on vital responsibilities as the Academy's leaders. Proctors help the dorm parents run the dormitories and, most importantly, are strong role models and mentors for all students.

All dorms have resources from the Dean of Students' Office to fund social activities. Dinners, ice cream sundaes, movie rentals, pizza study breaks, and other on- and off-campus activities help foster dorm unity.

Nearest International Airport: Logan International Airport, Boston.

Nearby Lodgings: Sheraton Tara Hotel at Ferncroft, 978-777-2500; Best Western, 987-373-1511; Fairfield Inn, 978-388-3400; Hampshire Inn, 603-474-5700.

The Gow School

Location: South Wales, New York (U.S. East Coast, New England)

P.O. Box 85, South Wales, NY 14139-0085
Phone: 716-652-3450; Fax: 716-652-3457
Website: www.gow.org; Email: admissions@gow.org

Mr. Robert Garcia, Director of Admission
Phone: 716-652-3450; Fax: 716-687-2003
Email: admissions@gow.org

Mission Statement: Established in 1926 and located on 100 acres of woodlands,The Gow School is an internationally renowned boarding school that specializes in the education of young men who have dyslexia or other language-based learning differences. Our academic program offers a strong college preparatory curriculum balanced by a rewarding interscholastic athletic program. With a 4:1 student-faculty ratio and a focus on languaqge development and study skills, The Gow School celebrates a boy's talents while strenghtening his intellectual foundation. We offer a 5-week summer camp experience for boys and girls from around the world providing an outstanding curriculum for students who have experienced academic difficulties or have language based learning differences. The progam balances remediation with recreational activities.

Grade Level: 7-12.

Student Gender: Boys only.

Enrollment: 143 boys, 143 boarders.

Accredited by: NYSAIS

Head of School: M. Bradley Rogers, Jr.

Faculty: The faculty consists of 43 teachers and administrators who teach, 28 of whom live in the dormitories or in other campus housing. They hold 27 baccalaureate degrees, 15 master's degrees, and a doctor degree.

Tuition: Tuition and Boarding for 2003-2004 is $32,000.

Class Size: 3-6 students, with a 4:1 student-faculty ratio.

Curriculum: Instructors in The Gow School's academic program teach classes ranging in size from three to six students, provide individualized and extra help when needed, and regularly communicate with parents on their children's progress. All faculty members at Gow are specially trained in the teaching methods that are most effective in helping dyslexic students succeed in the classroom.

Gow students attend classes six days per week and take a minimum of five academic courses that meet daily. Their schedule includes a course in Reconstructive Language, which is designed to improve their individual language skills. A mandatory, two-and-half-hour study hall is held six nights a week, giving students ample time to prepare for tests and complete homework assignments.

College Placement: Recent graduates of Gow have been accepted to Bates, Centre, Cornell, Davis & Elkins, Denison, Elon, Gannon, Long Beach State, Loyola New Orleans, Marshall, Mount St. Joseph, Muskingum, New England, Northeastern, Regis, RIT, St. Lawrence, Syracuse, West Virginia Wesleyan, and the Universities of Arizona, Denver, Michigan, Missouri–Kansas City, Utah, and Vermont.

Academic Requirements: Graduation requirements for grades 9 - 12 include four credits in English, three in history, three in mathematics, two in laboratory science and one in art or music.

Sports: Gow believes that a healthy, disciplined student makes the best pupil. That's why physical fitness and athletics will always be an integral part of life at The School. Besides fielding varsity and junior varsity teams in soccer, basketball, lacrosse and tennis, Gow offers 12 additional activities that promote the concept of teamwork and health.

While Gow's picturesque landscape and fields are an ideal setting for outdoor sports, the School's 49,600 square foot athletic facility makes playing and training indoors a special experience as well. Completed in 2002, Gow's state-of-the-art gymnasium houses areas for basketball, tennis, indoor soccer, squash, weight training, and cardiovascular fitness.

Extracurricular Activities: Weekends present a variety of entertainment options for Gow students. Buffalo's world famous art gallery, prestigious symphony, or intimate theatre district are available to those with an affinity for cultural endeavors. Leisurely activities include dances with public and independent schools, shopping at local malls, ethnic festivals, NHL and NFL games, and skiing at local resorts. Because classes are held six days per week, "designated weekends" are offered to students each semester. During this six-day weekend, students may return home or visit another family. In the rare instances that students remain on campus, faculty members will arrange and supervise activities for them. Designated weekends and regular vacations occur about every six weeks during the academic year.

Campus: The 120-acre campus, which is traversed by a trout stream, includes hilly woodland, athletic fields, tennis courts, a ski/snowboard slope and a ropes course. The Main Building contains the business office, ten classrooms, infirmary, and the Gow Bookstore. Orton Hall provides 12 classrooms, including a tutoring room, a science laboratory, two computer classrooms, the computer writing lab, and a study hall. The Green Cottage furnishes living quarters for students and tw2o masters' apartments. Other facilities include The Admissions Building and the School House, which contains the Art Department. Students and masters reside in Cornwall House, Templeton Dormitory, Brown House, Ellis House, Whitcomb Dormitory, and Warner House. A 49,000 square foot athletic /activities facility, opened in the fall of 2001, will provide a student union, classrooms, two indoor tennis courts, two basketball courts, three squash courts, and a fitness center. The Isaac Arnold Memorial Library, with a capacity of 10,000 volumes contains a reading room, seven classrooms, a faculty room, and the Headmaster's office. The Andrew Thompson Memorial Gymnasium houses a basketball court, a stage, two locker rooms, a lounge, an exercise room, and a general recreation area.

Dormitories: All students attending Gow live in supervised dormitories where they learn to share their experiences with one or more roommates. Time spent in the dorm – whether studying for an exam, listening to music, emailing their family, watching TV or engaging in conversation – gives students a sense of belonging that is absent in non-residential settings.

Nearest International Airport: Buffalo International Airport.

Nearby Lodgings: Hampton Inn, 716-655-3300; The Roycroft Inn, 716-652-5552; Garden Place Hotel, 716-635-9000; Radisson Hotel, 716-634-2300; Sheraton Four Points, 716-681-2400; Marriott Hotel. 716-689-6900; Hyatt Regency Buffalo, 716-856-1234.

The Grand River Academy

Location: Austinburg, Ohio (U.S. Central, Midwest)

3042 College Street, Austinburg, OH 44010
Phone: 440-275-2811; Fax: 440-275-3275
Website: www.grandriver.org; Email: academy@grandriver.org

Mr. Sam Corabi, Director of Admission and Financial Aid
Phone: 440-275-2811; Fax: 440-275-1825
Email: academy@grandriver.org

Mission Statement: Nationally recognized as one of the few remaining boarding schools of its kind in the United States, Grand River Academy offers a non-military, nonsectarian, all-male college preparatory education. There has been an academic institution on campus for 168 years. The modern academy, founded in 1962, upholds a mission to develop and foster the emotional and academic maturity necessary for its students to graduate and launch successful college careers. The Academy's curriculum is college preparatory, with an emphasis on helping those students who can benefit from the extra attention offered in a boarding program. Our location, in the small rural community of Austinburg, Ohio, allows for a harmonious blend of the traditional past and the practical present. Our size, 120 students, allows for much individual attention, both in class and out, and ultimately gives all students the chance to gain real identity.

Grade Level: 9-12.

Student Gender: Boys only.

Enrollment: 120 boys, 120 boarders.

International Students: 17 Students, from Korea, Taiwan, Venezuela, Saudi Arabia and Spain.

Accredited by: ISACS

Head of School: Randy Blum, B.A. Milligan College, Master of Education, Ashland University. Email: rblum@grandriver.org

Faculty: The vision of the Grand River Academy instructor extends beyond the narrow focus of the classroom and the textbook. Through their own personal experiences, instructors are able to breathe life into the courses they teach and exude an enthusiasm they hope will be contagious. Often it is. The GRA faculty is comprised of a group of men and women with diverse interests. Our teachers are from varied walks of life, different regions of the country and each has a personality that adds to the originality of the Academy. This incredibly assorted group of men and women share one common desire - the desire to teach. All of our teachers are dedicated to the success of their students. These teachers devote their lives to helping young boys grow into men. They monitor the success of our students from the time they arrive at the Academy until the time they turn their tassels and move on into the 'real' world. GRA teachers are special people that influence our students' education, maturity and life experiences.

What holds this group of men and women together is their common interest in children of all ages and their dedication to improving their skills in "dealing with" these young men. Most of our instructors maintain contact with children during the summer break through volunteerefforts or by working at the Academy's summer school. Academy students are taught and supervised by adults who like their chosen field - and enjoy young people. GRA provides a winning combination for boys who are looking for a role model, an educator, and a positive life long mentor! Most students in larger schools have never been fortunate to have a teacher as a friend. In the non-threatening environment of the Academy, such a relationship is possible.

Tuition: Tuition and Boarding for 2003-2004 is $23,650.

Class Size: 7 students with a student/teacher ratio of 7:1.

Curriculum: Our college preparatory curriculum is rich in tradition, with college acceptance required for each student prior to graduation. Small classes are the hallmark of The Grand River Academy's education; with an average class size of seven, students have the opportunity to experience tremendous academic growth. The school day, lasting from 8:30 a.m. until 3:30 p.m., includes seven academic periods and a break for lunch. To help guarantee our students' academic success, study hours from 7:30 until 9:30 Sunday through Thursday evenings are mandatory. Most students study in their own dorm rooms under the guidance of the dorm master. Students who have not completed homework assignments and those who have trouble concentrating in their dorm rooms are assigned to a more structured study period, which is held in a classroom under the supervision of a faculty member. Students are encouraged to seek special help from their classroom teachers during this time period; this individual help quite often means the difference between success and failure in a subject. Students who are experiencing difficulty in their classes are assigned formal help sessions during the evenings, in addition to Saturday mornings. Under the guidance of their regular classroom teachers, they are assisted in studying for upcoming tests or are given drills to further explain material they are having difficulty understanding. The Resource Center is available as an aid to students in all disciplines. The Academy does assist students with learning differences in the Resource Center on a limited basis and networks with individual teachers to accommodate different learning styles.

ESL Program: Individually tailored courses are offered to those students whose native language is other than English. The Secondary Level English Proficiency (SLEP) and ELPT (English Language Proficiency Test) are employed for placement and diagnostic purposes. Students who "test out" of classes conducted within one band of difficulty receive credit, and then go on to the next until they no longer need or want ESL support. A whole-language method of instruction blends language acquisition activities with content-based lessons from academic courses where ESL students may be encountering difficulties because of as yet unrealized English fluency.

College Placement: Recent graduates of Grand River have been accepted to colleges such as Boston University, Michigan State, Ohio State, Penn State, Purdue, and Rutgers.

Academic Requirements: Four units of English, three units of Math, three units of Natural Science, three units of Social Studies, one- half unit of physical education, one-half unit of Health, one-half unit of

Computer Application, one unit of Fine Arts, five and one-half units of foreign language and electives. Each senior must also complete a research paper and be accepted by a college.

Sports: A wide range of rewarding and stimulating activities, both athletic and non-athletic, are available to the Grand River Academy student. Every student is required to participate in one activity every weekday afternoon. By offering a variety, we assure that everyone's interests will be satisfied. While athletics are not mandatory, all students are encouraged to participate, regardless of age or ability. The Academy fields interscholastic teams in soccer, basketball, tennis, cross-country, golf and baseball. Students who do not wish to make the commitment to inter-scholastic athletics will participate in the afternoon activities program, which includes an intramural sports program along with several other opportunities. The students participate in volleyball, basketball, tennis, soccer, bocci ball, croquet, flag football, ultimate frisbee, bowling and many other intramural sports.

Campus: The Grand River Academy campus consists of two hundred acres in northern Ohio's Western Reserve. The physical plant consists of five academic buildings, five dormitories, and ten faculty homes directly across from the campus. Bauder Hall (1961) houses the math and social studies department, along with a Computer Lab and Resource Center. English, and foreign language classes are located in Green Hall, as is the library and multimedia center. Skeggs Hall (2001) house the science and art departments and includes both a digital photography and ceramics classroom. All buildings are close to each other and can be easily reached within the five minutes allotted between classes. Juniors live in North Hall and West Hall. Both dormitories house 24 students in double-occupancy rooms. Both dorms were constructed in 1969 and then renovated in 2002. Shepard Hall, on the opposite side of campus, was built in 1918 and renovated in 1983. It has room for 40 seniors and juniors. Mastin Hall, completed in 1982, is a dormitory for 20 sophomore students. Warren Hall was built in 1997 and is home to our freshmen class. Each dormitory has one or more residences for faculty families. The Academy gymnasium is the center of campus. Its facilities include a 7000-square foot gym and locker rooms on the main floor, a rock-climbing wall located in the lobby and a modern health and fitness center upstairs. Faculty residences are just beyond the outside avenues and are within easy reach for students finding it necessary to talk with instructors during evenings or weekends.

Dormitories: The Academy promotes a home-like environment. Although instructors are provided their own housing in the dormitory, it is not unusual to see them in the student lounges during their off-duty hours. They and their families eat with students in the dining room. Faculty couples are never without a babysitter, and students usually can find a reliable source of coffee sugar, refrigerator space, and card players from among the faculty. The environment is family-like, yes, but like any family, the Academy has its rules and regulations. And there are penalties for their violation. But those rules are designed to create a more livable environment, not a military atmosphere.

At an extra cost, optional restricted telephones are available in every dormitory room on campus. Students may also decorate their rooms pretty much as they like. They may bring their stereos, skateboards, roller blades, bicycles, and PC's. But they may not bring televisions, cellular phones, beepers or hot plates. They need not wear blazers every day. But neither may they wear jeans and T-shirts to class. A visit to the Academy would convey its focused and structured way of life. Except for seniors, students share duties in the kitchen and dining room. All students must keep their own living quarters tidy. The faculty and faculty families all live in the dormitories or in houses on campus; they share and shape that social climate. They try their best to assure a living experience that is meaningful, comfortable, and entertaining, yet supportive of the learning program.

Nearest International Airport: Hopkins International Airport, Cleveland, Ohio.

Nearby Lodgings: Comfort Inn, 440-275-2711; Holiday Inn Express, 440-275-2020; Travelodge, 440-275-2011; Hampton Inn, 440-275-2000.

The Greenwood School

Location: Putney, Vermont (U.S. East Coast, New England)

14 Greenwood Lane, Putney, VT 05346
Phone: 802-387-4545; Fax: 802-387-5396
Website: www.greenwood.org; Email: smiller@greenwood.org

Mr. Stewart Miller, Assistant Headmaster
Phone: 802-387-4545; Fax: 802-387-5396
Email: smiller@greenwood.org

Mission Statement: The mission of The Greenwood School is to research, design, and provide the best academic program and learning environment possible for the comprehensive education of students who have dyslexia and related language difficulties. Our goal is to facilitate the development of self-confidence and to provide our students with the academic foundation necessary for them to reach their true potential and enjoy a successful experience in higher education.

Admission Requirements for International Students: Cognitive and achievement testing, as well as an interview required.

Grade Level: Ungraded (Ages 9-14)

Student Gender: Boys only.

Enrollment: 40 boys, 40 boarders.

Accredited by: NEASC, AISNE

Head of School: John Alexander, M.Ed. Harvard University. Email: jalexander@greenwood.org

Faculty: Faculty love of learning is at the heart of the enthusiasm and dedication Greenwood teachers bring to their work. Greenwood's faculty members are highly qualified and experienced, many hold advanced degrees, and their average tenure is over nine years. To address the needs of students with dyslexia and other language-based learning issues, our teachers have demonstrated competency either at the Greenwood School or elsewhere, and they work continually to improve the practice of their skills.

Our teachers are fully trained and certified in multi-sensory remedial language techniques through the Greenwood Institute. They have received training in the "Knowledge of Language," an approach promoted by Dr. Louisa Moats, Ed.D, and in "Structured Language Teaching," a multi-sensory approach based on the highly respected Orton-Gillingham method. Both are proven learning techniques recommended by leading researchers and highly regarded by educational consultants and are integral components of The Greenwood School academic program. This in-depth training deepens Greenwood teachers' knowledge of the structure of language and prepares them to apply competently remedial techniques and to tailor lessons to address each student's specific needs. Ongoing teacher training and supervision is also provided by a master teacher, independent consultants, and by The Greenwood School's Headmaster. 11 teachers live on campus, 3 of whom are dorm supervisors. They undertake after-school, evening, and weekend commitments to supervise, mentor, and assist students in all aspects of student life, as well as academics, music, the arts, school projects, sports and recreational activities. There are also 5 part-time teachers who live off campus

Tuition: Tuition and Boarding for 2003-2004 is $43,400.

Average Class Size: 4 students, with a student/teacher ratio of 2:1.

Curriculum: Language and mathematics are learned skills and as such they are acquired easily by some students and with varying degrees of difficulty by others. Genetic, neurological, and psychological factors may all contribute to a child's readiness and ability to master the basics in the environment of a mainstream classroom. Since the ability to read is so essential in our society, it is understandable that many remedial schools focus their programs almost entirely on remedial language skills. In so doing, many special programs fail to explore the dimensions of each student's unique talents. We agree that competent language skills are a requisite part of every child's education, and individualized remedial language training is the core of Greenwood's curriculum. But a true education provides students with more than skills. We believe the ability to reason, critique, debate, create, to enjoy a fund of general knowledge, to set personal goals and to persevere in achieving them, are essential components of personal, as well as of academic success.

If a child's reading level is used to determine the content of academic classes, the bright language-disabled student is intellectually deprived. If a student believes his scholastic progress is dependent on his weakest skill, his search for knowledge is discouraged. If he is convinced that all facets of his learning require clinical instruction and support, he is robbed of the joy of exploring his creative independence. Through a unique curriculum, strong in creative as well as functional studies, The Greenwood School strives to reawaken the enthusiasm for learning inherent in all children. A full pre-preparatory academic program, including science, history, literature, art, music, and athletics, assures that our students are intellectually challenged, creatively inspired, and factually informed.

Sports: Athletic activities include soccer, basketball, baseball, and intramural track as well as rugby, cricket, badminton, hiking, mountain biking, rock climbing, softball, volleyball, bowling, archery, outdoor leadership, martial arts, equestrian, and cross-country and downhill skiing.

Extracurricular Activities: The weekend schedule includes a variety of both group and individual activities. Saturday mornings are devoted to special programs and cooperative projects. During winter term, the whole school skis on Fridays, and we make up class work on Saturday morning. On Saturday afternoons, students can learn martial arts, play field games, and share other leisure activities. The Saturday evening meal is usually off-campus and is followed by an on-campus movie. Occasionally, we may be invited to attend local events. Sunday's schedule allows for individual worship, letter writing, and an all-school meeting. Faculty members, who live on or near campus, play an integral role in the students' weekends. They have a wide range of skills and interests, including fly-fishing, canoeing, music and cooking, and they enjoy sharing these activities with the students. Greenwood does not employ anyone solely as a dorm resident or weekend monitor; the faculty who are teaching the boys within the classroom are with them in the dorms as well as on the weekends.

Campus: The Greenwood School campus is located in southeastern Vermont in the rural township of Putney. Our campus overlooks the Connecticut River Valley and the mountains of nearby New Hampshire. The school owns 100 acres of rolling fields and woodland, including a two-acre pond, and is surrounded by several hundred acres of privately owned forest with a network of trails for hikers, mountain bikers, and cross-country skiers. A 2-acre pond is available for science classes, fishing, and recreation. Through the generosity of parents and friends, many new buildings and spaces have been constructed, including: an art/science wing, faculty residences, dining hall, and multipurpose recreation classroom building that houses a full sized gymnasium and climbing wall.

Dormitories: Dormitory life is an important part of Greenwood's program and is the hub of its extra-curricular activities. To create a good environment for community living, all faculty members participate in dorm life and assist the teachers who live in the dorm.

Parenting is important for all children, and we do our best to make Greenwood a home away from home. Although our program is structured and maintains definite behavioral expectations, the atmosphere here is relaxed and friendly. Students are encouraged to and assisted in taking responsibility for harmonious interpersonal relationships. We nurture a sense of partnership in the school family. For example, students and faculty are on a first name basis, one small way in which we help engender familial feelings and relaxed communication. Founders Hall, the main dormitory has 18 rooms, 3 faculty apartments, and two common rooms.

Nearest International Airport: Bradley International Airport, Hartford, CT; Albany International Airport, Albany NY; Logan International Airport, Boston MA.

Nearby Lodgings: Colonial Motel, 802-257-7733; Days Inn, 800-329-7466; Econo Lodge, 802-254-2360; Meadowlark Inn, 802-257-4582; Quality Inn & Suites, 802-254-8701; Holiday Inn Express, 802-257-2400.

Hackley School

Location: Tarrytown, New York (U.S. East Coast, New England)

293 Benedict Avenue, Tarrytown, NY 10591
Phone: 914-631-0128; Fax: 914-366-2636
Website: www.hackleyschool.org
Email: admissions@hackleyschool.org

Mrs. Julie Core, Director of Admissions
Phone: 914-631-0128 or 914-366-2642; Fax: 914-366-2636
Email: admissions@hackleyschool.org

Mission Statement: Hackley School, founded in 1899 by Mrs. Caleb Brewster Hackley, is a non-sectarian co-educational, college-preparatory school enrolling day students in kindergarten through grade twelve, and five-day boarding students in grades nine through twelve. The School believes in a diverse student body and assigns a significant percentage of its budget to scholarships.

Hackley offers a rigorous, traditional, and personalized education to able and motivated students whose parents value education.

The program is rigorous: Students encounter serious classes, demanding homework assignments, and an insistence on unreserved effort.

The School is traditional: Students are expected to dress and conduct themselves decorously. More important, Hackley exposes its students to classic texts and traditional disciplines, maintains an informed skepticism of educational fads, and attempts to inculcate the more serious elements of American culture – the democratic ethic and the work ethic.

The School is personalized: Hackley offers small classes, extra help, frequent communication with parents, student-teacher interaction outside the classroom, a predominantly residential faculty, and a high level of participation in team sports, coached primarily by the academic faculty. Hackley believes that students will grow in character and responsibility by participating in structured activity that serves the needs of people outside the spheres of home and school.

By committing their energy, time, and imagination to serving those needs, students can experience the satisfaction of helping others and can gain some appreciation of the complexity and concerns of the larger community. Hackley students are expected to be good citizens. The School shares with its parent community an active commitment to character development as well as academic excellence. Students are encouraged to have respect for and to act responsibly toward themselves and others. The School strives to provide an overall environment that supports the development of virtuous qualities and good personal habits. Hackley students are expected to go beyond mere observance of the rules and to strive to make Hackley a civilized community where courtesy, kindness, and forbearance reign, and incivility and intolerance are shunned.

Admission Requirements for International Students: Hackley will only accept international students after extensive testing is completed. To evaluate a student's ability to perform in English in mainstream classes, prior to enrollment she/he must present a TOEFL computer based exam score of at least 250 or 600 on paper based exam with at least a 6/31 in the Writing Section.

Grade Level: 9-12.

Student Gender: Boys & Girls.

Enrollment: 780 students, 400 boys, 380 girls, 30 boarders, 750 day.

International Students: None currently enrolled.

Accredited by: NYSAIS

Head of School: Walter C. Johnson. Email: wjohnson@hackleyschool.org

Faculty: No two teachers practice their craft in the same way, but they do share some common traits: love of their subject, sense of humor, high standards, and the ability to connect to children's minds and hearts. Whether serving as mentors, advisors, leaders, or partners, our teachers provide the raw material for the intensely personal endeavor of education.

Tuition: Tuition and Boarding for 2003-2004 is $23,000.

Class Size: 17 students, with a student/teacher ratio of 7:1.

Curriculum: The Upper School is specifically college preparatory. The demands of the Upper School academic program require that students demonstrate increasing self-discipline and motivation as they encounter sizable homework assignments, longer papers, and serious scholarship. For the most talented and ambitious, the program offers seminars and Advanced Placement courses in many disciplines. These courses and independent study offer extensive choice to students and are a distinctive feature of the Upper School experience. Each student's program is individually chosen, and choices increase as the student moves through the four years of Upper School. With the exception of English, ninth grade Anthropology, and several electives limited to Seniors, classes include students in several grades. Music and drama performances, athletics, Chapel-homerooms and assemblies provide further fora for association, friendship and learning among the four grades. Because of the flexibility of the curriculum, students are able to choose a program that reflects not only immediate interests but also long-term educational goals. For example, a student wishing to go to engineering school is advised to take four years of math and four years of science, and should plan accordingly. Extensive course counseling is available from Advisors, Class Deans, Upper School Director and Assistant Director.

Advanced Placement: Advanced Placement courses are offered in Calculus, Statistics, Computer Science, Physics, Chemistry, Biology, French Language, French Literature, Spanish Language, Spanish Literature, Latin, Music Theory, Art History, and Studio Art/Portfolio.

ESL Program: Not available.

College Placement: Hackley graduates attend a four-year college or university in the fall following their graduation from Hackley. The college-counseling department is staffed with two full-time college counselors and an office assistant. The primary goals of the college counseling office are to introduce our students to their collegiate options, to help them make good decisions, and to support them during the college search and application process. While many of our students attend the most selective colleges in the nation, we believe that it is more important that they find schools that "fit" them – schools where they are most likely to meet their full potential academically and personally. The college counseling office provides information and experience to families through parent nights, weekly student information sessions (with second-semester juniors and first-semester seniors), and a variety of mailings and publications. Students and their parents are invited to arrange meetings with their college counselor in the spring of junior year. Students may meet with the college counselor as often as they like thereafter, with or without their parents, until they make a final matriculation decision in the spring of senior year. In addition, our supportive alumni network is available to discuss their own college choices with prospective students.

Over the last four years, graduates of Hackley have been accepted by colleges such as Boston College, New York University, Columbia University, Johns Hopkins University , Princeton University, Cornell University, University of Chicago, Harvard University, University of Pennsylvania, Wesleyan University, and Yale University.

Academic Requirements: Four years of Upper School English, three years of Mathematics including Algebra II and Trigonometry, Spanish, French, or Latin through Level III, History 9,

U.S History to 1900, The 20th Century World, three years of Upper School science including one laboratory science, and one year of performing or visual arts.

A minimum course load must consist of five major (3 credit) courses; seniors may select four major (3 credit) courses and two minor (2 credit) courses.

Sports: A member of the Ivy Preparatory School League of the metropolitan area, Hackley competes against league members and independent, public and parochial schools in Westchester and Fairfield counties. All students must attend physical education twice a week or play on a junior varsity or varsity team. Upper School students may choose from a wide variety of offerings, ranging from co-ed and single sex teams to non-competitive fitness activities during each season. Athletic courses offered include Aerobics, Open Gym, Squash, Fitness Center, Golf, Cross Country, Field Hockey, Soccer, Tennis, Football, Fencing, Squash, Swimming, Indoor Track, Basketball, Wrestling, Track & Field, Lacrosse, Softball and Baseball.

Extracurricular Activities: Art Society, Black and Grey Key, Community Service Club, Cultural Diversity Awareness Club, The Dial student newspaper, Film Club, Gaelic Society, Gay/Straight Alliance, Hilltop Yearbook, International Students Service Organization, Latin Club, Math Team Midnight Run, Mock Trial Club, NEALSA (New England African American and Latino Student Alliance), Opera Club, Outdoor Club, Peer Tutoring, Photo Club, Physics Club, Poetry Club, Princeton and Harvard Model Congress, Prom Committee, SADD (Students Against Destructive Decisions), VAASA (Varsity Athletes Against Substance Abuse), The Vision Literary Arts Publication, and Writing Tutors.

Campus: Our 285-acre campus includes an award winning library, performing arts center, computer centers, tennis courts, photography, art and ceramic studios, basketball courts, and indoor pool.

Dormitories: Currently, Hackley boards boys and girls in grades 9 through 12, but only five days a week. While we do have foreign students among our boarders, they do not stay here on Saturdays, Sundays, holidays or vacations. Instead, they have been able to make arrangements to stay either with relatives or family friends in our immediate area. We would need to know what these arrangements are, in detail, before completing the admissions process.

Nearest International Airport: JFK International Airport, New York.

Nearby Lodgings: Castle On The Hudson, 914 631 1980; Courtyard Tarrytown, 914-631-1122; Dolce Tarrytown House, 914-591-8200.

Hackley School

Happy Valley School

Location: Ojai, California (U.S. West Coast, Southern California)

P.O. Box 850, Ojai, CA 93024-0850
Phone: 805-646-4343; Fax: 805-646-4371
Website: www.hvalley.org; Email: admin@hvalley.org

Ms. Adrian Sweet, Director of Admission/Development
Phone: 805-646-4343; Fax: 805-646-4371
Email: asweet@hvalley.org

Mission Statement: Our mission is to provide students with the necessary skills of both mind and heart that will enable them to approach life with a sense of inquiry and purpose. The Happy Valley Education: Prepares students for college study and lifelong learning. Promotes compassion, understanding, respect, and responsibility toward others. Promotes self-inquiry and the fullest expression of one's talents. Challenges and supports each student.

Celebrates beauty, diversity, and wonder. Fosters a sense of appreciation for the worldviews, arts, and histories of diverse cultures. Teaches skills of self-learning, sound thinking, effective reading, clear writing, and objective inquiry. Promotes altruism, ethical reflection, independent thought, and creative expression. Develops a harmony of mind, body, and spirit. Fosters an appreciation for the interdependence of all species and a spirit of responsibility and reciprocity toward our earth community.

Grade Level: 9-12.

Student Gender: Boys & Girls.

Enrollment: 96 students, 50 boys, 46 girls, 66 boarders, 30 day.

Accredited by: WASC, CAIS/CA

Head of School: Dennis H. Rice, B.A. English and philosophy, M.Ed. University of California, Berkeley, Institute of School Climate and Governance, Harvard Graduate School of Education.

Faculty: The HVS faculty is made up of a diverse group of professional educators devoted to the process of learning. As the role models in our community they take on multiple roles in the classroom, as dorm parents, as academic advisers and athletic coaches, educating our students on many different levels. Our faculty are actively participating in their fields and very passionate about sharing their experience with the students.

Tuition: Tuition and Boarding for 2003-2004 is $30,700.

Average Class Size: 11-15 students.

Curriculum: Happy Valley offers a rigorous college preparatory curriculum for grades 9 through 12. Based on the Socratic method of teaching, classes are facilitated by generating questions, which arouses a sense of inquiry and interest, and encourages students to develop logical assessment skills for problem-solving. The course of study at HVS has been carefully designed to develop cognitive growth. Skills of thinking, research, writing, and creative expression are stressed and reinforced. All of our courses meet standard UC requirements.

Advanced Placement: Advanced placement (AP) courses are offered in Spanish, French, Physics, English and Calculus.

ESL Program: The ESL program at HVS provides international students with a whole language learning experience in English and mainstreams them into the college preparatory curriculum. First year ESL students take classes in English reading, writing, speaking and grammar. After the first year, students are mainstreamed according to their English abilities. Sheltered classes in history, science, literature and writing are provided along with the college preparatory curriculum. TOEFL preparation is provided along with an institutional administered TOEFL test which occurs three times per year. These tests are used to prepare students for taking an external TOEFL for college admissions.

College Placement: The journey from high school to college is a long one. HVS provides help for this transition by having each student and their family work with a college counselor. The preparation for this begins in the students junior year by evaluating their academic record, test scores, extracurricular activities and community participation. The school regularly receives visits from Colleges/ Universities, giving students exposure to different schools. By the senior year, most students have narrowed their list and, with the help of the college counselor, applications are completed. Recent graduates of Happy Valley have been accepted to Bard, Occidental, Reed, Sarah Lawrence, and various campuses of the California State University and University of California Systems.

Academic Requirements: To graduate students must complete 4 years of English, 4 years of social studies, 3 years of mathematics, 2 years of science, 2 years of a foreign language, 2 years of fine arts, and sufficient electives to complete the required number of units.

Sports: Competitive interscholastic sports include soccer, volleyball, softball, tennis, cross-country, and basketball.

Extracurricular Activities: Recreational activities include surfing, rock climbing, museums, movies, concerts, plays, skating, and bowling, as well as frequent weekend trips to Los Angeles, Santa Barbara, and Ventura.

Campus: Located on 450 acres of land, ninety minutes north of Los Angeles, the Happy Valley School features a quiet, rural setting of unusual beauty. Surrounded by spectacular panoramic views of the Topa Topa Mountains and the Ojai Valley, the Happy Valley School provides a serene, natural environment in which students can pursue their educational goals.

Incorporating a modern design, the classrooms offer ample space for study. Our library houses over 8,000 volumes and serves as a learning resource and technology center.

Dormitories: The Happy Valley School offers separate boarding facilities for boys and girls. Residents are housed, two per room. Bedrooms contain study and storage facilities and incorporate fantastic views of the surrounding land. Each dorm includes a common room, kitchen and laundry facilities. A large playi8ng field, along with tennis, basketball, and volleyball courts are located on campus, as are a variety of natural trails which provide the opportunity for exploration and hiking.

Nearest International Airport: Los Angeles International, California.

Nearby Lodgings: The Blue Iguana and Emerald Iguana Inns, 805-646-5277; Casa Ojai - Best Western, 800-225-8175; Hummingbird Inn, 800-228-3744; The Moon's Nest Inn, 805-646-6635; Oakridge Inn, 805-649-4018; Ojai Valley Inn & Spa, 805-646-5511; Rose Garden Inn, 805-646-1434; Theodore Woolsey House, 805-646-9779.

Hargrave Military Academy

Location: Chatham, Virginia (U.S. Mid-Atlantic, East Coast)

200 Military Drive, Chatham, VA 24531
Phone: 434-432-2481; Fax: 434-432-3129
Website: www.hargrave.edu; Email: admissions@hargrave.edu

CDR Frank Martin, III, Director of Admission
Phone: 800-432-2480; Fax: 834-432-2481
Email: martinf@hargrave.edu

Mission Statement: Located in Southwest Virginia, Hargrave Military Academy is a private, Christian boarding school serving boys from grades seven to one postgraduate year. Hargrave offers a 'How to Study' program, discipline, and challenging college preparatory classes in a meaningful, structured environment for each student.

The "whole-person" is addressed at Hargrave. Development of personal responsibility, fitness, academic grades and moral character are important goals for each Cadet. Opportunities for personal achievement lead each Cadet to a more successful, rewarding life.

Grade Level: 7-12.

Student Gender: Boys & Girls.

Enrollment: 418 students, 400 boys, 18 girls, 353 boarders, 65 day.

Accredited by: VAIS, SACS

Head of School: Dr. Wheeler L. Baker, Ph.D. in Education.

Faculty: Hargrave has a faculty of 48 full-time teachers, 60 percent of whom hold advanced degrees. Twenty faculty members reside on campus.

Tuition: The enrollment fee of $20,550.00 (covers the full 9 month school term) includes tuition, room and board, uniforms, book rental, laundry, dry cleaning, haircuts, lab fees, infirmary fees and student activities.

Average Class Size: 12 students.

Curriculum: Grades 9-12 feature a college preparatory program. Students take six subjects and attend three subjects per day, alternating those subjects with the following day. The Academic day also allows students time to meet with their teachers should they have questions or difficulties in a particular subject area. These are called tutorials. The night prior to class, all students are required to attend study hall, mentored by the Hargrave faculty and staff. Hargrave Post-Graduate Cadets gain the time to focus on critical English and math SAT skill in their first post-high school year. It also allow time for students to increase their grade point average for a stronger college acceptance.

Students are assigned to academic classes based on their academic goals, their grade performance and the results of achievement tests administered on arrival.

When Cadets are not engaged in either academics or sports, Hargrave's TAC Officers in the military department ensure that they remain on task. Building personal character, self-discipline, leadership skills and self-esteem in each Cadet is the focus of Hargrave's military structure. The Academy's rules and regulations are designed to help a Cadet mature. One of the most important lessons Hargrave teaches is adherence to moral and behavioral standards. And, that a violation of these standards has consequences. This is very important for each Cadet's personal development and for their future success later in life. Cadets also play an important role with each other. Normal student interaction among the Corps of Cadets produces leaders. At Hargrave, these raw leadership aptitudes are directly nurtured and developed by the military department with the assignment of rank and responsibilities. It is also taught academically with Hargrave's General Colin Powell Center for Leadership and Ethics. Hargrave provides a one-two punch in an area where most school talk, but few actually put into practice. Almost all Hargrave graduates are practiced leaders.

ESL Program: The ESL program is offered on an as needed basis. Students will enroll in the ESL program in addition to their normal classes. This full immersion program, coupled with ESL, is continued until the student is able to continue without ESL assistance.

Average SAT Scores of Graduating Students: 521 verbal and 531 math (1052 total).

College Placement: Recent graduates of Hargrave Academy have been accepted to College of William & Mary, Florida State University, Georgia Institute of Technology, Howard University, Penn State University, Purdue University, The Citadel, U.S Military Academy, U.S. Naval Academy, University of Miami, and Vanderbilt University.

Academic Requirements: Hargrave offers two types of diplomas, a Hargrave Diploma and a Hargrave Advanced Studies Diploma. To earn a Hargrave Diploma, a student must complete 22 credits: English, 4; mathematics, 3; science, 3; social studies, 3; computer application, .5; health, 1; fine arts/practical arts, 1; Bible, 1; military 1; and electives, 4.5. To earn Hargrave's Advanced Studies Diploma, a student must complete 24 credits: English, 4; mathematics, 4; science, 4; social studies, 4; foreign language, 3; health, 1; fine arts/practical arts 1; computer application, .5; Bible, 1; military, 1; and electives, .5. The required course in Bible, which students take during the senior year, provides a general survey of the Old and New Testaments. The military grade is specific to a Cadet's over-all behavior. Electives include a variety of classes designed to meet students interests and provide exploratory learning experiences.

Sports: Hargrave Cadets enjoy a thorough line-up of athletic activities. Twenty sports, including twelve varsity sports and one club, provide Hargrave Cadets with plenty of options for competitive activity.

Hargrave sports programs are very competitive. Our teams are frequently either the Virginia Independent Conference (VIC) champions or contenders in several sports every year. About 70 percent of the students participate on one or more athletics teams each year. Middle school, junior varsity, and varsity competition ensures something for every Cadet at different levels of play. Staying fit and active is a required part of Hargrave. Students who choose not to participate on an athletic team are required to participate in an organized, supervised intramural activity in the afternoon. Athletic teams and courses offered are Baseball, Basketball, Cross Country, Football,

Golf, LaCrosse, Rifle Team, Soccer, Swimming & Diving, Tennis, Volleyball, and Wrestling.

Extracurricular Activities: During the weekends, Hargrave Cadets enjoy a healthy mix of activities of their choice. Adventure is available throughout the year. Cadets are only limited by their willingness to participate. Student Activities works hard to ensure that the Cadets have maximum number of opportunities possible for relaxation and enjoyment during their free time. Activities include Basketball courts, Boy Scout trips/activities, Church Service, Community Service, Field Days, Mall trips to Danville or Lynchburg, Movies/videos, Paintball, Ping-pong tables, Pool tables, Shuffleboard, Ski trips, Super Bowl Party, Swimming pool, Trips to fun centers/arcades, Trips to historical sites, Weight room, Junior retreat (One weekend in the spring; juniors only), and Senior picnic (Farewell picnic for seniors; seniors only). Clubs include Book Club, Boy Scouts, Chess Club, Chorus Club, Computer Building Club, Drama Club, Fellowship of Christian Athletes, French Club, Forensics/Debate Team (NFL), Golf Club, Hargrave Aquatics (Competitive swimming), Historical Movie Club, Honor Council (Elected positions), Junior Beta Club (Honor Society - must earn nomination), Magazine Club, Paintball Club, Photography Club, Sabre Club (seniors only), Science Club, Scuba Club, Senior Beta Club (Honor Society - must earn nomination), Skate Club, Ski Club, Spanish Club, United Nations (Model) and Venturers (see Boy Scouts).

Campus: As Hargrave implements its "enhanced Learning Through Technology" program, access to technology resources has been expanded through wireless computer networks in every class and study room on campus. With the Academy's laptop computers, Cadets have expanded availability to class material, learning resources and their instructors at any time, from any place on campus. Hargrave has recently (2003, 2001) completed two major projects that have provided significant upgrades to the Academy's academic space. In the last few years, the Academy has witnessed the addition of four new state-of-the-art laboratory areas, a new art studio, a distance learning center, a leadership center and a greatly expanded video production classroom. A completely refurbished

200+ seat auditorium, featuring the latest in educational video technology, has provided ideal modern place for visiting guest lectures, artists and drama productions. Six new standard classrooms have been added and five classrooms have been completely refurbished.

Cadet technology resources include a twenty-station computer learning center, an SAT prep program, and a variety of computer based teaching labs in mathematics, English and psychology. A darkroom is also available to students who wish to learn black-and-white photography. Hargrave's library retains more than 10,000 volumes and subscribes to over fifty newspapers and periodicals all while incorporating a greater degree of electronic media. Back issues of 120 journals and magazines are available either on online or on microfiche. There are also three online databases, which include a wealth of reference books, periodicals, newspapers and dictionaries. Two complete online encyclopedias, the Encyclopedia Britannica and Worldbook, are also available.

Dormitories: Boys are housed in double rooms on 10 dormitory floors, which include two recreation rooms, three television lounges, a snack bar and a 24-hour infirmary.

Nearest International Airport: Dulles International, Washington DC.

Nearby Lodgings: Comfort Suites, 434-369-4000; Holiday Inn, 434-369-4070; Sims-Mitchell House, 434-432-0595; The Columns, 434-432-6122; Courtyard by Marriott, 434-791-2661; Holiday Inn Express, 434-793-4000.

High Mowing School

Location: Wilton, New Hampshire (U.S. East Coast, New England)

P.O. Box 850, Abbot Hill Rd., Wilton, NH 03086
Phone: 603-654-2391; Fax: 603-654-6588
Website: www.highmowing.org; Email: admissions@highmowing.org

Mr. Sam Rosario, Director of Admission
Phone: 603-654-2391; Fax: 603-654-6588
Email: admissions@highmowing.org

Mission Statement: Inspired by a love and respect for the highest potential in each human being, High Mowing School awakens capacities of creativity, intellect, compassion, and the will to make life choices with integrity and responsibility.

Working from the ideals of Waldorf education, adapted to the needs of the American soul and spirit, we deeply value: Our natural environment and New England campus, beauty and simplicity, the uniqueness of each individual, the truth, beauty, and goodness of knowledge, the artistry and creativity that harmonizes all that we experience, finishing each task we begin, and passion for all that lives.

Grade Level: 9-12.

Student Gender: Boys & Girls.

Enrollment: 111 Students, 51 boys, 60 girls, 51 boarders, 60 day.

Number of International Students: About 10% of our students come from foreign countries. Every year, we welcome students from all over the world to study, live, and learn together on our campus. In the past five years we have had students from Austria, Korea, Japan, Canada, Germany, Switzerland, Denmark, Bermuda, Russia, and Brazil.

Accredited by: NEASC

Head of School: Doug Williams, B.A., Amherst College, M.Div., Virginia Theological Seminary, Diploma, C.G. Jung Institute, Zurich,

Switzerland.

Faculty: High Mowing is also the people who work here and come to school here. We are dedicated and enthusiastic about what we do. This is evident in the number of teaching years represented within the faculty. Two of our faculty members came to High Mowing over fifty years ago; another five joined us over twenty-five years ago and four others have lived and worked on the Hill for more than ten years. A further nine have joined us in the past five years.

Tuition: Tuition and Boarding for 2003-2004 is $29,360.

Class Size: 8-15 students with a teacher/student ratio of 1:4.

Curriculum: High Mowing is a Waldorf school with a curriculum that challenges a student's intellect, imagination, and social responsibility. College-preparatory academics are integrated with a rich program of studio and performing arts. The Naturalist Program offers students the opportunity to encounter nature in a holistic manner. The athletic program includes competitive and recreational sports. International exchanges are available with Waldorf schools worldwide. The outdoor trekking program, projects week, and weekend activities offer off-campus learning. In broad strokes, each year of the high, school curriculum embodies an underlying theme and method that helps guide students not just through their studies of outer phenomena, but through their inner growth as well. Obviously, these themes and methods are adapted to each specific group of students and take account of the fact that teenagers grow at their own pace. Hence the "broad strokes". And yet, one can identify struggles common to most any teenager; even though adolescents pass through developmental landscapes at varying speeds, they nonetheless have to cover similar terrain.

ESL Program: There are ESL tutorials for intermediate and advanced students. These sessions serve as a support for the student in their other classes.

College Placement: In the past three years, our graduates have attended colleges such as Boston University, Brown California Polytechnic, University, New York University, and Sarah Lawrence

College.

Academic Requirements: In order to more clearly represent our program on student transcripts, we have recently changed the system used to account for student credit. Note, however, that graduation requirements and required courses have not changed.

One unit of credit represents one successfully completed course (roughly 25-30 hours of class time).

Each block class earns 1 unit. Each trimester of a track class earns 1 unit. Each trimester of a "double-period" (2 hour) track earns 2 units. Each trimester of afternoon activity earns 1 unit.

To receive a diploma from High Mowing School, a student must be enrolled and in good standing at High Mowing School to the end of the senior year, must successfully complete the senior research paper, and must have earned the following units:

Academic Subjects: English 18, Social Science 12, Foreign Language 6, Math 12, Natural Science 12, Additional Academics 6.

Non-Academic Subjects (10 units): Studio Art/Performing Arts 24, Physical Education 6.

The Academic Committee will determine graduation requirements for students in special programs.

Sports: Our competitive sports teams are known throughout the league for having great sportsmanship and a good time. You may be (but do not have to be) on a soccer, cross country, running, basketball, cross country skiing, baseball or lacrosse team. HMS students have also joined local wrestling and swim teams.

Extracurricular Activities: You may become a member of one of our athletic teams, or engage in individual and non-competitive sports such as volleyball, frisbe, weight training, running, or skiing. You will have the opportunity to help others by working in soup kitchens, after-school care, nursing homes or other community centers. Some of your time during the afternoon program might be rehearsing for plays, music or eurythmy performances.

Weekend activities include Annual opera trip to NYC, baking cookies, basketball and baseball games, biking, bowling, cleaning rooms, coffee house for students and faculty, cross-country skiing, Drama performances, flea markets, gardening, games parties, visits to nearby cities, hanging out, hiking, movies, musical performances, peace rallies, playing outdoors, poetry readings, sporting events and traditional holiday parties.

Campus: High Mowing is the oldest Waldorf high school in North America and the only one to offer a boarding program. In 1942, Mrs. Beulah Emmet, inspired by the work and thought of Rudolf Steiner, converted her family country home into a Waldorf high school. The old and charming hilltop farm ideally suited the warm, home-like atmosphere she sought for her students, and it even suggested the school's name (mowing is an old New England term for "hayfield"). Since that time, High Mowing has offered teenagers the unique combination of Waldorf education and community living (9th to 12th Grade). In the 1970s, the school formed a partnership with Pine Hill Waldorf School (an elementary Waldorf school now located just across the road) to offer a complete K-12 Waldorf program in Wilton, New Hampshire.

Dormitories: Students are assigned double or single rooms by dorm counselors who live on campus. All dorms include recreational and laundry facilities.

Nearest International Airport: Logan International Airport, Boston.

Nearby Lodgings: Stepping Stones, 603-654-9048; Bedford Inn, 603-472-2001; Sheraton-Wayfarer, 603-622-3766; Crowne Plaza, 603-886-1200; Comfort Inn, 603-883-7700; Marriot, 603-888-9970.

Hillside School

Location: Marlborough, Massachusetts (U.S. East Coast, New England)

Robin Hill Road, Marlborough, MA 01752
Phone: 508-485-2824; Fax: 508-485-4420
Website: www.hillsideschool.net
Email: admissions@hillsideschool.net

Mr. Thomas O'Dell, Director of Admission
Phone: 508-485-2824; Fax: 508-485-4420
Email: admissions@hillsideschool.net

Mission Statement: The School's mission is to help young adolescent boys develop in their formative years. Our students develop academic and social skills while building confidence and maturity. Program highlights include a student teacher ratio of 6:1, academic and social skills tutorials, a working farm and farm curriculum, and wonderful cultural opportunities in Boston.

We seek not only boys of average to above-average intelligence who are looking for a supportive, structured school, but also students who have been underachieving in other school settings. Hillside's students matriculate at leading independent secondary boarding or day schools as well as local parochial and public high schools.

Grade Level: 5-9.

Student Gender: Boys only.

Enrollment: 105 boys, 65 boarders, 40 day.

International Students: Boys enrolled at Hillside School came from ten states and five countries.

Accredited by: AISNE

Head of School: David Z. Beecher

Faculty: Hillside's faculty and staff represent a wide spectrum of diverse talents and interests. The responsibility of all faculty is to serve as warm, patient role models and mentors. Through a generous professional development program, Hillside encourages its faculty to build strength in subject content areas and to develop active teaching strategies that engage the attention of middle school boys. The advisor program is the cornerstone of the academic program. All Hillside faculty members serve as advisors. Through regular meetings, advisors come to know their advisees well and, as a result, serve as primary points of contact for parents. In addition to teaching, advisors coach and work actively in the residential program as well, which affords them maximum opportunity to develop multi-dimensional levels of contact with students.

Tuition: Tuition and Boarding for 2003-2004 is $35,950.

Class Size: 6-12 students, with a student teacher ratio of 6:1

Curriculum: Hillside School's academic program aims to prepare students for a challenging and successful future in the school of their choice through a balanced exposure to the arts and sciences. Inquiry, activity, and experiential learning characterize the rhythm of the classroom. Through technology, bridges across the curriculum are created which unite all learners.

Hillside School offers carefully structured academic and social skills tutorials aimed at supporting the learning needs of all students. Tutorial classes are very small and can be flexibly scheduled to afford maximum effectiveness in learning new study strategies and in building self-esteem.

ESL Program: For over five years, Hillside's ESL program has proudly been servicing international students with their language needs. Taught by experienced professionals, the classes are small, in adherence to Hillside's philosophy and style. ESL classes meet Hillside's tutorial wing of the new Student Center Building four times a week for fifty minutes per class. In the case of seventh, eighth and ninth graders, ESL replaces foreign language electives. In the case of the fifth and sixth graders, ESL takes the place of reading and / or writing classes in the self-contained classes. ESL courses are credited with the equal importance to the other core classes at Hillside, and as such, homework is given on a daily basis and tests, quizzes, and exams are administered.

The focus of the ESL classes at Hillside is on the major strands of the English language: reading, writing, structured grammar, listening, speaking, and vocabulary. In an effort to aid international students in acclimating to life at an American boarding school, additional time is spent learning about American environment and culture. Quite often as well, the ESL classes are aid in supporting students' success in other core academic classes (such as English and history). Frequent and regular communication is shared by ESL teachers and other general education teachers, so that learning across the curriculum is optimized.

Upon arrival to the school, students are administered an English proficiency test, and as soon as their ability level is determined, ESL teachers set to work instructing students in English based on individual strengths and needs.

Sports: Athletics plays an integral role in the lives of Hillside students and is an important part of the educational program of the school. Athletics promotes social skills that can be essential to childre n's development. Cooperation with others, perseverance, school spirit, accepting of failure and working toward success, building self-confidence, improving skills, physical activity and play are but a few of the components the program promotes.

Children with different skills and skill levels benefit from a wide array of choices in each season that offers something for a variety of interests. Finding an activity or sport in which a child can find interest, success or even passion is the hope of our program and is a building block of healthy child development.

Each season students are offered four to five activities/sports in which to choose. After a short period in which they are encouraged to try out different activities they must choose one to participate in for that season.

Activities/sports choices reflect the varied student interest and abilities of our students. Students with athletic skill can excel in competitive sports on the varsity level or more participatory on the junior varsity level. Students with less interest in competitive sports can find fun and success in non-competitive activities. Athletic courses offered include Soccer, Cross Country, Eco-Team, Golf, Sailing, Basketball, Wrestling, Ice Hockey, Skiing, Outdoor Program, Lacrosse, Baseball, Track and Field and Drama.

Extracurricular Activities: Weekends at Hillside - For our seven-day boarders, and any day students and/or five-day boarders who remain on a given weekend, the weekends are a time of exciting activities, rest and good old-fashioned fun. Off campus activities - Hillside /School is centrally located between Boston and Worcester, which affords us a great deal of variety in off campus cultural and fun activities. Regional sporting events, art and science museums, theater, state and national parks, shopping, movies and skating are some regular activities that are within a thirty-minute drive. Additionally, some annual activities are a visit to the Basketball Hall Fame, the Big E (Eastern State Exposition), Georges Island in the Boston Harbor, Merrimac Repertory Holiday show, and Six Flags Amusement Park. Hillside School strives to balance the weekend schedule in such a way that our students can enjoy the many enrichment activities our location provides.

Campus: Founded in 1901, Hillside is situated on over 250 acres of fields, forest, and ponds in Marlborough, Massachusetts, less than a mile from the intersection of routes 495 and 290 (30 miles from Boston; 70 miles from Hartford, Connecticut and Providence, Rhode Island; and 3-1/2 hours from New York City. Hillside features a working farm and farm curriculum, and wonderful cultural opportunities in Boston.

Dormitories: Dorm Life - Hillside is blessed with four housing units - 2 family styled farmhouses and 2 dormitories - to which the boys are assigned based on age and grade. The dorms are staffed by Hillside faculty members. The dorm parents are supervised by the Dean of Residential Life.

Roommates - The Dean of Residential Life oversees the placement of students into the dormitories in consultation with other senior administrators, school counselors, dorm parents and families.

Generally, boys are divided into age/grade appropriate groups and then each group of three to four roommates is selected based on chemistry, boarding status, family/student needs and preferences. Living in community is a very important aspect of boarding and Hillside School's program teaches to this.

Common Rooms/Dorm Activities - Each of our dormitories has a common room that boys may gather in with their dorm mates and dorm parents to play games, hold a community meeting each Tuesday or just relax and watch a little TV. Computer/video games are not allowed during the school week as we stress the importance of interacting with others in the community. Dorm parents are ever aware of boys that may not find it easy to make friends or join a group activity and they coach and encourage them quietly.

Dorm Chores - No community can flourish without the experience of shared responsibilities. The care and cleanliness of the dorm is therefore shared with a custodial staff that clean and sanitizes the restrooms and showers while the boys are responsible for their own personal area which includes making their bed each morning, keeping their closet neat and orderly and completely a given chore each day that rotates on a weekly basis. These include taking out the trash, lost & found, windows and lights, etc.

Nearest International Airport: Logan International Airport, Boston.

Houghton Academy

Location: Houghton, New York (U.S. East Coast, New England)

9790 Thayer Street, Houghton, NY 14744
Phone: 585-567-8115; Fax: 585-567-8048
Website: www.houghtonacademy.org
Email: admissions@houghtonacademy.org

Mr. Ron Bradbury, Director of Admissions
Phone: 585-567-8500 or 585-567-8115; Fax: 585-567-8048
Email: admissions@houghtonacademy.org

Mission Statement: Houghton Academy is a coeducational, college preparatory school established in 1883. Houghton Academy recognizes and is committed to modeling and teaching spiritual values which draw their vitality and strength from a personal commitment to Jesus Christ.

The mission of Houghton Academy is to teach and nurture its students so that each young person makes a personal commitment to Christ; understands the importance of a life of service; grows toward a mature understanding of our society, history, and natural world; develops in physical ability and strength; and exhibits appropriate social courtesies.

Admission Requirements for International Students: Complete and return an application with supporting documents/references. Students entering in grades 11 or 12 must submit a score from either TOEFL, SSAT, SAT, ACT or SLEP and must demonstrate reasonable English proficiency (appx 500 on paper-based TOEFL)

Grade Level: 9-12.

Student Gender: Boys & Girls.

Enrollment: 270 students, 143 boys, 127 girls, 62 boarders, 203 day.

International Students: 25-40, from Korean, Japan, Hong Kong, Taiwan, Saudi Arabia, Jordan, several African countries, Central Amercia, Europe.

Accredited by: MSACS, ACSI, NY State Board of Regents

Head of School: Philip G. Stockin, BA Houghton College, MA School Administration, Grace Theological Seminary. Email: headmaster@houghton.edu

Faculty: It would be no exaggeration to say that a school's faculty is the school. Textbooks, chalkboards, desks, computers, laboratories - even buildings - are merely tools, put to use by the faculty as it inculcates a group of young people with its knowledge, wisdom, and world view.

At Houghton Academy students receive a superior education because the faculty has a superior education to impart. Whether their chosen discipline is English literature or calculus, history or foreign languages, members of the Academy faculty bring to the classroom not just a mastery of the subject and an uncommon gift for teaching, but more importantly, a thoroughly Christian perspective—a thoughtfully considered, unashamedly Christ-centered approach to education and life.

This combination of knowledge, teaching expertise, and uncompromising Christian philosophy gives Houghton Academy its distinctive character. Faculty statistics: Full-time 25, Part-time 5, Holding advanced degrees 13, Men 12, Women 18.

Tuition, Room, Board, Fees: $ 18,410. Summer ESL $2500 (Mid July to end of August), Year-long ESL if required: $2100.

Average Class Size: 17 students

Curriculum: Since its founding in 1883, Houghton Academy has based its entire educational program on a simple but profound conviction. We believe that nothing in creation can be properly examined or understood apart from an acknowledgment of the Creator's hand in it; that faith and learning are inseparable.

Today, as we look ahead to the next century, we're encouraged to see God taking this educational philosophy not only to the counties of western New York but to the countries of the world.

SAT: The range of SAT scores for the past ten years is as follows: Verbal: 290-800 (median 570), Math: 350-730 (median 580).

College Placement: Members of the class of 2003 were accepted at these universities: Alfred State, Asbury College, Biola University, Brooklyn College, Calvin College, Cedarville College, Clarion University, Colorado Christian University, Eastern University, Elim Bible Institute, Fashion Institute of Technology, Genesee Community College, Geneva College, Gordon College, Grove City College, Hofstra University, Holy Cross, Houghton College, Indiana University, Indiana Wesleyan University, John Carroll University, Lake Erie College, Lancaster Bible College, Medaille College, Millersville University, Montreat College, Northern Ohio University, Nyack College, Ohio Valley College, Oral Roberts University, Otis College of Art, Parsons School of Design, Penn State University, Renssalear Polytechnic Univeristy, Rochester Institute of Technology, Savannah College of Art and Design, Seattle Pacific University, Skidmore College, St. Bonaventure University, St. John's University, State University of New York, SUNY-Binghamton, Swarthmore, Syracuse University, Taylor University, Temple University, The New England Conservatory, The University of Wisconsin, Tri-State University, University of Akron, and Valparaiso University.

Academic Requirements: Graduation requirements include four credits each of English and social studies, three credits each of math and science, five elective credits, one credit of fine arts, and one-half credit of health. Credit in Bible and in physical education is required for each year of attendance. Elective subjects include ESL (English as a Second Language), accounting, biology, chemistry, physics, advanced math, computer applications, desktop publishing, Spanish, art, choir, band, and speech. Advanced students may take courses at Houghton College for both high school and college credit.

Sports: Houghton Academy's athletic program is built with the realization that sports can play a vital role in the development of character. We field a variety of teams for boys and girls. Houghton Academy is a member of the New York State High School Athletic Association, and thus we compete against both public and private schools in our area. Team sports include girls volleyball, girls basketball, girls soccer, boys soccer, boys basketball, girls softball, boys baseball, and golf. Several teams have advanced to state tournaments, including the 1997 state champion girls volleyball team, and a number of individual athletes have gone on to become successful at the collegiate level. Sports alone, however, is not why anyone has ever enrolled here.

Extracurricular Activities: Ski Club, Chess Club, Service Club, Interscholastic sports including Soccer, Volleyball, Basketball, Baseball, Soccer, Golf; fine arts including drama, choir, handbells.

Campus: Houghton Academy occupies two separate campuses. Our Main Campus in Houghton houses students in grades 7-12, as well as our boarding students. Our elementary program (K-6) is located on our Angelica Campus, 14 miles from here. **Please describe in more detail. The Phillipe complex and the Angelica campus are comprised of classrooms, gyms, auditoriums and offices.

Dormitories: Each dorm has student rooms (typically double occupancy), lounge, phones, and kitchens. The Boy's dorm has a large recreation area.

Nearest International Airport: Buffalo, New York.

Nearby Lodgings: Inn at Houghton Creek, 585-567-8400; Just-a-"Plane" B&B, 585-567-8338; Belfast B&B, 585-365-2692; Angelica Inn B&B, 585-466-3295.

Houghton is a small town in a rural area. Public transportation (busses, taxis, trains, and subways) is not available. Because Houghton Academy is able to provide only limited transportation services to visiting families, we highly recommend the Inn at Houghton Creek. The Inn at Houghton Creek is within walking distance of both the Academy and College, and it is both modern and very comfortable. We can provide logistical support with advance notice of your visit.

Idyllwild Arts Academy

Location: Idyllwild, California (U.S. West Coast, Southern California)

P.O. Box 38, 52500 Temecula Rd., Idyllwild, CA 92549-0038
Phone: 909-659-2171; Fax: 909-659-4383
Website: www.idyllwildarts.org; Email: admission@idyllwildarts.org

Ms. Anne Behnke, Dean of Admission
Phone: 909-659-2171 ext. 343; Fax: 909-659-2058
Email: admission@idyllwildarts.org

Mission Statement: The Idyllwild Arts Foundation exists to promote and advance artistic and cultural development. The mission of the Idyllwild Arts Academy is to provide pre-professional training in the arts and a comprehensive college preparatory curriculum in an environment conducive to positive personal development for gifted young artists from all over the world. The mission of the Idyllwild Arts Program is to provide for students the opportunity to benefit from arts instruction of the highest caliber.

Admission Requirements for International Students: Same as those for domestic students.

Grade Level: 9-12 (8th grade is only for beginning ESL students)

Student Gender: Boys & Girls.

Enrollment: 262 students, 95 boys, 167 girls, 238 boarders, 24 day.

International Students: 83 students from 15 countries, including Australia, Bulgaria, China, Denmark, England, Germany, Israel, Japan, Mexico, New Zealand, Saudi Arabia, Singapore, South Korea, Taiwan, and Thailand

Accredited by: WASC

Head of School: Bill Lowman, University of Redlands. Email: bill@idyllwildarts.org

Faculty: see website.

Tuition: Tuition and Boarding for 2003-2004 is $33,800.

Class Size: 18 students, with a student/teacher ratio of 11:1.

Curriculum: At Idyllwild, we're here to educate the whole you, the artist and the scholar. So that means every weekday morning, starting at 7:30 AM, you'll be taking a range of academic coursework. Our academic curriculum provides a strong college-preparatory program, challenging you to think critically, to creatively blend your intellectual and artistic perspectives, and to discover a passion for life-long learning. As a result, our graduates are well prepared to enter the leading colleges and universities, as they often do.

Idyllwild's diverse arts curriculum reflects our commitment to training the whole artist. Our demanding pre-professional training challenges students to work to their highest levels of achievement, and encourages them to be proud of their accomplishments. Throughout this process, students are supported by Idyllwild's highly regarded faculty. As practicing arts professionals, faculty members are able to work closely with students to assess and guide their growth as artists.

Advanced Placement: Advanced Placement courses are offered in the Humanities Department, Science/Math Department, Visual Arts Department, and the Music Department.

ESL Program: Placement of ESL students is based on the SLEP Test and a personal interview with the ESL faculty. When applying credits for graduation, only one unit of ESL credit may be applied toward the English requirement.

Beginning ESL students have four or five hours of classroom instruction each day focusing on basic reading, literature, writing, listening and speaking skills as well as essential grammar, vocabulary and study skills. A one-semester course in math language proficiency is included. High-Beginning level ESL students have a proficiency in basic English skills. A student at this level is scheduled for four hours of ESL each day and might also attend a math class appropriate to his/her mathematical ability. Instruction focuses on the same skills as Beginning ESL but is given at a faster pace and in more depth. Also included is a formal study of world history and geography. Intermediate ESL consists of two or three hours of ESL instruction each day. Typically, students at this level are also enrolled in both math and science classes. At this level the concentration is on developing vocabulary and writing skills as well as strengthening grammar. Reading comprehension is improved through studying literature, and readings in U.S. History are introduced. Advanced ESL meets one period each day to strengthen grammar and writing skills. Emphasis is placed on vocabulary building. In addition, TOEFL preparation and support in the mainstream humanities courses are provided at this level. Advanced ESL students may also enroll in a sheltered literature class.

College Placement: Graduates of Idyllwild have been accepted at colleges such as Boston University, Boston Conservatory, California Institute of the Arts (CalArts), California State University, Chicago College of Performing Arts, Peabody Conservatory of Music of the Johns Hopkins University, Pratt Institute, Purdue University, Ringling School of Art and Design, University of London, Royal College of Music, San Francisco Art Institute, San Francisco Conservatory of Music, San Francisco State University, Sarah Lawrence College, Smith College, School of the Art Institute of Chicago, School of the Museum of Fine Arts, Boston School of Visual Arts, Studio Art Central International (Florence, Italy), The American Musical and Dramatic Academy (New York), The Juilliard School, University of the Arts, University of California at Berkeley, University of California at Los Angeles, and Wimbledon School of Art (London).

Academic Requirements: Arts Academy students are expected to enroll in a minimum of four academic courses (credits) each year as well as those courses required by their arts major. In order to graduate, students must complete the following academic courses: 4 years of English; 3 years of History/Social Studies including World History, U.S. History, Government/Economics, 2 years of a Foreign Language (must be consecutive courses in the same language), 3 years of Mathematics- Algebra I, II, Geometry; 2 years of Laboratory Science, 1 Life Science, 1 Physical Science; 1 semester Computer Literacy; and 2 years Physical Education.

Sports: We do not have a formal athletic program due to the time commitment required by each students art classes, rehearsal needs and performance schedules. Students work with a faculty member individually to complete their physical education requirements for graduation. This may include walking, running, biking, yoga, weightlifting and/or ping-pong.

Extracurricular Activities: At the end of the day, students might wind down with a game of basketball on the outdoor court, or challenge each other to a ping-pong tournament. Additionally, a weight-room is available to students, and activities such as Tae-bo, yoga, aerobics, baseball, flag football, soccer and ultimate frisbee are offered throughout the year. Occasionally, faculty and students square off in ultimate frisbee or basketball, providing an opportunity to lambaste each other good-naturedly. In the evenings, the common areas in each dormitory serve as social gathering places where students can relax, share stories of the day, play games, or watch movies. Dorm parents, who are also faculty members, often join in student activities. Dorm parents are the primary caregivers, listeners, organizers and overseers of students, creating a family atmosphere away from home.

On weekends, students often go into the village of Idyllwild. A popular tourist attraction, Idyllwild offers a variety of restaurants, specialty shops, antique stores, and art galleries, as well as a movie theatre. The Visitor's Center houses historical photographs of early Idyllwild and artifacts of the Cahuilla Indians who used to reside in the area. Public campgrounds, picnic areas and fishing lakes are nearby, and impressive views of Tahquitz Peak, Lily Rock, and the 10, 804' summit of Mt. San Jacinto greet the eye. Transportation is provided between the Academy and the town throughout Saturday afternoon and evening, and all day Sunday.

Weekend trips to Los Angeles, San Diego or Palm Springs for shopping, museums, plays, opera, concerts, or to visit theme parks such as Universal Studios or Disneyland, afford students an opportunity to get off "the hill" once in a while. Additionally, ski trips to local resorts occur throughout the winter, and other activities suggested by students or faculty can be arranged by demand. The

Academy's mountain location offers students a variety of outdoor recreational opportunities such as hiking, rock climbing and cross-country skiing. Roads and extensive trails in and around the campus encourage running and cycling.

Students are encouraged to become involved in the production of student publications, which include the yearbook, the literary / photography magazine.

Campus: The campus, situated on 205-forested acres in the San Jacinto Mountains in Southern California, is a safe and inspiring setting for young students/artists. The Bruce Ryan Sound Stage, our newest facility on campus for the Moving Pictures Majors, opened April 8, 2002.

Dormitories: When you are not involved in classes, rehearsals or other activities, chances are you'll spend much of your time studying and relaxing in your dorm room or the common room. With a little time, the dormitory becomes a comfortable and friendly "home away from home." We do our best to provide a family-like atmosphere in our dorms. There is close interaction between students and dorm parents, fostering an atmosphere of care and mutual understanding. The dormitories are supervised at all times. Faculty/dorm parents reside in or next to the dormitories. They are visible, available, and approachable for students. Dorm parents are responsible for the well being of residents and the implementation of dormitory policies. The two Residential Life Coordinators also serve as dorm parents. Among other things, they are responsible for the daily activities and smooth operation within the dorms. Student Prefects assist in dormitory supervision. These older students provide good role modeling, experience, and leadership for the younger students. Each student, with the exception of prefects, has at least one roommate. Students are assigned roommates at the beginning of the year, with student requests for roommates given careful consideration. Students are encouraged to decorate their room with pictures, posters, plants, and personal objects. In addition, each student receives a phone voice line in his/her room for telephone, fax or computer use. The phone service includes voice message box and call forwarding features. Coin-operated washers and dryers are available to students either in or next to their dorm. Students are requested to have a laundry bag, and all clothes should be well marked. Students are expected to keep their clothes neat and clean. After dinner, from the hours of 8:30 PM to 10:00 PM, quiet time is maintained in the dorm so students may complete their homework. Quiet Hours coincide with the evening study hall period. Each evening, students must be in their rooms at curfew, which is 10:00 PM Sunday through Friday. Lights-out is at 10:30 PM. On Saturday nights, curfew is 11:00 PM.

Nearest International Airport: Los Angeles International Airport.

Nearby Lodgings: Silver Pines Lodge, 909-659-4335; Creekstone Inn, 909-659-3342; Cedar Street Inn, 909-659-4789; Atipahato Lodge, 909-659-2201.

Indian Mountain School

Location: Lakeville, Connecticut (U.S. East Coast, New England)

211 Indian Mountain Road, Lakeville, CT 06039
Phone: 860-435-0871; Fax: 860-435-0641
Website: www.indianmountain.org
Email: admissions@indianmountain.org

Mr. Mark Knapp, Director of Admission and Financial Aid
Phone: 860-435-0871 ext. 115; Fax: 860-435-0641
Email: admissions@indianmountain.org

Mission Statement: Indian Mountain School provides a traditional education for boys and girls from grades five through nine in a boarding and day environment. We promote individual academic and moral growth in a setting that fosters a respect for learning, the environment, and each other. We celebrate our community which is internationally and culturally diverse. We guide and challenge girls and boys through proper middle school scholastic, athletic and arts curricula, combining instruction and coaching with a system of personal support where needed. We involve each student in our Adventure Education program which ties into the spirit of IMS. We help our students gain confidence in their own innate abilities and develop the necessary academic and personal skills to be successful in secondary education. A well-defined and articulated set of values - honesty, compassion, respect and service - is at the heart of IMS.

Admission Requirements for International Students: WISC and SLEP.

Grade Level: 6-9.

Student Gender: Boys & Girls.

Enrollment: 110 boys, 80 girls, 70 boarders, 120 day.

International Students: 24 students, from Bahamas, Bermuda, Columbia, Haiti, Hong Kong, Japan, Korea, and Mexico.

Accredited by: CAIS/CT

Head of School: C. Dary Dunham, B.A University of Pennsylvania,

M.Ed. Boston University. EMail: D.D@indianmountain.org

Faculty: Energetic and dedicated, the IMS faculty numbers 46, (22 men, 24 women). Nineteen hold advanced degrees, and 75 percent live on campus. Really, it is the faculty who make the difference at IMS. These teachers, coaches, and advisors encourage our students to explore their potential. In doing so, we enable IMS students to become critical thinkers, confident academicians, spirited athletes, inspired artists, and responsible citizens of not only our own community, but of the larger world as well. With enthusiasm and passion, our faculty members offer themselves as examples of the character and the principles that IMS embodies.

Tuition: Tuition and Boarding for 2003-2004 is $29,450.

Curriculum: At IMS, a well-developed academic program, combined with a system of personal support, promotes strong study skills and reinforces good study habits. Class size is kept small and individual attention is readily available. Students learn to be active and responsible participants in their own education. Teachers ask questions, draw out opinions, and engage students in the conversation of learning. Students gain confidence in expressing themselves, in defending their opinions, and in public speaking. The Middle School program (grades 5 and 6) takes place in a modified self-contained classroom setting apart from the Upper School. In a comfortable environment, a core team of teachers directs the academic day. There is ample time for personal attention, close supervision, and frequent communication with parents. Upper School students (grades 7, 8 and 9) enter a departmentalized program that builds knowledge in each discipline while continuing to stress fundamentals and study skills. Understanding the process of how to organize the material gives students the best possible foundations for secondary school.

Sports: Over the course of the year, IMS offers over thirty teams to our students. The fall term allows children to participate competitively in soccer and football and provides a recreational alternative through our dance program and a hiking club. During the winter, students may choose from basketball, hockey, skiing (both recreational and alpine racing) and dance. The school year concludes with students involved with baseball, lacrosse, and tennis. While most teams are separated into varsity and junior varsity levels, several of our teams also offer a developmental squad on which a student can learn the skills and the rules of the game without the pressure of interscholastic competition.

IMS has six playing fields and three all-weather tennis courts to accommodate our athletes during the fall and spring seasons. During the winter months, our athletes make use of our own gymnasium, the basketball courts and ice hockey rink at the Hotchkiss School, the ice hockey rink at the Salisbury School, and the alpine training facilities available at Catamount Mountain.

Extracurricular Activities: Our weekend program is designed to promote healthy community living through a variety of dormitory activities as well as time for academic studies. One of the most popular aspects of our Residential Life Program is the Friday Night Activity. Every Friday night each dormitory participates in its own activity with the other residents and dorm parents such as meals in the dorm parent's apartment, dinner at a local restaurant, a sleep-over in a dorm parent's apartment, Bombardment in the gym or Manhunt on the mountain. It is a time for residents to bond and the develop long-lasting friendships that IMS boarding students cherish. Saturday and Sunday afternoon students can sign up for a variety of different cultural and recreational trips, such as the New York Yankees, the Albany Symphony, Riverside Amusement Park, and The Skate Factory. Other trips include: movies, shopping at the mall, bowling, fishing, apple picking and do-it-yourself ceramics.

Campus: The Main Building houses the Lower School academic classes, Lower School computer room and music room. The new wing is home to the library, which contains more than 10,000 volumes, a video collection, and audio equipment. Moreover, the library includes an automated card catalog, an electronic library, IBM-compatible computers, and access to the Internet and email. In addition to three new science rooms and a new technology center, more than forty new computers have been connected to the campus-wide network. These additional computers provide access to technology not only in the library and computer labs but also in the core classrooms and residential spaces. Connected to the Main Building are the Upper School academic classes, Upper School computer room, study hall, assembly hall, studio art center, gymnasium, and newly expanded and renovated dining hall. A new performing arts center has been added, providing space for music and theater arts.

Dormitories: Our dormitories serve as a "home away from home" for boarding students. Dorm parents and their families live in the dormitories with the students and integrate much of their lives with those of the students. Other members of the faculty work in the dormitories on a regular basis and make up the six person dorm teams. There is a faculty member "on duty" at any time when the dormitory is open. Even in the middle of the night, students may knock on a dorm parent's door for emergency reasons.

Dorm parents are a vital component of the success of our Residential Life Program. They wake up our students in the morning, get them ready for school, eat breakfast with them and then welcome them home in the afternoon following sports. Our dorm parents are experienced and compassionate faculty members who have chosen to live and raise their own families with our boarding students. The bonds that are created between boarding students and their dorm parents are among the strongest at our school.

Boarding students participate in a Weekly Work Program that includes jobs such as monitoring the food closet, taking out the trash and recycling and cleaning the common rooms. Every Monday evening after study hall each dormitory has a Monday Night Dorm Meeting to discuss any issues or concerns as well as any upcoming activities and events. Students are often invited to make suggestions for weekend activities as their input is valuable in our planning of fun and appropriate recreation. Elected members of the Dormitory Council serve as representatives to the Director of Residential Life and the residential faculty for all student issues. The Dormitory Council meets on a bi-weekly basis.

Nearest International Airport: Bradley International, Hartford CT.

Nearby Lodgings: Blackberry River Inn, 860-542-5100; Chambery Inn, 413-243-2221; Monument Mountain Motel, 413 528-3272; Holiday Inn Express, 413-528-1810.

Indian Springs School

Location: Indian Springs, Alabama (U.S. Southern Central)

190 Woodward Drive, Indian Springs, AL 35124
Phone: 205-988-3350; Fax: 205-988-3797
Website: www.indiansprings.org
Email: admissions@indiansprings.org

Mr. Charles Ellis, Director of Admission
Phone: 205-988-3350; Fax: 205-988-3797
Email: cellis@indiansprings.org

Mission Statement: Indian Springs School was the brainchild of
Harvey G. Woodward, a Birmingham industrialist who had attended
M.I.T. and who wanted to establish a school in his home state that
would train young men for a lifetime of learning. Mr. Woodward left
a sizeable estate and a detailed description of his program when he
died in 1930. The will survived legal challenges and the program
was refined, and finally the school opened its doors in 1952 with ten
faculty members and sixty boys. The school served as a boarding
school for boys from Birmingham and rural parts of Alabama, and
from the start the graduates went off to distinguished colleges
around the nation.

The founding head of the school, Dr. Louis Armstrong, made certain
that an Indian Springs education was far more than sound preparation for college. A program was put into place that was designed to
awaken the intellectual curiosity of the students by making them
aware of problems facing American society. Students were encouraged to keep open minds and become determined to change things
in society for the better.

From the start, students and faculty worked together in a model of
"shared governance." A constitution was written that explained
clearly the responsibilities of students and faculty in the day-to-day
operation of the school. The school ran like a small town, and the
student government was given a strong voice in determining how
the school would evolve. Town meetings were called regularly to
discuss issues.

Student directed learning in the classroom and in activities has always been encouraged at Indian Springs School. The school's choir has a tradition of presenting concerts all over the globe. The first soccer program in the state was initiated at Indian Springs. By the 1970's the school had an equal number of day students and boarders. An eighth grade was added and the school became coeducational. The school boasts of its 2000 alumni, all of whom have experienced Harvey G. Woodward 's vision of "learning through living."

Grade Level: 9-12.

Student Gender: Boys & Girls.

Enrollment: 264 students, 137 boys, 127 girls, 70 boarders, 194 day.

Accredited by: SACS

Head of School: Melville G. McKay III, A.B. Harvard University, M.A.T. University of North Carolina, Chapel Hill.

Faculty: most of our teachers have graduate degrees and live on campus. Number of faculty: 35. Faculty living on campus: 21. Average number of years at Indian Springs: 15. Average number of years in education: 22. Master's degrees: 24. Doctorates: 6.

Tuition: Tuition and Boarding for 2003-2004 is $22,150.

Average Class Size: 15 students, with a student/teacher ratio of 9/1.

International Students: 22 students from 7 countries.

Curriculum: Indian Springs offers challenging courses for bright, motivated students in a supportive and informal environment. There is a clear structure to each day at Indian Springs School, but students don't feel "programmed." You work with an advisor to select courses that are right for you. There are tons of extra-curricular activities, and you are welcome to try any of all of them ... or to start a new one. You work hard, but you also know that it is okay to take a break and simply relax. In such an environment you get to know others well, as you get to know yourself better.

ESL Program: No

Advanced Placement: Advanced Placement courses are offered in English Literature, French Language, Spanish Language, Statistics, Biology, Chemistry, Environmental Science, and Music.

Average SAT Scores of Graduating Students: Verbal: 657, Math: 653, SAT II Writing: 668

College Placement: 100 percent of Indian Springs students enroll in college, and each year at least three-quarters of the seniors are accepted at top-ranked colleges and universities. Recent graduates of Indian Springs have been accepted at colleges such as Boston University, Brown University, Columbia University, Cornell University, Dartmouth College, Duke University, George Washington University, Georgia Institute of Technology, Harvard University, Massachusetts Institute of Technology, New York University, Princeton University, Smith College, and Yale University.

Academic Requirements: 4 credits of English; 3 credits of History: World History, European History, and U.S. History; 3 credits of one Foreign Language; 3 credits of Math: Algebra I & II and Geometry; 3 credits of Science; ½ credit of Art; ½ credit of Music; and 2 ½ credits of Physical Education.

Sports: Indian Springs recognizes the need for physical exercise and the development of healthful attitudes and life-long habits. All students who are not involved in interscholastic athletics are required to attend P.E. They choose from a variety of sports and recreational activities which fit their interests and skills. Class sizes are small to allow for individual instruction. In addition to tennis courts, cross-country trails, softball, baseball and soccer fields, the school's field house contains two gymnasiums, an aerobics room, recreation center, weight room and training facilities. Interscholastic athletics include soccer, basketball, tennis, golf, volleyball, cross country, baseball, softball, fencing, and ultimate frisbee,

Extracurricular Activities: Abundant extracurricular activities include sports, debate and academic teams, 8 to 10 plays a year, and a choir composed of almost half the students in the school.

Campus: Indian Springs School has a 350-acre campus in a valley surrounded by the most southwestern hills of the Appalachian Mountains. Among the hickory, oak, maple, and sweetgum trees that reflect the changing seasons, there are trails for hiking, biking and cross-country running. The spring-fed lake provides for canoeing and swimming and sunning on the sandy beach. Sharing our southern boundary is Oak Mountain State Park, with thousands of wooded acres and rock faces for climbing.

To take advantage of the climate and the campus, there are few halls. Dorm rooms and classrooms open directly to the outdoors, connected by breezeways. Students speak of ours as "an outdoor campus." With everything on the ground floor, there are no barriers for handicapped students.

Yet this pastoral setting is only 15 minutes by Interstate 65 from Birmingham, Alabama. The international airport is a 30-minute drive. Atlanta is a two-and-a-half-hour drive to the east.

Nearest International Airport: Birmingham International Airport.

Nearby Lodgings: ; Hampton Inn, 205-313-9500; Holiday Inn Express, 205-987-8888.

Kents Hill School

Location: Kents Hill, Maine (U.S. East Coast, New England)

P.O. Box 257, Rt. 17, 1614 Main Street, Kents Hill, ME 04349-0257
Phone: 207-685-4914; Fax: 207-685-9529
Website: www.kentshill.org; Email: info@kentshill.org

Ms. Loren Mitchell, Director of Admission
Phone: 207-685-4914; Fax: 207-685-9529; Email: info@kentshill.org

Mission Statement: At Kents Hill, we believe every person wants to make a difference, to have his or her life count for something. Each individual has the capacity to be a leader in our school. We look for opportunities to help each student be successful, and we encourage every person in our community to live up to high standards of behavior. In our dining hall, there are ten plaques presented under the heading Kents Hill Leadership. Each plaque displays a value. They are: Courage, Compassion, Tolerance, Altruism, Scholarship, Honesty, Sportsmanship, Perseverance, Responsibility, and Friendship. These values form the core of the Kents Hill experience. They encourage us to look beyond self-interest to ask what is right, what is good for the community and the environment? They challenge us to aspire to higher moral standards and to have our lives count for something.

Grade Level: 9-12.

Student Gender: Boys & Girls.

Enrollment: 215 students, 140 boys, 75 girls, 155 boarders, 60 day.

Accredited by: NEASC

Head of School: Rist Bonnefond, Phillips Exeter Academy, Cornell University (B.A., 1971).

Faculty: We have a faculty of 50 teachers, 23 of whom hold advanced degrees. Most live on campus and also serve as coaches, advisors, dormitory parents, and extracurricular coordinators.

Tuition: Tuition and Boarding for 2003-2004 is $31,850.

Average Class Size: 8-15 students with a 6:1 student/teacher ratio.

Curriculum: The goal of the Kents Hill School academic program is to prepare our students for college and to be lifelong learners. Our students come from a wide variety of backgrounds. Some are ready to tackle the most advanced courses, while others need to be challenged at a level appropriate to their abilities. Advanced placement courses are present in virtually every academic discipline, as are basic courses for those needing more help and guidance. Our goal is to assist each student to succeed by finding the academic area in which his or her strengths lie.

Advanced Placement: courses are offered in English, History, Calculus, Biology, Chemistry, Physics, Environmental Science, Studio Art, Spanish and French.

ESL Program: The ESL Program at Kents Hill offers students of many levels of English proficiency the opportunity to study in a mainstreamed environment and receive a high school diploma. Students enrolled in the program are able to mix regular and advanced math and science courses with excellent English language, culture and conversation classes for all levels. Three levels within the program promote small classes and allow students to maximize their proficiency. Students are tested at the beginning and end of each school year to determine placement.

College Placement: Recent graduates of Kents Hill have been accepted to Babson, Bates, Bowdoin, Cornell, Colby, Connecticut College, Fordham, Harvard, Hobart, McGill, Michigan State, Pratt Institute, Rensselaer, Rhode Island School of Design, St. Lawrence, Smith, Tufts, Vassar, Wheaton, and Yale.

Academic Requirements: A student needs 18 credits to graduate. 1 credit=1 year. 4 credits of English, 3 credits of Math, 3 credits of Science, 3 credits of Social Studies, 2 credits of Modern Languges, 1/3 credit of Environmental Studies, 1 1/3 credits of Fine Arts, and 1/3 credit of Health.

Sports: Our philosophy is that a healthy body goes hand in hand with a healthy mind. Coaches focus on the ethics of competition, teaching teamwork, integrity, discipline, and above all, sportsmanship. The School has earned the MAISAD Sportsmanship Award many times in the last decade. The Kents Hill community continually enforces the concept of fair play. The varsity level teams are members of the Division II NEPSAC (New England Prep Schools) and aspire to develop in student athletes the ability and character to succeed at a higher level, while the junior varsity squads concentrate on skill development. Throughout the entire athletics program, the sheer enjoyment of sport is central to each activity. Athletic courses offered include Field Hockey, Football, Soccer, Cross-Country, Mountain Biking, Outdoor Skills, Golf, Equestrian, Competitive Alpine, Snowboarding, Recreational Alpine Skiing & Snowboarding, Ice Hockey, Basketball, Cross-Country Skiing, Lacrosse, Baseball, Softball, and Tennis.

Campus: The 600-acre campus is located in a rural community on a hill overlooking the Belgrade region of Maine. The campus is just 12 miles from the state capital, and is also within close proximity to ski resorts, the ocean, and Portland International Airport.

Dormitories: students live in residence halls staffed by faculty members. Most students are grouped according to age and grade, and live in double rooms. On average, the three halls (two boys' and one girls') operate at a 10:1 student to faculty ratio. Halls are supervised daily and monitored nightly by faculty members. Each hall is equipped with common rooms, microwaves, pool tables, cable television and drink machines. Students are responsible for maintaining the cleanliness of their rooms and the common area. Faculty members oversee regular room checks and assigned hall jobs. Students have hall and room curfews during the week and weekend. Each week the students meet formally to discuss community issues and to plan residence hall activities. The meetings are supervised by the faculty and help students to develop skills for living together.

Nearest International Airport: Portland International Airport.

Nearby Lodgings: Best Western Senator Inn & Spa, 207-622-5804; Comfort Inn, 207-623-1000; Holiday Inn, 207-622-4751; Travelodge Hotel, 207-622-6371; Maple Hill Farm, 207-622-2708; Village Inn, 207-495-3553.

The Kildonan School

Location: Amenia, New York (U.S. East Coast, New England)

425 Morse Hill Road, Amenia, NY 12501
Phone: 845-373-2013; Fax: 845-373-2004
Website: www.kildonan.org; Email: admissions@kildonan.org

Ms. Bonnie Wilson, Director of Admission
Phone: 845-373-8111; Fax: 845-373-2004
Email: bwilson@kildonan.org

Mission Statement: The mission of The Kildonan School is to empower students with dyslexia to reach their academic potential and to equip them for future success. Our threefold mission remains consistent. We strive to remediate skills in reading, writing, and spelling, to provide intellectually stimulating subject matter courses in mathematics, literature, science, and social studies, and to foster confidence.

Grade Level: 7-12.

Student Gender: Boys & Girls.

Enrollment: 138 students, 96 boys, 42 girls, 83 boarders, 55 day.

Accredited by: NYSAIS

Head of School: Ronald Wilson, B.S. in psychology from the State University of New York College, M.S. in counselor education from Western Connecticut State University.

Faculty: Many members of the Kildonan faculty subscribe to the academy of Orton-Gillingham Practitioners and Educators. While teachers are certified at different levels, four members of the Kildonan community are Fellows. Teachers at Kildonan assume many important roles. As instructors, coaches, advisors, and dorm masters, they interact with students throughout the day. They become mentors nd role models. The faculty bring diverse talents and extensive varied educations, and share a strong commitment to skilled teaching and the promotion of a nurturing boarding school life. The Kildonan faculty is comprised of 59 teachers—26 men and

33 women, one of whom has a doctorate, 9 have master's degrees, and 49 have bachelor's degrees.

Tuition: Tuition and Boarding for 2003-2004 is $38,850.

Curriculum: The academic program is unique in that it revolves around intensive, daily one-to-one Orton-Gillingham tutoring for each student. The language training instructor is responsible for devising a sequential learning program in language skills in accordance with Dr. Samuel T. Orton's principles and with his belief that "...such disorders should respond to specific training if we become sufficiently keen in our diagnosis, and if we prove ourselves clever enough to devise the proper training methods to meet the needs of each particular case." Orton-Gillingham tutoring is multi-sensory, direct, and effective. The tutorial setting makes it possible to tailor the teaching to the unique brain of each individual. The instructor is also responsible for inculcating orderly study habits; students are held accountable for daily independent reading and writing assigned to reinforce the skills taught during the tutorial. Students learn to work through periods of frustration and even temporary failure. Ultimately, the goal is for students to become independent learners.

Subject matter courses in mathematics, history, literature, and science are designed to meet the learning style of students with dyslexia. Visual, auditory, and kinesthetic presentations supplement textbooks. Class size is small; courses stimulate thinking and provide opportunities for creativity. The approach to mathematics is closely aligned with language training both in its logical, sequential approach and its daily assignments. Reading and writing demands are reduced or removed entirely from other content courses while the student is building reading and writing skills. Classes are structured to ensure that success is possible even for the student with minimal skills.

College Placement: Graduates of Kildonan have been accepted at colleges such as American International College, Boston University, New England College, Rhode Island School of Design, Wesleyan Georgia, and the University of West Virginia.

Academic Requirements: Requirements for graduation: 4 units of

English, 4 units of social studies, 4 units of mathematics, 3 units of science; 1 unit of art; 2 units of physical education, and 2 ½ units of elective courses, for a total of 20½ units.

Sports: Athletic activities at Kildonan include basketball, biking, golf, hiking, horseback riding, lacrosse, skiing, soccer, softball, tennis, and weight training.

Extracurricular Activities: Weekend activities include bowling, miniature golf, movies, biking, skiing, and white-water rafting, professional sporting events, theater performances, movies, dinner with dorm supervisors, and church services. Wednesday afternoons from 2 p.m. to 3:15 p.m. students participate in a community service project such as clearing trails painting, gardening, maintaining computers, operating the school bookstore, and cooking for the elderly.

Campus: Located between the towns of Amenia and Millerton, the Kildonan campus is set on a hillside with academic life at the foot of the hill and dining and residential life at the crest. The academic quadrangle includes the main building which houses administration, tutorial rooms, the computer center, and classrooms; the Francis St. John library with additional classrooms, the admissions building, the elementary schoolhouse, the wood shop, and the Howard Simon Art Studios. The playing fields, stables, tennis courts, and pond surround the quad. The 450- acre campus extends well into the surrounding fields and woods, offering an abundance of space for communing with nature.

Dormitories: Students are comfortably accommodated in doubles in the two modern dormitories, the Stephan D. Goldman Hall for 62 boys and the Diana Hanbury King Founder's House for 28 girls. The dormitory lounges are popular places to spend time with friends. Faculty live in dormitory apartments and housing interspersed throughout the campus.

Nearest International Airport: Bradley International Airport, Hartford, CT; JFK International Airport, New York, NY.

La Lumiere School

Location: La Porte, Indiana (U.S. Central Midwest)

6801 N. Wilhelm Road, La Porte, IN 46350
Phone: 219-326-7450; Fax: 219-325-3185
Website: www.lalumiere.org; Email: admiss@lalumiere.org

Mr. John Imler, Director of Admission
Phone: 219-326-7450; Fax: 219-325-3185
Email: admiss@lalumiere.org

Mission Statement: LaLumiere School assists talented young men and women to reach their potential. Through our academic, athletic, and co-curricular programs we create the circumstances that inspire our students to meet their personal bests and to aid them to be productive members of our school community. We challenge each of our students to reach for higher goals and to prepare for college and a fulfilling life through the development of character, scholarship, and faith.

Admission Requirements for International Students: applicants should have studied English in their home country and scored above 400 on the paper-based or 97 on the computer-based Test of English as a Foreign Language (TOEFL) or at least 39 on the Secondary Level English Proficiency Test (SLEP).

Grade Level: 9-12.

Student Gender: Boys & Girls.

Enrollment: 58 boys, 56 girls, 51 boarders, 63 day.

International Students: 15 Students from Canada, Chile, China, Japan, Mexico, Philippines, Saudi Arabia, South Korea, Nigeria, Taiwan and Tanzania.

Accredited by: ISACS, NCA-CASI

Head of School: Larry Sullivan, B.S. in Mathematics, Loyola University (Chicago), Graduate Studies in Math/Edu, Michigan State University, 44 years of teaching (35 at LaLumiere.) Email:

sullivan@lalumiere.org

Faculty: The La Lumiere faculty of 17 teachers includes 9 men and 8 women, all of whom are full-time. 11 live on campus, and all of the faculty members hold baccalaureate or master's degrees in the subjects they teach. In addition to teaching and coaching, the faculty also sponsors extracurricular activities.

Tuition: Tuition and Boarding for 2003-2004 is $20,644.

Class Size: 12 students, with a student/teacher ratio 7:1

Curriculum: LaLumiere School offers a traditional college-preparatory education on a rural campus with a private, boarding/day school environment. Because of our commitment to the education of the whole student, the school's faculty cultivates a positive, encouraging environment that reinforces responsibility for one's learning within each cooperative, energized school day. Implicit in each course are skills that promote critical thinking and problem solving as well as the integration and relevance of new ideas. Students respond to the academic challenges and opportunities as they grow and discover the integrated curriculum. A cross-curricular writing program provides structure and organizational skills for all facets of the academic program.

Advanced Placement: courses offered in English, French, and U.S. history.

ESL Program: La Lumiere provides a program in English as a second language (ESL) to qualified international students. The ESL program is a one-year, fully integrated, intensive curriculum emphasizing language, social studies, and study skills. Each ESL student is mainstreamed during at least two class periods per day. Levels are determined by ability. La Lumiere 's goal is to assist and support ESL students in moving as quickly as possible into the School's common program.

Average SAT Scores of all Graduating Students: 930-1340.

College Placement: Recent graduates of La Lumiere have been accepted into colleges such as Boston University, Duke University,

Emory University, Illinois Institute of Technology, Marquette University, Michigan State University, Purdue University, Pennsylvania State University, University of Chicago, University of Notre Dame, and Vanderbilt University.

Academic Requirements: To graduate, a student must complete 4 years of English, 4 years of math, 2½ years of social studies, 2 years of foreign language, 2 years of science with labs, 2 years of theology, a semester of art, and 2 years of electives.

Sports: La Lumiere regards athletics as an integral part of its program. All students participate in one of several sports offerings each season. Two hours of participation on sports teams follow classes each weekday. Programs are designed to teach skills and to give every student the experience of representing the School, demonstrating sportsmanship, and enjoying teamwork. Students can choose from a variety of sports programs, including baseball, basketball, football, soccer, tennis, track, and volleyball.

Marsch Gymnasium provides facilities for basketball, volleyball, track, and tennis. In addition, there is an extensive weight-training building and a practice gym with lockers and a whirlpool. There are four tennis courts on a hill overlooking the football field. A track beside the campus lake encircles the soccer field.

Extracurricular Activities: Every Wednesday afternoon the normal academic schedule is set aside for special interest activities. Offerings arise from teacher and student interests and expertise. Some of the offerings in 2002–03 included the yearbook, drama production, photography darkroom, computer gaming, portfolio preparation, golf, Science Olympiad, fitness and weight training, chess, and multiple opportunities for community service. A student council with a president, a vice president, and 2 representatives from each class is elected by the students. The council sponsors activities and represents student interests to the faculty and Headmaster. Admissions tour guides and National Honor Society members are chosen annually.

Scheduled throughout the year are all-school and class trips, athletic events, and speech and drama competitions and performances. The

Parents Association provides special events such as cookouts and Halloween and Christmas parties.

The weekend faculty team designs a variety of activities. These might include off-campus trips to theaters, museums, shopping malls, sporting events, movies, and parks.

Campus: LaLumiere is a coeducational, boarding and day, college-preparatory high school. It is situated on a beautiful rural estate in northwest Indiana, 25 miles west of South Bend, 60 miles east of Chicago, and 8 miles north of LaPorte. At the center of its 155 rolling acres is a picturesque country lake fed by a number of natural springs. The main facility is one large multilevel complex that features ten classrooms, two science labs, an art studio, two computer labs, and a library. The library houses more than 8,000 books and has a large reading room and an audio-visual room. La Lumiere has a state-of-the-art computer lab with T-1 connection and a dual-processing server.

Dormitories: There are five dormitories with large double rooms and a home-like atmosphere that encourages the growth of lifelong friendships. A faculty member and his or her family also reside in each dormitory.

Nearest International Airport: Chicago O'hare Airport.

Nearby Lodgings: Holiday Inn Of Michigan City, 219-879-0311; Hampton Inn Of Laporte, 219-362-6100.

Lawrence Academy

Location: Groton, Massachusetts (U.S. East Coast, New England)

P.O. Box 992, Groton, MA 01450-0992
Phone: 978-448-6535; Fax: 978-448-9208
Website: www.lacademy.edu; Email: admiss@lacademy.edu

Andrea O'Hearn, Director of Admissions
Phone: 978-448-6535; Fax: 978-448-9208
Email: admiss@lacademy.edu

Mission Statement: The aim of Lawrence Academy is to help students to learn and to develop a sense of identity. Young men and women need to understand the world, to determine who they are, and to establish a healthy set of values. Through their studies, students work to acquire knowledge and master the academic skills that are essential for success in college. The faculty and curriculum are dedicated to developing the students' capacity for creative and independent thought.

Committed to coeducation of a diverse population of boarding and day students, Lawrence recognizes the existence of many paths to learning. Some students learn best by reading and memorizing; some, through actual experience; some, by pursuing a deep interest. At Lawrence many paths exist in partnership, and students are guided to find paths that are most effective for them. Athletic and extracurricular activities combine with academic life to provide opportunities for personal growth. Students learn to work with others, to assume leadership responsibilities, and to take constructive risks.

Lawrence respects young people for who they are as well as who they can become. Close relationships among teachers, staff members, and students with varied backgrounds, interests, and aspirations lead to respect for individual and cultural differences and to an appreciation of achievement and excellence in its varied forms.

Admission Requirements for International Students: Application, Application Fee of $100, Math Letter of Recommendation, English Letter of Recommendation, Guidance/Personal Letter of ecommendation, Science Letter of Recommendation (for 10th and 11th grade applicants), Transcripts, Interview (on-campus preferred), TOEFL and/or SSAT.

Grade Level: 9-12.

Student Gender: Boys & Girls.

Enrollment: 201 boys, 182 girls, 181 boarders, 202 day.

International Students: 45 students, from China, Colombia, Germany, Dominican Republic, Hong Kong, Jamaica, Japan, Korea, Mexico, Phillipines, Singapore, Spain, Taiwan, and Thailand.

Accredited by: NEASC

Head of School: D. Scott Wiggins, Boston University (B.A., 1977), Arizona State University College of Law (J.D., 1988).

Faculty: The 62-member faculty of Lawrence Academy includes 39 men and 23 women who hold 56 baccalaureates, 34 master's, and 2 doctorates. 35 faculty members and their families live on campus. Many faculty members coach, supervise dormitory and student activities, and act as counselors.

Tuition: Tuition and Boarding for 2003-2004 is $32,800.

Class Size: 12 students, with a student-teacher ratio of 7:1.

Curriculum: Students at Lawrence Academy learn by doing. While having emphasized all the important academic skills and study habits over our 208-year history, we are particularly proud, today, of our innovative people and programs. Active learning begins in the Ninth Grade Program (NGP). Within a carefully integrated curriculum, students learn to drive their own seminar discussions, challenging and stimulating each other to personalize their own education. From hands-on experiments to spirited debates over current social issues and topics, students in Lawrence's NGP learn that education is not a spectator sport. Other schools have toyed with programs like Winterim, but LA' s commitment to experiential education since the early 1970s is only growing stronger. Both on and off our 100-acre campus in the picturesque town of Groton, students learn to redefine the boundaries of their own education. Pepperell or Peru, Headstart or the homeless, museums or marine biology – there is an astonishing variety of entrées on this menu of exciting opportunities. Lawrence II has an equally long history of preparing students for a career of active learning with its program of intensive independent study. This program is specifically for students with a clear purpose and compelling proposal for shaping part of their Lawrence Academy education. More about Lawrence II. Students from all over the United States and around the world come to stretch themselves intellectually and personally, shaping an identity along the way.

Advanced Placement: Advanced Placement preparation courses are available in environmental science, English, French, Spanish, Latin, government, calculus, and computer science.

ESL Program: Lawrence Academy offers a year-round ESL program with a full-time faculty and director.

Average SAT Scores of Graduating Students: The middle 50 percent of the most recent class scored between 500 and 610 on the verbal SAT I and between 520 and 640 on the quantitative.

College Placement: Recent graduates of Lawrence Academy have been accepted to American University, Boston University, Brown University, Chicago Art Institute, Columbia University, Cornell University, Dartmouth College, Emory University, George Washington University, Harvard University, Johns Hopkins University, McGill University, New York University, Northeastern University, Pennsylvania State University, Rhode Island School of Design, University of Massachusetts, and Vassar College.

Academic Requirements: To graduate, students must complete 18 credits and their Winterim courses. Minimum credit requirements are 4 credits of English, 3 credits of mathematics, 2 credits of foreign language, 2 credits of history 3 for ninth graders), 2 credits of science, and 2 credits of arts. Winterim is a two-week period of intensive experiential learning, including backpacking, mountain biking in Utah; cultural study trips to Russia, Italy, and Ireland, quilting, field studies in marine biology in Central America, or performing volunteer work with the homeless in Worcester.

Sports: Athletics at Lawrence Academy are an important part of the school program and, therefore, many students participate in athletics. Whatever your ability and your goals, you will find coaches at LA who will help you improve your skills and "raise your game." Most importantly, though, you will stand to learn the valuable personal lessons about character and teamwork that last a lifetime. The Lawrence Academy athletic curriculum includes soccer, cross-country, field hockey, basketball, ice hockey, wrestling, volleyball, baseball, golf, lacrosse, tennis, and softball. Outdoor programs include rock climbing, hiking, camping, bicycling, cross-country skiing, and snowshoeing. Dance is offered year round. The Academy's Stone Center athletic facilities include locker rooms for boys and girls, weight room, Nautilus equipment, training room, wrestling room, offices, meeting room, and gymnasium with two basketball courts, a climbing wall, and a volleyball court. The athletics outdoor facilities include 14 acres of playing fields, ten tennis courts, and a covered artificial-ice skating rink.

Extracurricular Activities: Lawrence Academy provides a variety of extracurricular, social, and academic activities including Chorus, Consortium literary magazine, Drawing, Early Music Ensemble, Envirothon, Faculty/Student Senate, French Club, Jazz Band, Junior Varsity Dance Company, Main Stage Productions, Multicultural Association, Performing Artist Series, Private Vocal or Instrumental Instruction, S.A.B.A. (Students Against Boring Assemblies), SLACS (a co-ed a cappella singing group), Spectrum Newspaper, Spring One-Act Play Festival, Student Government, Technical Theatre, Tour Guides (and Elm Tree Society), Varsity Dance Company, WRLA Radio and Yearbook. Also available are computer classes, academic skills classes, and driver education, SAT preparation, athletics competition and outdoor program trips. Supervised off-campus activities include trips to Boston, as well as to beaches, sporting events, games, dances and skiing.

Campus: Lawrence Academy is in Groton, Massachusetts, which is located in the Nashoba Valley region, eight miles south of the New Hampshire border and thirty-five miles northwest of Boston. A traditional New England town steeped in history, Groton has a Main

Street lined with maple trees and white colonials. Among its other charms are majestic old homesteads, faded red barns, apple orchards, centuries-old stone walls, family farmstands and an abundance of conservation land ideal for hiking, cross-country skiing and canoeing. It is in this setting that Lawrence Academy was founded by Groton residents in 1793. Governor John Hancock made it official when he put his famous signature on the school's bill of incorporation. The Academy's rolling, 100-acre campus, which features its share of maples and colonials as well as classical red brick buildings, is only a stone's throw from town hall, the post office and the bank. Standing in the middle of the campus quad one can see the distant outline of Mt. Wachusett to the west, the Angus-dotted pastures of Gibbet Hill Farm to the north, and the sloping fairways of the Groton Country Club to the east. LA' s natural backdrop helps to create a setting that is conducive to learning and reflection. Just as they have for over 200 years, students at Lawrence feel secure and comfortable on campus and in town. They breathe fresh air, they see friendly faces, they wake up to familiar views from the hilltop. And while they may catch the train to Boston on weekends or visit friends in nearby towns, Groton is the place they call homes.

A new academic building is planned to open in fall 2004, which will supplement the current academic building that includes new biology and chemistry laboratories. Classrooms with computers are equipped with seven workstations with PCs, a teacher workstation, an HP printer, and access to the Ethernet network. In addition, students may independently use three more rooms that contain computers with Internet and e-mail access and online resources similar to those in the library. The Ferguson Building contains the library (with 20,000 volumes, fifty-two periodical subscriptions, and computers with educational software, online resources, CD-ROM databases, Internet access, and an automated card catalog), an art gallery, the theater, the studies office, and the college office. The Williams Art Center provides classrooms for visual and performing arts, a performance studio for the Academy's expanded dance and theater program, a recital hall, five practice rooms, an art library, a photography lab, a state-of-the-art recording studio, a radio station, and the art faculty offices.

Dormitories: Dormitory facilities include ten buildings, seven of which are 18th and 19th century Colonial homes, and a newly constructed dormitory which opened in 2003. Each dorm room is networked for Internet access. Students are assigned to double rooms, with a few single rooms available. There are two school nurses in the expanded health center, and 2 doctors are on call, and a hospital is located 4 miles from campus.

Nearest International Airport: Logan International Airport, Boston.

Nearby Lodgings: Stage Coach Inn, 978-448-5614; Lyttleton Inn, 800-344-4715; Residence Inn by Marriott, 800-331-3131; Holiday Inn Boxborough Woods, 978-263-8701; Sheraton Tara, 603-888-9970.

Linden Hill School

Location: Northfield, Massachusetts (U.S. East Coast, New England)

154 South Mountain Road, Northfield, MA 01360-9681
Phone: 413-498-2906; Fax: 413-498-2908
Website: www.lindenhs.org; Email: admissions@lindenhs.org

Ms. Ruth Zealand, Interim Headmaster
Phone: 888-254-6336; Fax: 413-498-2908
Email: admissions@lindenhs.org

Mission Statement: Linden Hill's mission is to narrow the gap between poor performance and high potential. Our goal is to help boys make the most of their individual capabilities and thus enable them to succeed not only in school, but in life. The program is designed to address the academic, social, emotional and athletic needs of 9 to 16 year old boys, with average-to-superior intelligence, who have dyslexia or language based learning differences. Additionally, boys who need to learn English as a second language find our program ideally suited to progress and master reading, writing, and speaking in English. Prior to attending Linden Hill, many boys experienced academic failure and frustration because they received instruction that did not match their learning needs. For boys who struggled in other schools, a safe, nurturing environment is essential At Linden Hill, all boys are given the opportunity to be successful in a community of their peers who share an understanding of learning differences and are encouraged to realize their potential.

Grade Level: Ages 8-16.

Student Gender: Boys only.

Enrollment: 56 boys, 56 boarders.

Accredited by: NEASC

Faculty: The Head of the school, most of the full-time faculty members and their families, and additional support staff live on campus. All instructors are trained in the Orton-Gillingham method and are experienced in the teaching of students with learning differences. The support staff includes a psychologist and counselors, a full-time registered nurse, occupational and speech and language therapists, and Northfield Mount Hermon School Health Services, with a 24-hour clinic.

Tuition: Tuition and Boarding for 2003-2004 is $39,160.

Average Class Size: Class size ranges from two students in Orton-Gillingham language training sessions to an average size of four students in all other courses. The ratio of students to faculty is approximately 3:1

Curriculum: The curriculum of Linden Hill School begins with the idea that we strive to unlock the intellectual potential in each student by providing him with tools which work toward making the best of his own learning style. Each of the students is held to possess a unique and above average intelligence which our program seeks to access and foster. Therefore the student's own intellect plays a vital role in our curriculum.

The teaching method used at Linden Hill School is based on the principles of Anna Gillingham, a pioneer in the field of language tutoring. Working under the guidance of Dr. Samuel T. Orton, she was able to formulate a multi-sensory approach to remedially train students with language based learning differences. Multi-sensory teaching is a way of utilizing all of a child's senses. It reinforces learning: listening to the way a letter or word sounds; seeing the way a letter or word looks; and feeling the movement of the hand or mouth when producing a written or spoken letter, word or sound. Teachers are trained in a variety of programs and it is through this eclectic approach that the students are able to succeed and develop individually.

While the methodology of our curriculum is geared toward unlocking the intellectual capacity within our students, it must also be emphasized that the anxiety level for the students must be lowered for our methodology to be most effective. Our first step is to build confidence in the students and lower this anxiety level of the learning difference. Therefore our program is ungraded for the junior boarding students and success-oriented. Through reinforcement of learned skills, confidence grows and the student moves along the learning continuum.

Interactions within the Linden Hill community offer many opportunities for social and emotional growth. All members of the school community are key in providing a structured environment in which each boy will employ positive social behaviors. Communicating effectively, problem solving, and conflict resolution are addressed on a daily basis through modeling, role playing, and social reinforcement. By way of daily morning meetings, the Linden Hill student learns respect for himself and others. Social pragmatics are stressed throughout the day, from table etiquette to maintaining a presentable dorm room and being a good roommate. Each boy learns that he is a valued member of the school community and, in turn, that his community offers guidance and support.

We do offer a formal, traditional Freshman opportunity for students requiring a small, nurturing and academically supportive program. The young men enrolled in this class also gain leadership experiences usually associated with upper classmen. They continue to develop the skills necessary for future success in other educational settings.

ESL Program: Boys who need to learn English as a second language (ESL), find our program ideally suited to progress and master reading, writing and speaking in English. The English as a Second Language (ESL) class offers students, whose native language is something other than English, direct instruction in speaking, reading, spelling, and handwriting. The class incorporates many of the multi-sensory techniques within the Orton-Gillingham framework. Students are introduced to the sound symbol relationship of the language with a specific emphasis on pronunciation and phonemic awareness. Students are introduced to the first 300 words (a list of the most common words in English ranked by frequency and which make up 65 percent of all written material). Students engage in conversation daily and topics relating to the American English speaking culture are highlighted.

Sports: Linden Hill has an extensive athletic program. The School has its own full size indoor gymnasium with climbing wall and an outdoor soccer field, hiking trails, and a pond. Indoor swimming and ice hockey facilities are enjoyed by Linden Hill boys at Northfield Mt. Hermon school, a 10 minute shuttle ride from our campus. Horseback riding*, downhill skiing, snowboarding and golf* are available nearby. The school also offers archery, basketball, biking, cross-country-skiing, cross-country running, fishing, ice skating, roller blading, soccer, softball, tennis, and wrestling. Team sports are emphasized and all students participate. The focus is on learning skills and good sportsmanship. The school competes with other schools in interscholastic sporting events

Extracurricular Activities: Some of Linden Hill's extracurricular activities include: arts & crafts, board games, ceramics, chess, community outreach, Holiday play, culinary arts, maple sugaring, model building, vocal and instrumental music lessons, poetry night, photography, RC cars, woodworking, and more.

Campus: The school's location in the Pioneer Valley provides a farm-like environment while having easy access to transportation and to major cities. The heavily wooded, 300-acre campus overlooks the Connecticut River. It includes six major buildings, an athletic field, and cross country running and skiing trails. The main school building is the former Bennett farmhouse (circa 1835). Its ground floor houses the School's new kitchen and food storage area, offices, private meeting/ dining rooms, and a music room. On the second floor are two newly renovated faculty residences. Haskell Hall contains classrooms, an art room, a library, a greenhouse, and a large room that serves as both study hall and auditorium. The Duplex extension has classrooms, science laboratories, a technology center, a wood shop, and housing for 16 students and three faculty apartments. A multi-use gymnasium, with a full-size hardwood floor basketball court and a climbing wall, opened in 1998. White Cottage (1999) connects with the Headmaster's residence and houses the administrative offices, nurse's office, infirmary, and school store. In addition, there is another faculty residence, a maple-sugar shack, and several small buildings on campus.

Dormitories: There are three dormitories that provide students with a nurturing, "home away from home" environment. The Bennett Farmhouse extension, the school's latest million-dollar improvement, has three floors. The top floor is a dormitory with faculty residence. The main dining room, with expansive views of the surrounding valley, covers the middle floor, and a student activity center occupies the lower level. The Hayes Hillside Dormitory (1971) provides housing for 25 students, living quarters for dormitory parents and 1 or 2 collegians, a common room, large shower/bathroom, and a locker area for each boy to store his athletic gear and other equipment.

Nearest International Airport: Logan International Airport, Boston.

The Madeira School

Location: McLean, Virginia (U.S. Mid-Atlantic East Coast)

8328 Georgetown Pike, McLean, VA 22102
Phone: 703-556-8200; Fax: 703-821-2845
Website: www.madeira.org; Email: admissions@madeira.org

Ms. Cheryl Plummer, Director of Admission and Financial Aid
Phone: 703-556-8273; Fax: 703-821-2845
Email: admissions@madeira.org

Mission Statement: The Madeira School believes in the lasting value of single-sex education for girls. Young women expect more of themselves and learn to take pride in their individual effort when their community focuses solely on them and on their success. In this natural setting of woods and fields above the Potomac River, boarders and day students from ninth to twelfth grades prepare to take their place in the wider world. The Madeira education occurs in three arenas simultaneously; the classroom, the workplace, and the international community of the campus. It is both our duty and privilege to help young women to understand the changing world in which thy live and to have the confidence to live lives that are of their own making, their own passions, their own dreams.

Admission Requirements for International Students: Applicants for whom English is a second language are required to take the TOEFL.

Grade Level: 9-12.

Student Gender: Girls only.

Enrollment: 307 girls, 161 boarders, 146 day.

International Students: 13% of students, from 16 countries.

Accredited by: VAIS

Head of School: Elisabeth Griffith, PhD.

Faculty: Exceptional teachers run Madeira classrooms. Our teachers love teaching and have devoted their lives to the profession and their individual classrooms. Madeira teachers' passions are as high as their standards, and whether a girl is being taught verb endings in Spanish I or an advanced theory in an AP-level science course, the lesson is artfully designed, carefully delivered, and rigorous. Because our teachers are committed to investing a love of learning and thinking in each student, they may spend more time in the classroom on problem-solving and abstract reasoning, less time on review of rote material. Madeira's faculty includes 52 teachers, 27 of whom hold Masters degree or higher. 36 are full time, 16 part time, 9 men and 43 women.

Tuition: Tuition and Boarding for 2003-2004 is $32,800.

Average Class Size: 12 students.

Curriculum: The Madeira School recognizes that every student learns differently. This recognition is evident in the school's enticing, rigorous, college prep curriculum that offers many paths toward graduation; in the attention the faculty pay in the classroom not only to content but also to the process of learning; and in the experiential Co-Curriculum program in which all students partake each Wednesday. Obviously, Madeira's small classes, built-in conference times, and academic support system echo the school's philosophy that learning is an ongoing, individual, exquisite experience for each student at the school.

At Madeira, there is flexibility within the curriculum for individual journeys. At Madeira, not every girl is on the same journey or the same path. Miss Madeira's philosophy, that each girl should learn here how to achieve her personal best, allows for the creation of many paths, with many destinations.

Advanced Placement: Advanced Placement courses are offered in English Literature, U.S. History, Government and Politics, European History, Latin, French Language and Literature, Spanish Language and Literature, Calculus, Computer Science, Biology, Chemistry, Physics, Art History and Studio Art.

Average SAT Scores of Graduating Students: Math 625, Verbal 619.

College Placement: Colleges attended by recent graduates include Boston College, Brown University, Columbia University, Cornell

University, Dartmouth College, Duke University, Georgetown University, Harvard University, Johns Hopkins University, New York University, Princeton University, Stanford University, University of Pennsylvania, Vanderbilt University, Vasser College, and Yale University.

Sports: The Madeira athletic curriculum includes Cross-country, Dance, Field Hockey, Riding, Soccer, Tennis, Volleyball, Basketball, Diving, Riding, Soccer, Squash, Swimming, Lacrosse, Softball and Tennis. Madiera's outstanding athletic facilities include three playing fields, a cross-country course, eight tennis courts, and extensive riding facilities. The Hurd Sports center houses an indoor pool, volleyball and basketball courts, aerobics and weight training facilities and dance studios.

The purpose of The Madeira School Athletic Department is to encourage, facilitate, and support the participation of our students in Athletics. As a member of the Independent School League, which consists of seventeen schools in the Metropolitan D.C. area, Madeira has over 200 girls competing on 22 teams each year.

Participation on an athletic team is an excellent means of learning about oneself and developing strategies for the world beyond sports. Not only does athletics provide a vital ingredient in the physical development of girls, it also lays the foundation for developing self-confidence and discovering the value of teamwork. Madeira seeks to consistently emphasize to its students, both as players and spectators, the importance of integrity and good sportsmanship. The Madeira community having won the Gary T. Blackman Sportsmanship Award for six consecutive years evidences the extent to which our student-athletes take this to heart.

Extracurricular Activities: Madeira's extracurricular programs include the Asian Club, BSU (Black Student Union), "The Cabinet" Newsletter, Chai (Jewish Religion and Culture), Community Service Club, Cultural Club, Donkeyphants, Feed the Mind, FFM (Future Farmers of Madeira), Food Critics Club, GSA (Gay Straight Alliance), Habitat for Humanity, Kidsave International, Latin Club, Madeira Auto Club, Math Team, MESA/Roots and Shoots, Model UN, Museum Club, Muslim Student Association, Opera Club,

Outdoor Interest Group, Poetry Club, Riding Club, SADD (Students Against Destructive Decisions), Singing Club, Ski/Snowboard Club, Spanish Club, Spectator (school newspaper), STAMP (Peer tutoring), Sychronized Swimming Club, Thespians, TRANS, and YAA! (Youth Advocates for Awareness).

Campus: The dorms, classroom building, dining room, and Main Building surrounding the lawns and walkways of the Oval reflect the classic Georgian architecture of Madeira's spectacular 382-acre campus, overlooking the Potomac River. The primary classroom building is Schoolhouse, but classes are also held in the Science Building, which features laboratories, classrooms, and a fully equipped photo lab. The Art Building/Studio has facilities for painting, sculpture, printmaking, and ceramics. You will take performing arts courses in the Auditorium, which boasts a 500-seat theater with a professional lighting and scene shop, voice and instrument practice rooms, rehearsal space, a costume room. The Huffington Library houses 20,000 volumes. The campus also features the fully-equipped Hurd Sports Center, indoor and outdoor riding facilities, a General Store, a Post Office and Bank, six dormitories, a Health Center, Dining Hall, faculty housing and a Student Center with a natural amphitheater.

Dormitories: The residential program at Madeira houses approximately 165 boarding students in six houses. Approximately 28 students live in each house. Each house contains rooms of varying sizes. Students are housed in either single rooms or double rooms. Returning students select their house, their room and their roommate in the spring during Room Draw. See the Student-Parent Handbook for details of Room Draw. New students are assigned to double rooms and always have roommates in their grade. Each house has a vestibule at the entrance, a commons room which houses a television/VCR and a Cyberpod (a group of three computers that provide access to the world wide web), a small kitchen with a washer and dryer for laundry, a storage room for luggage and telephones.

Nearest International Airport: Dulles International Airport, Washington DC.

Maine Central Institute

Location: Pittsfield, Maine (U.S. East Coast, New England)

125 South Main Street, Pittsfield, ME 04967
Phone: 207-487-2282; Fax: 207-487-3512
Website: www.mci-school.org; Email: cwilliams@mci-school.org

Mr. Clint Williams, Director of Admission
Phone: 207-487-3355 or 207-487-2282; Fax: 207-487-3512
Email: cwilliams@mci-school.org

Mission Statement: MCI pledges to provide a rigorous, comprehensive educational program to a multicultural student body with a wide range of abilities and interests. In a safe and caring atmosphere, students will acquire knowledge, self-esteem, social responsibility, and the critical thinking and communication skills necessary for global citizenship and lifelong learning.

Grade Level: 9-12.

Student Gender: Boys & Girls.

Enrollment: 512 students, 303 boys, 209 girls, 90 boarders, 422 day.

International Students: students come from 18 different countries.

Accredited by: NEASC

Head of School: Joann Szadkowski, B.A. Lake Erie College, M.A. Kent State University.

Faculty: Faculty members are selected on the basis of three main criteria. They must possess a strong subject-matter background, the ability to relate to students, and an educational philosophy consistent with that of the institution. Faculty members are also expected to become actively involved in coaching, supervising dormitories, advising, counseling, and student affairs. The faculty consists of 54 members. Twenty-eight percent of the faculty and staff members live on campus.

Tuition: Tuition and Boarding for 2003-2004 is $29,000.

Curriculum: MCI offers a rigorous, comprehensive curriculum to accommodate various learning styles and academic abilities. MCI's math and science programs exceed national standards and utilize state-of-the-art technology. Students in MCI's well-known humanities program understand the culture of an era through a study of its history, literature, art, and music. The foreign language program includes four levels of French and Spanish. In addition to the traditional offerings, students may take courses in psychology, music composition, the Internet, sociology, child development, computer-assisted drawing, human sexuality, vocational subjects, and philosophy.

MCI offers a strong program in instructional support. Students who have a diagnosed learning difference and have struggled in academic content areas may receive individual or group support with a learning specialist. These services are available for an additional cost.

ESL Program: MCI's comprehensive English as a Second Language Program offers a complete curriculum for students with limited experience speaking English. In small-enrollment classes of five or six students, courses in mathematics, history, literature, speaking, and listening offer an unusual opportunity for one-on-one instruction. Students who complete this outstanding ESL program find success in mainstream classes and college programs. First class enrolled: $2,500; Each additional class: $1,500.

College Placement: MCI graduates have gone on to some of the finest colleges and universities in the world, including Harvard University, Georgetown University, Rochester Institute of Technology, Bates College, Fairleigh Dickinson University, Colby College, Boston College, Bowdoin, Colgate, Cornell, Maine Maritime Academy, Marquette, Miami, Providence, Purdue, Tufts, U.S. Naval Academy, and Wellesley.

Academic Requirements: For grades 9–12, 20 credits are required for graduation. Students must successfully complete units in English (4), mathematics (4), social studies (3, including U.S. history), science (4), physical education (1), fine arts (1), humanities (2), computer science (½), and health (½). Students are required to take the equivalent of at least 5 units each semester.

Sports: At MCI, we believe that athletics is an important part of the educational process, a dynamic lesson in teamwork and personal dedication. We offer a comprehensive athletic program for student-athletes of varying levels of ability. There are seventeen sports teams for boys and girls, including football, field hockey, soccer, basketball, golf, skiing, softball, track, wrestling, cheering, rifle, baseball, and tennis.

Wright Gymnasium and Parks Gymnasium are multiple-use athletic facilities, and each contains a weight room and locker facilities. Located on the main campus are a football field, a practice field, a ¼-mile track, two tennis courts, and a rifle range. Manson Park has fields for soccer, field hockey, baseball, and softball as well as three tennis courts. The school has the use of a local golf course and ski areas for competitive teams and recreation.

Extracurricular Activities: MCI's extracurricular program includes drama production, foreign languages, international travel, chess, hiking, weight lifting, science and reading clubs, Key Club, computer science, public speaking, Student Council, concert band, concert choir, chamber choir, vocal jazz ensemble, instrumental jazz ensemble, jazz combo, percussion ensemble, pep band, Math Team and the Science Olympiad.

On weekends, after a leisurely brunch, the campus springs to life. Options abound - sports activities and competitions; a bus trip to some of Maine's finest skiing areas; a trip to nearby shopping areas in Newport, Bangor, or Portland. MCI requires residential students to attend at least two cultural events each quarter. Choices include our own campus offerings: our nationally renowned vocal and instrumental jazz ensembles as well as our world class Bossov Ballet Theatre. Students might choose to attend a Broadway show or international performance at the Maine Center for the Arts. Fine films are enjoyed at Maine's Arts and Foreign Film Theater in nearby Waterville. The "Maine Experience" is another area of participation by our residential students. Hiking in the famed Acadia National Park and Baxter State Park, white-water rafting on the Kennebec River or Penobscot River, whale watching, and snowboarding down the Pinnacle are popular activities. MCI residential students can also experience the hospitality of our community by becoming involved in our Host Family Program. Students enjoy having "a home away from home" and joining with members of a local host family for weekend activities.

Campus: Currently, there are seven main academic buildings. The new Math and Science Center is a 23,000-square foot, state-of-the-art building that provides fourteen instructional spaces, two computer classrooms, and a botany area. More than 190 computers are available for student use campuswide, many of which have Internet and e-mail access. The 12,000-volume Powell Memorial Library has a computerized card catalogue and Infotrac as well as Internet access. The Pittsfield Public Library and the Pittsfield Community Theater are also available for school use.

The rural town of Pittsfield (population 4,500) is situated in an area that provides opportunities for hiking, skiing, biking, fishing, skating, and snowmobiling. It is 35 miles from the Atlantic Ocean and 70 miles from the mountains of western Maine.

Dormitories: Boarding students are housed in single-sex residence halls on campus, supervised by resident faculty and staff members. Each residence hall has its own recreation room and laundry facilities. Weymouth Hall houses the Student Services Center, consisting of the student lounge, snack machines, a bookstore, a post office, and a game room.

MCI offers a unique Host Family Program. Participating students are assigned to a family from the community that will make the student a part of the family for the school year. Students may spend time with their host family on weekends, after school, and during vacations, if so desired.

Nearest International Airport: Bangor International Airport, Bangor, Maine.

Marianapolis Preparatory School

Location: Thompson, Connecticut (U.S. East Coast, New England)

P.O. Box 304, Rt. 200, Thompson, CT 06277-0304
Phone: 860-923-9565; Fax: 860-923-3730
Website: www.marianapolis.org
Email: admissions@marianapolis.org

Mr. Daniel M Harrop, Director of Admissions
Phone: 860-923-9565; Fax: 860-923-3730
Email: dharrop@marianapolis.org

Mission Statement: The mission of Marianapolis Preparatory School is to educate students in the Catholic tradition of academic excellence with a commitment to an active faith in God and a dedication to building character with content, compassion and integrity. Its aims and purpose are: to encourage scholarship and mature character; to develop critical and analytical thinking skills; to build communicating and problem-solving skills; to promote the love of learning and the highest standards of academic achievement; to foster aesthetic sensitivity and creativity; to encourage the classical ideal of "mens sana, in corpore sana" (sound mind and body); to appreciate the value of cultural diversity; to nurture active and intelligent citizenship in the world; and to affirm Catholic principles through ethical and moral values.

Admission Requirements for International Students: International students who want to join the ESL program must plan to enter the U.S. on a Student Visa (F1). They must have transcripts and letters of recommendation forwarded from their secondary school. Complete and submit an application from with application fee. Submit a certified letter of financial guarantee on bank or other official letterhead that shows a specific amount of money available to pay for program costs and living expenses while in the U.S. All students must present evidence of a current medical examination and immunizations.

Grade Level: 9-12.

Student Gender: Boys & Girls.

Enrollment: 229 students, 126 boys, 103 girls, 87 boarders, 142 day.

International Students: 80 students, from Bosnia and Herzegovina, Brazil, Bulgaria, China, Cameron, Columbia, Germany, Japan, Kazakhstan, Korea, Mexico, Nigeria, Poland, Puerto Rico, Russia, Saudi Arabia, Taiwan and Vietnam.

Accredited by: NEASC

Head of School: Marilyn S. Ebbitt, A.B. Marquette University, M.S. from Georgetown University. Email: mrs.ebbitt@marianapolis.org

Faculty: The Marianapolis faculty features 25 full- and part-time teachers. In addition to classroom teaching, they serve as advisers to 8 to 10 students each and meet with their advising groups four days a week. Faculty members also moderate student clubs and coach athletic teams.

Tuition: Tuition and Boarding for 2003-2004 is $24,512.

Class Size: 13 students, with at student/teacher ratio of 8:1

Curriculum: Marianapolis Preparatory School is a Roman Catholic college-preparatory school; however, admission is open to all, regardless of religious persuasion. The School seeks to prepare young men and women for life intellectually, emotionally, physically, ethically, and spiritually by having them master, through self-discipline and a hunger for excellence, the core curriculum, which provides the basis for a traditional classical education, and by challenging them to be mature stewards of their talents.

Advanced Placement: Courses available are American History, Art, Music Theory, Biology, Calculus, Chemistry, English Language, English Literature, European History, Government, Physics, and Psychology.

ESL Program: The goals of the English as a Second Language Department are to prepare non-native English speaking students to focus their learning on the nature and structure of language; to refine their language skills so that they will be able to achieve the appropriate TOEFL scores necessary for placement in a U.S. college or university; and to develop their linguistic proficiency for entry into a U.S. college or university with no ESL assistance.

The Marianapolis ESL Program is structured to test students for their English skills and then place them at appropriate levels from beginning to intermediate and advanced levels of ESL. Students are expected to remain in ESL courses until they have sufficiently advanced to be accepted into the regular English program. The ESL Department comprises students with a wide range of abilities and interests, and it strives to develop the skills and confidence needed by these students to succeed in an unfamiliar environment. All new international students are encouraged to attend our six-week summer ESL program. The ESL curriculum endeavors to expand knowledge of the English language and to focus on the diversity of students' own capabilities while providing an atmosphere of challenge. The program will provide the communication skills for international students that will enable them to participate more fully in the educational process and provide a multi-cross cultural atmosphere for the campus.

Average SAT Scores of Graduating Students: Math-700, English-500, Total-1200.

College Placement: Among the colleges and universities to which recent seniors have been accepted are Harvard, Brown, Amherst, Williams, Notre Dame, Carnegie-Mellon, Colby, Colgate, Boston College, Boston University, Holy Cross, Vanderbilt, Rensselaer, Trinity, Tufts, Wellesley, and Worcester Polytechnic Institute, Providence College, George Washington University, Rhode Island School of Design, School of the Art Institute of Chicago.

Academic Requirements: All students are required to fulfill the following course of study to earn a Marianapolis diploma: Four years of English, Three years of math (including Algebra I, II and Geometry), Three years of history (including U.S. History), Three years of lab science (including IPS, biology, and chemistry), Three years of foreign language (may be waived for international students)

Six semesters of theology (including Old Testament, New Testament, Morality, and Church History), One year of either art or music, One semester of computer applications. All students are expected to take six academic courses as a minimum load.

Sports: Marianapolis feels that students' participation in athletic activities complements their overall development, helping them to become well-rounded individuals and good citizens. The values of fair competition and good sportsmanship are encouraged. The School requires that each student participate in one athletic activity or two alternative sports throughout the school year. Marianapolis features comprehensive athletic opportunities for students. Athletic offerings include boys' and girls' soccer, cross country, track and field, wrestling, yoga, aerobics, boys' and girls' basketball, lacrosse, golf, baseball, softball, and tennis on both junior varsity and varsity levels. The athletics facilities include soccer fields, a baseball and softball diamond, a gymnasium, and tennis courts. The gymnasium serves as the Student Sports Center. It contains basketball courts, a wrestling room, a Universal weight room, and a training room.

Extracurricular Activities: Boarding students are offered a variety of activities on weekends. On Friday nights and on Saturdays, trips are scheduled to local malls and areas of cultural, social, and historical interest. School dances are sponsored by various clubs and classes each month.

Various extracurricular clubs and activities are offered throughout the school year. Clubs and activities include Amnesty International, computer, math, science, and ski clubs, Art/Spirit Club, Yearbook, Literary/Art Magazine, Student Government, Matulaitis Nursing Home Volunteers, Honor Board, Drama Club, National Honor Society, Chorus/Band/Jazz Ensemble, and Dance Club. Traditional events each year include the Annual Rake Day in the fall and the Sports Day in the spring.

Campus: Adjoining the Town Common in the center of Thompson, Marianapolis Preparatory School occupies a 300-acre rural campus boasting woodlands and meadows, manicured lawns, and a pond. Blessed George Matulaitis Hall lies at the heart of the campus, housing the academic wing, administrative offices, computer and science labs, study hall, student lounge, dining room, and chapel. There are three dormitories on campus, one male and two female.

St. John's Hall houses all male students, while St. Albert 's and Bayer House provide housing for female students. The gymnasium provides a double basketball court with seating for 350 spectators, while the lower gymnasium offers room for aerobics classes, athletic department offices, and locker room facilities. Other facilities include tennis courts, trails for cross country running, biking, and walking, as well as baseball, lacrosse, softball, and soccer fields.

Dormitories: The dormitories are important centers of activity where students form lasting friendships with each other, their teachers, and prefects. Boys and girls are housed in separate dormitories where they are supervised by religious, lay, or resident faculty prefects who live in close proximity. All resident boys live in St. John's Hall and the girls are housed separately in St. Albert 's and Bayer House. St. John's is the boys' dormitory on campus and has the capacity to house 85 boys. This dormitory environment reflects the composition of the school. In the dormitories, as well as the classrooms, students from all four grades representing many different ethnic and cultural backgrounds form the Marianapolis community. St. John's is staffed 24 hours a day 7 days a week. It is supervised by resident faculty members and religious or lay prefects who serve as advisers to students and ensure that an adult is always available for assistance with any concern. Boys have the use of two recreational lounges with televisions and game rooms with foosball, table tennis, billiard tables, and a variety of games. A student store sells snacks and other items. The boys' laundry facilities are located on the lower level. Dry cleaning is available at a discounted price for the resident students.

In 1974, girls were first admitted into Marianapolis. Fifteen years later the girls resident program was established. Through the years the resident program for girls continues to grow. Two restored historic mansions on campus provide housing for girls "St. Albert 's" and "Bayer House". These are smaller living communities which foster a family atmosphere. St. Albert 's and Bayer House are staffed 24 hours a day, 7 days a week. Both are supervised by resident faculty members and religious or lay prefects who serve as advisers to students and ensure that an adult is always available for assistance with any concern.

Recreational lounges within the houses offer television, board games, and table tennis. The girls' laundry facilities are located in each of the dormitories. The resident program for girls is supervised by lay faculty members.

St. John's, St. Albert 's, and Bayer House are all closed during Thanksgiving, Christmas, and Easter recesses. Arrangements with local families are provided for international students who, because of distance, cannot travel home during vacations.

Nearest International Airports: T.F. Green International Airport, Providence, CT; Logan International Airport, Boston, MA; Bradley International Airport, Hartford, CT.

Nearby Lodgings: Lord Thompson Manor, 860-923-3886; Holiday Inn, 860-779-3200; Ramada Inn, 508-832-3221; Inn at Woodstock Hill, 860-928-0528; Baymont Inn & Suites, 508-832-7000.

The Marvelwood School

Location: Kent, Connecticut (U.S. East Coast, New England)

476 Skiff Mountain Road, P. O. Box 3001, Kent, CT 06757
Phone: 860-927-0047; Fax: 860-927-0021
Website: www.themarvelwoodschool.net
Email: marvelwood.school@snet.net

Mr. Todd Holt, Director of Admission
Phone: 860-927-0047; Fax: 860-927-0021
Email: marvelwood.school@snet.net

Mission Statement: Marvelwood's mission is to strengthen the foundation that leads to personal growth and academic success. We seek young people willing to get involved in their own education and committed to the challenge of preparing for college. Our school is an optimistic place that provides a structured, supportive and challenging environment, celebrates diversity, and awakens untapped potential. Marvelwood School's commitment has always been to the potential that resides in each of its students. The advisor system, small classes, dedicated faculty, optional skills support, and whenever possible, a hands-on approach to teaching and learning are some of the methods used to help students achieve their goals. The school strives always to be familial and to be a place where each student is known, valued, and treated with respect. Programs are designed and continually reviewed to enable each student to experience success in several different areas with a view to building self-confidence and optimism.

Grade Level: 9-12.

Student Gender: Boys & Girls.

Enrollment: 157 students, 108 boys, 49 girls, 150 boarders, 7 day.

Accredited by: NEASC

Head of School: Anne Davidson Scott, Wellesley College, B.A. Southern CT State University, Alliance Francaise, Paris; Diplome Surperieur.

Faculty: There are 42 full- and part-time faculty/administrative members (19 men, 23 women). 17 hold advanced degrees. 16 hold master's degrees and two hold Ph.D.'s. There are also 20 staff members. Marvelwood's faculty members experience ranges from one to 25 years in private school education. All faculty members and most administrators also act as dorm supervisors, and student advisors. Every faculty member advises four to five students, oversees their progress, and communicates with their parents.

Tuition: Tuition and Boarding for 2003-2004 is $30,500.

Class Size: 8 - 10 students, with a student/teacher ratio of 4:1.

Curriculum: The Marvelwood School, founded in 1957, is for average to above-average students who have not yet reached their potential as well as for young people who have not been successful in traditional school settings. The School's small, supportive, family-like environment is ideal for students who are struggling to reach their potential but have a serious commitment to their education and development. Students have a wide variety of backgrounds and learning styles requiring a flexible curriculum. Small classes, dedicated faculty members, a strong adviser program, and supervised study time ensure that each student receives the individual attention he or she needs. "Hands-on learning" in every facet of the academic program is a major emphasis at Marvelwood.

Hallmarks of a Marvelwood education include: A strong college-preparatory curriculum with a variety of interesting classes to challenge students at every level of ability; an advantageous 4:1 student-to-teacher ratio which enables close supervision and easy access to academic support; small classes that both enable and require students to be actively involved in their education; a skills program for those students requiring more intensive academic support; a caring, qualified faculty committed to bringing out the best in each student; an outstanding noncompetitive outdoor education program and a strong competitive sports program; a commitment to community service as an integral part of the curriculum.

ESL Program: The ESL program includes ESL Beginning Reading and Vocabulary, ESL Beginning Writing and Grammar, ESL

Intermediate Reading and Vocabulary, ESL Intermediate Writing and Grammar, ESL Literature, ESL World History, and ESL U.S. History.

SAT: SAT I score ranges for the class of 2001 were 290–670 verbal and 290–650 math.

College Placement: Recent graduates have been accepted to colleges such as Michigan State University, Syracuse University, University of Connecticut, University of Hartford, UMass Boston, Wellesley, and Washington State University.

Academic Requirements: Marvelwood requires a minimum of 20 credits for graduation in the following distribution: English - 4 credits (one year at each grade level), History- A minimum of 3 credits including U.S. History, Science - A minimum of 3 credits including Biology and one other lab science, Math - 4 credits including Geometry and Algebra 2, Foreign Languages - 2 credits (waived for some students), Arts/Electives - A minimum of 2 credits.

Sports: Marvelwood believes that participation in athletics is an important part of a student's growth. Students participate in sports in lieu of gym classes. Marvelwood competes with other schools at the varsity and JV levels. Marvelwood's athletic curriculum includes cross-country, volleyball, soccer, ice hockey, wrestling, basketball, downhill skiing, lacrosse, softball, tennis, and golf. In addition to the competitive sports, Marvelwood also offers recreational activities such as a Wilderness Ways program, including rock climbing, hiking, survival, and wilderness skills. Other noncompetitive offerings include a mountain biking program, Ultimate Frisbee, skiing/snowboarding, yoga, and white-water canoeing. Marvelwood has five playing fields, eight tennis courts, and a gymnasium.

Extracurricular Activities: activities included the yearbook, drama, guitar lessons, photography, chess, student government, admissions tour guides, driver's education, literary magazine, creative writing, and private music lessons. Students also attend the Hartford Stage and Hartford Symphony subscription series. A special part of students' education is participation in the School's Community Service Program which includes volunteer work at local hospitals, day-care centers, elementary schools, nursing homes, soup kitchens, nature conservancies, an animal shelter, and Habitat for Humanity.

On weekends, Marvelwood's rural campus provides opportunities for numerous out-of-doors activities including: hiking, camping, bicycling, fishing, and skiing. On Saturday evenings, students enjoy movies, off-campus trips, plays, concerts, dances or special events. Students enjoy games or other sports activities on Wednesday afternoons. On Saturdays, students attend four classes, a cafeteria lunch and athletics in the afternoon. On Sundays, students enjoy a 10:30 brunch, dorm cleanup and a free afternoon.

Campus: The school is located on 83 rural, hilltop acres. The land and the buildings comprise the former Kent Girls' School campus. The campus includes 20 buildings, eight tennis courts, four playing fields, two ponds, and large open spaces and woods. The Appalachian Trail passes close by and the land sits above the Housatonic River in the foothills of the Berkshire Mountains. The school is 55 miles west of Hartford and 80 miles north of New York City. Because of its rural location, hiking, biking, camping, skiing, and field studies are all normal activities at Marvelwood. Classes are held in the main schoolhouse in fifteen classrooms including two up-to-date science labs. The Bodkin Library contains more than 9,000 books and 70 periodicals. It also houses a computer lab. The gymnasium building contains a large stage, student lounge, and music room as well as the main indoor athletic facilities.

Dormitories: Each dormitory houses students from all grade levels, with roommates matched with students of the same grade level or age. The dorm rooms are homey and comfortable with faculty supervisors who live on the premises.

Nearest International Airport: Bradley International Airport, Hartford, CT.

Maur Hill - Mount Academy

Location: Atchison, Kansas (U.S. Central Midwest)

1000 Green Street, Atchison, KS 66002
Phone: 913-367-5482; Fax: 913-367-5096
Website: www.maurhillmountacademy.com
Email: admissions@mh-ma.com

Mr. Mike McGuire, Director of Admission
Phone: 913-367-5482 or 913-367-5482 ext. 210; Fax: 913-367-5096
Email: admissions@mh-ma.com

Mission Statement: Maur Hill-Mount Academy is a Catholic, college preparatory school educating young men and women in the Benedictine tradition of prayer, work, and love of learning. Through emphasis on loyalty, obedience, honesty, humility, and good works, we help local, national, and international youths mature as individuals who respect and care for others and understand their world.

Grade Level: 9-12.

Student Gender: Boys & Girls.

Enrollment: 168 boys, 105 girls, 117 boarders, 156 day.

Accredited by: NCA-CASI

Tuition: Tuition and Boarding for 2003-2004 is $19,500.

Class Size: 18 students, with a Student/Teacher Ratio of 8/1.

ESL Program: A super-intensive English program for international students is operated on an 11-month basis (July through May). Beginning to advanced levels are taught. Some combinations of English with regular curriculum are allowed to students in advanced levels until they test out of the English program. Maur Hill-Mount Academy offers 8 hours a day and 440 hours per quarter of English training and between 20 and 25 hours of classwork along with academic trips and summer activities per week. Those who are interested in super-intensive English but are unable to work with the scheduled programs are invited to write and inquire about special short-term courses to accommodate their schedules.

Academic Requirements: The following courses are required and must be completed before graduation: English - 4 Units; Mathematics - 4 Units; Science - 3 Units; Social Studies - 4 Units; Physical Ed./Health - 2 Units; Debate/Speech - 1 Unit; Religion (Optional for non-Catholics) - 4 Units; Fine Arts - 1 Unit; Foreign Language - 2 Units; Computer Technology - 1 Unit; Minimum Total Units Needed: 28 (with 4 Religion), 26 (with 2 Religion).

Sports: Interscholastic Team and Individual Activities include Baseball, Football, Soccer, Basketball, Wrestling, Tennis, Cross-Country, Track, Golf, Forensics, Debate, Journalism, Math & Science Contests, Volleyball, Weightlifting, Pool, Air Hockey, Swimming, Ping Pong, Tennis, Handball, Soccer, Bowling

Extracurricular Activities: Weekend activities include Professional sporting events, shopping in Kansas City and Topeka, Renaissance Festival, ski trips, museum and special events, rodeo, demolition derby, monster truck show, haunted houses, horseback riding, on-campus dances, Cookouts, amusement parks, and fishing trips.

Nearest International Airport: Kansas City International Airport, Kansas.

Middlesex School

Location: Concord, Massachusetts (U.S. East Coast, New England)

1400 Lowell Road, Concord, MA 01742
Phone: 978-371-6524; Fax: 978-402-1400
Website: www.middlesex.edu

Mrs. Sibyl Cohane, Director of Admissions
Phone: 978-369-2550 or 978-371-6524; Fax: 978-402-1400
Email: scohane@middlesex.edu

Mission Statement: In everything we do, we are committed to excellence and to the growth and development of our students. Throughout the past century, students at Middlesex have pursued the school's goal, "to find the promise" within themselves as they grow into their interests and talents and become the people they want to be. You can share in that tradition of self-discovery with an energetic, diverse, and committed peer group and work with talented and engaging teachers. We believe that each of us adds his or her talents and energies to those of the community to make us all stronger, more energetic, and more powerful people.

Grade Level: 9-12.

Student Gender: Boys & Girls.

Enrollment: 328 students, 164 boys, 164 girls, 240 boarders, 88 day.

Accredited by: NEASC

Head of School: Kathleen Carroll Giles, B.A., Harvard College, J.D., Harvard Law School.

Faculty: Middlesex faculty members, 51 of whom hold graduate degrees, are integrated into their students' experiences at every level. Students at Middlesex choose their own adviser to assist with course selection and provide support and counsel on other concerns. Many of the 80 Middlesex faculty members of live on campus, some even in the student dormitories. The accessibility and opportunity for friendship help faculty members get to know each student's strengths, weaknesses, interests, and goals.

Tuition: Tuition and Boarding for 2003-2004 is $32,800.

Class Size: 11 students, with a student-teacher ratio of 6:1.

Curriculum: Critical thinking, verbal classrooms, and a spirited community all define Middlesex School. There are four broad principles which shape the content of the curriculum. First, we want students to take some courses by grade level so that they can comfortably express understandings, discuss confusions and share triumphs with classmates. All freshmen, therefore, take a common English course and most elect biology. Similarly, all sophomores take a common English course with a writing workshop, modern European history, and most elect chemistry.

Second, we encourage students to advance in some disciplines (math, science and foreign language, in particular) at a rate that is appropriate for their level of training and interest. With this in mind, all students are carefully placed in math and foreign language sections each semester by the respective department. Two examples illustrate our commitment to this principle. In math, incoming freshmen last September were placed in five different levels of mathematics; in science, we offer three levels — regular, honors, and Advanced Placement — in biology, chemistry, and physics.

Third, we want students to progress as rapidly and as far in any discipline as their ability and their ambition will allow. To that end, we offer a full complement of Advanced Placement courses in virtually every discipline (we prepared students for 24 different AP exams last year), but we do not stop there! Almost every department offers courses beyond the AP level.

Finally, we want students to experience the freshness of newly created courses. The faculty is encouraged to imagine and plan new courses, even as they constantly update courses that are standard parts of the curriculum.

Advanced Placement: Preparation for Advanced Placement examinations is offered in twenty-four subject areas. Permission of the Department is required for student enrollment in all AP courses. The requirement for admission to AP courses varies from department to department. For instance, admission to AP Economics is based on performance in both United States History and previous courses in mathematics, and admission to AP Art History is based on performance in Art 1, United States History and English 3. In general, admission to all Advanced Placement courses depends on demonstrated mastery of the subject in preceding courses and permission of the Department.

Average SAT Scores of Graduating Students: The median scores on the SAT I for Middlesex's class of 2003 were 660 verbal and 660 math.

College Placement: The members of the class of 2003 are attending fifty-four colleges and universities including Brown, Colby, Cornell, Harvard, Yale, Columbia, Vanderbilt, New York University, Boston University, Stanford, and Dartmouth.

Academic Requirements: Departmental requirements include 8 semesters of English, mathematics through trigonometry and analytic geometry, a foreign language through the third-year level, 2 years of laboratory science, 1 year of American history, 1 year of European history, and ½-credit courses in the arts (freshmen and sophomores only). In addition, juniors and seniors are required to distribute their courses among the four divisions of the curriculum: 8 in the humanities, 5 in the natural sciences, 3 in the social sciences, and 1 in the arts, with 3 unrestricted.

Sports: Interscholastic competition is available at all levels in cross-country running, soccer, Alpine skiing, basketball, ice hockey, squash, lacrosse, crew, golf, and tennis, football, wrestling, baseball, and field hockey.

The Atkins Athletic Center features two basketball courts, as well as a fitness center, a dance studio, eight international squash courts, an indoor hockey rink, indoor tennis courts, and a wrestling arena. The campus also has a boathouse and a ½-mile rowing course.

Extracurricular Activities: Extra curricular activities include, Model United Nations, dramatic productions, a one-act-play festival, singing groups, instrumental ensembles, and community service.

The School encourages an "if we don't have it, start it" approach to extracurriculars, which allows the program to remain as lively and creative as the students involved.

One of the School's oldest traditions requires that every senior carve a wooden plaque. The week before graduation, each plaque is mounted on the walls in the corridors of the School buildings.

The Student Activities Committee (SAC) plans events for every weekend of the school year. Traditional favorite activities include the opening Square Dance, Hypnotist Russ Burgess, a Video Dance, Casino Night, the Senior Prom, a Luau, and the Spring Carnival. The SAC also plans dorm competitions, more affectionately referred to as "Dorm Wars". Competitions in the last few years have consisted of a Field Day (volleyball and relay races), Brain Bowl (Jeopardy-style), Air Guitar, Name That Tune, Dorm Lights, Gladiators, and Family Feud. Occasionally, the school offers trips to Boston for theater or sporting events.

The Student Activities Committee, a joint student-faculty venture, plans exciting events for students on non-school days. The committee organizes dances, parties, weekend movies, and live music performances. Major dramatic and musical presentations in the theater arts center draw full houses of students, parents, and visitors. The proximity of Cambridge and Boston provides an almost inexhaustible supply of interesting off-campus cultural options for students and accompanying faculty members. Eleven weekends of the year are designated as "campus weekends," during which the students remain on campus.

Most of the weekend activities enjoyed by boarding and day students are informal. Many students use the School's extensive woodlands for hiking, running, biking, and cross-country skiing. The School's athletic facilities are open for spirited student and faculty competition. In the winter, students skate in the rink and on the pond. On weekends, students are active in the woodworking, metal-welding, ceramics, and photography studios and in the music rooms.

Campus: Located on a rural campus of 350 acres just 20 miles from

Boston, Middlesex enrolls 340 students from 27 states and 10 countries. These students pursue academic excellence in small, Socratic-style classes that average twelve students. Additionally, a deep commitment to the arts is supported by a modern theater arts complex, and a competitive athletic program is enhanced by a newly renovated athletic center. The Clay Centennial Center houses math and science classrooms and laboratories for biology, chemistry, physics and environmental science as well as a state-of-the-art observatory with an 18-inch Centurion telescope for the astronomy program. Selected students may also participate in summer science research internships, most recently at Harvard's Smithsonian Center for Astrophysics.

Most classes and administrative activities take place in Eliot Hall, one of the eight Georgian brick buildings that surround an oval green known as "The Circle." With its extensive studio space, large main stage, and small teaching theater, the Cornelius Ayer Wood '13 Theatre Arts Center has served as a model for a number of secondary schools. The Warburg Library supports student research with 34,000 carefully selected volumes, nearly 200 periodical subscriptions, an online catalog of all library materials, and a growing collection of CD-ROM services. The Warburg Library has its own wide area network (WAN) that includes the online card catalog as well as access to the Internet, CD-ROM multimedia information, and word processing software. The new Clay Centennial Center includes lab/classrooms, math classrooms, an observatory, a rooftop "telescope garden," a project room to support independent study, and a student lounge.

Technology and computers play a significant role in the lives of students and faculty members at Middlesex. Two state-of-the-art technology centers contain multimedia computers and full Internet access. Middlesex also has several lab classrooms equipped with interactive computers for the study of mathematics, computer science, modern languages, science, and economics. In addition, all dormitory rooms have access to the School's academic and library networks, the Internet, and email.

Beyond the dormitories, the academic facilities, and the athletic center, the simple, dignified chapel gives the campus its stately center. Four of the dormitories, the athletic center, and the chapel have all been recently renovated. The dining hall includes a student center complete with snack bar, game rooms, and lounge area. The health center is affiliated with Emerson Hospital, which is located less than 5 miles from the campus.

Dormitories: Residential life at Middlesex centers around the nine dormitories on campus. Proctors live on each floor so that they are available for all students. Two to three faculty families live in every Middlesex house and oversee the activities of the 24 to 30 resident students. New students are usually assigned single rooms for their first year and may choose their rooms, roommates, and dorms in subsequent years.

Nearest International Airport: Logan International Airport, Boston.

Millbrook School

Location: Millbrook, New York (U.S. East Coast, New England)

School Road, Millbrook, NY 12545
Phone: 845-677-8261; Fax: 845-677-8598
Website: www.millbrook.org; Email: admissions@millbrook.org

Mrs. Cynthia McWilliams, Director of Admission
Phone: 845-677-8261; Fax: 845-677-1265
Email: admissions@millbrook.org

Grade Level: 9-12.

Student Gender: Boys & Girls.

Enrollment: 240 students, 133 boys, 107 girls, 188 boarders, 52 day.

Accredited by: NYSAIS

Head of School: Drew Casertano, Choate School and Amherst College, Master's in education, Harvard Graduate School of Education.

Faculty: Millbrook has assembled a talented group of men and women who happen also to be gifted, devoted teachers. To their chosen profession, the faculty bring an array of accomplishments and experience: all are graduates of highly selective college, university, and graduate school programs; many are accomplished athletes, scholars, and artists. Regardless of where they might have been before, all faculty members share a passion for their disciplines, a commitment to and belief in the power of education, and a desire to involve themselves deeply in the lives of young people.

Of the 72 member faculty, all hold a bachelor's degree, 23 hold a master's degree, and 3 hold a doctoral degree. Most faculty members live on campus, many in dormitory housing.

Tuition: Tuition and Boarding for 2003-2004 is $31,465.

Class Size: Student/faculty ratio of 4.5:1

Curriculum: of Millbrook's academic program exists not only in the quality of its offerings or the ability of its teachers, for while both are components of a flourishing and broad program, neither can guarantee its success. Rather, the program's strength resides in the attitude, the ethos that fills each class period, each singular exchange between faculty and students. Classes are places where respect for one another, for the free exchange of ideas and opinions, is a most prized commodity. Within a traditional, rigorous college preparatory course of study, Millbrook students are encouraged to be curious, involved, active learners, for the teachers with whom they work understand that the success of any educational pursuit lies in the vigor and commitment that students bring to it. The acquisition of knowledge and skills, though critical to our mission, is but a component of a Millbrook education. The ability to read effectively, write clearly, and think independently are of greatest use when students challenge themselves, listen carefully to their classmates, test their own limits, and question their assumptions.

SAT: Mean SAT I scores are 550 verbal and 540 math.

College Placement: Recent graduates of Millbrook have been accepted to Boston University, Columbia, Cornell, and Duke.

Academic Requirements: The minimum graduation requirements are 4 years of English, 3 years of mathematics, 3 years of one foreign language, 2 years of laboratory sciences, and 1 year of fine arts. The history/social science requirement varies with the grade level at which the student enters.

Sports: Millbrook School has a long history of strong, competitive athletics with a high standard of sportsmanship. Millbrook students are required to play team sports for at least two out of three seasons of the academic year. Team sports offered are: soccer, cross-country, field hockey, ice hockey, basketball, squash, tennis, lacrosse, golf, baseball, and softball. While many students choose to play team sports all three terms, electives such as zoo squad, F.L.I.P. (Forest Land Improvement Project), dance, or recreational sports may be selected as alternatives one term per year. The school also has stable space for five horses and hundreds of miles of riding trails available on and surrounding the campus. The Coole Park Equestrian Center, one of the major showplaces in the Northeast, is adjacent to our campus and provides horses, instruction and indoor riding to the students at an additional cost. Millbrook's athletic program was greatly enhanced with the recent completion of the $9 million, 86,000 square foot Mills Athletic Center. A center of student life on the campus, this spectacular new facility houses an interscholastic basketball court, four international squash courts, a training complex and fitness center, and the indoor Bontecou Hockey Rink (convertible to four indoor tennis courts off season).

Extracurricular Activities: Scheduled weekend activities might include dances with other boarding schools, a coffee house, Autumnfest, Winter Weekend, poetry readings by the library fireplace, shopping trips, on- or off-campus movies, video games night, meals at nearby restaurants, or camping in the Catskills. For the athletically inclined: intramural triathlons, cross-country skiing or running sessions, bowling, golf, broom ball or free skating at the Bontecou rink, mountain bike races, ultimate frisbee matches, and much more. A much-anticipated yearly event on campus is Intersession, a weeklong program held just before spring break in March. During this week, students may select one of the twenty different courses offered by the faculty, ranging from film making to gourmet cooking, from woodworking to exploring Manhattan, from building with Habitat for Humanity to Adirondaction - hiking and skiing in the Adirondack Mountains. Intersession is designed to allow Millbrook students to work with adults in ungraded situations, to develop collaborative skills, and to learn experientially.

The school encourages its students to participate in summer activities which reinforce their Millbrook academic program. Among these might be international travel and language study (including home study programs), community service programs, outdoor adventures, scientific study, visual and performing arts programs, and sports-related programs. Millbrook students have participated lately in some of the following: American Field Service, Youth for Understanding, World Horizons, Interlochen, Visions International, Where There Be Dragons, Teton Science School, World Learning, The School for Field Studies, Putney Student Travel, Outward Bound, Carnegie Mellon Summer Pre-College Program for Theater and Acting, Rustic Pathways, Trails Wilderness, Deer Hill

Expeditions, ACS British Studies, Broadreach, and Academic Study Associates at Stanford and Oxford.

How about a trip with one of your teachers? We've done that, too. During the past few years, Millbrook faculty members have sponsored scientific data-collecting trips down the Amazon, and to Machu Picchu, Peru; language-immersion visits to Mexico and Costa Rica, and just-plain-fun visits to Baja. Even the baseball and lacrosse teams have traveled south at spring break to warm up for the coming season.

Community Service periods are included in the formal class schedule four times per week, but since students often choose their services based on their individual interests, they may find themselves devoting extra time to their volunteer work. From managing money in the Strong Box (the school bank), to caring for the animals at the zoo, to working on the library 's computers, all Millbrook students learn to be actively involved in their community. Among the community services currently offered are the following: Activities, Admission Tour Guides, Arts, Athletic Association, Bird Banding/Science, Computer Services, Conservation Action Center, Dorm leaders/Managers, Fire Safety, Food Service, Greenhouse, Headwaiters, Library, Maintenance, Millbrook School Website, Outreach, Peer Counselors, Post Office, Recycling, School Store, "The Silo" (student newspaper), Spiritual Life, Strong Box (student bank), Student Council, Student Tutors, "The Tamarack" (yearbook) and Trevor Zoo.

Campus: Incredible natural beauty defines the Millbrook School campus which is located 90 miles north of New York City (Dutchess County) in the lovely countryside of the Mid-Hudson Valley region. Its rural 600 acres contain rolling hills, forests, wetlands, playing fields, trails (used by those on foot or on horseback) and the campus proper which is arranged around the main quadrangle. The quad is reminiscent of a traditional New England village with the Flagler Memorial Chapel at its head and red brick and white clapboard buildings completing the square. The entire campus is comprised of 68 buildings, including seven dormitories, the Schoolhouse, the Mills Athletic Center, the Holbrook Arts Center (completed in December, 2000), Pulling House (the headmaster's residence), the Barn (informal theater/student center), and the six-acre Trevor Zoo. Sixty-nine years' worth of students have enjoyed Millbrook's sweeping lawns, tree-lined country lanes, acres of woodlands – all amid a breathtakingly gorgeous natural setting.

Dormitories: Living with a group of people from diverse backgrounds twenty-four hours a day is a unique experience, one seldom found outside of boarding school. In many ways a student's dormitory will become his or her new home - where best friends and teachers live next door or down the hall. Dorm life is such a special part of Millbrook, that day students also have their own beds as well.

Evenings for Millbrook students begin with a buffet-style dinner in the Prum Dining Hall six nights per week and a formal dinner one night each week. Just before formal dinner, students assemble for a chapel talk (sponsored by the school's Spiritual Life Committee) given by a student, a faculty member, or a visiting speaker on a relevant and timely topic. And on special Friday nights, the school community gathers once again in the chapel to listen to an outside speaker, a panel discussion, a musical or theatrical performance, etc., as part of the forum series.

At 7:45 evening study hall begins - a quiet period set aside for serious studying in the dorms through 9:30 - after that, the dorm comes alive with music and laughter and impromptu pizza or popcorn parties until "lights out."

Nearest International Airport: JFK International Airport, New York.

Miss Hall's School

Location: Pittsfield, Massachusetts (U.S. East Coast, New England)

492 Holmes Road, Pittsfield, MA 01201
Phone: 413-443-6401; Fax: 413-448-2994
Website: www.misshalls.org; Email: info@misshlls.org

Ms. Kimberly Boland, Director of Admission
Phone: 413-443-6401 or 413-499-1300; Fax: 413-448-2994
Email: info@misshalls.org

Mission Statement: We affirm that Miss Hall's School is a school committed to preparing young women for full and satisfying lives in the modern world. We incorporate experiential learning into a comprehensive, college preparatory education, adapting students' programs to build on their strengths. We discover and invigorate the unique qualities of each young woman, motivating her to respect her own special abilities and those of others. We honor sensitivity, ethical behavior, trust, and compassion and nurture these qualities in the Miss Hall's School family. We embrace diversity and, through instruction and example, foster understanding of the full spectrum of human and cultural differences. We commit to the principle of serving, endeavoring to teach the grace of giving, the warmth of community, and the dignity of a cooperative spirit.

Admission Requirements for International Students: Miss Hall's requires the TOEFL for all international students. In addition to the regular application, there is an international student supplement that is one additional page.

Grade Level: 9-12.

Student Gender: Girls only.

Enrollment: 175 students, 125 boarders, 40 day.

International Students: 15% of total enrollment, from Bahamas, Bermuda, Canada, Ecuador, Hong Kong, Japan, Korea, Mexico, Nigeria, Serbia-Montenegro, Taiwan, Thailand, Ukraine, and Venezuela.

Accredited by: NEASC

Head of School: Jeannie K. Norris, Pittsburgh State University
(B.M.Ed.), Temple University (M.M.)

Faculty: Miss Hall's School has a 52-member faculty, 26 of whom
hold advanced degrees, and 19 reside on campus. In addition to
teaching, faculty members act as academic instructors, class
advisers, club facilitators, coaches, and dorm residents. Each Miss
Hall's student also selects a faculty advisor for both academic and
personal guidance.

Tuition: Tuition and Boarding for 2003-2004 is $31,800.

Class Size: 10 students, with a student-teacher ratio of 7:1.

Curriculum: Miss Hall's School offers a comprehensive college
preparatory curriculum, providing students with an outstanding
academic foundation. The size of our School permits a thorough
knowledge of each student's abilities and achievements. Advanced
Placement courses in all disciplines and honors courses are available
to those students who seek greater challenges in their academic
program. In addition to courses in English, history, math, science,
and foreign language, broad offerings in the visual arts, music, and
theater provide avenues of learning in which students may excel.

We believe that not everything girls need to learn about the world
and themselves can be learned in the classroom. Every Thursday
throughout the school year, all students participate in Horizons - a
unique, experiential learning and internship program that provides
girls with opportunities to participate in work and service to the
larger communities of Miss Hall's School and Berkshire County.
This unique program allows each student to develop new skills,
explore areas of interest for college majors and careers, test values in
the real world, and increase financial literacy.

Advanced Placement: Advance Placement courses are available in
English, French Language, Spanish Language, Latin, Calculus,
Chemistry, Biology, U.S. History, European History, and Studio Art.

ESL Program: The Program is designed to help students develop proficiency in English as they compete academically in an all-English language culture. Our ESL program is dedicated to facilitating this integration. International students are tested in all areas of English and individually placed in appropriate class sections. The School offers three levels of English as a Second Language.

The International Student Program at Miss Hall's School provides services to girls and their families who may need assistance in understanding the American Educational system and the boarding school culture. International students begin their Miss Hall's experience at a three-day orientation program just for them. The girls learn their way around school, schedule classes, begin to make friends, and have a few days to feel at home before returning students arrive.

Classes for international students are carefully selected so that each student's language needs are met and her academic interests and talents are strengthened. We offer three levels of English as a Second Language, and have graduation requirements for international students to ensure their ability to succeed at American universities.

Miss Hall's offers one-on-one weekly college counseling meetings for each international senior. Her counselor will help the student research appropriate schools, complete her application, appraise her essay, and help her to meet deadlines. The School also helps to schedule college visits and to prepare financial and legal documents for the university-bound graduate.

The International Student Alliance is a club that traditionally includes international and American students who work together to provide programs about diversity and other cultures to the school community. This club, the largest on campus, presents several dances, banquets, and cultural events each year.

From pre-admissions questions right through college counseling services, we answer questions and solve problems as they arise. The following are a few of our recent projects: Placed students in summer school programs at Tufts, Cornell, Johns Hopkins, UCLA, Exeter, Andover, and Other U.S. institutions; arranged special tutoring services in the girls' first languages; found luggage that disappeared on its way to New York from Europe; added special foods to the school menu to accommodate different meal preferences.

For 100 years, Miss Hall's School has been providing outstanding education and wonderful care to young women from the United States and all corners of the globe. We hope that you will consider joining us.

College Placement: Recent graduates of Miss Hall's have been accepted to colleges such as Boston University; Chicago Art Institute; Cornell; Georgetown; George Washington; Smith; Wellesley; Yale; Universities of Massachusetts, and University of Southern California.

Academic Requirements: Rigorous academic courses combined with Horizons, an innovative experiential program, and athletics comprise college preparation at Miss Hall's. The School's curriculum provides students with a range of requisite and elective courses to meet the diverse talents and interests of the student body.

Graduation requirements are as follows: Four (4) years of English; Three (3) years of history, including United States History; Three (3) years of a foreign language; Three (3) years of mathematics, including Algebra I, Geometry, and Algebra II; Three (3) years of science; Two (2) additional credits, for a minimum of 18 credits; Successful completion of Horizons and three seasons each year of athletics.

Sports: The Miss Hall's School athletic program provides varied environments for girls to learn the benefits of teamwork, physical fitness, and healthy competition while instilling and strengthening an appreciation of athletics. A variety of offerings are available, including varsity and junior varsity sports and non-competitive activities. Athletics teach girls skills, enhance self-discipline, encourage confidence, and provide leadership opportunities. A variety of offerings is available, including varsity and junior varsity sports as well as non-competitive activities. Girls must play three seasons each year of athletics, one of which must be a team sport. Our offerings include the following: Cross-Country, Field Hockey, Soccer, the Outdoor Program and Tae Kwon Do, Riding, Tennis, Modern Dance and Choreography, Skiing, Snowboarding, Basketball, Volleyball,

Fitness, Aerobics, Lacrosse, Softball, and Tennis. The Anne Meyer Cross '37 Athletic Center and Thatcher Family Gymnasium is an 18,720 sq. ft. state-of-the-art indoor fitness and sports facility, which supports the School's commitment to healthy competition, teamwork, and school spirit. Features include: Full-size basketball and volleyball courts, Lockers and team rooms, Fitness Center with treadmills, stationary bikes, Stairmasters, elliptical machines, and more, Aerobics Room, Wilderness Program Center, and Climbing Wall.

Extracurricular Activities: Extracurricular activities at Miss Hall's include Student Council, the Social Committee, Athletic Association, Judicial Committee, Student-Faculty Advisory Committee, Essence Diversity Club, Environmental Club, Photography Club, French Club, Latin Club, International Student Alliance, Hallways student newspaper, Hallmark yearbook, Sol literary magazine, performance groups, such as Grace Notes, Vocal Ensemble; Merrie Melodies, various instrumental ensembles, and theater productions.

For half a day on Thursdays, there are no classes at Miss Hall's. Instead, students roll up their sleeves and get to work. This is Horizons – a chance for each girl to participate in work and service as a way of gaining new skills, testing values and moral positions in society, learning about other people, and increasing financial literacy. Freshmen learn to run a business, sophomores do volunteer work, juniors learn through community service organizations, and seniors explore careers through internships.

Weekend activities at Miss Hall's include dances and social events, volunteer and community service opportunities, trips to Boston and New York, games and sports, movies, shopping, theater, music, and dance performances.

Campus: Miss Hall's School is located on a scenic 80-acre campus. The main school building at Miss Hall's is a Gorgian-style mansion originally built in 1923 and renovated in 1966. The building houses classrooms, offices, dormitory rooms, and faculty apartments. It's also where we eat, where we hang out with each other, where we live, where we learn. The 90,000-square-foot Main Building building also houses laboratories, choral and instrumental music rehearsal space, Humes Euston Hall Library, the Melissa Leonhardt Academic Skills Center, and the Pamela Humphrey Firman Technology Center. Other campus facilities include the Anne Meyer Cross Athletic Center, Ara West Grinnell Teaching Greenhouse, Elizabeth Gatchell Klein Arts Center, and Jessie P. Quick Ski Chalet, the Humes Euston Hall Library, the Gustafson Family Lending Library, and the Klein Arts Center, which features a theater with dressing rooms, costume and prop-storage rooms, and a design workshop, dance, art, ceramics, and photography studios.

Dormitories: Most students live in the Main Building on campus, where almost all the rooms are doubles. Witherspoon Dormitory gives seniors their own space and more independence. Roommates are assigned for the first year, but students can change roommates in the following years. Half of Miss Hall's faculty lives on campus and many serve as resident dorm parents. Seniors also serve as dorm proctors – big sisters who can provide peer counseling and support.

Nearest International Airport: Albany, NY; Bradley International Airport, Hartford, CT; Logan International Airport, Boston, MA.

Nearby Lodgings: Crowne Plaza, 413-499-2000; The Yankee Inn, 413-499-3700; Cranwell Resort, 413-637-1364; The Red Lion Inn, 413-298-5545.

Miss Porter's School

Location: Farmington, Connecticut (U.S. East Coast, New England)

60 Main Street, Farmington, CT 06032
Phone: 860-409-3530; Fax: 860-409-3531
Website: www.missporters.org; Email: admissions@missporters.org

Ms. Deborah Haskins, Director of Admission
Phone: 860-409-3530; Fax: 860-409-3531
Email: admissions@missporters.org

Mission Statement: Miss Porter's School excels at preparing young women for college and for life. Our attentive, diverse boarding and day community provides a demanding curriculum—academic, artistic, athletic, and residential. We challenge our students to become informed, bold, resourceful, and ethical global citizens. We expect our graduates to shape a changing world.

Admission Requirements for International Students: Application - Part I and Part II with essay, Graded paper; Transcripts for current year and two previous years; Recommendations from Head of School or counselor, current English teacher, and current math teacher; TOEFL (if English is not the applicant's first language) and SSAT scores.

Grade Level: 9-12.

Student Gender: Girls only.

Enrollment: 325 girls, 219 boarders, 106 day.

International Students: 7%

Accredited by: NEASC

Head of School: Burch Ford, B.A. English, Boston, M.S.W. Simmons College, Ed.M. Harvard University.

Faculty: Miss Porter's has a faculty of 45 teachers, 33 of whom have advanced degrees. The school hires teachers who are dedicated to academics as well as to the intellectual, moral, and personal development of its students. Faculty members participate in every aspect of boarding school life, and each student has her own advisor, who helps manage her academic program as well as life on campus.

Tuition: Tuition and Boarding for 2003-2004 is $32,860.

Class Size: 12 students, with a student / teacher ratio of 8:1

Curriculum: Miss Porter's School offers a demanding college preparatory curriculum that includes Honors, Advanced Placement, and elective courses, as well as internships and independent studies. Emphasis is placed on literature, expository writing, public speaking, mathematics, foreign languages, science, and history.

Honors courses are available. Juniors and seniors are encouraged to investigate career opportunities by working at internships in the Hartford area or at other locations across the U.S. They may also participate in the School Year Abroad program in France, Spain, Italy, or China.

Advanced Placement: Advanced Placement courses are offered in Art History, Biology, Calculus, Chemistry, Computer Science, English Language and Composition, Environmental Science, European History, French Language and Literature, Latin Literature, Microeconomics, Macroeconomics, Music Theory, Physics, Spanish Language and Literature, Statistics, Studio Art, and U.S. History.

ESL Program: Yes

Average SAT Scores of Graduating Students: Math 616/Verbal 622

College Placement: Recent graduates of Miss Porter's have been accepted to Harvard, Yale, Columbia, Smith, Georgetown, Vassar, McGill and University of Michigan.

Academic Requirements: To graduate, each student entering in 9th grade must have a total of 36 semester units, including 8 units of English; 6 units of a foreign language; 4 units of history; algebra I, geometry, and algebra II; 6 units of science; 2 units in the arts (art, music, theater, dance, art history, or photography); and a ½-unit each in computers, ethics, and leadership.

Sports: The athletic curriculum includes badminton, basketball, crew, cross-country, downhill skiing, field hockey, golf, lacrosse, soccer, softball, squash, swimming, tennis and volleyball. Each student participates daily in organized sports, and Miss Porter's features numerous playing fields and courts, including eight tennis courts, an athletics center with two gyms, an indoor track, three squash courts, a weight room, basketball and volleyball courts. Riding stables are also available nearby.

Extracurricular Activities: Miss Porter's provides many opportunities for cultural and recreational entertainment, including concerts, art exhibits, speakers, poetry readings, and drama productions. Extracurricular organizations offered include Salmagundy school newspaper, Daeges Eage yearbook, Chautauqua expository writing, Haggis Baggis creative writing, French, Spanish, Archives school history, Glee clubs; Debate Team; Concordia social services; Stagecrafters and Players drama group, and Watu Wazuri multicultural organization. Students also operate a radio station, which broadcasts on the campus. Theater performances are staged three times a year, and annual held events include Parents' Weekend, Spring Musical, Grandparents' Day, and Graduation. A variety of weekend activities include dances, movies, theater performances, special dinners, and concerts.

Campus: Miss Porter's School (MPS) is located in the town of Farmington, 9 miles from Hartford, Connecticut. The 50-acre campus is conveniently located near the town center. The school is surrounded by woods and fields and is a short walk from the Farmington River. The nearby city of Hartford offers a wide variety of cultural resources and both New York City and Boston are within driving distance for social, cultural, and athletic events. Miss Porter's classroom buildings include the Hamilton Building for English and history studies, the Ann Whitney Olin Center for the Arts and Sciences, a modern theater/gymnasium complex for athletics and performing arts, the Dance Barn, the foreign languages building featuring a state-of-the-art language laboratory and classrooms for foreign language instruction, and a library with more than 20,000 volumes. The dining room and administrative offices are located in Main Building, which also features a student snack bar. The campus has a bookstore, and a student health center staffed by registered nurses with a physician on call 24 hours a day.

Dormitories: Miss Porter's has 9 dormitories, many of which were once elegant private homes. They are supervised by House Directors, many of whom are couples with children.

Nearest International Airport: Bradley International Airport, Hartford, CT.

Nearby Lodgings: Avon Old Farms Hotel, 860-677-1651; Centennial Inn, 860-677-4647; The Farmington Inn, 860-677-2821; Farmington Marriott Hotel, 860-678-1000.

The Northwest School

Location: Seattle, Washington (U.S. West Coast, Pacific Northwest)

1415 Summit Avenue, Seattle, WA 98122
Phone: 206-328-1129, ext. 18 or 19; Fax: 206-328-1776
Website: international.northwestschool.org/start.html
Email: gek.stevens@northwestschool.org

Ms. Gek Stevens
Director of International Programs and Boarding Admission
Phone: 206-682-7309; Fax: 206 328-1776
Email: gek.stevens@northwestschool.org

Mission Statement: The Northwest School offers a faculty who engage each student in sequential, cross-disciplinary study in the Humanities, Sciences, and Performing and Fine Arts. Faculty, trustees and parents are committed to bringing together a diverse group of students to work in an atmosphere of respect for themselves, their teachers and the environment. Our students graduate with historical, scientific, artistic and international perspective, enabling them to think and act with integrity.

Admission Requirements for International Students: International students seeking admission to The NWS must have a strong desire for serious study. Those who apply to our Regular College Preparatory Program must score at least 540 on the paper TOEFL or 205 on the computer-based TOEFL before we begin to consider the applicant for acceptance. The Northwest School is strongly college preparatory and academically rigorous. Virtually all our seniors are accepted into competitive colleges because they have been well prepared in our program.

Grade Level: 9-12.

Student Gender: Boys & Girls.

Enrollment: 429 students, 209 boys, 220 girls, 45 boarders, 384 day, 50 International Program.

International Students: The school has a uniquely international character; the fact that 18% of its population comes from 14 countries gives students a truly global perspective.

Accredited by: PNAIS

Head of School: Ellen Taussig

Faculty: At The NWS, teachers pursue their disciplines, artists practice their arts. They share their inspiration with students through lectures, discussion seminars, one-on-one tutorials, performing ensembles, theater groups, and studio instruction. Teachers are mentors and allies in the academic adventure. In their daily treatment of students, they also are powerful role models who bring to life the school's culture of respect for the individual and for the community.

Tuition: Tuition and Boarding for 2003-2004 is $18,935.

Class Size: 12 to 18 students, with a student-teacher ratio of 9 to 1.

Curriculum: Discovery, synthesis, critical thinking and clear articulation are the goals of academic studies at The NWS. Students analyze facts and concepts to discover and integrate new relationships for themselves. They wrestle with the classic themes they encounter in each area of study. Surrounded by an atmosphere of passion for learning and exuberant participation in all aspects of the school's curriculum, students explore far beyond what they already know about the world and themselves.

Because the artist-teachers of The NWS take joy in their own arts, they believe that every student will gain by direct experience in all four art forms. Required classes in Music, Dance, Theater and Visual Arts allow students to develop self-discipline and self-esteem. Performances in concerts, plays and arts festivals become community events in which students celebrate and support each other.

We also have a well-regarded International College Preparatory Program for non-native English speakers (see details below.)

Advanced Placement: We do not offer advanced placement courses. We believe that our curriculum is sufficiently rigorous for students who are aspiring to attend reputable colleges and universities in the

U.S.A. Our college acceptance record supports our philosophy.

ESL Program: The NWS has a well-regarded International College Preparatory Program for non-native English speakers who have studied the language for at least three years. Students in this program increase their English proficiency while immersed in a content-based curriculum that allows them to earn academic credits towards graduation. Whether taking courses in the regular or international college preparatory program students participate equally in all other aspects of community life and assume the same responsibilities as their U.S. classmates: They lead environment teams, they mentor younger students, they participate in all grade level activities and are expected to be fully contributing members of The NWS community.

SAT: We do not tabulate SAT scores. Our college acceptance record confirms for us that our graduates are not handicapped by our policy.

College Placement: Recent graduates of the Northwest School have been accepted at Art Institute of Chicago, Boston University, Brown University, Bryn Mawr College, California College of Arts and Crafts, Columbia University, Cornell University, Dartmouth College, Duke University, George Washington University, Harvard and Radcliffe Colleges, Johns Hopkins University, Julliard School, MIT, New York University, Parsons School of Design, Princeton University, San Francisco Art Institute, Sarah Lawrence College, Smith College, Stanford University, University of Pennsylvania, Vassar College, Wellesley College, and Yale University.

Sports: A variety of sports teams, including Girls' and Boys' Soccer, Basketball, Cross Country, and Crew take part in league competition. Several NWS teams have won division titles. Camaraderie sets the tone for PE classes in team and individual sports such as rock climbing, Aikido, swimming, racquet games, soccer, basketball, cross country, and rowing.

Extracurricular Activities: Weekly community meetings bring the whole school together to listen to each other and to outside speakers. Students can join interest groups such as peer-mentoring, the Outdoor Program, the Latin Club, and Kibali, which addresses issues of diversity. Student publications, class activities, and community service projects offer other opportunities to get involved.

Campus: We are located in the heart of Seattle on a quiet, tree-lined street just above downtown. The School is housed in the 1905 Summit School Building and is listed on the National Historic Register. Our beautiful old building, whose ample spaces are rooted in tradition, provides an environment of warmth and character, engendering respect for the past and confidence in the future.

Dormitories: At the NWS, we always encourage friendships and group activities. Just a minute's walk from campus, the dormitory, which houses approximately 50 students, was renovated in 1988 from a classic 1915 building. Inside you will find student rooms, common living areas, a laundry room, bathroom and shower facilities, cable television and a small kitchen area. A dormitory director and resident advisors professionally supervise the dormitory and boys and girls live on separate floors. Our staff matches roommates by gender and age, and from different countries, as the opportunity to make new friends from around the world will enhance The NWS experience. Boarding students are expected to join two sports a year, attend a minimum number of extra-curricular activities and events and participate in occasional all-dormitory excursions to build community. Because of our small size, the residential program is run more like a large family than an institutional facility.

Nearest International Airport: Seattle International Airport, Seattle Washington.

Nearby Lodgings: Summerfield Suites by Wyndam, 206-682-8282; Executive Inn, 206-448-9444; Paramount Hotel, 206-292-9500; Roosevelt Hotel, 206-621-1200.

Oak Grove School

Location: Ojai, California (U.S. West Coast, Southern California)

220 West Lomita Avenue, Ojai, CA 93023
Phone: 805-646-8236; Fax: 805-646-6509
Website: www.oakgroveschool.com
Email: enroll@oakgroveschool.com

Ms. Ellen Sklarz Shapiro, Admission Director
Phone: 805-646-8236 ext. 102; Fax: 805-646-6509
Email: enroll@oakgroveschool.com

Mission Statement: Oak Grove is a place where graduates not only acquire the academic foundation for college but also develop a global view, a sensitivity toward the environment, and investigate the nature of their own thinking. Serious inquiry and questioning are considered vital as is a balanced and holistic approach to living. The intent of the Oak Grove School is for students to develop the skills necessary to function in the modern world, and at the same time to develop a foundation for inquiry into perennial questions of human life. Consistent with the views of its founder, J. Krishnamurti, the school does not subscribe to any creed or ideology. Rather, it assists students in the open-minded investigation of enduring human issues. Krishnamurti said about the school, "The school is concerned with freedom and order. Freedom is not the expression of one's own desire, choice or self-interest. That inevitably leads to disorder. Freedom of choice is not freedom, though it may appear so; nor is order, conformity, or imitation. Order can only come with the insight that to choose is itself the denial of freedom. In school one learns the importance of relationship which is not based on attachment and possession. It is here one can learn about the movement of thought, love and death, for all this is our life. From the ancient of times, man has sought something beyond the materialistic world, something immeasurable, something sacred. It is the intent of this school to inquire into this possibility."

Grade Level: 9-12.

Student Gender: Boys & Girls.

Enrollment: 15 boys, 28 girls, 8 boarders, 35 day.

Accredited by: WASC

Faculty: Oak Grove has a faculty of 7 teachers and 6 elective specialists. Oak Grove's experienced and creative teachers share a distinctive approach to all academic subjects. An inherent interest in the spirit of inquiry naturally translates into innovative and exciting curriculum development. Education is experienced in its broadest context, where both teacher and student are free to investigate, question, respond to ideas, and talk together in friendly conversation about the material they are learning. Students are able to develop a strong foundation in communication, reasoning, speculation, and problem solving in an environment of genuine affection and support.

Tuition: Tuition and Boarding for 2003-2004 is $27,650, ($32,950 with ESL).

Curriculum: Oak Grove provides an engaging college preparatory program while striving to develop in each student a self-reflective capacity that leads to honesty, independence, and integrity. A foundation in English, Math, Science, Social Studies, and Foreign Language is enriched by art and life skill classes. In addition, all students benefit from complementary programs in human relationship, physical education, sports, outdoor education, community service, and travel. An essential aspect of student life at Oak Grove High School is the underlying curriculum that asks students and staff to study a most intriguing subject—themselves. Students are given the opportunity to explore a broad spectrum of subjects including psychology, philosophy, culture, interpersonal relationship, and the nature of our human condition. Developing a capacity for serious inquiry and questioning are considered vital for academic work as well as for a balanced and holistic approach to living.

Advanced Placement: Advanced Placement courses are offered according to student requests and need. Recent offerings include Computer Sciene, Permaculture, Personal Fitness, Studio Art, Ceramics, Photography and Music.

ESL Program: Strong emphasis at Oak Grove School is communication in its broadest and deepest sense. In order to facilitate cross-cultural communication, Oak Grov accepts students of all nationalities in an English as a Second Language program. ESL is only available for students entering 9th grade. Students must possess an advanced level of English proficiency to be considered for enrollment. During the transition year of 9th grade, students are prepared to enter the college preparatory 10th grade the following year. In addition to the academic and ESL classes, students are offered the electives, sports, and life skill classes that all students participate in. The primary goal of the ESL program is to give students competence in spoken and written English enabling them to freely express themselves in the school and in the community. The program encourages communication and the development of friendly relationships between students of different cultures and backgrounds. No more than two or three students speak the same native language to encourage English as the only language spoken. The multi-cultural environment creates an exciting learning experience. In addition, the curriculum provides a foundation for a successful completion of a college preparatory high school. Utilizing the language acquisition approach of TPR (Total Physical Response), students learn to speak English through movement, mime and storytelling. Focusing on speaking and writing in English, students learn English in a safe and fun learning environment.

Average SAT Scores of Graduating Students: The SAT mean scores are Verbal 587, Math 647.

College Placement: Recent Graduates of Oak Grove have been accepted at Bard, Barnard, Bates, Brown, California Polytechnic, Columbia, Lewis and Clark, Mills, Oberlin, Occidntal, Pepperdine, Pitser, Pomona, Sarah Lawrence, Scripps, Stanford, Wellesley, Wesleyan, Vassar and all University of California campuses.

Academic Requirements: 4 years of English, 4 years of History and Social Studies, 3 years of Math, 3 years of Science, 3 years of the Arts, 2 years of Foreign Language,

Sports: A variety of team sports are available through participation in the California Interscholastic Federation. Ok Grove is a member of the Condor League, a group of nine independent schools in Ventura, Santa Barbara Counties. The school offers teams in volleyball, soccer lacrosse, basketball and baseball. All students participate in physical education that includes fitness, cooperative games, skill development, physical challenges, sportsmanship dynamics, and health curriculum reading.

Extracurricular Activities: Extracurricular activities include trips to Santa Barbara, Ventura, or Los Angeles for shopping, movies, museums, festivals and community events. The School also hosts concerts, dances, and other community events on campus.

Campus: Founded by internationally recognized author J. Krishnamurti, Oak Grove is located in Ojai California, fifteen minutes from the Pacific Ocean at Ventura. Santa Brbara is a short drive north and Los Angeles is an hour and a half south. The small town of Ojai and the Los Padres National Forest provide a beautiful and culturally exciting environment for students and their families. The campus consists of 150 acres of oak woodland ad buildings of award-winning architecture. Oak Grove's Main House includes a comfortable meeting room with a fireplace, administrative offices and he campus' main kitchen facility where vegetarian lunches are served on week days using produce from the school's large organic garden. Students also have easy access to numerous hiking and biking trails. Computers are available for student use at Besant House and at the school.

Dormitories: Boarders at Oak Grove enjoy a family-style vegetarian atmosphere, art facilities, recording studio, PC/i-Mac labs, and ESL, if needed. Boarding students reside at Besant House, a co-ed, family-style dorm for 15 high school students. A private room is provided to each boarding student. Besant House is cooperative living adventure that requires a responsible and respectful attitude from everyone. The focus of Ok Grove's boarding program is to consider a balanced approach to living by examining our relationship o the environment and o each other. Besant House functions like a large family, depending on open and honest communication between all members. Weekly meetings and Council Talks facilitate communication. Healthy vegetarian meals and snacks are a basic component of life at Besant House, as is daily study and quiet time. Residents take personal responsibility for their behavior and schoolwork maintain their rooms, do their own laundry and participate in house chores. Facilities include a living room, study, kitchen, dining room and laundry facilities. An outdoor patio area provides additional recreational space for ping-pong and other games. Oak Grove's soccer field and tennis and basketball courts are adjacent to Besant House.

Nearest International Airport: Los Angeles International Airport.

Nearby Lodgings: The Blue Iguana and Emerald Iguana Inns, 805-646-5277; Casa Ojai - Best Western, 800-225-8175; Hummingbird Inn, 800-228-3744; The Moon's Nest Inn, 805-646-6635; Oakridge Inn, 805-649-4018; Ojai Valley Inn & Spa, 805-646-5511; Rose Garden Inn, 805-646-1434; Theodore Woolsey House, 805-646-9779.

Oakwood Friends School

Location: Poughkeepsie, New York (U.S. East Coast, New England)

22 Spackenkill Road, Poughkeepsie, NY 12603
Phone: 845-462-4200; Fax: 845-462-4251
Website: www.oakwoodfriends.org
Email: admissions@oakwoodfriends.org

Mr. Robert Suphan, Director of Admission
Phone: 845-462-4200; Fax: 845-462-4251
Email: bsuphan@oakwoodfriends.org

Mission Statement: Oakwood Friends School, guided by Quaker principles, educates and strengthens young people for lives of conscience, compassion and accomplishment. Students experience a challenging curriculum within a diverse community, dedicated to nurturing the spirit, the scholar, the artist and the athlete in each person.

Grade Level: 9-12.

Student Gender: Boys & Girls.

Enrollment: 167 students, 88 boys, 79 girls, 41 boarders, 126 day.

International Students: 8%

Accredited by: NYSAIS

Head of School: Peter F. Baily, Earlham College, Nasson College (B.A., M.E.), Bryn Mawr College (M.A.).

Faculty: There are 20 full-time teachers and 12 administrators, most of whom reside on campus. 38 have baccalaureate degrees and 23 have advanced degrees. Oakwood hires teachers based on the depth of their academic background, their extensive teaching experience, agreement with the school's philosophy, and the capacity to support the intellectual, personal, and social growth of its students. Faculty members also serve as student advisers, and many supervise activities or serve as coaches.

Tuition: Tuition and Boarding for 2003-2004 is $29,060.

Curriculum: We offer a progressively challenging college-preparatory curriculum, in which students are placed according to their ability in mathematics and foreign language. By their senior year, students may advance to college-equivalent classes. Elective classes include vocal ensemble, jazz ensemble, music theory, musical production, art history, music history, drawing, painting, printmaking, playwriting, directing, ceramics, photography, drama, portfolio, algebra, pre-calculus, writing seminar, chemistry, biology, and physics. Independent or accelerated study may be arranged for advanced students.

Advanced Placement: Advanced Placement courses are available in art, English, French, Spanish, calculus, and biology.

ESL Program: Oakwood is a microcosm of the world. Many cultures, languages, religions and ethnicities are represented in our community. This speaks to our commitment to diversity. In living and learning with people from backgrounds different from one's own experience, lives are enhanced and perspectives are enriched. Special needs of international students are addressed through our International Student Advisor.

Students whose native language is not English are given a placement test during the interview process. Results of this test will determine whether the student will be able to manage Oakwood's rigorous and demanding college preparatory curriculum. It may be determined that the student needs additional language training through the American Language Academy (ALA) or another intensive English language training program. Oakwood is fortunate to be one of two secondary schools in the United States to have the privilege of hosting the ALA. ALA is an intensive English language training program which is available to qualified Oakwood applicants who have not yet reached the English proficiency entrance requirements. Upon successful completion of the ALA program, students can then apply for admission to Oakwood.

College Placement: Recent graduates of Oakwood have been accepted to Marymount, NYU, Northeastern, Smith, St. Mary 's of California, SUNY at Buffalo, Syracuse and the University of Chicago.

Academic Requirements: 4 credits of English, 3 credits of Math, 4 credits of History, 3 credits of Foreign Language, 3 credits of Science, 1.3 credits of Visual & Performing Arts, ½ credit of Health, 1/3 credit of Quakerism, 1/3 credit of Computer, 4 years of Electives and Physical Education. Total credits required 19.4.

A unified year-long senior program is the final requirement for graduation, which begins with a camping trip to the Adirondacks and continues through process of personal and group goal-setting at weekly Core Group meetings. The focus of the program is provided by challenging courses on topics such as 21st century moral dilemmas, comparative political systems and geopolitical studies, comparative religion, and classic film and literature.

Sports: Oakwood's Physical Education Program emphasizes participation. Several levels of interscholastic sports opportunities allow all students to enjoy the excitement, discipline and camaraderie of team play. We are members of the Hudson Valley Athletic League and the Western New England Preparatory School Athletic Association. All students are required to participate in one team sport. Most students, however, choose to participate on teams all three trimesters. There are levels appropriate for all students allowing those who are particularly talented in athletics and those who have never played on a team to share equally. Interscholastic Teams includes Cross Country, Soccer, Volleyball, Basketball, Swimming, Baseball, Softball, and Tennis. Other athletic courses include Yoga, Table Tennis, Aerobics, Martial Arts, Running, and Fitness.

Extracurricular Activities: each student is required to participate in one extracurricular activity per year. The students produce two dramatic performances and one musical. Other activities include: the yearbook, photography, choral performance, drama, instrumental groups, cabaret and the school newsletter. Weekends are relaxed at Oakwood. Each weekend has scheduled, supervised activities ranging from hikes in the Catskill Mountains to Broadway shows, and students may pick and choose those that interest them. Or, they may choose to spend time shopping, seeing a movie, catching up on homework or just hanging out with friends on campus. Most campus facilities are open on weekends, including the gym, ceramics lab and music room. Special weekend activities such as coffeehouses, dances and trips to New York City are open to both day and boarding students. The senior year also includes an off-campus community service program in which students volunteer at the project of their choice one day a week.

Campus: Oakwood is located in New York's historic Hudson River Valley, where views of the river and Shawngunk Mountains to the west inspired many 19th century painters. Although stores and restaurants are nearby on Route 9, the campus retains the pastoral ambiance of its farmland origins. Acres of well-trimmed lawns and stately maple trees line the entrance to the campus. The buildings are situated well off the main roadway in a comfortable, quiet, and secure environment. The main building houses administrative offices, the meeting room, four classrooms, the art room, the ceramics studio, the dance studio, and the infirmary. Stokes and Crowley classroom buildings contain Middle School classrooms and a lounge. The Turner Math and Science Building has state-of-the-art biology, chemistry, and physics laboratories. Collins Library contains 12,000 volumes and a computer laboratory with eighteen Intel-based systems in a local area network with Internet connections. Lane Auditorium provides the performing arts facilities, including two music studios. Craig dormitory includes a darkroom and photography classroom. Connor Gymnasium has basketball courts, volleyball courts, and a weight room. Boys' and girls' playing fields include soccer and baseball, as well four tennis courts.

Dormitories: Oakwood has one dormitory. Although it is co-ed, there are appropriate guidelines for visitation, study halls and activities. Dorm life is a special part of the Oakwood experience. It is here that one can be independent within a structure, live next door to best friends and down the hall from a teacher, but more importantly, learn what it takes to live harmoniously with a group of people from diverse backgrounds. Our dormitory has a resident adult on each floor. The dorm is also staffed with student proctors who serve as peer counselors - helping with homework, mediating disputes, or just sharing student concerns. Evening study hall provides an important opportunity to concentrate on homework. Weeknight study halls are held from 7:00-9:00 P.M.

Nearest International Airport: JFK International Airport, New York.

Ojai Valley School

Location: Ojai, California (U.S. West Coast, Southern California)

723 El Paseo Road, Ojai, CA 93023
Phone: 805-646-1423; Fax: 805-646-0362
Website: www.ovs.org; Email: info@ovs.org

Mr. John Williamson, Director of Admission
Phone: 805-646-1423; Fax: 805-646-0362; Email: jhw@ovs.org

Mission Statement: The philosophy of Ojai Valley School is contained in the motto: "Integer Vitae" - meaning wholeness of life, symmetry of life, soundness of life, and, therefore, poise and strength of life. To accommodate the school philosophy every effort is made to create an atmosphere for students and staff which is conducive to learning and growing through the framework of a warm family environment. Guided by this stated philosophy, OVS has as its goals and objectives the development of each student's character through the advantageous use of Ojai's natural surroundings, its diverse educational community and through a strong, professional staff. More specifically, the goals and objectives for each student are outlined in the school philosophy as follows: Wholeness of Life - OVS students are presented with a wide variety of experiences through college and university preparatory studies, campus life, educational field trips, student activities, athletic programs, outdoor education and camping. These activities allow students to explore the extent of their interests and abilities, to know themselves, and to develop an appreciation and respect for other people. Symmetry of Life - OVS students are exposed to a well balanced program, both academic and social, with consistent standards set for each discipline and activity. Soundness of Life - Towards the development of character, OVS students are given responsibilities which relate to their personal lives and to school affairs. Students have an opportunity to learn, perhaps to fail and to try again. With staff support and guidance, students begin to develop the knowledge and strength needed to make sound judgments. By the time OVS students are ready to graduate, they will have developed the academic strength, the character, and the self-confidence, to meet life's future challenges.

Admission Requirements for International Students: Application, Transcripts, TOEFL or SLEP test results, Personal Interview or Phone Interview, Writing Sample, Affidavit of Support, and Teacher Rrecommendations.

Grade Level: 3-12.

Student Gender: Boys & Girls.

Enrollment: 398 students, 193 boys, 205 girls, 190 boarders, 208 day.

Accredited by: WASC, CAIS/CA

Head of School: Carl S. Cooper, OVS Class of 1968, B.A. California State University, Northridge, M.Ed. California Lutheran University.

Michael Hall-Mounsey, Headmaster of the Lower, St. Paul's College, Bristol University, King Alfred's College, Winchester, England, M.Ed. California Lutheran University.

Faculty: Faculty are recognized for their nurturing attention to the individual. OVS employs a faculty of 55 full-time and part-time instructors, 22 of whom teach at the Upper School, 8 hold advanced degrees. The Upper and Lower Schools have their own headmasters. Students are also assigned faculty advisers who meet them on a weekly basis. Faculty also act as activities leaders and off-campus trip supervisors.

Tuition: Tuition and Boarding for 2003-2004 is $32,600.

Class Size: 12-16 students, with a 1:5 faculty-to-student ratio.

Curriculum: Since 1962, OVS Upper School has given young men and women a curriculum for life based on the school's motto Integer Vitae which means "Integrated Life". What does that mean for you? A challenging college preparatory curriculum, overnight camping trips, fine and performing arts, team sports, horseback riding and variety of exciting extracurricular activities. One of the attractive features of the Upper School is that it is small, and that each student has considerable opportunity for individual attention and growth. OVS knows you face a challenging, competitive world.

Our goal is to help you succeed, to be happy and productive while also caring about the world around you. College is probably on your mind, and the OVS curriculum can give you the tools you need to make it in the college of your choice. With a 1:5 faculty-to-student ratio and fewer than 12-16 students per class, your teachers will know you as an individual. An OVS education will give you the academic edge, individualized attention, and motivating environment you need to succeed in life.

Advanced Placement: courses are available in English, French, Spanish, biology, chemistry, math, music theory, and studio art.

ESL Program: International students comprise 20% of the student body at OVS, bringing diversity and a world perspective to daily life. English as a Second Language (ESL) programs are available throughout the year to students of all ages and proficiency levels. International students working on their English skills find OVS's nurturing, safe, and warm environment ideal for mastering a new language while embracing a different culture and lifestyle. Many international students ages 8 to 18 attend the August English Language Camp, a 4-week program which offers intensive English instruction with teachers and peer tutors, recreational activities, and trips to southern California theme parks.

Average SAT Scores of Graduating Students: Verbal 587, Math 600.

College Placement: Boston University, Brown University, California State University, Cornell University, George Washington University, Purdue University, Rhode Island School of Design, Seattle University, Syracuse University, Stanford, Cal Tech, Johns Hopkins, New York University, Tufts University and University of California (Berkeley, Davis, Los Angeles, Riverside, Santa Barbara and Santa Cruz).

Academic Requirements: Graduation requirements for students in the Upper School (grades 9–12) include 4 years of English, 3 years of a foreign language, 3 years of history, 3 years of mathematics, 2 years of laboratory science, 1 year of fine arts, and 1 additional year of credit.

Sports: Team sports include soccer, volleyball, baseball, softball, basketball, lacrosse, track, cross-country, tennis, and equestrian events. Recreational sports include aerobics, yoga, fitness programs, cycling and mountain biking, weight training, fencing, karate, surfing, swimming, ocean kayaking, bowling, rappelling, skiing, skating, and golf.

Extracurricular Activities: School is more than class work at OVS. All students are expected to participate in community service. We also offer an exciting variety of extracurricular activities: performing arts, yearbook, swimming, fine arts, computers, ropes course, rock climbing, and fencing, to name but a few. Team sports, such as soccer, lacrosse, tennis, basketball, baseball, cross-country, and volleyball, are an important part of OVS life, as is our acclaimed competitive Equestrian Program. In addition, a variety of weekend activities are planned throughout the year and students have the opportunity to participate in travel during school breaks and for special studies.

OVS Upper Students use weekends to surf at area beaches, step out at school dances, enjoy "town-time" in Ojai, and shop in Santa Barbara. Weekend outings have included movies, Karaoke singing, Magic Mountain, Disneyland, Raging Waters Park, Universal Studios and City Walk, fishing, camping, rock climbing, skating, concerts, and museums. In addition to scheduled events, small groups of teachers and students take impromptu trips. When homework's done, there 's plenty of fun!

Campus: OVS Upper School is located in a spectacular setting of orange groves and horse ranches just five miles from the village of Ojai, a short drive away are incredible hiking trails, the beach, and the city of Santa Barbara. The city of Ojai (population 8,000) is a rural resort community surrouned by the Los Padres National Forest. It is located 70 miles north of Los Angeles, 15 miles inland from the coastal city of Ventura.

Upper School campus facilities include Wallace Burr Hall which houses eight school classrooms, a library, computer lab, science lab, and tutoring room. The Upper school also includes a separate Fine arts and photography studio.

Lower School facilities include six elementary classrooms, five junior high classrooms, an ESL classroom, a science lab, a library, and a technology center with a computer room and language lab. Each classroom also has its own computer.

Dormitories: Think dorms and you think of rows of beds in a long room? Not at OVS. Our dorms are actually small group housing units. Resident supervisors make them warm and home-like, safe and supportive. In addition, OVS has delicious food. Our bakery features homemade breads, cakes, and cookies. There is also a dress dinner held weekly. Weekends are filled with special activities from trips to Santa Barbara to concerts to backpacking.

Nearest International Airport: Los Angeles International Airport.

Nearby Lodgings: Ojai Valley Inn & Spa, 805-646-5511; Hummingbird Inn, 805-646-4365; Rose Garden Inn, 805-646-1434; Holiday Inn Ventura, 805-648-7731.

Perkiomen School

Location: Pennsburg, Pennsylvania (U.S. East Coast, New England)

200 Seminary Ave., P.O. Box 130, Pennsburg, PA 18073
Phone: 215-679-9511; Fax: 215-679-1146
Website: www.perkiomen.org; Email: cdougherty@perkiomen.org

Mrs. Carol Dougherty, Assistant Head of School
Phone: 215-679-9511; Fax: 215-679-1146
Email: cdougherty@perkiomen.org

Mission Statement: As a school, Perkiomen strives to develop individuals who appreciate learning, and who work to acquire the skills necessary to learn. We endeavor to develop an inquisitive student who knows how to set appropriate goals, and who can work independently once those goals are established. Our environment provides support and challenge.

Grade Level: 7-12.

Student Gender: Boys & Girls.

Enrollment: 160 boys, 110 girls, 150 boarders, 120 day.

International Students: 20%, from countries including Canada, China, Hong Kong, Indonesia, Japan, Korea, Russia, Saudi Arabia, Spain, Taiwan, and Thailand.

Accredited by: MSACS

Head of School: George K. Allison, A.B., Union College, M.A., Trinity College. Email: gallison@perkiomen.org

Faculty: Perkomien School has a faculty of 41 full time teachers, 32 of whom reside on campus. 40 hold baccalaureate degrees and 21 hold advanced degrees. All instructors must be academically qualified as well as athletically qualified for coaching sports and coordinating extracurricular activities. Every teacher also serves as an adviser for up to 8 students.

Tuition: Tuition and Boarding for 2003-2004 is $31,200.

Class Size: 7:1 student/teacher ratio.

Curriculum: The academic program at Perkiomen School offers students in grades 5 through 12 and postgraduates a structured and challenging college preparatory program. In the process of developing a community conscious individual, a concerted effort is directed toward nurturing and sustaining an appreciation of learning. Within our structured and traditional environment, we seek to develop an inquisitive student who can work independently after goals have been established and procedures outlined.

The Upper School curriculum prepares students for challenging college programs. Each student carries five major courses and the required minor courses. A sixth major course may be elected only with the permission of the Director of Studies. Senior year students must attend all classes on campus. In order to graduate, students must accumulate a minimum of 19 academic credits distributed as follows for an Advanced Academic Diploma:

Advanced Placement: The curriculum is college preparatory, offering Honors and Advanced Placement courses in all academic departments.

Average SAT Scores of Graduating Students: Verbal 533, Math 529, Total 1062.

College Placement: Recent graduates of Perkiomen have been accepted to St. Mary 's College of California, American University, Bryn Mawr College, Temple University, University of Massachusetts, Loyola University New Orleans, University of Miami, Michigan State University, Wesleyan College, and Penn State University.

Academic Requirements: English (4 units), Social Studies (2 units), United States History (1 unit), Laboratory Science (2 units), Algebra (2 units), Geometry (1 unit), Foreign Language (3 units), Fine Arts (1 unit), Electives (3 units).

Sports: Athletic teams and courses offered are Cross Country, Field Hockey, Football, Golf, Soccer, Tennis, Basketball, Cheerleading, Power Lifting, Swimming, Tae Kwon Do, Wrestling, Baseball,

Lacrosse, and Softball.

Extracurricular Activities: Perkiomen believes in providing students with an excellent education within the classroom as well as beyond the classroom. At Perkiomen, students have a wide variety of extracurricular activities from which to choose. These clubs and organizations are lead by faculty members and the students who are involved. Some of these extra-curricular activities are Amnesty International, Chess Clubk, Debate Team, Environmental Club, French Club, Griffin (yearbook), History Club, International Club, Middle School Eye (newspaper), Middle School Senate, National Honor Society, Palantir (literary magazine), Perkiomenite (newspaper), S.A.D.D., Spanish Club, Student Senate and Thespian Society. Each year, the students produce 3 plays, and a musical revue. Musical activities include chorus, show choir, band, and jazz combo.

Weekend activities offer many recreational opportunities both on and off campus. The student center, the gymnasiums, and the pool are open for use on weekends and planned activities include movies, dances, athletic events, theater productions, and special entertainment. Nearby restaurants, stores, and a movie theater are within walking distance of the school, and students often take trips to go skiing, hiking, horseback riding, and skating. They also visit historic sites and museums; attend concerts and other cultural and sporting events; and go shopping in nearby malls. Speakers, concerts, and fine arts exhibits are featured on campus, and trips to New York City, Baltimore, and Philadelphia are organized to provide a variety of cultural opportunities.

Campus: Perkomien School is located in the small town of Pennsburg, Pennsylvania, surrounded by open space and farm land. Although the campus is removed from the distractions and potential dangers of large cities, it is not isolated. Philadelphia is just over 50 miles away and New York, Baltimore and Washington DC are also within easy driving distance for school outings. The nearby Pocono Mountains offer popular destinations for weekend fishing, white water rafting, skiing and other outdoor activities. The hub of the campus is Kriebel Hall, the original school building which has recently undergone a modernization. It houses Upper School boys' dorm rooms, faculty apartments, classrooms, chapel, administrative offices, an academic hall, lounge, and a state-of-the-art computer center. Other buildings include Carnegie Library, Kehs Hall, the fine arts center ad art gallery; Parents Hall, the school dining hall; five dormitories; a science center; a health center; numerous faculty houses; a gymnasium with swimming pool and weight room; tennis courts; and playing fields for baseball, field hockey, football, lacrosse, softball and soccer.

Dormitories: Perkiomen's campus has five dormitories. The dorms are single sex (three male dorms, two female dorms) and all dorm rooms are doubles. Each room is wired with two phone lines and two data jacks. Faculty members live in the dormitories to provide supervision, structure and extra help. An extensive weekend activity program offers four to six activities each weekend. The movies and mall trips are the most popular events. Also, professional sporting events and cultural events are frequent offerings. New York, Philadelphia and Washington, D.C. are all easily accessible for day trips.

Nearest International Airport: Philadelphia International Airport.

Nearby Lodgings: Globe Hotel, 215-679-5948; Hampton Inn, 215-536-7779; Holiday Inn Express, 215-529-7979; Rodeway Inn, 215-536-7600.

Phillips Academy Andover

Location: Andover, Massachusetts (U.S. East Coast, New England)

180 Main Street, Andover, MA 01810-4161
Phone: 978-749-4050; Fax: 978-749-4068
Website: www.andover.edu; Email: admissions@andover.edu

Mrs. Jane Fried, Dean of Admission
Phone: 978-749-4000 or 978-749-4050; Fax: 978-749-4068
Email: admissions@andover.edu

Mission Statement: Phillips Academy, a residential secondary school, seeks students of intelligence and integrity from diverse cultural, racial, socioeconomic and geographic backgrounds. The school's residential structure enables faculty to support students in their personal, social and intellectual development. The academic program fosters excellence in all disciplines within the liberal arts tradition. Faculty members guide students in mastering skills, acquiring knowledge and thinking critically, creatively and independently. The school strives to help young people achieve their potential not only intellectually, but also artistically, athletically and morally, so that they may lead responsible and fulfilling lives. The academy is committed to establishing a community that encourages people of diverse backgrounds and beliefs to understand and respect one another and to be sensitive to differences of gender, ethnicity, class and sexual orientation. In its programs the school seeks to promote a balance of leadership, cooperation and service, together with a deeper awareness of the global community and the natural world. Andover's 1778 Constitution charges the academy to prepare "Youth from every quarter" to understand that "goodness without knowledge is weak...yet knowledge without goodness is dangerous." This obligation challenges students in mind, body and spirit to see beyond themselves and to go beyond the familiar; to remain committed to developing what is finest in themselves and others, for others and themselves.

Admission Requirements for International Students: All international students must be diploma candidates. Therefore, if a student applies for the 10th grade, it is understood that the intention of this student is to remain at Phillips Academy until his/her graduation three years later. We do not entertain exchanges in the middle of the high school program.

Fluency in the English language: We do not offer any ESL courses (English as a Second Language). However, for one year seniors, we offer academic support in the form of specialized English and United States history courses.

Personal interview: If you are unable to visit our campus, you may schedule an interview with one of our Alumni Admission Representatives, located in 25 countries. If there is no alumni representative in your area, the interview may be conducted by the headmaster or principal of your current school.

Standardized testing: For students applying for grades 9-11, we require the SSAT (Secondary School Admission Test). For students applying for grade 12 or a post graduate year, we require the SAT. Students who are non-native speakers of English may choose to take the TOEFL (Test of English as a Foreign Language).

Please note that the TOEFL is designed for college-bound students. Therefore, younger students may be better off taking the SSAT rather than the TOEFL. Students are welcome to take both exams if they so desire.

Grade Level: 9-12.

Student Gender: Boys & Girls.

Enrollment: 1087 students, 536 boys, 551 girls, 785 boarders, 302 day.

International Students: 82 students from 30 countries.

Accredited by: NEASC

Head of School: Barbara L. Chase, A.B. Brown University, M.L.A. Johns Hopkins University.

Faculty: Andover has 212 faculty members, 154 full-time and 58 part time, most of whom live on campus and serve as dormitory counselors, academic advisers and/or coaches. 36 hold Ph.D.

degrees, 123 hold Master's degrees.

Tuition: Tuition and Boarding for 2003-2004 is $30,100.

Class Size: 13 students, with a student/teacher ratio: 6 to 1

Curriculum: The curriculum of Phillips Academy comprises a required core of studies believed to be fundamental to a liberal education and elective courses designed to fit the interests of the individual student. Instruction is given in all subjects usually required for entrance to higher learning institutions. The diploma requirements, chosen by and voted on by the entire faculty as essential elements of the academic program, are designed to ensure that Phillips Academy graduates successfully complete a course of study in a broad range of disciplines and skills which, in the judgment of the faculty, provide the appropriate foundation for a liberal education. The requirements are further specified as to skill level and content by the academic divisions and departments with the oversight of the Academic Council. Certain requirements vary in keeping with the length of time a student attends the academy. Classroom groups are small enough to permit individual attention, and students are placed in sections fitted to their skill level. Accelerated sequences and advanced courses offer particularly able and well-prepared students opportunity to progress at a rate commensurate with their ability and ambition. Most departments offer courses beyond the level of preparation for college. The academic year is separated into three trimesters. There are two types of weekly class schedules: one during which classes meet only Monday through Friday, and the other during which classes also meet on Saturday morning. Within a given week, classes are scheduled to meet according to varying patterns. Many departments offer yearlong courses as well as those that are term-contained (completed in one trimester). The diploma requirements are stated in terms of full-year courses or trimester courses, depending on the academic area involved.

Qualified students may join the School Year Abroad program in France, Spain, China, and Italy. Advanced language students may attend a local school in Göttingen, Germany; Burgos, Spain; Antibes, France; Kyoto, Japan; Santo Domingo, Dominican Republic;

Salamanca, Spain; and Yokohama, Japan.

Advanced Placement: A large number of Phillips Academy students take College Board Advanced Placement Tests in May to establish advanced placement in college courses or credit toward the college degree. Advanced Placement examinations are offered in American History, Art History, Art Studio (2), Biology, Chemistry, Computer Science (A and AB), Economics (2), English Language and Literature, Environmental Science, European History, French Language and Literature, German, Government and Politics (2), Latin Vergil and Literature, Mathematics (AB and BC), Music Listening, Music Theory, Physics (C), Psychology, Spanish Language and Literature, and Statistics.

ESL Program: Phillips Academy does not offer remedial courses, training in English as a Second Language (ESL), or tutoring by faculty members other than out-of-class help offered by teachers to students enrolled in their courses.

Average SAT Scores of Graduating Students: 670 verbal; 679 mathematics.

College Placement: Recent graduates of Phillips Academy Andover have been accepted to Harvard, Brown, Cornell, University of Pennsylvania, Georgetown, Princeton, Yale, Columbia, Wesleyan, Chicago, and Dartmouth.

Academic Requirements: The basic diploma requirement is the satisfactory completion of a four-year secondary school program, of which at least three trimesters must be at Andover; the student must be in good standing (not on probation or under suspension) at the time of graduation. A student who has been dismissed is ineligible for a diploma unless readmitted.

Trimester credits required for the diploma are: for entering Juniors 54, for entering Lowers 51, for entering Uppers 48, for entering Seniors 48. A student's required program includes nine trimester credits in English, nine in world languages, eight in mathematics, seven in history and social science and six (two full-year courses) in laboratory science. Details about the manner in which these requirements are to be fulfilled can be found in the opening descriptions of the departments concerned.

In order to be eligible for a diploma, all students must satisfy the swimming requirement of the Department of Physical Education. Certain diploma requirements vary with the class level at which the student enters Phillips Academy. Entering Juniors must earn two credits in art and two in music and a half credit in theatre. Entering Juniors and Lowers must pass Physical Education 100 and a one-trimester course offered by the Department of Philosophy and Religious Studies, usually inthe Lower year. Entering Lowers must earn a total of three credits in art and music, with at least one in each area. Entering Uppers need pass only one trimester of either art or music at the academy. Some modifications of the language requirement are made for entering Uppers and Seniors. Entering Seniors with no previous world language experience must pass a 195/0 course in a world language or Latin 190. A Senior must earn a minimum of 12 graded trimester credits during the Senior year. Seniors must have passing trimester grades for all courses taken during their spring trimester. Independent Projects are counted as graded courses.

Academic Guidelines: In order to promote both breadth and depth in a student's academic program, the faculty has voted the following guidelines, which are in addition to the diploma requirements listed above. These represent what the faculty strongly urges students to do. The advisers recognize that there will always be some acceptable student programs that do not follow these guidelines. All students, including Seniors, normally carry five courses each term, but students who take at least three courses designated advanced or honors courses may carry a four-course program. All Juniors and Lowers should take English, mathematics and a world language every term. By the end of Lower year, each four-year student should have taken some science. All Uppers should take English all year.

In their Upper and Senior years, students should take a total of at least four trimesters of mathematics and science, with at least one trimester in each of these two areas. All four-year students should take a year of science (a yearlong course or three terms) in addition to the two-year requirement. All Seniors should take, during each term, a course in which they do some writing in the English language. All one-year Seniors should take one term of art, music or theatre.

All three- and four-year students will be advised to take more than the minimum diploma requirements in the arts (art, music, theatre and dance).

Sports: Facilities for 30 sports include 2 hockey rinks, 2 swimming pools, 8 squash courts, 2 basketball courts, 2 dance studios, fitness center and wrestling room, 2 fully staffed training rooms; outside track, 18 playing fields, 18 tennis courts, nearby crew boathouse; indoor facilities for track, tennis and team practice. In addition to all major competitive team sports, Andover also offers dance, aerobics, yoga, kayaking, swim instruction, Search and Rescue, and many others. All students participate in daily afternoon athletics and fitness activities.

Extracurricular Activities: Andover offers many extracurricular opportunities, including numerous academic clubs such as literary and political magazines, a weekly newspaper, a campus radio station, the debate and math teams, and several drama and dance groups, and a community service program, as well as 4 orchestras, 4 choral groups, several singing groups, a concert band and a jazz band. On weekends, dances, concerts, drama productions, movies, museum exhibits and cultural events are scheduled on campus. Public transportation is also available for students who wish to attend cultural and sporting events in Boston.

Campus: The school is located 21 miles north of Boston, on a scenic hilltop in the historic town of Andover, Massachusetts. The campus facilities are comprised of 160 buildings, including the Oliver Wendell Holmes Library, fully automated, with 120,000 vols.; the Addison Gallery of American Art, with a collection of 12,000 works by such artists as Winslow Homer, Edward Hopper, Georgia O'Keefe, Jackson Pollack, and Andrew Wyeth; the Audio-Video Center & Polk-Lillard Center for video electronic imaging; the R.S. Peabody Museum of Archaeology, which houses one of the most extensive collections of Native American artifacts in the country; the Isham Health Center; the Language Learning Center; the Elson Art

Center; the Brace Center for Gender Studies; the Gelb Science Center (opening January 2004); the music center; the counseling center; the theatre complex; and the minority counseling office. The 500-acre campus also features a 125-acre bird sanctuary, a greenhouse, an FM radio station, an astronomy observatory

Dormitories: Andover has forty-three dormitories which accommodate 4 to 42 students. Larger dorms also house several faculty supervisors and their families. Single rooms are available to 1/3 of the resident students, and the other 2/3 are housed in large double rooms. All rooms are equipped with Internet access and each student is provided with an e-mail account, a private telephone line, and a personal voice mailbox.

All Andover students and faculty members are assigned to one of the school's five residential clusters, which serve as students' academic advisory, personal counseling, intramural sports, social functions, and any disciplinary measures.

Nearest International Airport: Logan International Airport, Boston.

Nearby Lodgings: Andover Inn, 978-475-5903; Andover Country Club, 978-475-1263; Courtyard by Marriott, 978-794-0700; Hawthorn Suites - Andover, 888-729-7705; Residence Inn Boston Andover Hotel, 978-683-0382; SpringHill Suites Boston/Andover Hotel, 978-688-8200; Staybridge Suites by Holiday Inn, 978-686-2000.

Rabun Gap-Nacoochee School

Location: Rabun Gap, Georgia (U.S. East Coast, Southern Central)

339 Nacoochee Drive, Rabun Gap, GA 30568-9850
Phone: 706-746-7467; Fax: 706-746-2594
Website: www.rabungap.org; Email: admission@rabungap.org

Mr. J. Timothy Martin, Director of Admission
Phone: 706-746-7467; Fax: 706-746-2594
Email: admission@rabungap.org

Ms. DaRel Christiansen, Assistant Director of Admission
Email: dchristiansen@rabungap.org

Mission Statement: To create an environment of order, truth, caring, and concern where students of diverse economic and cultural backgrounds learn to live together with new understanding, and prepare for college by beginning the habit of life-long learning, and achieve personal and spiritual development. The school motto is Work, Study, Worship. Rabun Gap is committed to Judeo-Christian values, a strong work ethic, and rigorous academic preparation in small classes. The program is broadly based by design and global in nature. It promotes personal achievement, self-esteem, a sense of community, and commitment to protecting the environment.

Admission Requirements for International Students: Application Form & Fee, Transcript, Parent Questionnaire, References Entrance Examination (Official Record Of Standardized Entrance Examination Scores, Which May Be SLEP, TOEFL or SSAT), Supplemental Information, Oral Proficiency Interview, Campus Visit & Tour (strongly encouraged, but not mandatory for application or acceptance.) Once a student is admitted we follow the procedure for issuing I-20's.

Grade Level: 7-12.

Student Gender: Boys & Girls.

Enrollment: 273 students, 127 boys, 146 girls, 126 boarders, 147 day.

International Students: 14%, from Germany, Kenya, Korea, Nigeria, Pakistan, Russia, Rwanda, Saudi Arabia, Slovakia, Spain, Taiwan, the Turks and Cacaos Islands, Uganda, and Vietnam.

Accredited by: SACS

Head of School: Gregory D. Zeigler, B.A. English, Washington and Jefferson College, M.Ed. University of Utah.

Faculty: We have about 50 teaching faculty, with more than half having earned advanced degrees. Most live on campus and often work with students outside of regular class hours. Current students and alumni both say that our caring and professional faculty is our greatest asset.

Tuition: Tuition and Boarding for 2003-2004 is $21,500.

Class Size: The maximum class size is 17 students.

Curriculum: As a college preparatory school, Rabun Gap-Nacoochee School offers an educational program designed to provide the student with a solid foundation in the liberal arts. We offer a program that will both challenge and nurture each student. We encourage natural curiosity, and by example we demonstrate that discovery and learning are lifelong pursuits.

We know that a student's total education is far more than what is learned in the classroom; however, the formal aspects of the class-room compose the core from which a student's education develops at Rabun Gap-Nacoochee School.

Our program includes core subjects, many of which have an honors section, and several elective courses for special interests. We also offer Advanced Placement (AP) courses for sophomores, juniors and seniors. Most colleges and universities grant credit for AP course work, depending on the examination grade.

Advanced Placement: Advanced Placement courses are offered in English Literature, Calculus, Biology, Chemistry, U.S. History, European History, World History, French, Spanish, Studio Art and Art History.

ESL Program: The ESL program at Rabun Gap-Nacoochee School seeks to prepare international students for entry into mainstream classes and to provide them with the working knowledge, strategies, and skills necessary to function comfortably in an American high school setting, as well as to prepare them for entry into American colleges. As students are placed in mainstream courses, they continue to be supported by the ESL program. Students placed in higher level ESL courses are taught important second language skills, grammar, and vocabulary which are not covered in courses geared toward native speakers. Effective second language acquisition is accomplished through accurate placement in level-specific, in-depth communicative classes in reading, oral/aural communication, grammar, writing and ESL history content courses. Core ESL classes (ESL I & II, World Literature) are required for all international students except where an OPI (Oral Proficiency Interview), the SLEP (Secondary Level English Proficiency) Test, or the TOEFL test indicates that a core class is not needed.

Average SAT Scores of Graduating Students: SAT Verbal Mid 50% 640-530, SAT Math Mid 50% 590-510.

College Placement: Colleges and universities to which RGNS graduates have been accepted include: Agnes Scott College, Birmingham-Southern College, Brown University, College of Charleston, Davidson College, Denison University, Dickinson College, Emory University, George Washington University, Georgia College and State University, Georgia Institute of Technology, Mary Washington College, Mount Holyoke College, Pepperdine University, Presbyterian College, Randolph-Macon Woman's College, Rhodes College, Stetson University, Tufts University, University of Georgia, University of Miami, University of North Carolina-Chapel Hill, Vanderbilt University, Wake Forest University and Yale University.

Academic Requirements: English (I-IV) 4 credits, Mathematics 4 credits, Science 3 credits (entering 9th graders will take Concepts of Physics, Biology, and 1 credit from either Chemistry or Physics), History 3 credits (entering 9th graders will take Ancient & Medieval World History, Modern World History and United States History), World Language 3 credits (the same language), Personal Fitness 1 credit (or 0.5 credit Personal Fitness and participation in 2 seasons of competitive sports), Fine Arts 2 credits (for the four-year student, or 0.5 credit per year of attendance), Bible 1 credit, and Senior Project 0.5 credit.

Sports: Athletics is an integral part of the educational experience in which we strive for excellence. All students are encouraged to participate in the athletic program, the equestrian program or the outdoor program at the level most challenging to them. The primary goal of the Athletic Department is to challenge students to grow and mature in ways that will enable them to reach their fullest potential. It is also an athletic department goal to field competitive teams, which exhibit discipline, the desire to excel, and pride in themselves and the school. Coaches work with individuals and teams to improve performance and to promote qualities of character and leadership through competitive athletics. It is our intention to promote a healthful lifestyle, to encourage daily opportunities for personal improvement, and to encourage growth and excellence through organized practices and competitions. We expect our athletes to excel in the classroom, and we expect the same excellence to be demonstrated in the effort and performance of our teams. Individual commitment and a strong sense of responsibility in all student activities are the keys to success. We feel that academic pursuits and athletics complement one another and thrive together. Rabun Gap teams compete in the Georgia High School Association. The school also competes independently to best satisfy the needs of each team. Interscholastic Sports include Soccer, Volleyball, Softball, Equestrian Show Team, Cross-Country, Basketball, Swimming, Cheerleading, Tennis, Track, Baseball, and Golf.

Extracurricular Activities: Rabun Gap students participate in a full range of interscholastic and competitive athletics, as well as a work program, outdoor program and community service. They produce the yearbook, literary magazine and newspaper and join the band, the chorus and the equestrian program, as well as a variety of service, scholastic, and artistic clubs. Once a year the entire school participates in a Shakespearean Festival and also MADFest (Music, Art, Dance and Drama).

Campus: On a 1200-acre campus in the north Georgia mountains only 2 hours from Atlanta, students pursue arts, athletics, and outdoor adventures. The 200-acre central campus on 1,400 acres of property includes: seven dormitories, upper and middle school classroom buildings, chapel, library, health center, dining hall, student center, art and music studios, industrial arts building, science labs, computer lab, gymnasium, herbarium, natatorium, 20 acre lake, all weather track, baseball and softball fields, cross country trail, tennis courts, soccer field, equestrian center, ropes course, climbing wall, and working farm. We have completed a $22 million facility improvement program including a new Arts & Technology building that contains classrooms and studios for performing, visual, graphic, and musical arts; a theater/auditorium; and a video technology facility. We have five electronic classrooms, including two exclusively for middle school use. Every student has supervised Internet and intranet access and a personal email address. Computers are available in every dorm and many classrooms. Boarding students are allowed to bring computers for use in their rooms. The library has terminals for online research and reference. We have also remodeled and redistributed the use of current spaces in order to expand the science labs, general classroom areas, administration, bookstore, archives/alumni center and have also completed construction of a new, two-story state-of-the-art library/media center. A new 'suite-style' residence hall for senior students was opened in August of 2003.

Dormitories: Every dorm has a non-teaching full time resident faculty member. The staff at Rabun Gap plan a wide variety of trips and activities for weekends, including trips to Atlanta Braves games, white water rafting, concerts and movies. Shopping trips are frequently arranged for the convenience of students. The school has an attractive student center on campus, and hosts a variety of dances and parties throughout the year. Rabun Gap parents provide birthday cakes and monthly deliveries of treats for boarders.

Nearest International Airport: Hartsfield International Airport, Atlanta, Georgia.

Nearby Lodgings: The York House, 706-746-2068; The Dillard House, 706-746-5348; Holiday Inn Express, 706-746-3585.

Southwestern Academy

Locations: San Marino, California (U.S. West Coast, Southern California) and Rimrock, Arizona (U.S. Southwest)

San Marino Campus
2800 Monterey Road, San Marino, CA 91108

Beaver Creek Ranch Campus
HC64, Box 235, Rimrock, AZ 86335
Phone: 626-799-5010; Fax: 626-799-0407
Website: www.southwesternacademy.edu
Email: admissions@southwesternacademy.edu

Mr. Alex McDavid, Director of Admissions
Phone: 626-799-5010 ext 1-205; Fax: 626-799-0407
Email: amcdavid@southwesternacademy.edu

Mission Statement: Southwestern offers and shall continue to offer programs to strengthen students through small classes - normally of eight to twelve students - with personalized lessons, achievement grouping, two unique campuses in safe environments, and especially by supporting student achievements through an involved, nurturing, caring staff who create an environment for individual student success.

Southwestern balaces enrollments by actively promoting cultural diversity and social heterogeneity in its student body. We seek to admit motivated, successful students who want smaller classes and personalized instruction. We believe also in giving a chance to students who may have experienced unsuccessful schooling elsewhere, when they have the abilities and willingness to try. We believe in giving students love and encouragement to overcome obstacles, and in providing and stimulating participation in a wide variety of activities and athletics that they might not encounter in a larger setting. We work with students who want to be here and who will help their fellow students; if a student continues to hurt the community, we will help find more appropriate placement for that student. Our staff decisions about students will be based on the assessment of each case, rather than a comparison with inflexible standards. We will work to recruit American and international students who will benefit from and add to our school.

Support and encouragement for students will be our standard in all academic and disciplinary decisions. We will work to remove obstacles from students who want to reach their full potentials, and to encourage students at each step. We will pay special attention to each individual, particularly those needing our guidance. We shall keep building our caring and loving of students, using patience and the extra time we gain because of our small class sizes. Our object is never to fail students unless they give us no choice, but to help them be successful. This takes all our best teaching skills, and we are pledged to use those skills.

Admission Requirements for International Students: Completed application and $100 application fee. 2 Letters of recommendation from current teachers or school officials. Transcripts of a student's school records for the past 3 years. Health report and immunizations. Student Visa: The I-20 application form for a student visa to enter the United States is sent by Southwestern when a student is accepted and has paid tuition.

Grade Level: 9-12.

Enrollment: 12 boys, 16 girls, 28 boarders.

Accredited by: WASC

Head of School: Kenneth Veronda, Headmaster, History, Stanford University, MA. Headmaster Kenneth Veronda was born at the San Marino campus founded by his father.

Faculty: Southwestern Academy has a faculty of 22 instructors in California and 9 in Arizona, most of whom hold advanced degrees. Each teacher acts as an advisor to several students, and an on-campus counselor is also available to assist students with college and career plans.

Tuition: Tuition and Boarding for 2003-2004 is $ 28,800.

Class Size: Student/teacher ratio is 5:1

Curriculum: Southwestern Academy is a college preparatory school for secondary grades at the San Marino Campus, and grades 9 - 12 at the Beaver Creek Ranch campus. Postgraduate students select from the curricula as needed to strengthen their skills. There is Internet access in all classrooms, libraries, and dorms. While high school classes are offered at both campuses, some specialized courses may be offered at only campus from time to time. Some classes listed may only be offered in alternate years.

ESL Program: Since 1924, Southwestern has offered high quality educational programs to bring out the best talents of each boy and girl attending. The school is fully accredited and approved for attendance by international students. Some students continue at Southwestern, and some attend for just the summer program, sometimes before entering American universities in the fall, so English skills are strengthened. Southwestern offers a friendly, caring home in America for visitors from many other countries.

International students are carefully tested shortly after arrival at Southwestern to determine their levels of English abilities in each aspect of the language. Each student is then given a schedule of classes to improve English proficiency based on our placement test results. At each level, students are assigned to appropriate high school classes, suitable to their abilities. These include mathematics, art, computer literacy and others. There are transition classes as well, including, Expository Writing, and introductions to literature and physical science, which stress vocabulary, writing and reading with a context already familiar to the students. Other transition classes, such as United States History, introduce the international student to American culture, history, and traditions.

Southwestern offers a special summer semester exclusively for international students. This fifteen week session offers an accelerated program for students to quickly improve their knowledge and use of English and to earn credits towards high school graduation. It is also possible for students to attend just the summer session for an introduction to English language and American culture. Many special daily activities are included, from baseball games at Dodger Stadium to concerts, beaches, and theme parks. The goal of the International Student Program is to mainstream each student into a regular high school program as quickly as possible. This normally takes from eighteen to twenty-four months for a beginning student who puts forth consistently good effort and attends as least one summer semester. International students are completely integrated into all school activities, sports and trips and share dormitory rooms with students from the Untied States and from other countries. Southwestern sets enrollment limits to avoid overcrowding from any one country or native language. International students are required to live on our campuses and be under our care and supervision. No "guardian" or local families are needed. The school provides the needed forms and assistance for visas to enter the United States, and meets students at Los Angeles International Airport (LAX) on arrival. Enrollment is through secondary school graduation unless a shorter term is agreed to in advance by the school. Payment must be made in advance. Payments are refunded should the United States deny the visa, but no payment is refunded if a student is withdrawn or otherwise fails to attend. Application and enrollment terms and payments are outlined in the International Student Application and Contract. Students live at the San Marino Campus, in an elegant residential area near Pasadena, ten miles from the center of Los Angeles. Meals, activities and supervision are provided each day of the week. The campus has a full range of sports and other facilities for an exciting school experience.

College Placement: Among those colleges that Southwestern graduates of the 1990's have attended are Amherst, Bennington, Boston, Brigham Young, Brown, California State Universities, Chapman, Georgetown, Lewis and Clark, Occidental, Pasadena, Pepperdine, Pitzer, Pomona Purdue, Texas Tech, West Point, Whitman, and the Universities of Arizona, California (UC, UCI, UCSB, UCSD, UCLA), Mississippi, New Orleans, Northampton, Pacific, San Francisco, Southern California, Texas, Washington, and Wisconsin.

Academic Requirements: Requirements include: four years of English; three years of mathematics; two years of a foreign language; two years of laboratory sciences; one year each of U.S. history and world cultures, plus one semester of U.S. government and economics; two years of visual/performing arts; and one semester of computer literacy.

Sports: As a member of a federated league, Southwestern offers competitive team sports at both campuses in all major sports except tackle football. Both the San Marino and Beaver Creek campuses feature gymnasiums and outdoor playing fields for physical education requirements and recreation.

Extracurricular Activities: The activities vary at the two campuses according to environment, interest and availability. Several activities are planned for each weekend throughout the year. Some of these adventures include: San Marino: visits to concerts, plays, shopping centers, amusement and theme parks, ice skating, beaches, skiing, movies, zoos, museums, hiking and camping in nearby mountains and deserts, watching baseball, hockey, soccer, football, and basketball games; golf, horseback riding, ethnic centers (Japanese, Chinese, Korean, etc.), and other places as suggested by student dorm groups. Beaver Creek: hiking, camping, golf, mountain climbing, skiing, fishing, trail biking, canoeing, water skiing, boating, swimming, horseback riding, movies, roller skating, museums, national parks, shopping trips, and other activities as suggested by a student committee.

Campus: Southwestern is a unique school. Boys and girls from across the United States and around the world prepare for university studies and a rewarding life as they receive a thorough education in a safe, supportive, caring environment at their choice of superb campuses, city and country, with summer and winter programs. The California campus is in the peaceful residential suburb of San Marino, near the world-famous Huntington Library and Pasadena, with all the the Los Angeles area cultural and recreational centers nearby. The 8.5 acre campus has full facilities for complete academic and athletic programs. Boarding boys and girls from around the world are accepted in grades 6 - 12 and for a postgraduate year when needed, while a few commuting boys and girls are also accepted. All dormitories have been recently renovated, as have the library, computer rooms, science labs and ESL facilities. The metropolitan area offers much, from skating, shopping, skiing, and Disneyland, to whale-watching cruises, plays, beaches, hikes in the local mountains, and varied concerts.

The northern Arizona campus is near the famous redrock resort community of Sedona, in the verdant valley of Beaver Creek, 100 miles north of Phoenix. The 180 acre campus has a full range of facilities, and features a heated indoor swimming pool, gym, computer lab, and well-equipped recreation room. All dorms are of modern, masonry construction. Student activities feature outdoor adventures, including camping, hiking, golf, mountain biking, and skiing.

Students in grades 9 - 12 may divide their time between campuses, and all San Marino students have opportunities for study trips to the Beaver Creek campus during the school year. Academics are coordinated between campuses. Electronic tools such as computers in each class, Internet on fast DSL lines to all our computers, CD-ROM towers, voice mail, pagers, and e-mail for all students and staff, help facilitate thorough learning, supporting dedicated teachers who have time to assist each student.

Dormitories: San Marino campus has 4 dormitories that accommodate 20 boys in double and single rooms. There are 2 off-campus dormitories located nearby that accommodate 30 girls.

Beaver Creek features 4 residence halls that accommodate 56 students. The campus includes recreation rooms, a gymnasium, several large activity fields, and an indoor, heated swimming pool. Each dormitory is supervised by a resident counselor who has an apartment adjacent to the dormitory. The counselor is responsible for the personal cleanliness and well-being of each student under his or her care. Parents and students are given a list of dorm needs before the beginning of a school term. Dorms have TVs, VCR's, and computers with Internet / e-mail access. Dorm residents organize activities, sports, and barbecues or other special meals.

Nearest International Airport: Los Angeles International Airport.

St. Andrew's School

Location: Barrington, Rhode Island (U.S. East Coast, New England)

63 Federal Road, Barrington, RI 02806
Phone: 401-246-1230; Fax: 401-246-0510
Website: www.standrews-ri.org; Email: admissions@standrews-ri.org

Mr. R. Scott Telford, Director of Admissions and Financial Aid
Phone: 401-246-1230 ext. 3025; Fax: 401-246-0510
Email: admissions@standrews-ri.org

Mission Statement: The history of St. Andrew's revolves around our mission statement that informs all that we do. We are intent on discovering ways to help students succeed in all areas of their lives including academics, athletics, and activities. Students and parents say that you cannot get lost at St. Andrew's. We are a small school with a first rate faculty and wonderful facilities that concentrates on the success of each student. When families visit they often talk about the wonderful community spirit they feel on campus.

Admission Requirements for International Students: Our admissions process for International Students is designed to help you learn more about S. Andrew's School, and for us to learn bout you. Most importantly, the results of a Secondary Level English Proficiency Test (SLEP) is required because we have to ensure that the students will be successful in our International ESL Program. To apply to St. Andrew's School, please submit an application and parent questionnaire, an application fee of $100, a student questionnaire completed by the student candidate in English in his or her own handwriting, three teacher recommendations, a transcript of grades over the last three years, and the results of a recent SLEP test.

Once the student has been accepted to St. Andrew's School, the family must designate someone to be the local guardian. The Guardian must live within three hours of the school. This person will handle all issues that would be normally handled by parents living in the U.S. Also, if a student attends St. Andrews, it is mandatory that the student be covered by ISM International Student Accident ad Health Insurance.

Grade Level: 9-12.

Student Gender: Boys & Girls.

Enrollment: 167 students, 104 boys, 63 girls, 50 boarders, 117 day.

International Students: from Germany, Bermuda, Japan, and Korea.

Accredited by: NEASC

Head of School: John D. Martin, Bachelor of Arts degree from Tufts University Master of Divinity Yale University, Master of Education American International College.

Faculty: St. Andrew's has a faculty of 42 full-time faculty instructors, 16 of whom reside on campus. All full-time faculty members serve as activities coordinators and student advisors.

Tuition: Tuition and Boarding for 2003-2004 is $30,400.

Class Size: 8 to 12 students , with a 5:1 student-teacher ratio.

Curriculum: We are intent on discovering ways to help students succeed in all areas of their lives including academics, athletics, and activities. This involves not only a strong college prep curriculum with innovative programs to help those students with learning differences, but also a co-curricular program that sees athletics, the arts, and boarding life as part of the learning environment.

ESL Program: St. Andrew's International Program has been developed to meet the needs of students who arrive from various parts of the world to take advantage of our small classes and structured curriculum. The program addresses both academic and social needs, and it aims to make students feel comfortable as they immerse themselves in a new culture and to thoroughly prepare them for their academic futures. A warm and cohesive community, St. Andrew's provides a 'home away from home' for its international students. We are happy to be ble to provide students at varying levels of proficiency with ESL courses appropriate to their academic needs, and we know that these small, specific ESL classes increase the efficacy of our program. All international students are required to be enrolled in ESL classes while at St. Andrew's ; placement is determined based on SLEP test results, teacher recommendations, and previous experience in studying English.

College Placement: On average, ninety percent of our graduates enter a four-year or two-year college every year. Some of the colleges our students have been accepted to during the past three years are as follows: Art Institute of Boston, Bentley College, Boston University, Bryant College, Clark University, Colby-Sawyer College, Curry College, Fordham University, Johnson and Wales University, Keene State College, Mitchell College, Mt. Ida College, New England College, Northeastern University, Rhode Island College, Roger Williams University, Rutgers University, Salve Regina University, Tufts University, University of Connecticut, University of Hartford, University of Massachusetts at Amherst, University of Massachusetts at Dartmouth, University of Rhode Island, Wentworth Institute of Technology.

Academic Requirements: To graduate, a student must complete 26 credits and pass four major courses during the senior year. Minimum requirements are 4 credits in English; 3 credits in social studies, including 1 in U.S. history; 3 credits in mathematics; and 3 credits in science, including 2 in a lab science; 2 credits in physical education; and 1 credit in art.

Sports: Sports at St. Andrew's equals opportunities: the opportunity to play, the opportunity to be challenged, the opportunity to compete, the opportunity to win, the opportunity to develop the values and integrity that form winning individuals.

Our intention is to develop a student athlete's character, mental discipline, and physical abilities. Competitive sports and physical education are important aspects of St. Andrew's life. All students are required to participate in an afternoon athletic or activity program. Varsity and J.V. sports offered include: soccer, cross country, basketball, lacrosse, tennis, and golf. St. Andrew's also offers activities for recreational athletes, including: Project Adventure Ropes Course consisting of high and low ropes elements, bicycling (with mountain biking trips), kayaking, conditioning, lawn games, intramural sports, theater and arts, weight lifting, and fitness classes.

Extracurricular Activities: Who'd want to go home for the weekend? Students at St. Andrew's have the opportunity to take advantage of cultural and recreational events in Rhode Island as well as in the greater Boston area. A faculty member accompanies students on each trip. Every weekend brings choices, including off-campus activities as well as on-campus options — if there's something going on, you can bet that St. Andrew's students will be there! Sample Weekend Activities include Mall Trips, Boston Red Sox Games, Plays and Concerts, Movie Trips, Open Gym, Shopping in Harvard Square, Pool Tournament in the Student Center, Ski Trips, Swimming at the Y, Trips to Newport and Mansion Tours, Sailing on Narragansett Bay, Rhode Island School of Design Museum, Pizza-Tasting Tour, Hiking in New Hampshire, On-Campus Film Festivals, Amusement park trips, Rock 'N Bowl Rollerskating and ice skating.

Campus: The St. Andrew's campus is located in Barrington, Rhode Island, a suburban community on Narragansett Bay, within easy driving distance of Providence, Boston, and New York. Stone Academic Center, the main building, features fifteen classrooms, a student resource center, two computer labs, a fine arts classroom, an art gallery, a theater, academic offices, and a faculty workstation. Hardy Hall includes the library, the Middle School facilities, and a computer lab. The Karl P. Jones Gymnasium features a gymnasium, and locker rooms, as well as a stage, a music room and an art room. The Annie Lee Steele Adams Memorial Student Service Center includes the Health Center, additional classrooms, and offices. The campus also includes a fitness center, the Brown Science Center, and the Sage Gymnasium.

Dormitories: Small, family-like dorms form the core of the St. Andrew's boarding program. Each dorm is staffed by two faculty members with the assistance of one or more Student Prefects. Other faculty members play an active role in the dorms, supervising study halls and participating in special activities. Over the course of the year each dorm develops its own personality and culture as boarders from all over the world form friendships, find solutions to problems, celebrate birthdays and holidays, and generally transform the dorm into a home away from home. The Dorms include Bill's House - 20 residents (boys), Cady House - 16 residents (girls), Coleman House

- 9 residents (boys), Perry Hall - 8 residents (girls). The mission of St. Andrew's School, "helping students succeed," is magnified for boarders. With their lives centered on campus, they have the opportunity to explore their abilities in co-curricular activities like theatre, yearbook, or softball as well as experience community service and leadership roles as dormitory, library, or student center prefects. They learn, through structured evening study halls, to manage their workload and to take responsibilities seriously, yet they do all of this with the support of a caring community of adults. In short, a boarder at St. Andrew's is both nurtured and challenged. A typical day for a boarder includes morning meeting classes, sports, meals, extra help, study hall, co-curricular activities, dorm meeting and dorm chores and of course, and socializing. Sample Dorm Activities include Dorm vs. Dorm basketball, Movie trips, Everybody Cooks dorm dinners, Boarders' Beach Party, and more!

Nearest International Airport: Providence International Airport, Rhode Island.

St. Johnsbury Academy

Location: St. Johnsbury, Vermont (U.S. East Coast, New England)

P.O. Box 906, 1000 Main Street, St. Johnsbury, VT 05819
Phone: 802-751-2130; Fax: 802-748-5463
Website: www.stjohnsburyacademy.org
Email: admissions@stj.k12.vt.us

Mr. John Cummings, Director of Admission
Phone: 802-751-2130; Fax: 802-748-5463
Email: admissions@stj.k12.vt.us

Mission Statement: This is the mission of St. Johnsbury Academy, a diverse, comprehensive, and independent educational community grounded by our traditions, our deep optimism regarding young people, and our commitment to academic excellence. Character: To teach good character by modeling and fostering compassion, respect, responsibility, and integrity. Inquiry: To foster a love for learning by challenging individuals to pursue knowledge, creativity, and intellectual self-reliance. Community: To encourage each individual to understand his or her relationships, rights, and responsibilities within a community that is itself part of the larger world.

Grade Level: 9-12.

Student Gender: Boys & Girls.

Enrollment: 976 students, 502 boys, 474 girls, 172 boarders, 804 day.

Accredited by: NEASC

Head of School: Thomas W. Lovett, Providence College (B.A.), Brown University (M.A.)

Faculty: Our faculty members have two preeminent strengths: their professional preparation and their dedication. To be selected to teach at the Academy is an honor and a privilege. We have always had the luxury of a pool of candidates from which to select our teachers. Thus, our teachers have strong credentials from very good colleges and universities. A further strength of our faculty is that many of them are alumni/ae of the Academy. They understand the Academy and its traditions quite well, having been students here for four years. Many of them left the area and the state and taught in other places before returning to the Academy. They have come back with a perspective of other places, yet with an abiding love for this place. St. Johnsbury has a faculty of 125 teachers, 62 of whom have advanced degrees. 26 faculty members live on campus.

Tuition: Tuition and Boarding for 2003-2004 is $25,469.

Class Size: 15 students, with a student/faculty ratio of 10:1

Curriculum: At St. Johnsbury we tailor our curriculum to meet the needs of each student. Courses are taught at four levels of difficulty. Advanced Placement, acceleratd, standard and basic. You can select each course at he appropriate level. For example, you may pursue science and math courses at the accelerated level while making standard lvl English and social studies courses.

Advanced Placement: Advanced Placement courses are available in English, history, math, science, foreign language, and art.

ESL Program: We have designed ESL courses, within a full academic learning environment in English, to provide direct instruction in the English language in order to enhance the proficiency level of each student. We also wish to encourage authentic practice of English in a supportive atmosphere so that each student can achieve fluency, accuracy, and confidence. Our ESL program focuses upon the integration of all language skills, such as listening comprehension, speaking, reading, writing, grammar, and vocabulary development. We then ask that our students apply their newly acquired or improved language skills to real life situations. We firmly believe that we prepare the students in our program for college admission, as well as for college level work.

College Placement: Recent graduates of St. Johnsbury have been accepted to Amherst, Barnard, Bates, Boston College, Carleton, Carnegie Mellon, Champlain, Colgate, Cooper Union, Fashion Institute of Technology, Johnson State, Lafayette, Lyndon State, McGill, Oberlin, RIT, Sarah Lawrence, U.S. Air Force Academy,

Chicago, Vassar, Wesleyan, Worcester Polytechnic, and the Universities of Colorado, New Hampshire, North Carolina, Vermont, and Wisconsin.

Academic Requirements: English 4 credits, Science 3 credits, Mathematics 3 credits, Social Studies 3 credits, Physical Education 11/2 credits, Keyboarding 1/2 credit, Health Education 1 credit.

Sports: The Academy offers a wide variety of sports activities and encourages all students to participate. Although the work is hard, the rewards are great. Teams and courses offered include Football, Field Hockey, Cheerleading, Cross Country, Soccer, Ice Hockey, Wrestling, Gymnastics, Alpine Skiing, Nordic Skiing, Basketball, Baseball, Golf, Softball, Lacrosse, Tennis, and Track.

Extracurricular Activities: The club and activity program is an integral part of our schoolwork and offers unusual opportunities to all who participate, including Academy Theater, Alternative Activities Leadership Fun – AALF, Amnesty International, Art Club, Audio Visual Club, Band, Cheerleaders, Chess Club, Chorus, Close-Up Program, Creative Writing Club, Cycling Club, French Club, Future Business Leaders of America, Golf Club, HAM Radio Club, Improv Club, International Club, Intramural Program, Japanese Club, The Lamp, Lyceum, Math League, National Honor Society, Naturalist Club, Office Assistants, Peer Tutoring, Photography Club, Political Leaders Club, Russian Club, Scholars Bowl, Science Club, Spanish Club, Student Government, The Student, Ushers Club, Vocational Clubs of America, "We the People", and Wilderness Club.

Each weekend, the Resident Program schedules activities for resident students. These activities occur almost every Friday evening, Saturday, and Sunday. In addition to the sporting, choral, theater and other events taking place on campus, the Resident Program organizes: Day trips to Boston and Montreal, Skiing and snowboarding every weekend in the winter (the nearest mountain is 25 minutes away!), Shopping at the outlets in North Conway, NH, Sightseeing in Burlington, VT, Rockclimbing, Go-cart racing, Miniature golf, Paintball, Battle of the Bands and Dances. Brunch and dinner are served on weekends.

Campus: The town of St. Johnsbury (population 8,000) is 180 miles north of Boston, 330 miles north of New York City, and 150 miles south of Montreal. The town is located in the mountains, and offers opportunities for skiing, canoeing, camping, and hiking. The campus is also located in the heart of maple sugar country. Proximity to Dartmouth College and the University of Vermont offers students access to additional educational and cultural resources.

Colby Hall is St. Johnsbury 's main building, with administrative offices and 20 classrooms. Carl Ranger Hall is the English and writing center, withs 13 classrooms and a writing lab. Severance Hall houses the Boarding Students Office and eight classrooms. The St. Johnsbury Athenaeum library contains 45,000 volumes. Streeter Hall is the center for math, science, and technology. Newell Hall serves the foreign language department and features two computerized language learning systems. The campus also features a dining hall, the Common Ground Café, a television studio, and a 450-seat outdoor amphitheater. For performnc arts, Fuller Hall seats 800. The Morse Center for the Arts offers 6 Fine Arts classrooms, an art gallery, a print and photography studio, two music performance and recording studios with practice rooms, a dance studio, and a 200-seat theater. A new 23,000-square-foot facility houses the Grace Stuart Orcutt library, a student center with study space and state-of-the-art information technology, as well as a café.

Dormitories: St. Johnsbury 's 8 dormitories accommodate 152 students, as well as resident faculty members in each building. Boarding students are responsible for maintaining their own rooms. A school nurse is available 24 hours a day, and emergency services are available nearby at nearby Northeastern Vermont Regional Hospital.

Nearest International Airport: Burlington International Airport, Burlington, Vermont.

St. Stanislaus College

Location: Bay St. Louis, Mississippi (U.S. Southern Gulf Coast)

304 South Beach Boulevard, Bay St. Louis, MS 39520
Phone: 228-467-9057 ext. 227; Fax: 228-466-2972
Website: www.ststan.com; Email: admissions@ststan.com

Mrs. Dolores Richmond, Admissions Director
Phone: 800-517-6257; Fax: 228-466-2972
Email: admissions@ststan.com

Mission Statement: The mission of St. Stanislaus, a Catholic residency and day school for young men, is to teach Gospel values and to nurture the total development of each student according to the charism of the Brothers of the Sacred Heart. The school fosters character formation and integrates faith development within a curriculum which is primarily college preparatory. As an integral pert of its mission, Saint Stanislaus maintains a residency program which offers students opportunities for educational success and personal growth within a disciplined and structured environment.

Grade Level: 6-12.

Student Gender: Boys only.

Enrollment: 558 students, 201 boarders, 357 day.

Accredited by: SACS

Head of School: Brother Ronald Hingle, SC, Principal.

Faculty: St. Stanislaus has a faculty of 60 instructors, 12 of whom are Brothers of the Sacred Heart. More than half of the faculty have advanced degrees.

Tuition: Tuition and Boarding for 2003-2004 is $16,650.

Curriculum: Through its philosophy, admissions policy, curriculum and facilities, Saint Stanislaus College strives to create an atmosphere for holistic learning and self-growth. This atmosphere provides each student the opportunity to realize his potential and to develop the healthy attitudes and responsible behavior that will permit him to pursue continued studies and to assume his place in society as a concerned Christian gentleman, a Man of Character.

Saint Stanislaus College conducts a junior high program (sixth through eighth grades) and a four-year high school program. Students must complete four years of high school studies in order to graduate.

The curriculum is primarily college preparatory. Because of the wide variety of interests, needs and abilities found among students, the curriculum is regularly evaluated and revised. Honors courses are available to challenge intellectually gifted students. An Academic Assistance Program is also available to students who have been diagnosed with a learning difference.

In establishing its curriculum, Saint Stanislaus strives to provide educational opportunities that will enhance the growth and development of all its students. In order to encourage students to work to their fullest potential, to use their talents most effectively and to give themselves the broadest possible education, Saint Stanislaus College encourages each student to plan his own academic schedule with the assistance of his teachers, his guidance counselor and his parents. The student is guided in developing his future plans and in assuming responsibility for meeting his goals.

Offerings are designed, within budgetary constraints, to permit a student to elect courses that are within his range of ability and interest. In the areas of English, foreign languages, mathematics, science and social studies, courses are available to meet a broad scope of student needs. A fine arts program encourages the student to develop his musical and artistic abilities. Business, computer education, physical education and religion programs promote the formation of a well-rounded, well-informed individual.

ESL Program: The English as a Second Language program at St. Stanislaus is designed for students whose first language is not English. International or bilingual students who do not demonstrate proficiency on the Language Assessment Scale (LAS) which will be administered at the beginning of the year, are required to take this course. Proficiency is a score of 4 or 5 on the LAS scale. An additional fee of $600 per semester is charged for this course. This program includes instruction in both small groups and individualized settings and offers strategies to help with the acquisition of English as a second language. The goal of the course is to improve a student's use of English in everyday conversation as well as to assist in the understanding of subject area materials encountered in the regular classroom. Instruction focuses on proper usage of English in reading, writing, and speaking. The regular textbooks used in the student's subject areas are supplemented with related print and non-print materials to improve vocabulary, spelling, and grammar. Reading short high-interest stories and giving oral talks to classroom peers provide further practice in English. At the end of the first semester of work in ESL a student is assessed for proficiency in English provided that his performance in his other subjects is at the "C" level or higher. A score of a 4 or a 5 on the Language Assessment Scale allows a student to enroll in another subject. Otherwise, he remains in the ESL program for the second semester. A student whose performance in any academic subject is below the "C" level continues in the ESL program for a second consecutive semester. At the end of the second semester of ESL, the LAS is administered to determine the English proficiency of each student.

College Placement: Recent graduates of St. Stanislaus have been accepted to Boston University, the College of Charleston, Florida State, LSU, Loyola, the Merchant Marine Academy, Mississippi State, NYU, Notre Dame, Oxford University, Spring Hill College, Tulane, the U.S. Military Academy, the U.S. Naval Academy, and the Universities of Chicago, Florida, Miami, and Pennsylvania.

Academic Requirements: 4 units of religion, 4 units of English, 4 units of history, 4 units of science, 4 units of mathematics; 2 units of foreign language; 1 unit of art; 1 unit of computer education; and 1 unit of health and physical fitness.

Sports: Competitive team sports include baseball, basketball, cross-country, football, golf, sailing, soccer, swimming, tennis, track and field, and powerlifting. Each sport offers junior high, junior varsity, and varsity teams. Recreational sports include football, Ultimate Frisbee, beach volleyball, baseball, tennis, and swimming, pool, air hockey, bumper pool, Foosball, and table tennis.

Extracurricular Activities: Saint Stanislaus sponsors an array of student organizations designed to engage and develop its students after school. From Band to Youth Legislature, and everything in between, extracurricular organizations have developed around areas in which students have shown an interest, and often play a significant role in developing each student's appreciation of his own unique gifts and talents.

Clubs and organizations include Student Council, Key Club, Student Ministry Program the Reflections yearbook, the Rock-A-Chaw student newspaper, National Honor Art Club, Archaeology Club, band, Computer Club, Drama Club, literary magazine, Magic Club, Photography Club, Radio Club, Scuba Club, Sports Card Club, Varsity Quiz Bowl, band concerts, the Arts Festival, drama productions, drum line, and flag.

Weekend activities include cultural events in New Orleans, and waterskiing on the Jourdan River. Attendance at Sunday Eucharist is required, and daily Eucharist with the Brothers is encouraged.

Campus: St. Stanislaus is located on the Gulf of Mexico, with a 30 acre campus that overlooks the beach and extends into the town coastal town of Bay St. Louis. An elevated highway overpass connects the campus to a 1,000-foot pier for fishing, boat launch and access to the beach. The campus itself includes the main classroom and administrative building, the Student Chapel, the Kleinpeter-Gibbens Memorial Library which houses more than 13,000 volumes. The campus also features the latest in computer technology and Internet access. A two-story structure houses a gym, weight room and laundry. The campus also features a dining hall, swimming pool, three lighted tennis courts, handball and basketball courts, playing fields, the Brother Peter Memorial Gymnasium, a new fitness center, the Brother Philip Memorial Stadium complete with a football field and a 400-meter all-weather track, soccer fields, a field house, a baseball field and concession stand.

Dormitories: The Residency Department is responsible for the needs of SSC's resident students outside of the school day. Each resident student is assigned to an age-approrpiate dormitory, where he shares a room with other students under the supervision of the residency staff. The Residency Department provides additional recreational and learning opportunities for students under its care. The Brother Aurelian Dormitory accommodates 230 resident students and 11 dorm supervisors. This air conditioned building features rooms with private baths for 2 or 3 students each.

Nearest International Airport: New Orleans International Airport.

St. Timothy's School

Location: Stevenson, Maryland (U.S. Mid-Atlantic East Coast)

8400 Greenspring Avenue, Stevenson, MD 21153
Phone: 410-486-7401; Fax: 410-486-1167
Website: www.sttimothysschool.com
Email: admis@sttimothysschool.com

Mr. Patrick F. Finn, Director of Admission and Financial Aid
Phone: 410-486-7400; Fax: 410-486-1167
Email: admis@sttimothysschool.com

Mission Statement: Our motto, "To seek the truth and uphold it, to be worthy of trust, and to be kind" is the bedrock of a St. Timothy's School education. These virtues are as important today as they were when St. Timothy's School and Hannah More Academy were founded in 1882 and 1832, respectively.

The founders of St. Timothy's School and Hannah More Academy knew instinctively what it has taken years of research to prove. Girls and boys learn differently and a single-sex education can make a significant difference in the success of young women, especially at the secondary level. Girls' schools sustain a predominately female culture whose hallmarks are caring, challenge, collaboration, competition and an interest in developing each girl to her fullest potential, as well as providing a moral context that will serve them all their lives. The girls' school environment affirms and encourages young women in their capacities as confident individuals, leaders, and agents for social change.

Since our founding, St. Tim's has devoted itself exclusively to preparing young women for all the possibilities of the future. Over time, those possibilities have expanded, so the School's curriculum has broadened accordingly to accommodate our changing world and the needs of each new generation. On this website you will find information about the School's history, its curriculum, and its alumnae and students.

At St. Tim's, tradition and values blend with our academic and residential programs. St. Tim's is a place where excellence, intellectual curiosity, and independent thinking are celebrated. St. Ti m's is a boarding/day school. We are grounded in the Episcopal tradition but affirm all faiths. It is a place where every star athlete and every student leader is a girl. It is a place where friendships are formed to last a lifetime. At St. Ti m's students are prepared for the possibilities of the future. Everything we do is for girls and every girl deserves to attend a school that puts her needs first!

Grade Level: 9-12.

Student Gender: Girls only.

Enrollment: Girls: 100, 55 boarders, 45 day.

Accredited by: MSACS, AIMS

Head of School: Randy S. Stevens, B.A. in Government and International Studies from the University of South Carolina, Master of Public Administration from Cornell University.

Faculty: St. Timothy's has a faculty of 32 full-time and 9 part-time instructors, 18 of whom hold advanced degrees, and 70% of whom live on campus with their families. Faculty members also serve as dorm supervisors, advisors, and coaches. Each faculty member is assigned 4 to 6 students and meets regularly with them during scheduled advisory periods.

Tuition: Tuition and Boarding for 2003-2004 is $30,725.

Class Size: 7 to 10 students, with a student/teacher ratio of 4:1

Curriculum: St. Timothy's School curriculum focuses exclusively on a college-preparatory program. The School offers both a liberal arts curriculum, and an EFL (English as a foreign language) program for international students. The EFL program is limited to 6 students, who assimilate into the standard curriculum after one year. Seniors may also enroll in an independent study project, which might include internships at the White House and NASA, or journalism assignments with national newspapers.

Advanced Placement: Advanced Placement courses are available in English, biology, art history, U.S. history, European history, calculus,

French, Spanish, and Latin.

ESL Program: For students who may not speak English as their first language, St. Timothy's School offers the English as a Foreign Language program. The one-year program is geared toward students with an intermediate level in English (420 - 500 on the TOEFL). Instruction is both one-on-one and in small groups, as the program is limited to about six students. Students study with EFL teacher Alyson Shea in English reading, writing, and grammar. They attend classes in math, science and art with their other classmates. The EFL curriculum prepares students to do well on their TOEFL exam and to join mainstream English and history classes at St. Timothy's the following year.

Average SAT Scores of Graduating Students: The SAT middle 50% verbal, 530–660, and math, 530–640.

College Placement: Recent graduates of St. Timothy's have been accepted to colleges such as Boston University, Columbia, George Washington, Georgetown, Johns Hopkins, Penn State, Vanderbilt, Vassar, Wesleyan and Wellesley.

Academic Requirements: To graduate each student must earn a minimum of 18 academic credits and 1 athletic credit. Minimum requirements include the following number of credits in each subject area: Art: 1 credit awarded for 1 year of studio art, photography, drama, music theory, 2 years of piano or dance, or participation in concert choir each year; Athletics: 1 credit, ¼ credit given for each year of participation; English: 4 credits; Foreign Language: 3 credits, Spanish, French or Latin; History: 3 credits, Including U.S. History and World History II; Laboratory Science: 2 credits, Including at least 1 year each of Biology and Chemistry; Mathematics: 3 credits, Including Algebra I and II, and Geometry; Religion: 1/2 credit, Comparative World Religions.

Sports: The athletic program at St. Timothy's School is an integral part of the overall curriculum. Every student participates in the program each season, and we ask that each girl join an interscholastic team each year. The school has a very high rate of participation. The emphasis at St. Tim's is for our girls to have an enjoyable athletic experience on both competitive and non-competitive teams. Varsity teams enjoy a competitive schedule with other Baltimore-area private schools. Our interscholastic teams are in Tennis, Basketball, Softball, Field Hockey, Indoor Soccer, Volleyball, Riding, Lacrosse, and Ice Hockey. In addition we offer dance, physical education and riding classes.

St. Timothy's School maintains regulation-size fields for field hockey, lacrosse and softball, as well as six hard-surface tennis courts. In 2003, we dedicated our new athletic complex. The state-of-the-art facility has a basketball court (large enough to also provide two regulation-size cross courts), a fitness center, a classroom and locker rooms. The Center can put any trendy health club to shame, equipped with Stairmasters, treadmills, crosstrainers, bikes, free weights and state-of-the-art weight machines. The Center also has fitness studios for yoga and aerobics, well-appointed locker rooms, a training room, and is wired with a sound system, TV and DVD throughout.

Extracurricular Activities: Students decide each year which clubs will be organized, with membership open to all. This year, students have chosen to participate in SADD, Amnesty International, the Black Awareness Club, Social Services Club, Formal Club, Prom Club, International Club, Equestrian Club, Chapel Committee, Environmental Action Club, Double Helix, Current Events Club, Art Club, Film Club, Book Club and Flame (a student-run choreography and dance group). A new club, Shalom, has been inaugurated this year, to promote Jewish studies. In addition, students are elected to serve as Tour Guides and as class officers in or liaisons to the Self-Government association.

St. Tim's is especially proud of its award-winning student publications, produced as part of the Creative Writing and Publications Journalism course in the English Department. The Steward has garnered the Marylander Award — or best in the state—for best yearbook in its division, awarded by the Maryland Scholastic Press Association. The most recent edition of The Moongate, our literary arts magazine, ranked second place in a similar competition for 2002. In addition, numerous student contributors to these publications have received accolades for their work.

As all students are required to complete 10 hours of community service each year, they choose from many opportunities offered. This year, over 10% of the student body volunteers weekly at Gallagher Services, a residential facility for adults with developmental disabilities. Students spend two hours each Sunday — from October to May — as "special friends" to these adults. In addition to bringing joy into the lives of others, St. Tim's girls make new friends in Baltimore as they work alongside high-school students from other area schools.

Another popular social service activity is the yearly Special Games Day in May, when we host a day of music, games, and special food for children with developmental disabilities. Students from local day schools join us each spring to sponsor this event.

St. Timothy's School is in an ideal location. Situated 15 minutes from the Inner Harbor of Baltimore and one hour from Washington, D.C., we have a full array of activities each weekend.

Along with over twenty other boarding schools in Maryland, Washington DC, Virginia, and North Carolina, St. Tim's is a member of the Boarding Schools Social Activities Committee (BSSAC). BSSAC works to provide a variety of social activities for the schools, such as mixers and trips to see the Orioles play or to King's Dominion theme park. In addition, there are frequent trips Starbucks, Baskin Robbins, Lotte (an Asian grocery store), Giant Supermarket and, of course, the movies and the mall.

Campus: St. Timothy's is located on 145 acres, 15 minutes from the city of Baltimore. The campus features 22 buildings, including a Performing Arts Center that seats 350, the Ella R. Watkins Library with 22,000 volumes, a Visual Arts Center, 3 science labs, and computer labs in both dorms as well as the academic building.

Dormitories: About 60% of St. Timothy's girls are seven-day boarders living in Carter House or Heath House. Day students also enjoy time in the dorms with their friends, because they can spend up to 25 nights a year on campus free of charge. Each dorm has a student living room for socializing and watching TV and a computer lab for homework, research, or just checking e-mail. In Heath

House, a private living room and kitchen are set aside for seniors. All students have personal e-mail and voice mail accounts, making it easier to keep up with friends and family.

Each girl has an advisor, and meeting times are scheduled every other morning. Teachers are also frequently free to meet with students after lunch. In addition, students can readily seek extra help after the school day is over, as over 70% of the teachers and administrators live on campus and serve as coaches, dorm parents, study hall proctors, and weekend duty staff. Three faculty live in each dorm as dorm parents, and most other faculty reside in houses on campus. Students enjoy spending time getting extra help, watching movies, or baking brownies.

The dining room serves three hot meals a day, with plenty of options - including vegetarian ones - for students to choose from. A salad bar is open for lunch and dinner, and students regularly scribble special requests or a quick "thanks" on a napkin to post on the "napkin board" in the kitchen. Our dining staff likes to cook special meals for the girls, and cooks everything from a meal for an international dinner to a huge birthday cake for 110! Parents can order special fruit baskets and cookies during exams, or cake and balloons for a daughter's birthday.

Nearest International Airport: Baltimore/Washington International Airport.

Nearby Lodgings: Gramercy Mansion, 410-486-2405; Baltimore Marriott Inner Harbor, 410-962-0202; Renaissance Harbor Place Hotel, 410-547-1200; Sheraton Inner Harbor, 410-962-8300.

Stevenson School

Location: Pebble Beach, California (U.S. West Coast, Northern California)

3152 Forest Lake Road, Pebble Beach, CA 93953-3200
Phone: 831-625-8300; Fax: 831-625-5208
Website: www.rlstevenson.org; Email: info@rlstevenson.org

Mr. Thomas Sheppard, Director of Admission
Phone: 831-625-8309; Fax: 831-625-5208
Email: info@rlstevenson.org

Mission Statement: Stevenson's educational philosophy may be different from that of any other school you are considering. Our approach to education starts with you. As a student at Stevenson, you have three main responsibilities:

You are here to prepare for your college years - so work constantly to sharpen your mind, to expand your academic knowledge, and to stretch your intellectual reach. In the meantime, remember that you are more than an academic machine. We want you to love learning and achievement - but we also want you to love the arts, nature, recreation, friends and your own evolving perspective on the world. Respect yourself, and respect everyone else whose life touches yours.

We believe that if you can meet these requirements - within an environment as beautiful as Stevenson's, and among people as intelligent and congenial as the ones here - your high school years will turn out to be more fulfilling than you had ever expected.

Grade Level: 9-12.

Student Gender: Boys & Girls.

Enrollment: 530 students, 265 boys, 265 girls, 260 boarders, 270 day.

Accredited by: WASC

Head of School: Joseph E. Wandke, St. Olaf College (B.A., 1967),

Stanford University (M.A., 1972).

Faculty: Stevenson has a faculty of 60 full- and part-time instructors, 34 of whom hold advanced degrees, and 30 of whom reside on campus . All full-time faculty members also serve as advisors to students, and many act as coaches or club sponsors.

Tuition: Tuition and Boarding for 2003-2004 is $31,500.

Class Size: 15 students with a faculty-student ratio of 1:11.

Advanced Placement: Advanced Placement courses are offered in art, English, foreign languages, American and European history, economics, mathematics, biology, chemistry, environmental science, and physics.

ESL Program: The Stevenson School does not have an ESL program. Therefore, international applicants should demonstrate proficiency in English by taking the TOEFL or the SSAT.

College Placement: Recent graduates of Stevenson have been accepted to Boston University, Brown, California Polytechnic State University, Columbia University, Culinary Institute of America, Dartmouth College, Georgetown University, Johns Hopkins University, New York University, Northwestern University, Smith College, Sophia University, Japan, Stanford University, The School of the Art Institute of Chicago, University of California, (Berkeley, Davis, Irvine, Los Angeles, San Diego, Santa Barbara, and Santa Cruz), University of Chicago, and University of Pennsylvania,

Academic Requirements: Stevenson has a traditional college-preparatory curriculum, requiring 60 course credits for graduation: English, 12; mathematics, 9; history, 9; foreign language (French, Latin, Spanish, German, and Japanese), 9; science, 9; word processing, ½; art or music, 1½; and expressive arts (forensics, drama, dance, radio broadcasting), 1. The remaining credits may be made up from electives.

Sports: Athletics are a part of everyone's day - and the cornerstone of the program is good sportsmanship. Our interscholastic teams have something for everyone. In the fall, we've got cross-country, field hockey, football, girls golf, girls tennis, volleyball, and water polo. In the winter, it's time for boys lacrosse, soccer and basketball. In the spring, try baseball, softball, swimming and diving, boys golf, girls lacrosse, track and boys tennis. After-school sports range from sailing and sea kayaking to horseback riding and rock climbing to fencing and yoga.

Extracurricular Activities: Stevenson's students enjoy a variety of non-academic activities all year long. Clubs usually meet once a month and create a booth for the Spring Carnival and a fun and educational assembly once each year. Check out a list of our clubs above. And then, explore the many other opportunities we offer outside the classroom:

Trips:Start small, by taking our shuttle into Monterey or Carmel. Then try an overnight or a weekend—backpacking, rock climbing, ocean kayaking, skiing, cycling. With a group, go to the Model UN or to Washington, D.C.; take a drama production on tour in Europe. When you're ready, try study abroad or summer trips on your own— in countries throughout the world.

Beach: Imagine jogging on firm white sand, next to cypress tress, craggy rocks, and foaming surf. Think of tide-pools, sunsets, picnics, friends—and golf courses with a world-famous backdrop.

Afternoons: Here 's open time—for sports, clubs, volunteer service, and your own pursuits. Head for the beach or the Equestrian Center; hang out in your room, at the pool, or on the lawn. Our student newspaper, our high-powered radio station, dozens of clubs, and plenty of friends are here for you to enjoy.

Sign up for trips: hiking, skiing, restaurants, museums, shows. We're down the road from Monterey and Carmel, three hours from San Francisco, and only 25 miles from the Los Padres National Forest. Pick up a game of tennis on our courts, have a swim in the pool, cheer for the football team at a home game. Buses take you into town for shopping or a trip to the movies; they also take you to away games so you can cheer for the Pirates when they're on the road.

Campus: Located at the tip of the beautiful Monterey Peninsula on the coast of California, Stevenson is 125 miles south of San Francisco and 350 miles north of Los Angeles. Stevenson's 60-acre campus is in the heart of the Del Monte Forest of Pebble Beach, a wooded coastal area of spectacular natural beauty, The campus buildings include Douglas Hall, housing administrative offices; Talbott Academic Center, Stevenson library, with a collection of 12,000 volumes; the Lindsley Science Center, containing laboratories, classrooms, a lecture hall, a computer and mathematics center, and faculty offices; the Morse Fine Arts Center, which features an art gallery, a theater, and facilities for art, publishing, photography, and music; the W. M. Keck Auditorium, a student-operated FM radio station; and the Erdman Memorial Chapel.

Dormitories: In our dorms, we care about light, space, reasonable cleanness and in-room phone lines and computer connections. We have five dormitories, each with a girls and boys wing: Atwood, Wilson, Silverado, Day, and Casco/Douglas. Faculty members live with you, in their own apartments. Our own Cafe Louie Louie offers three meals a day and a fantastic Sunday brunch. Monday nights are set aside for a special, family-style dinner. Our Health Center is available to you if you need a nurse's care. Our resident faculty members are there for you, even late at night. Our Residence Council, made up only of boarding students, works to improve resident life and organize fun events on campus.

Upperclassmen serve as prefects who help organize events in the dorms and help out when you have a question. Monday nights are for the resident formal dinner, a chance to dress up and enjoy a sit-down dinner, family-style. Impromptu pizza parties, movie nights, and coffee houses are common

Nearest International Airport: San Francisco International Airport.

Stoneleigh-Burnham School

Location: Greenfield, Massachusetts (U.S. East Coast, New England)

574 Bernardston Road, Greenfield, MA 01301
Phone: 413-774-2711; Fax: 413-772-2602
Website: www.sbschool.org; Email: admissions@sbschool.org

Ms. Sharon L. Pleasant; Director of Admissions
Phone: 413-774-2711; Fax: 413-772-2602
Email: admissions@sbschool.org

Mission Statement: Based on a heritage which dates back to 1869, Stoneleigh-Burnham School is a close-knit, culturally diverse, college preparatory boarding and day school for young women, grades 9-12. We assign top priority to academic achievement; our comprehensive curriculum incorporates innovation within a traditional structure. Students have opportunities to participate in exemplary programs in the visual and performing arts, championship athletics and renowned equestrian training. Deeply committed faculty encourage students individually, challenging them to explore, question and attain their full potential in the world at large. Our warm, caring community supports its members and exemplifies unifying values of honesty, respect, personal responsibility, and service to others. Through their own efforts, students develop the intellectual skills and self-awareness to lead informed and significant lives as adult women. Respect for academics, commitment to community and appreciation of diversity define the Stoneleigh-Burnham graduate.

Requirements for International Students: TOEFL or SLEP.

Grade Level: 9-12.

Student Gender: Girls only.

Enrollment: 150 Girls, 90 boarders, 60 day.

International Students: 22, from Azerbaijan, China, Korea, Rowanda, Saudi Arabia, Switzerland, Taiwan, United Kingdom.

Accredited by: NEASC

Head of School: Martha W. Shepardson-Killam, Ohio Wesleyan University (B.A., 1974), Middlebury College/La Sorbonne (M.A., 1975).

Faculty: Stoneligh-Burnham has a faculty of 70 instructors and administrators, 23 of whom hold advanced degrees. Among them are also riding instructors, a veterinarian, and professional counselors and faculty advisors who are available for consultation at all times.

Tuition: Tuition and Boarding for 2003-2004 is $29,700.

Class Size: 11 students, with a Student/Teacher ratio of 5:1

Curriculum: Classes at Stoneleigh-Burnham emphasize connections - connections between what you are studying in history and science, for example, and connections between your ideas and those of your classmates and teachers. The curriculum is tailored to meet the needs of students at all levels, both within a single section of a course to courses designed to provide differing levels of challenge. Because classes are small, with an average of just 11 students, the contributions of each person count. You will find that your teachers know you well, as a student and as a person with varied interests outside the classroom. This helps teachers provide the support and encouragement you need to do your best academically - and to discover new talents and explore new interests. Stoneleigh-Burnham offers a challenging academic program with a wide range of courses and electives. Advanced and honors sections are available in all disciplines to provide the appropriate level of instruction for each student. In addition, we offer advanced placement courses in science, history, English, foreign languages, and studio art. Strong programs in math and science focus on interactive learning that often takes place in groups. The majority of students take four full years of both math and science, with some taking more by enrolling in two science or math courses in junior and senior year. In English and history, you may choose from a variety of electives ranging from the Villains of Shakespeare, Latin American Literature, Introduction to Political Science, and Gender Studies. Other electives include Website Design, Ecology, and Sports Medicine. A Stoneleigh-Burnham education emphasizes proficiency in writing in all subject areas and helps you learn to analyze ideas and share your opinions with others. Students say what they gain most in their time at the school is confidence. Along with a strong academic program, this is the best preparation for college and for the choices you will make in your career and personal life.

Advanced Placement: Advanced Placement courses are offered in English, French, Spanish, European History, US History, Calculus, Biology, Art.

ESL Program: Stoneleigh-Burnham School is committed to enhancing its community life by the inclusion of students from all over the world from many different cultures. The School provides valuable educational opportunities for its international students while broadening the cultural and geographical horizons of their American counterparts. In order to offer the best possible experience for our international students, we provide the following: A comprehensive ESL program which typically attracts students whose English abilities range from intermediate to advanced.

The International Programs Director works with the school community to ensure the academic well-being of international students and to facilitate cross-cultural exchange and understanding. Special orientation activities which take place a day earlier than the arrival date for our American students. Ongoing orientation activities with new International students during the first trimester to address pertinent topics. Various trips to local areas of interest, dinners at faculty homes, etc. College counseling by advisors who are experienced in International student college application issues.

Contact, a forum which gives international students an opportunity to speak about their countries to small groups of American students and faculty.

International News, a newspaper published several times a year. Led by an Editorial Board of International and American students, this paper focuses on cross-cultural issues.

MECCA (Multi-Ethnic Club for Cultural Awareness), open to all students, is dedicated to promoting cultural awareness in our school community. The club sponsors many activities such as coffee houses, talent nights, dinners, etc., which help to further this goal. MECCA's activities, including the creation of a scholarship fund which it has established for a deserving international student, are supported through a variety of fund raising projects.

College Placement: Recent graduates of Stoneleigh-Burnham have been accepted to colleges such as Babson, Bates, Boston University, Bowdoin, Bucknell, Columbia, Drew, Hamilton, Lafayette, Mount Holyoke, Sewanee, Skidmore, St. Lawrence, Smith, Tufts, Wheaton, and the Universities of Colorado, North Carolina, and Vermont.

Sports: Teachers and students take pride in Stoneleigh-Burnham's tradition of excellence in athletics. A full program of junior varsity and varsity teams gives you the opportunity to try new sports and to advance to experienced levels of play. Athletics is an important part of school life that brings people together to experience the excitement of achieving shared goals. In all sports, we emphasize learning to work with others in a spirit of cooperation and the enjoyment of physical exercise. Every student participates in athletics throughout the year. We offer interscholastic competition in basketball, cross country, field hockey, lacrosse, skiing, soccer, softball, tennis, and volleyball. Both dance and riding fulfill the requirement for team sports. Stoneleigh-Burnham teams compete against coed and girls' schools with much larger enrollments and post outstanding records. We play in the Western New England Preparatory School Athletic Association (WNEPSAA) and in the Girls' School League. Since the founding of the Girls' School League in 1991, Stoneleigh-Burnham has won nine titles in softball and ten in basketball. Other recent accomplishments include four WNEPSAA titles in softball, runner-up titles for the Western New England Championships in basketball and softball, semi-final finish in field hockey in the Class B Tournament, and a ranking of third in volleyball in the WNEPSAA.

Extracurricular Activities: Stoneleigh-Burnham gives you lots of opportunities to learn - and not just during the day while you are in class. Students pursue a wide range of interests and gain practical skills through an extracurricular program that offers many clubs and activities. From editing the literary magazine to organizing pep rallies, students take initiative for projects on and off campus

Stoneleigh-Burnham School

throughout the year. Students produce publications, plan and execute a variety of events, and raise money for charitable causes. Student Council plays an important role in making decisions that affect school life and presenting school issues to the administration.

The Debate Society has a history of excellence and involves many students in debate competition against such schools as Deerfield, Loomis-Chaffee, St. Paul's, and Phillips Exeter. In the past 17 years, seven Stoneleigh-Burnham students have ranked as world competitors in debate. Recently, three students attended the International Debate Tournament in Vancouver, with two placing in the top five finishers, and another student placed 24th in the world at the Championship Competition in Botswana. Clubs and Activities offered in recent years include: Athletic Association, Blue Key (admissions guides), Community Service, Dance Performance Project, Debate Society, The Hoot (student newspaper), Literary Society, Multi-Ethnic Club for Cultural Awareness (M.E.C.C.A.), Octet (singing group), PANGAEA, Peer Tutors, Resident Assistants/Proctors, Riding Club, Student Activities, Student Council and Yearbook.

Weekends are full of activities, from community service projects to dances with other area schools. The Student Activities club plays an important role in planning weekend events for students. Stoneleigh-Burnham provides a shuttle into town on Friday and Saturday nights for students who want to eat out or attend a movie. Weekend activities have included trips to Boston and the National Horse Show in New York City, cultural events at area colleges, and excursions to ski resorts.

Campus: The School is located on 100 acres of woodland, just outside Greenfield, a community of 20,000. This historic region is home to such academic institutions as University of Massachusetts, and Smith, Amherst, Mount Holyoke, and Hampshire Colleges. The main buildings on the Stoneleigh-Burnham campus contain classrooms, a greenhouse, a math and computer center, and a library of more than 10,000 volumes. The Jesser Science Center houses laboratories and lecture rooms. Emerson Hall is a multi-purpose gymnasium and auditorium for athletics events, plays, and student dances. The 9,000-square-foot Student Art Center features studios for fine arts, ceramics, photography, music, and dance, with a student lounge and art gallery. The campus also has an indoor riding ring and equestrian stables.

Dormitories: In the dormitory, students live on hallways that house from 12 to 18 students in a small, home-like community. Resident teachers or dorm parents live on the hallways and provide supervision and support. Day students, who make up a third of the student body, are assigned rooms in the dorms where they can leave belongings and stay overnight on occasion. Day students frequently spend time on campus during the weekend and participate fully in after school programs.

Nearest International Airport: Bradley International Airport, Hartford, CT.

Nearby Lodgings: Howard Johnson Motor Lodge, 413-774-2211; Candlelight Motor Inn, 413-772-0101; Deerfield Inn, 413-774-5587; Red Roof Inn, 413-665-7161; Whately Inn, 800-942-8359.

Storm King School

Location: Cornwall-on-Hudson, New York (U.S. East Coast, New England)

314 Mountain Road, Cornwall-on-Hudson, NY 12520
Phone: 845-534-9860; Fax: 845-534-4128
Website: www.sks.org; Email: admissions@sks.org

Dr. Stephen Lifrak, Director of Admission
Phone: 845-534-9860; Fax: 845-534-4128
Email: admissions@sks.org

Mission Statement: The mission of the Storm King School, an independent, co-educational boarding and day school, is to provide a personally supportive, safe learning environment. Individual attention is offered to a multicultural student body, with a broad range of abilities, by caring faculty who help young people reach their full intellectual potential. A traditional curriculum, enhanced by co-curricular programs and a strong emphasis on moral development, prepares students for higher education.

We believe that: Young people learn best in a personally supportive and safe environment.

Students should be assisted in realizing their fullest potential in their intellectual, physical, creative and moral growth. A diverse and multi-cultural community provides important learning opportunities for everyone.

Students should be guided to develop a strong a moral character. An open and receptive environment should be provided that respects and encourages the individual ideas and intellectual pursuits of every student and faculty member. Education is a developmental process for each individual.

Character development and education are inseparable.

The Storm King community should be encouraged to make healthy choices about body, mind and spirit.

The arts, athletics, cultural activities, outdoor education and community service enhance life and growth. Respect, dignity and acceptance should be accorded each individual regardless of race, creed, gender or orientation. Hiring and retaining the best faculty and administration possible is essential.

Faculty, staff, administrators and students should lead by example.

Grade Level: 9-12.

Student Gender: Boys and Girls.

Enrollment: 130 Students, 90 boys, 40 girls, 90 boarders, 40 day.

Accredited by: MSACS

Head of School: Philip D. Riley, B.S. West Point, M.A. University of North Carolina at Chapel Hill.

Faculty: Storm King has a faculty of 18 full-time and 12 part-time instructors, 20 of whom hold advanced degrees. 90% of the faculty at Storm King live on campus and are available to the students for help or discussion. Faculty and staff all eat meals together. During every school day there is a "Tutorial" period when neither students nor faculty have class. During this period, a student can seek out a teacher and receive extra help. Storm King faculty share their experience and expertise, strive to inspire, and personalize the educational process for each student. Teachers are available to students, helping those who need more of a guiding hand, and challenging those who break the confines of the syllabus. As students progress through the Storm King curriculum, increased personal responsibility results in more freedom. The result is an independent, knowledgeable, thinking, young person who has learned how to use the tools with which he/she will shape the future.

Tuition: Tuition and Boarding for 2003-2004 is $29,300.

Curriculum: The Storm King School curriculum is college preparatory, placing an emphasis upon a well-rounded education. As members of the learning community, students become increasingly involved in making decisions related to their education. Each student is given the opportunity to develop his/her own talents and independence. This development occurs in an environment characterized by a sense of self-worth, responsibility, and humor, combined with the structure needed to succeed. A close relationship between students and faculty fosters a community atmosphere conducive to learning in the classrooms, on the stage, in the dorms, and on the athletic fields.

ESL Program: All new international students are tested for their proficiency in English at the beginning of the school year and are placed at the appropriate level in the ESL program. The ESL curriculum features courses for the beginning student through TOEFL preparation.

College Placement: Recent graduates have been accepted to: Bennington, Boston University, Bucknell, Emerson, George Washington, Hamilton, Iona, Northeastern, NYU, Parsons, Roger Williams, Skidmore, several campuses of the State University of New York, Syracuse, Tufts, Virginia Tech, and the Universities of Colorado, Hartford, Massachusetts, Miami, Southern California, and Vermont.

Academic Requirements: The following requirements must be met in order to qualify for a Storm King diploma: A minimum of 23½ academic credits including: English (4), Social Studies (4), Mathematics (3), Science (3), Physical Education (4), Foreign Language (2), Visual Arts (1), Performing Arts (1), Health (½), Outdoor Education (½), and Community Service (½). Students are required to participate in the Physical Education program each semester and must play two competitive sports per year.

Sports: Athletics at Storm King include recreational and competitive activities as well as a physical education program that is part of the course curriculum. Each student must participate in an approved activity in each of the three sport seasons and in a competitive sport for one of the three seasons each year. The gymnasium provides basketball, wrestling, and weight lifting. There are also a dance studio and locker and shower facilities. There are interscholastic teams for boys in baseball, basketball, cross-country, lacrosse, tennis, and wrestling; and for girls in basketball, softball, tennis, and volleyball. Coed soccer is also offered as an interscholastic team sport. The recreational alternatives include karate, skiing, yoga, tennis, and weight lifting. The Wilderness Program takes advantage of the School's physical setting, offering outdoor-skill activities, such as mountaineering, canoeing, hiking, and rock-climbing as an alternative to sports as well as a series of weekend backpacking trips.

Extracurricular Activities: During the week, Storm King offers several options for activities, including theatre (acting and tech work), dance, The Quarry (year-book), the School's literary magazine and community service. There are also several options for clubs, such as ceramics or computer graphics. On the weekend, trips to the mall, movies and shops are offered, as well as special event trips to West Point, New York City, Boston and other New England areas for museums, shows, historical sites and outdoor adventures. The extracurricular program at Storm King enables students to pursue special interests outside of class other than athletics. Opportunities that are available to the student each year include theater (acting and tech work), dance, The Quarry (yearbook), the school's literary magazine, and service learning, which works toward improving both the campus and helping members of the local communities. In addition, students can learn to be leaders by joining some of the student organizations on campus. The activities director and student committee plan weekend activities, such as movies, dances, intramural athletics, hikes, horseback riding, visits to museums, and trips to special events.

Campus: Situated on the west bank of the Hudson River near the crest of Storm King Mountain just 55 miles north of New York City, the campus offers a commanding view of the Shawangunk Mountains and distant Catskills. Settled in the peaceful small town of Cornwall-on-Hudson, the campus also adjoins the Black Rock Forest, a 3,600-acre nature preserve. The proximity of New York City and the many local offerings provide our students with a wide variety of activities and opportunities. Storm King School is a member of the Black Rock Consortium, which administers the Black Rock Forest, a 3,600-acre wilderness that abuts the campus. The School makes maximum use of these natural surroundings for its science, environmental, and recreational programs.

The campus also features Stillman Hall which houses Math and

Science classes, faculty offices, a faculty apartment, and the Florence Wall Health Center. Dyar Hall contains five classrooms primarily where the humanities are taught. The Ogden Library contains two ESL classrooms, the Enrichment Center, and the Computer Center. The Cobb-Matthiessen Observatory serves the needs of the science department through use of its 16-inch Cassegrain telescope.

The 220-seat Walter Reade Jr. Theater supports theater productions, the study of music, and school assemblies and meetings. The Allison Vladimir Arts Center contains an art classroom, a studio that supports the A.P. Studio Art program, and a gallery on the main floor that is used to showcase student projects and is often used for special gatherings and meetings of the Board of Trustees.

The Gym serves as the focal point for the athletic program that not only includes fall, winter, and spring sports, but also supports the physical education program. The ropes course, located behind Tryon Cottage, features 21 elements (low and high ropes) and is used in conjunction with our Outdoor Education Program.

Dormitories: There are five dormitories, three for boys and two for girls, on the campus. The Cottage is a residence for girls grades 9-11. Stone Hall is a senior girls dormitory. Highmount is the senior boys dormitory. Dempsey Hall and McConnell Hall serve underclass boys. Most of the rooms are doubles, but several singles are available. The Student Commons contains lounges, a video room, modern kitchen and dining room facilities, and a Student Center for informal recreation. The health center is on the ground floor of Stillman Hall. Resident Assistants help and support dorm faculty during study hall and check-ins and also help students adjust to dorm life and work through problems. Their opinions on school life are sought and encouraged. RA's are appointed to live in specific dorms and are expected to lead the student body by example.

Nearest International Airport: JFK International Airport, New York.

Nearby Lodgings: The Storm King Lodge, 845-534-9421; Painter's Inn & Tavern, 845-534-2109; Cromwell Manor Inn, 845-534-7136; Marriott Courtyard Hotel, 845-567-4800.

Subiaco Academy

Location: Subiaco, Arkansas (U.S. Central Midwest)

405 N. Subiaco Ave., Subiaco, AR 72865
Phone: 479-934-1025; Fax: 479-934-1033
Website: www.subi.org; Email: admissions@subi.org

Mr. Jason Gaskell, Director of Admission
Phone: 479-934-1025; Fax: 479-934-1033
Email: admissions@subi.org

Mission Statement: Subiaco Academy, a boarding/day high school, is dedicated to providing young men with an opportunity for a college preparatory education in a stable and structured environment nourished by Christian values. The Subiaco experience creates an opportunity for a sense of community, which is a reflection of Catholic Benedictine traditions of service to God, respect for self and others, mutual support, and the value of work.

Admission Requirements for International Students: International applicants are expected to have a working knowledge of the English language.

In addition, applicants are required to take the SSAT, the TOEFL, or the SLEP Test. The results must be submitted to Subiaco Academy with the application and other required forms.

It is highly recommended that applicants visit the school for a personal interview.

To attend Subiaco Academy, an international student must have an F-1 (student) visa if he does not have other legal immigration status, U.S. citizenship, or a green card. After an applicant is accepted, the school issues a SEVIS I-20 in order for him to obtain his F-1 visa.

Grade Level: 9-12.

Student Gender: Boys only.

Enrollment: 165 boys, 106 boarders, 59 day.

Number of International Students: 30 students, 1 from Croatia, 15 from Mexico, 11 from South Korea, and 3 from Taiwan.

Accredited by: ISACS, NCA-CASI, ANSAA (Arkansas Nonpublic Schools Accrediting Association)

Head of School: Father Aaron Pirrera, O.S.B., M.A. Library Science, University of Iowa. ESL Certificate, University of California at San Diego.

Faculty: Subiaco Academy has a faculty of 35 instructors, 13 of whom are Benedictines residing on campus. Twenty-two faculty members hold advanced degrees.

Tuition: Tuition, room, and board for the 2004-2005 school year is $17,000 for international students, plus additional fees of approximately $825. An additional fee is charged for each class period of English as a Second Language (ESL).

Class Size: 14 students, with a 6:1 student/teacher ratio.

Curriculum: The liberal arts curriculum challenges each student to achieve his potential as he prepares for college and as he engages in community living that includes participating in interscholastic and extracurricular competitions and activities.

Advanced Placement: Advanced placement courses are offered in biology, calculus, chemistry, English language and composition, English literature and composition, European history, government, statistics, and U.S. history.

ESL Program: The ESL program includes ESL I, II and III.

Average SAT Scores of Graduating Students: For the class of 2003, the average verbal score was 533. The average math score was 560.

College Placement: Recent graduates of Subiaco Academy have been accepted to Case Western Reserve, La Salle, Michigan State, Rhodes, St. Joseph Seminary, Texas A&M, the United States Naval Academy, and the Universities of Arkansas and Notre Dame.

Academic Requirements: Students are required to complete 26 academic units to graduate (1 unit equals one full-year course).

Required are 4 years of English, math, and religious studies; 3 years of science, social studies, and foreign language; 2 years of art; 1 year of physical education, 1 year of senior project; and ½ year of computer applications, oral communications, and health.

Sports: Competitive interscholastic sports include baseball, basketball, cross-country, football, golf, soccer, tennis, and track and field. Recreational sports include fishing, hiking, racquetball, soccer, swimming, tae-kwon-do, and volleyball. The facilities include a swimming pool, tennis courts, Rebsamen Football Stadium, the Father Louis Duester Fieldhouse, the Alumni Baseball Field, and the Oskar Rust Gymnasium.

Extracurricular Activities: Student activities include Student Council, Quiz Bowl, the National Honor Society, the Drama Club, Benet Club (Benedictine life and culture), Blue Arrow (tour guides), The Pax (yearbook), and The Periscope (student newspaper). Weekend excursions include trips to Dallas, Memphis, Tulsa, and other cities for cultural events. A 9-acre campsite, complete with a cabin and a dock, is available to the students for fishing, boating, and waterskiing. The school is located near national and state parks that offer outdoor activities such as hiking, fishing, and hunting. The student council also arranges dances and other activities that include girls from nearby schools.

Campus: Subiaco is located in the Arkansas River Valley on 100 acres of campus adjoining 1700 acres of farmland. The nearby Ouachita Mountains offer many opportunities for outdoor activities. The campus facilities include a five-story Main Building, which contains the Martha Platt Library, featuring 15,000 volumes; the computer center; administrative offices; a dining room; a student recreation room; and dormitory rooms for upperclassmen. Classrooms are housed in Alumni Hall, Wardlaw Hall, and Centenary Hall, which also features an art gallery, a 360-seat auditorium and theater for the performing arts, music practice rooms, and a music library. The Fine Arts building contains a large art studio with facilities for visual media.

Dormitories: Freshmen are housed in double rooms in Heard Hall. The Main Building houses sophomores, juniors, and seniors in double rooms. Each dormitory features laundry facilities. Students in both dorms have access to Die Bunkerstube, a student-operated snack bar and entertainment center. The Health Center is staffed by a registered nurse and a licensed practical nurse.

Nearest International Airport: Dallas/Fort Worth International Airport, Texas; Will Rogers International Airport, Oklahoma City, Oklahoma.

Nearby Lodgings: Coury House (on Subiaco Academy campus), 479-934-1290; The Paris Inn, 479-963-2400.

Tabor Academy

Location: Marion, Massachusetts (U.S. East Coast, New England)

66 Spring Street, Marion, MA 02738
Phone: 508-748-2000; Fax: 508-748-0353
Website: www.taboracademy.org
Email: admissions@taboracademy.org

Mr. Andrew L. McCain, Director of Admission
Phone: 508-748-2000; Fax: 508-748-0353
Email: admissions@taboracademy.org

Mission Statement: We believe a worthwhile independent school education should demand hard work, intense exploration and a sense of intellectual and creative daring. Learning at Tabor is an adventurous enterprise, sparked by good teachers with a flair for creating imaginative assignments and curious students eager to discover new interests and passions. While we are justifiably proud of the quality and range of our academic program, it is the personal nature of learning here, the warm interaction between student and teacher and among classmates, that best characterizes academic life at Tabor.

Admission Requirements for International Students: Tabor's Admission Office warmly welcomes international applicants and will provide a catalogue and application on request. The Boarding School Common Application may also be used. A campus tour and personal interview are strongly recommended, both to help families choose the right school and for us to assess the candidate. For students and families who live overseas, a telephone interview may substitute for a personal interview and tour if necessary. Non-native English speakers should submit a TOEFL or SSAT score. International families are encouraged to contact the International Center during the application and admissions process for help and support.

Grade Level: 9-12.

Enrollment: 480 students, 260 boys, 220 girls, 342 boarders, 138 day.

Number of International Students: 43 students or 8% of student body, from Bahrain (2), Belarus (1), Bermuda (3), China (9), Germany (2), India (1), Japan (1), Korea (11), Russia (1), Saudi Arabia (1), Taiwan (3), and Thailand (5).

Accredited by: NEASC

Head of School: Jay S. Stroud, Graduate of Carleton, Dartmouth, and Columbia.

Faculty: Tabor has a faculty of 81 full-time instructors, 45 of whom hold advanced degrees. 60 faculty members reside on campus.

Tuition: Tuition and Boarding for 2003-2004 is $31,600.

Class Size: Student/faculty ratio: 6:1

Curriculum: Tabor offers a thoughtful and rigorous academic program that provides a solid foundation for study at competitive colleges. For a school of our size, the curriculum contains an especially broad spectrum of courses, from introductory levels to honors and AP courses to highly sophisticated opportunities for independent work; from traditional liberal arts fields such as the humanities, math and the sciences to unusual offerings - for a secondary school - in areas such as Greek, oceanology and lighting design.

Adapting to a new environment, perhaps, thousands of miles from home; working harder in freshman math or biology or English than you ever thought you could; learning to budget your time - these are among the personal challenges you will face as a new Tabor student. With helpful teachers and classmates at your side, you will soon settle in and experience the exhilaration of belonging to a spirited community where the mind's great adventures are pursued to the fullest - and in settings you can never imagine today.

Advanced Placement: Humanities: English Literature and Language, European History, French, German, Latin, Spanish, U.S. History, U.S. Government and Politics and World History. Math and Sciences: Biology, Calculus AB and BC, Chemistry, Economics, Environmental Science, Physics.

ESL Program: Tabor has welcomed international students for nearly a century. In 1992, A Center for International Students was established with a director and office to assist international students and promote ties with the larger school community. Tinker Saltonstall directed the Center for its first decade, strengthening ties to international families and initiating many annual events. Steve Downes and Merry Conway now direct the Center. In 2003-2004, 43 international students from 14 countries will join the Tabor community.

The Tabor International Center is authorized to issue the I-20 forms that allow students from other countries to apply at US Embassies for F-1 student visas to study in the United States. The Center provides travel assistance to students coming from overseas, and arranges home stays of short and medium duration at vacation times. Four International Center letters are faxed annually to international families, including student grades and comments. International Center students regularly rely on the International Center for support and advice in a variety of school-related areas.

Approximately one quarter of each year's incoming international student group is placed in our advanced English as a Second Language (ESL) class for the first year only, based on a test given during our orientation. The class replaces one year of English, and is taught by an experienced English teacher with the aim of reaching "mainstream" English the second year. An international section of sophomore (Modern World) History is also created for sophomores each year to smooth the path to "mainstream" US History for the junior year.

Tabor's excellent College Placement Office provides individual guidance and support for each student's college search beginning in the winter of the junior year. The International Center arranges college visits in southern New England and also provides support for applications and searches. The Class of 2003's non-native English speaking Tabor graduates will attend Princeton, Duke, Brown, Occidental, Bentley, University of Rochester, Boston University, and Bates. They are proud of their achievements and so are we.

Approximately 50 returning American and International students and 13 faculty members joined new International Students for a three-day orientation last September. Faculty and student Global Partners participate with the International Students in activities throughout the year. Orientation is the first of many International Center-sponsored events, including regular evening "coffees", senior gatherings, Chapel programs, and Asian and European dinners for the whole school. Significant opportunities for leadership exist within the International Center - Student Co-Heads, Orientation Co-Heads, Special Activity Heads - as well as in all school academic and co-curricular programs.

Average SAT Scores of Graduating Students: Verbal: 572, Math: 594.

College Placement: Recent graduates of Tabor have been accepted to Boston University, Brown University, Columbia University, Cornell University, Dartmouth College, Duke University, Emory University, George Washington University, Georgetown University, Harvard University, Massachusetts Institute of Technology, Princeton University, Sophia University (Japan), United States Naval Academy, University of Massachusetts at Amherst, University of North Carolina/Chapel Hill, University of Southern California, and Vanderbilt.

Academic Requirements: Required courses include 4 years of English, at least 3 of mathematics (algebra I, algebra II, and geometry), 2 of a foreign language (chosen from a number of modern and classical languages), 2 of history, and 2 of laboratory sciences, as well as involvement in the arts each year.

Sports: At Tabor, we offer all students the opportunity to become involved in competitive sports and fitness activities, from the elite level athlete looking for top competition and a stepping stone to collegiate athletics to the student with little or no experience wielding a squash racket or sailing a laser-class sailboat. With 55 different teams in 23 interscholastic sports and another 15 instructional programs, there is a place for everyone in Tabor's athletic program. Top these opportunities with a brand-new Athletic Center, which includes an indoor hockey rink and a fitness center, and an extensive waterfront, and you can understand why athletics play a big part in school life - for players and cheering fans alike. Seawolf teams claim a long-standing tradition of consistently winning league championships and tournaments. What truly sets Tabor's athletic program apart, however, is the people - teachers who coach and coaches who teach; students who share their coaches' and teammates' enthusiasm, commitment and passion. As you get to know your history teacher on the baseball diamond or your basketball coach in the math classroom and then in the dormitory, a sense of togetherness and support is solidified. Facilities include The Fish Center for Health and Athletics which houses nine squash courts, four basketball courts, an indoor hockey rink, state-of-the-art fitness and cardio equipment and free weights. Outdoor athletic facilities include eight athletic fields, seven tennis courts and a track. Tabor employs two full-time trainers.Tabor fields 50 interscholastic teams: 24 girls' 26 boys' and 5 coeducational. Boys' sports: cross country, football, soccer, basketball, ice hockey, squash, wrestling, baseball, crew, golf, lacrosse, sailing, tennis and track. Girls' sports: cross country, field hockey, soccer, basketball, ice hockey, Squash, softball, crew, golf, lacrosse, sailing, tennis and track.

Instructional activities include: crew, tennis, golf, sailing, and conditioning.

Extracurricular Activities: Tabor students enjoy taking time out from their studies to join an activity or club. It's a great way to develop new interests and skills, share your talents with the school community, and widen your circle of friends. Tabor students participate in the following activities: Student newspaper, The Log Yearbook, Fore and Aft, Speech and Debate Team, Community Service Program, Admissions Tour Guides, Bowsprit literary magazine, Student Council, Peer Listening, FM radio station, WWTA, Vocal and instrumental groups, International Student Organization, Student Activities Committee, Drama for Athletes, Mock Trial Team and Tabor Stock Club (on-line traders).

There 's lots to do at Tabor on weekends, including organized trips and spur-of-the-moment activities like pick-up games in the gym, a walk to the Marion General Store and talks with friends in the dorm lounge. In the winter, indoor activities are abundant on the Tabor campus. From open skating to athletic contests to dances and movies, students have a myriad of choices for their free time. Here 's a list of winter school activities to be enjoyed by Tabor students.

Campus: It is hard to picture a more stunning location for a school than Tabor's in southeastern Massachusetts. Our campus in the small town of Marion stretches along a half mile of Sippican Harbor on Buzzards Bay leading to the Atlantic. Views of water glistening in the afternoon sun and sailboats gently bobbing, the bracing salt air nourish our souls and raise our spirits when work loads overwhelm. Our students and teachers exploit the school's location through academic programs in marine and environmental science, research in our new oceanology research lab and a unique set of nautical science courses. Our interscholastic and recreational waterfront program - sailing and crew - ranks as one of the finest, and best-coached, high school programs in the country.

Situated directly on the oceanfront, the Schaefer Oceanology Center combines hands-on research with classroom space. Drama and music are housed in an exceptional facility hosting 8 productions annually. The 90-foot schooner "Tabor Boy" provides newly enrolled students week-long orientation cruises, as well as coral reef ecology courses in the Caribbean. Tabor's Fish Center for Health and Athletics opened three years ago, and a new girls dormitory, Heath House, opened in 2000.

Dormitories: Residential Life: A hallmark of the Tabor boarding experience is living in small to medium sized dormitories. This arrangement allows for maximum of interaction between the student, dormitory faculty and other dorm mates. Like our small classes, it is impossible to fade into the background in a Tabor dormitory. The freshman boarding class has a slightly different experience, with all members living in various corridors in Lillard Hall and a unifying freshman residential curriculum. There are 19 dormitories with a average dormitory enrollment of 18 students. The ratio of residential faculty to boarding students is 1:5, with a full-time weekend activities coordinator, and a comprehensive residential curriculum.

Living in a dorm with a group of interesting peers is one of the most memorable parts of the Tabor experience. Guided and supported by faculty residents, you will learn to appreciate the backgrounds and habits of others and enjoy the good times - and occasionally, the trials - of sharing daily life with students whose interests and opinions on everything from politics to bands to sports may be far different from - or exactly the same - as your own. This mingling of diverse personalities and cultures under one roof makes dorm life an education in itself. Our students particularly like the fact that most of Tabor's 19 dorms - some have as few as four girls or boys - are located in close proximity, helping to create a kind of residential neighborhood. Students also enjoy close relationships with their houseparents; the student-faculty ratio in dorms is 12:1. The school's location on Sippican Harbor brings gorgeous sunrises for those lucky boarders with waterfront views, although few would ever admit to being up so early.

Nearest International Airport: Logan International Airport, Boston.

Nearby Lodgings: Pineywood Farm, 508 748-3925; Village Landing, 508 748-0350; Fairfield Inn by Marriott, 508 946-4000; Holiday Inn Express, 508 997-1281; Marriott Residence Inn, 508 984-5858.

The Thacher School

Location: Ojai, California (U.S. West Coast, Southern California)

5025 Thacher Road, Ojai, CA 93023
Phone: 805-640-3210; Fax: 805-640-9377
Website: www.thacher.org; Email: admission@thacher.org

Mr. William McMahon, Director of Admission
Phone: 805-640-3210; Fax: 805-640-9377
Email: admission@thacher.org

Mission Statement: The Mission of the School today remains essentially unchanged from that of its modest beginnings over one-hundred years ago. While hewing to its traditional task of preparing students for admission to college and equipping them with the contemporary knowledge and tools for a successful course of higher education, Thacher continues to train young men and women in the art of living for their own greatest good and for the greatest good of their fellow citizens in the increasingly diverse society of a complex nation and ever-changing world. To these ends, a scholarly and able faculty encourages and expects excellence of students in the School's classrooms, laboratories, and studios; a lifelong love of truth and learning; exemplary levels of performance and sportsmanship on the playing fields and courts; high standards of conduct in all relationships and activities; and civil courtesy throughout the School's daily round. The School's extraordinary location and traditional family environment continue to promote the virtues of personal growth and self-reliance tempered by an increasing awareness of the needs of others and a shared responsibility for a healthy and happy community.

Grade Level: 9-12.

Student Gender: Boys & Girls.

Enrollment: 115 boys, 115 girls, 210 boarders, 20 day.

Accredited by: WASC, CAIS/CA

Head of School: Michael Mulligan, B.A. and M.A. Middlebury, Ed.M. Harvard.

Faculty: Thacher has a faculty of 44 teachers, 70% percent of whom hold advanced degrees. Teachers also act as coaches, club sponsors, dining room supervisors, weekend coordinators. All but a few of the faculty live on campus.

Tuition: Tuition and Boarding for 2003-2004 is $31,250.

Class Size: The student-faculty ratio is 6:1.

Curriculum: The academic program includes a core curriculum of English, mathematics, foreign language, science, history, and fine arts, along with a wide variety of electives. All seniors are required to complete a research project and make a presentation at the annual Senior Exhibitions. Independent study programs are also available, and students may also participate in off-campus study abroad and throughout various locations throughout the U.S.

Advanced Placement: 21 Advanced Placement courses are offered.

Average SAT Scores of Graduating Students: SAT I scores average 640 verbal and 640 math.

College Placement: Recent graduates of Thacher have been accepted to Brown, Colorado College, Columbia, Northwestern, Stanford, and the University of California at Berkeley.

Academic Requirements: Thacher's graduation requirements are based on the School's commitment to academic opportunity, rigor, and flexibility. Students must meet the departmental requirements outlined below, take the requisite number of courses each term, and successfully complete the Senior Exhibition. All Thacher students, however, go well beyond the minimum graduation requirements in areas of special interest, and the program is designed to allow and encourage the best mix, for each student, of broad, general background and advanced specialized study. To graduate from The Thacher School, students must complete the following departmental requirements: English: 8 semesters, Mathematics: 6 semesters (through Math III), Foreign Language: 6 semesters or third-level proficiency, Science: 4 semesters (Physics and Chemistry), History: 4 semesters (World History and United States History), The Arts: 4 semesters

Course Load Requirement: Each student must take five courses each term. Four of them must be solid courses, and the fifth may be either a solid or a non-solid course. A solid course is defined as one having substantial written homework. In general, studio classes such as sculpture and chorus receive full credit but are classified as non-solids. Courses in art history and music theory, like most courses in the other academic departments, are classified as solids.

Sports: Athletics enjoy great popularity at Thacher. While most Thacher students play sports throughout their careers, all students are required to play on at least one Third, JV, or Varsity team prior to graduation. Ninth-graders may practice and compete on teams on Wednesdays, Fridays, and Saturdays, provided they have met all of their Horse Department obligations. Thacher coaches emphasize participation, teamwork, and sportsmanship. Winning and losing are means for learning about commitment, friendship, cooperation, competition, limits, and stress.

Thacher fields the following competitive teams: Boys' and Girls' Cross Country, Boys' and Girls' Tennis, Girls' Volleyball, Dance Ensemble, Boys' and Girls' Equestrian, Boys' and Girls' Soccer, Boys' and Girls' Basketball, Boys' and Girls' Lacrosse, Boys' Baseball, and Boys' and Girls' Track.

Extracurricular Activities: All students, regardless of prior experience, are invited to participate in the Thacher Performing Arts Program. In addition to the faculty-directed activities below, many informal opportunities exist for students to dance, act, and play music. The afternoon dance program combines jazz, ballet, and modern dance, and is offered as an athletic activity in the fall. Classes focus on improving strength, flexibility, and alignment, and on learning a variety of dance styles. Students may also audition for the Dance Ensemble, a repertory dance company which performs each term. Performances are prepared for Family Weekend, the Holiday Concert, and winter and spring productions.

The Thacher Masquers is a theatrical ensemble which puts on a fall play, a winter musical, and a number of one-act plays in the spring. Auditions are open to all. The Chorus, Chamber Singers (a select singing group), and the Instrument Ensemble can be taken as half-credit elective courses. These musical groups give performances each term and often participate in the Winter Musical. Private instrumental and vocal lessons are also available.

The Community Service Program (CSP) serves two distinct -functions. First, it serves a very real need in the local community, providing bright and able volunteers to fulfill a wide variety of jobs. Second, it offers Thacher students an opportunity to provide service in a way that is meaningful, necessary, and appreciated. To do this, CSP has developed a broad program so as to involve, inspire, and inform as many students as possible. During the 1998-99 school year, students served as volunteers at local elementary schools, Head Start, the local Humane Society, Senior Day Care, the Braille Institute, Special Olympics, and Habitat for Humanity. Students and faculty volunteer two or three times a month at either the Oxnard or the Los Angeles Rescue Mission, and Thacher has become a sponsor of the seasonal Ojai Homeless Shelter program, providing both food and volunteers. In addition, Thacher students help feed patients at two convalescent hospitals four nights a week and have also been involved with the distribution of food through Food Share.

Although nonsectarian and nondenominational in nature, Thacher recognizes the importance of religious and spiritual study and insight for the overall growth and well-being of the individual and the community. Blessed with a magnificent outdoor chapel, the School offers nondenominational services at various religious holidays, as well as regular convocations for the purpose of investigating spiritual, religious, and ethical concerns. All students are encouraged to attend these services. The School also arranges transportation to various places of worship in Ojai each Saturday and Sunday for interested students. A World Religions course is offered for the purpose of intellectual inquiry into the sociology, history, and theology of the world's great religions.

Some clubs at Thacher are steadfast traditions, like The Cum Laude Society and the Radio Station (KROK). Others, like the Gourmet Society, wax and wane with student interest. Students can always start their own clubs by finding a faculty advisor and getting approval from the Community Council, making them eligible for student activities funds. Other clubs and activities at Thacher

The Thacher School

include: Bible Study, California Mathematics League, Computer Network Consultants, El Archivero (the yearbook), Film Society, Foreign Students' Club, French Club, Games Club, Gun Club, Latin Club, Literary Society and Symposium, The Notes (the newspaper), Sir Winston Churchill Debating Society, Ski Club (Mad-Bomber Skiing Society), Spanish Club, Thacher Pack & Spur Club, United Cultures of Thacher, and Instrumental Ensemble.

Campus: Thacher is located on 400 acres, 90 miles northwest of Los Angeles, inland the coastal towns of Ventura and Santa Barbara. The campus is bordered by the Los Padres National Forest, and was once a ranch named "Casa de Piedra" - house of stone. Campus facilities include the Boswell Library, with 28,000 volumes; the Anson S. Thacher Humanities Building, which houses classrooms, art studios, computer graphic design stations, music practice rooms, darkrooms, an art gallery, and the campus radio station; the Seeley G. Mudd Science and Math Center contains computer labs, a digital media lab, eight science labs, and several aquariums. The school is fully networked through the campus server and offers Internet access through multiple T1 connections.

Dormitories: Thacher students live by class in eight single-sex dormitories. Ninth-graders nearly always live in single rooms; after the first year, many students have roommates. The dormitories are arranged in sections of about six students and one senior prefect who helps administer dormitory rules and serves as a role model and informal advisor for other students. Dormitories are run by dorm heads with help from faculty advisors and prefects. While every dorm room comes with a bed, desk, closet, dresser, and direct connection to the Internet, students quickly decorate their rooms to reflect their own individual characters. It is the diversity of these characters that makes dorm life special. While living in a shared space comes with challenges - from sharing the laundry facilities to tolerating your roommate's choice of music - rising to these challenges lays the foundation for meaningful and lifelong friendships. Like the individuals who live in them, every dormitory at Thacher has its own character and history. Some dorms have more history than others: the Upper School was built in 1889, Los Padres in 1994. Traditions such as dorm songs (one lively, one slow, one in

Latin) illustrate the plentiful spirit of dorm areas.

Nearest International Airport: Los Angeles International Airport.

Nearby Lodgings: The Blue Iguana and Emerald Iguana Inns, 805-646-5277; Casa Ojai - Best Western, 800-225-8175; Hummingbird Inn, 800-228-3744; The Moon's Nest Inn, 805-646-6635; Oakridge Inn, 805-649-4018; Ojai Valley Inn & Spa, 805-646-5511; Rose Garden Inn, 805-646-1434; Theodore Woolsey House, 805-646-9779.

The Vanguard School

Location: Lake Wales, Florida (U.S. Southern)

22000 US Highway 27, Lake Wales, FL 33859-7895
Phone: 863-676-6091; Fax: 863-676-8297
Website: www.vanguardschool.org
Email: vanadmin@vanguardschool.org

Mrs. Melanie Anderson, Director of Admission
Phone: 863-676-6091; Fax: 863-676-8297
Email: mander@vanguardschool.org

Mission Statement: The mission of the Vanguard School is to provide an individualized program in a nurturing environment which enables students to develop to their fullest capabilities: Academically, Socially and Personally.

Grade Level: 5-12.

Student Gender: Boys & Girls

Enrollment: 141 students, 88 boys, 53 girls, 131 boarders, 10 day.

Accredited by: SACS, FCIS

Head of School: James R. Moon, Ph.D., M.B.A., Washington and Jefferson College, (B.A., psychology, 1977), Virginia Tech (M.S., clinical psychology, 1979, Ph.D., clinical psychology, 1982), Nova Southeastern University (M.B.A., 1997).

Faculty: The Vanguard School has a faculty of 29 teachers and specialists, 12 of whom hold advanced degrees. The School also staffs 40 residential and recreational supervisors who coordinate sports, clubs, weekend trips, social events and oversee dorm life and activities. The School has a resident psychologist who conducts evaluations and serves as a student counselor. A speech therapist is also available to work with students on an individual basis and to consult with teachers and staff.

Tuition: Tuition and Boarding for 2003-2004 is $31,400.

Curriculum: The Vanguard Upper School program is a fully accredited high school program that provides students with learning difficulties an opportunity to participate in an educational program that is individually designed for each student, based on their specific learning needs.

Individualized goals are devised for each student offering remedial and academic support in appropriate subject areas. Specialists in reading, math, speech and language evaluate students and offer individual clinical tutorials which promote and challenge the development of academic competencies. Reading and math are taught in classes of 8 or fewer students, with each student working at an individual level. Group taught courses have up to 12 students in each class.

A comprehensive educational program is offered in the Upper School program. In addition to the core reading and math classes, the students have a wide range of classes from which to choose. Graduation requirements give guidelines as to the courses that need to be completed before graduation. There are numerous elective courses.

Academic Requirements: English (Reading, Literature and Language) 4 credits, Mathematics 4 credits, Science (2 with labs: Biology + 1 other) 3 credits, Social Studies (U.S. History, World History, Economics and Government) 3 credits, Life Management ½ credit, Career Exploration ½ credit, Computer Science ½ credit, Physical Education 1 credit, Fine Arts or Vocational Arts 1 credit, Elective 6½ credits. Total credits required with a minimum 2.0 GPA: 24.

Sports: The athletic curriculum includes team sports in soccer, basketball, tennis, golf, weight lifting, track and field, and cross-country running, volleyball, cheerleading, and bowling. Students may also participate recreational basis in softball, swimming, volleyball, tennis, indoor hockey, soccer, and basketball. The Vanguard fitness center features a complete weight-training room. Aerobics classes are offered, and scuba diving lessons are available to students age 13 and older.

Extracurricular Activities: Extracurricular activities include the student newspaper and yearbook, an annual art and photography exhibition, clubs and activities, intramural sports, Key Club, and Student Government. Weekend activities include camping, canoeing, fishing, and off-campus trips to Disney World, Sea World, Cypress Gardens, the Kennedy Space Center, and the cities of Tampa and Orlando. Brunch is served on Saturday and Sunday mornings, and students may attend religious services. Dances, special activities, an annual field day, and several banquets are held throughout the year.

Campus: Located in the Florida city of Lake Wales, 70 miles east of Tampa and 45 miles south of Orlando, The Vanguard School is a 75-acre campus, conveniently accessible to beaches, entertainment, and cultural events. The Vanguard 's 13 buildings include 25 classrooms, and 2 science labs, the Aquatic Center, 3 dormitories, Harry E. Nelson Library, a dining hall, a fitness center, a visitors' reception center, the Edward Bartsch Memorial Gymnasium, three playing fields, three lighted tennis courts, a soccer field, and a fishing pier.

Dormitories: Our dormitories are home away from home for our students. There are two students to a room. The students take advantage of the spacious rooms and bring TV's, stereos, computers and other decorations to make their rooms feel like home. A lounge is available in each dormitory for watching television or visiting with friends. A telephone connection in each room allows parents to contact their child. With the voicemail system parents have an opportunity to leave messages when trying to catch up with an active child. High-speed access to the internet is available in each dormitory room for a fee.

West Dorm: Mr. Hewitt, the West Dormitory supervisor, and his staff provide 24-hour supervision and guidance for our youngest boys and the majority of our girls' population. The environment for the younger students is structured and extensively monitored by the house-parents and recreation staff. Daily responsibilities and activities are planned to provide a minimum of unscheduled time. A daily grading system is utilized to provide immediate reinforcement during social activities and the completion of responsibilities. Attempts are made to make expectations clear and consistent.

The grading of student performance takes into consideration effort, participation and cooperation. The older adolescent girls that reside in the West Dorm are provided more opportunity to demonstrate independent decision-making and self-monitoring skills that are consistent with their age and level of maturity.

East Dorm: The East Dorm is home to the majority of our adolescent boys. Mr. Whidden and his staff provide 24-hour monitoring and assistance to the young men who reside in the dormitory. Goals are established for each student emphasizing the development of independent living skills and acceptance of responsibility for their actions. The use of natural consequences for decisions is utilized and there is a reduction in staff intervention in the decision-making process. There is also more emphasis upon actual performance, progress and achievement in place of effort, participation and cooperation criteria used with younger students.

Sabbagh Hall: To reside in Sabbagh Hall is everyone's goal. Sabbagh serves as our honors dormitory for upper-level students and houses both boys and girls in an apartment-type environment. Mr. Mooneyham and his staff provide the guidance and assistance needed for these students to prepare for survival in postgraduate programs or independent living. The two students who share a spacious room also have a private bathroom. The common area with its lounge and kitchen facilities allows students to socialize and interact while under the monitoring of Mr. Mooneyham's staff.

Nearest International Airport: Orlando International Airport, Orlando, Florida.

Virginia Episcopal School

Location: Lynchburg, Virginia (U.S. Mid-Atlantic East Coast)

400 VES Road, P.O. Box 408, Lynchburg, VA 24503
Phone: 434-385-3605; Fax: 434-385-3603
Website: www.ves.org; Email: admissions@ves.org

Mrs. Pam Barile, Director of Admission
Phone: 434-385-3607; Fax: 434-385-3603; Email: pbarile@ves.org

Mission Statement: Virginia Episcopal School is committed to rigorous academic training and vigorous individual attention in a spiritual and ethical environment.

Grade Level: 9-12.

Student Gender: Boys & Girls.

Enrollment: 240 students, 150 boys, 90 girls, 150 boarders, 90 day.

Accredited by: VAIS

Head of School: Dr. Phil Hadley, B.S. Mathematics, Ohio University, M.A. Spanish Literature, Ohio University, Ph.D. Latin American History, University of Texas.

Faculty: When you think of friends in high school, you don't usually think of teachers, do you? You will here. Because here, our faculty and staff are not just friendly — they're friends. You can expect to play soccer with your teachers, shoot hoops with them, have dinner with their families, and go to the movies or a play with them. They're also your neighbors. More than 70 percent of VES faculty and staff live on campus with their own families. So your home is their home too. They're part of your family. The most fundamental element of the teacher-student relationship, or any relationship at VES, is respect. Our teachers show interest, notice the good things that students do, and are attentive to the students. We expect the same from our students. We believe that in a place where respect is a given, people have more freedom to explore, grow, and feel at ease. Virginia Episcopal School has a faculty of 46 full-time instructors and administrators, half of whom hold advanced degrees.

Faculty members also act as an advisors, coaches, club sponsors, and dormitory supervisors.

Tuition: Tuition and Boarding for 2003-2004 is $27,200.

Class Size: 12-14 students, with a student/faculty ratio of 6:1

Curriculum: At VES, we expect all of our students will attend college. So we design our curriculum to make our students as competitive for college as possible. We know that in order to inspire students to work hard, they must have curriculum choices that intrigue them. Here, students have a superb number of course options. Our curriculum provides more than 65 courses, including honors tracks and 16 advanced placement courses. You definitely won't be bored in our classrooms. Our approach is one-on-one — one teacher relating to one student. It's the way students learn the most, and the way we teach the best. We get to know students personally, challenge them individually, and encourage them to go beyond the talents they already possess. It requires hard work. It also inspires excellence.

Advanced Placement: Advanced Placement courses are offered in English, Music Theory, Studio Art, French, Spanish, Government, U.S. History, European History, Calculus, Statistics, Biology, Chemistry, and Computer Science.

Average SAT Scores of Graduating Students: The range of recent SAT I scores for the middle 50% were 990–1250.

College Placement: Recent graduates of Virginia Episcopal School have been accepted to Mary Washington, Rhodes, Virginia Tech, VMI, William and Mary, University of Alabama, University of Mississippi, University of North Carolina at Chapel Hill, University of Tennessee, and University of Virginia.

Academic Requirements: To qualify for graduation, each student requires 4 years of English, 3 years of mathematics through Algebra II/trigonometry, 2 years of one foreign language, 2 years of history, 2 years of laboratory science, 1 year of fine arts, 2/3 of a year of religion, 1/3 of a year of computer applications, and 1/3 of a year of life issues.

Sports: The Virginia Episcopal athlethic program offers team sports for baseball, basketball, cross-country, football, golf, indoor soccer, indoor track, lacrosse, soccer, tennis, track, wrestling, field hockey, golf, softball and volleyball. Recreational activities include aerobics, dance, and riding. The campus athletic facilities include two baseball diamonds, one softball fields, an outdoor track, two athletic buildings, with basketball/volleyball courts, basketball/soccer courts, an indoor track, a batting cage, a wrestling room, an athletic training room, and locker and shower facilities.

Extracurricular Activities: Extracurricular activities include the Vestige Yearbook, the school newspaper, the Alpha Order, the Student Vestry, the Earth Club, community service, and academic clubs in art, drama, photography, and science. The Activities Committee plans regular events including concerts, and class trips to Washington DC and other nearby cities. The School provides bus transportation to Lynchburg on the weekends. Students also attend dances at other nearby schools. Movies are shown every weekend at the dorms, and boarding students are allowed to visit the homes of day students.

Campus: Virginia Episcopal School is located on 160-acres in Lynchburg, Virginia, in the foothills of the Blue Ridge Mountains. Jett Hall is the main building on campus, with classrooms, a writing lab, an auditorium, administrative offices, dormitories and faculty apartments. Pendleton Hall and Randolph Hall both contain classrooms, the Banks-Gannaway building houses a library with 16,000 volumes, and the Zimmer Science and Activity Center features state-of-the-art laboratories, an audiovisual hall, lecture rooms, a computer center, and faculty offices.

Dormitories: Virginia Episcopal School has 6 six dormitories with double rooms. Each dorm room has two Internet connections and a phone line. All dormitories are staffed with counselors and resident teachers.

Nearest International Airport: Dulles International Airport, Washington DC.

Wasatch Academy

Location: Mount Pleasant, Utah (U.S. Western Central)

120 South 100 West, Mount Pleasant, UT 84647
Phone: 800-634-4690 ext. 121; Fax: 435-462-3380
Website: www.wacad.org; Email: admissions@wacad.org

Mr. Dan Kemp, Director of Admission and International Relations
Phone: 800-634-4690; Fax: 435-462-3380
Email: admissions@wacad.org

Mission Statement: Wasatch Academy provides a nurturing community that empowers young men and young women to develop academically, socially and morally, preparing them for college and for the challenges of living in the 21st century.

Grade Level: 9-12.

Student Gender: Boys & Girls.

Enrollment: 153 students, 83 boys, 70 girls, 125 boarders, 28 day.

International Students: students come from Belgium, Bulgaria, Canada, Cyprus, Germany, Japan, Kenya, Korea, Latvia, Lithuania, New Zealand, Peru, Russia, Rwanda, Sudan, Taiwan, and Tibet.

Accredited by: PNAIS

Head of School: Joseph R. Loftin, University of Texas, Utah State University, Klingenstein Fellowship Columbia University.

Faculty: The Wasatch commitment to diversity extends to our teaching staff as well. Our 35 faculty members have earned both undergraduate and advanced degrees from the leading institutions in the U.S., including Harvard, Yale, Duke, Amherst, Brandeis and Reed, as well as further afield, from McGill University in Canada and the University of Oxford in England. Many of our faculty members are attracted to Wasatch Academy by the abundant opportunities to enjoy recreation in what is one of the most spectacular states in the U.S. The faculty also very much enjoy sharing the wonders of nature with their students. Our small class sizes and close-knit community permit students get to know their instructors in a variety of settings both within and beyond the classroom. It is common for a student to attend class with a teacher in the morning, chat with that same teacher over lunch, meet the teacher's family in the dining hall at dinnertime and then participate in a weekend recreation trip supervised by that same teacher. At Wasatch, teachers and students benefit greatly from interacting in innumerable ways, seven days per week.

Tuition: Tuition and Boarding for 2003-2004 is $16,800.

Class Size: 10 students, with a student/teacher ratio of 4:1.

Curriculum: Wasatch Academy is the oldest college preparatory school in the state. The principal concern in every course is to train students in the essential skills they need for success at their college level studies.

The course offerings at Wasatch Academy are carefully sequenced across the four years from grades 9 - 12 (vertically)to reflect increasingly challenging levels of complexity, while the subjects at each grade level are interdisciplinary in emphasis (cross-curricular) such that each course is cross-referenced to all other subjects that a student will address at that time.

In addition to the core subjects (History, English, Math, Science) which a typical four-year student studies in preparation for college, a Wasatch student has opportunities to study (naming just a few of the more popular offerings in recent years) creative writing, visual arts, ceramics, photography, fabricarts, stained glassworks, choral music, instrumental music, dance, drama, debate, computer-assisted design, computer programming, furniture making, organic gardening, landscape design, rock-climbing, backpacking, snowboarding, skiing, and of course to pursue a full complement of varsity sports.

Advanced Placement: Wasatch offers Advanced Placement courses in English, U.S. History, Biology, Calculus, and Statistics.

ESL Program: At Wasatch Academy, international students have the opportunity to grow and develop socially, culturally, and of course, academically. Students at Wasatch have the chance to make friends from all parts of the world including Lithuania, Korea, Japan, Nepal, Bulgaria, Cypress, Pakistan, Kenya, Latvia, Taiwan, Rwanda. While living in the dorms, international students have the opportunity to interact with native English speakers from the United States and learn about American culture. This cultural and linguistic immersion necessitates that ESL students have no other choice but to speak English in order to communicate and many international students come to Wasatch to find that after a few months they are speaking English non-stop! Living in a dorm environment enables international students to add diversity to the student-body and to educate others concerning their own language, country and culture. International students develop emotionally as they face new challenges such as adapting to a new environment, language, and culture. Wasatch Academy is blessed with dedicated and caring teachers, dorm parents and student advisors to help our international students overcome any culture shock issues as they arise.

Wasatch Academy also allows students to grow culturally. Many students from foreign countries, form strong friendships with each other and visit each other in their home countries during the summer break. After graduation, international students leave Wasatch Academy with both American and international friendships and fond memories that last a lifetime.

Finally, the reason why most international students come to Wasatch Academy is to learn English. At Wasatch Academy, all ESL classes are small and interactive, varying from four to nine students in each class. The small number of students in all ESL, and in all academic classes for that matter, enables teachers to give individual attention and to recognize individual needs. Students feel more comfortable asking questions in a small, informal classroom setting and feel free to interact with other ESL and native English speaking students in English. International students learn English very quickly at Wasatch Academy, as they advance through the intermediate and advanced levels of ESL Grammar, Reading, Writing, Listening and Speaking, and U.S. History and Culture classes.

Eventually ESL students are mainstreamed into regular academic classes. After graduation from Wasatch Academy, international students are accepted into competitive colleges and universities in the United States or they decide to return to their native country to attend college. With the solid classroom instruction and practice they receive at Wasatch, students gain the knowledge base and grammatical background they need to succeed in university life. Meanwhile, each student is taking advantage of being immersed in the English language and American culture through dorm life, outdoor and sports recreation, academics and by building lasting friendships with other students and faculty. The ESL Program at Wasatch Academy is an opportunity no international student should miss.

College Placement: Wasatch Academy is the oldest university-preparatory school in the state of Utah. Students graduating from Wasatch enjoy numerous offers of admission to competitive colleges and universities from across the United States, including: NYU, U.S. Military Academy, San Francisco Academy of Art, Boston University, Oregon State, University of California, Westminster College, Loyola Marymount, and Cornell.

Academic Requirements: Wasatch requires 24 academic credits for graduation: 4 credits in English, 3 credits in math, 3 credits in the sciences (including biology), 3 credits in history/social science (including U.S. history), 2 credits in a single foreign language (3 for honors), 2 credits in fine arts, ½ credit each in health and computer proficiency, and ½ credit each year in religion or ethics.

Sports: Students are encouraged to learn teamwork and the spirit of competition by participating in at least one sport each year. In addition to requiring mandatory participation in sports, Wasatch Academy maintains an inclusive, no-cut policy which ensures that whoever goes out to try for a given team will be on board. There are a wide variety sports from which to choose, which effectively encompass all skill levels; Wasatch Academy offers more varsity sports than any comparable 1A school in the state. At Wasatch Academy, you're not watching the action from the sidelines, you're in the game! In addition to physical sports, students may choose to satisfy the sports participation requirement by joining the Speech and Debate team or the Choir or by selecting Theatre Sports as their elective, inasmuch as these activities also foster the virtue of teamwork. We hold a one week camp prior to the start of school designed for all students/athletes who choose to participate in one of the following sports: Cross Country, Tennis, Volleyball, Soccer, Baseball, Alpine Skiing, Basketball, Cheeleading, Martial Arts, Snowboarding, Golf, Soccer, Softball, Track and Field. Wasatch offers recreational sports such as yoga, mountain biking, rock climbing, skateboarding, and fly fishing.

Extracurricular Activities: Extracurricular activities include drama, music, yearbook, martial arts, drawing, pottery, photography, and community service. And each year, the students and staff climb to the 11,800 ft. summit of Mount Nebo. Weekend recreation is an important part of the Wasatch experience. We offer hiking, camping, rock climbing, fly fishing and cross country skiing through our Outdoor Education program. Students also have the chance to sign up for mall, movie, dinner, and amusement park adventures. Snowboarding and ski trips are a winter favorite. Extracurricular eligibility is a necessity to be able to participate in any recreational events that require leaving campus. We ask that all students broaden their recreational horizons. Each student will be required to attend two cultural recreational offerings and two outdoor offerings over the course of the year. There are a variety of events from which to choose. Much of our recreation goes on within the campus limits. Java the Hut (our traditional coffee house evening) , athletic contests, movies on the big-screen TV in the Tiger´s Den and residence hall open houses are a few examples of campus entertainment. The gym and weight-rooms have regular weekend hours and the Tiger´s Den is open for pool, ping-pong, air hockey and just relaxing with the satellite dish or a game of Monopoly.

Wasatch also offers weekend camping, hiking, mountain biking, skiing and snowboarding trips, as well as excursions to Salt Lake City for cultural or sporting events; off-campus dinners, shopping, movies, and festivals.

Campus: Located in the rural Sanpete Valley 100 miles south of Salt Lake City, Wasatch Academy is located in Mt. Pleasant, Utah, a safe and quiet rural community of approximately 3,000 people, 100 miles south of Salt Lake City, home of the 2002 Winter Olympics. The academy is located within easy reach of some of the most scenic natural areas in the world, including world-class white water rivers, mountains, deserts and the breathtakingly beautiful red rock canyon country.

Wasatch Academy is designated a National Historic Site, featuring antique brick buildings housing classrooms and residence halls, a spacious gymnasium, playing fields, faculty homes and a museum, all situated on a spectacular 17 acre campus nestled in the foothills of the Rocky Mountains. Students enjoy the fresh air, brilliant sunsets and bright starry skies Mt. Pleasant has to offer. It quickly becomes a home away from home.

Academic facilities at Wasatch include three main buildings: mathematics and science building which features four science labs, math classrooms, and a computer lab. The Craighead School Building serves the humanities and language departments with classrooms, a computer writing lab, an auditorium/theater, and a library linked to the Utah University Interlibrary System. The Hansen Music and Art Center features 5 music rooms, 4 art studios, a photo lab, and pottery kilns, The school is fully networked with wireless technology. The Student Center features a recreation area, a lounge, a bookstore, and a grill and snack bar. The campus also has an athletic center, a health center, a chapel, a museum, a student game room, several sports fields, tennis courts, and a mountain cabin for hiking and winter sports.

Dormitories: Wasatch Academy has a true boarding school feel, with all students, both day and residential, sharing in the lived sense of community. Boarding students are centered around dorm and campus life, though all students learn to live and work in an atmosphere of respect, forming friendships that last a lifetime. Wasatch Academy sets a high priority on the comfort and security of its residential population. At Wasatch, unlike 95% of the other boarding schools on the U.S., none of the dorm parents have to teach - their sole responsibility is providing a nurturing and supportive residential environment within our six dormitories. Wasatch has a total of 6 dormitory buildings with double rooms, student lounges, kitchens, storage space, and laundry facilities. Students and faculty members share all meals in the dining room.

Nearest International Airport: Salt Lake City International Airport.

Washington Academy

Location: East Machias, Maine (U.S. East Coast, New England)

P.O. Box 190, High Street, East Machias, ME 04630
Phone: 207-255-8301; Fax: 207-255-8303
Website: www.washingtonacademy.org
Email: admissions@washingtonacademy.org

Ms. Charlene Cates, Director of Admission
Phone: 207-255-8301; Fax: 207-255-8303
Email: admissions@washingtonacademy.org

Mission Statement: From your first sight of the tall white spire of the original Academy Building against the blue sky, you will feel the strength of Washington Academy's mission. Since John Hancock signed the school's charter in 1792, Washington Academy has had one goal: providing students with the finest secondary education possible. Over the years, Washington Academy has grown to meet the needs of today's high school students as they face modern challenges. As well as an extensive curriculum for college preparation, Washington Academy offers business and vocational studies, a large selection of sports and extracurricular activities. Affordable tuition rates make it one of the best values among boarding, private secondary and college prep schools in Maine and New England.

Admission Requirements for International Students: While many schools require a minimum TOEFL (Test of English as a Foreign Language) score before admission, we do not. This is because we have seen how quickly students at all levels progress once they are in an all-English environment. We do require that a student take either the TOEFL or the SLEP.

Grade Level: 9-12.

Student Gender: Boys & Girls.

Enrollment: 344 students, 171 boys, 173 girls, 34 boarders, 310 day.

International Students: 34 students from: Japan, Korea, Russia, Taiwan, Spain, Bermuda, Vietnam, China, and Serbia.

Accredited by: NEASC

Head of School: Judson L. McBrine III, University of Maine (B.S., 1990), University of Maine Graduate School (M.Ed., 1996).

Faculty: At Washington Academy, recruiting high caliber teachers is a top priority. All of our teachers are certified and over half have Master's degrees. But credentials are only part of the story. Our teachers love to teach, love to learn and love to talk and listen to students. Washington Academy has 26 full-time teachers, which means one teacher for every eleven students and an average class size of 14.

Tuition: Tuition and Boarding for 2003-2004 is $21,500. Tuition and host family placement for 2004-2005 is $17,500.

Class Size: 14 students, with a student-teacher ratio of 11:1.

Curriculum: Washington Academy is one of the oldest college preparatory schools in New England. With more than one hundred classes, students have plenty of options to tailor their studies to their interests and needs. In addition to excellent programs in traditional studies such as science, mathematics, English, and world history and culture, Washington Academy also offers hands-on programs like Boat Building and Environmental Science. Our extensive use of "nature as a classroom" sets us apart among boarding schools in Maine and New England. In addition to college preparatory courses, Washington Academy also offers many exciting electives. These include digital film and video production, music appreciation, creative writing, computer programming and web design. We also have many advanced placement (AP) classes for advanced students, as well as the opportunity for juniors and seniors to take free classes at the nearby University of Maine at Machias.

Advanced Placement: Washington academy offers the following Advanced Placement courses:, AP Calculus, AP Calculus BC, AP Biology, AP Java, AP Studio Art, AP English 4, and U.S. History.

ESL Program: No matter what your English level is now, at Washington Academy, you'll be speaking English fluently and understanding American culture sooner than you imagine! In our

English Language Classes (also called ESL - English as a Second Language) you will learn from everything around you. We listen to song lyrics, read magazines, act out scenes from movies and play computer games. We might take you to the bank to or a grocery store to practice your English. We also have advanced word recognition software to help you master your pronunciation. You will also learn to write college essays. Are you an advanced English speaker? Washington Academy's full time professional tutor will help you study for the TOEFL. She also works with you to improve any weaknesses in your speaking, writing or understanding English. Your parents understand how important "the language of global commerce" is to your future success. At Washington Academy, we do what it takes to make sure you graduate with the strongest English skills possible.

Average SAT Scores of Graduating Students: Average total SAT combined score - 1000.

College Placement: Recent graduates were accepted at Bates, Bowdoin, Boston University, Ithaca, Johnson & Wales, Maine Maritime Academy, Middlebury, Roger Williams, Worcester Polytechnic Institute, and the Universities of Arizona and Maine.

Academic Requirements: Washington Academy students are required to take twenty credits to graduate: four English credits, three social studies including U.S. History, three science, three mathematics, one fine arts, one physical education and one half credit each of health and computer proficiency.

Sports: Are you the sporting type? You'll love Washington Academy! We offer many of the sports you'd expect: basketball, baseball, soccer, softball, cross-country and cheerleading. Washington Academy also has strong programs in golf, tennis, and volleyball—no wonder so many of our students are on a team! Washington Academy also has something you cannot put a price on: school pride! Our gymnasium is ready for our teams with two courts and seating for 1,100 fans. Students, teachers and many people from the community show up for games to cheer for the Washington Academy Raiders.

We also provide boarding students membership as part of their activity fee at the University of Maine at Machias Center for Lifelong Learning. Daily transportation is provided from the school to the center. The Center includes a competition-size swimming pool, a fully equipped fitness room, racquetball courts, an aerobics/multi-purpose room, and the largest gymnasium in eastern Maine. The Center staff includes certified personal trainers, fitness instructors, and lifeguards. Students can use the facilities independently or take one of many courses included in the membership.

Extracurricular Activities: Music: The halls are alive with the sound of music at Washington Academy. From casual enjoyment to serious music scholars, there 's a music club for everyone: Jazz chorus, concert chorus, pep band, National Music Honor society, County Wide District and All-State music competitions. Our Tri-M Music Honor society has even traveled to Europe.

Drama: The WA players put on one-act plays and a musical production every year and even take the show on the road to compete statewide. Students can work on any aspect of theater: set design, stage management, lighting, sound, choreography, acting or costumes and make-up.

Visual Arts: A club for students who love drawing and painting, illustrating comic books, making sculptures, designing murals, taking pictures, making digital art and just about anything else creative!

Communication: The perfect word for every occasion! Our students try their hand at journalism on the student paper; fill the pages of the Silver Quill, the school literary magazine, with fiction and poetry; take photos; and write the school yearbook and say what's on their minds in Public Speaking.

Academics: For the students who want that extra edge, academic clubs pick up where classes leave off. Economic decathlon, academic decathlon and the Envirothon team are whirlwind weekend competitions, a statewide Olympics for the mind. Some clubs focus on a single interest like the math team, math help, science club, creative writing club or the foreign language club.

Interest Groups: A little bit of everything! Activities include International Club, Future Business Leaders, Student Librarians, Prom Committee, Student Council, Video and Digital Movie Club, Knitting Club, Yoga, Ski Outing, community service clubs, and Chess.

What about weekends? At WA, we have that covered! Boarding students at Washington Academy can take part in free weekend activities as part of their WA experience. Sometimes these trips are true "Maine outdoors adventures," such as a whale-watching excursion or downhill skiing. Sometimes, they are laid-back, such as a trip to the movie cinema or the Bangor Mall. During Thanksgiving vacation, February vacation and April vacation, Washington Academy offers students some exciting and educational trips with affordable prices. Trips are free to boarding students, with the exception of meals and personal spending. All student road trips are fully chaperoned, with at least 1 adult per 10 students. Students travel in comfortable buses and stay in nice hotels. Some of the memorable trips on our list include Boston: The trip to "Beantown" starts with walk along the freedom trail and see historic sites from the American Revolution. Favorite stops include the New England Aquarium, the Museum of Science or the MFA (Museum of Fine Arts.) We also try to visit potential future colleges and Universities such as Harvard, MIT and UMass. Sugarloaf, USA: If you don't know how to ski or snowboard, the professionals at Sugarloaf will teach you. This mountain has spectacular views, fresh air, and even a mountainside restaurant. This is a very popular trip! New York: Time Square is amazing. The museums are astounding. This trip even features a show at the Met or on Broadway. We also visit Ellis Island, the Statue of Liberty and the site of the 9/11 tragedy. Bar Harbor: Close by, and one of our students' favorite trips. We walk along Acadia National Park's famous Sand Beach, see the views from Cadillac Mountain, watch the boats from Bar Harbor's busy pier, and much more. Students and their chaperones rent bicycles to explore the trails that surround Bar Harbor. The trip also includes a tour of Jackson Laboratories, a world leader in genetic research.

Washington, D.C: Recent trips have included visits to the Capitol Building, the White House, the Lincoln, Washington and Jefferson

Memorials, Arlington National Cemetery, the Vietnam Memorial and the Smithsonian Museum.

Campus: East Machias, a small town on the eastern coast of Maine, is home to Washington Academy. Within two miles of the ocean, atop a hill, Washington Academy consists of seven buildings on a 45 acre campus. The school is a blend of history and modernization. As you approach, you will first see the tall white tower of the original Academy Building, built in 1823, which is home to foreign languages, mathematics and special education. From the front steps, you can see both the Cates House and the Larson House, both dorms for boarding students. Across the street, the newly renovated Alumni Building serves as the heart of Washington Academy. It includes many classrooms, guidance, five computer labs, the performing arts stage, and the cafeteria as well as an inviting library with over 10,000 books. Directly behind the Alumni building is the Gardiner Gymnasium, one of the best athletic facilities in the state. It has two courts and a seating capacity of 1,100, a weight room and a training room. Also within the gym complex are the music classrooms. As soon as you step inside, you'll see how seriously we take music: we have tiered seating and practice rooms as well as a computer lab for music composition. Beside the Gardiner Gymnasium is the Industrial Technology Building. This building contains the Marine Trades program, Industrial Arts and Computer Networking and Repair. The Marine trades classroom area has computerized numerical cutting equipment, a professional paint booth, fiberglass boat building machines, as well as equipment for the construction of historical bent lathe canoes! Behind the main buildings are the soccer, baseball and softball fields, and outdoor basketball courts. Behind the fields, a cross-country course winds its way up through steep and rugged blueberry fields.

Dormitories: Your new home at Washington Academy will be either in a dorm or with a host family. Washington Academy has two historic homes full of modern conveniences for International students; the Larson House for 15 male students and the Cates House for 14 female students. When you come to Washington Academy, you will feel right at home. Our dorms are safe, comfortable, and clean. Each room is wired for Internet access and cable TV.

A cook prepares your evening meal, and the kitchen stays open for evening snacks! If you wish, you can have your laundry washed and folded by a service, or you can wash your own clothes in the dorm.

Host parents live in the dorm 24 hours a day for supervision and support. Your dorm parents will take you to the store to buy new sneakers, help you cook your favorite foods for your new friends, or take you to the doctor if you get sick. Your dorm parents will help you have a happy, safe, and successful school experience! Dorm life gives you plenty of chances to practice your English with your new friends. When you study together, play tennis or soccer, or just relax, you'll be sharing and learning a new language.

Host Families. How did you learn to speak your native language? From your family, of course! A host family helps you learn English the way you learned your own language. You will be in a warm, caring environment — and you will speak and hear only English. A host family gives you a chance to be immersed in U.S. culture all day, every day. No class or book can do that! You don't just learn English and customs, you live them! Our host families are carefully chosen and we match your interests to theirs. All our host families are friendly, and eager to share their lives with international students. They are happy to learn about you and your country. You will share meals, go to movies, shop, and take family trips. Frequently, students and families stay in touch long after graduation.

Nearest International Airport: Bangor International Airport, Bangor, Maine; Portland International Jetport, Maine.

Nearby Lodgings: The Riverside Inn, 207-255-4134; Machias Motor Inn, 207-255-4861; The Seagull Motel, 207-255-3033; Four Points Hotel by Sheraton, 207-947-6721.

The Webb School

Location: Bell Buckle, Tennessee (U.S. East Central)

Sawney Webb Highway, P.O. Box 488, Bell Buckle, TN 37020
Phone: 931-389-6003; Fax: 931-389-6657
Website: www.thewebbschool.com
Email: admissions@webbschool.com

Mr. Matt Radtke, Director of Admission
Phone: 888-733-9322; Fax: 931-389-6657
Email: admissions@webbschool.com

Mission Statement: Founded in 1870 by noted scholar William R. "Old Sawney" Webb, Webb School Bell Buckle is the South's oldest continuously operating boarding school.

Sawney Webb's goal was to build moral character, make ladies and gentlemen of his students, and prepare them for any challenge that may come their way. This has been accomplished for over 130 years through a solid liberal arts education, a strong sense of honor, and an interactive school community. Over the years, Webb has produced 10 Rhodes Scholars and its graduates have gone on to attend prestigious colleges and universities across the nation and to lead important, successful and fulfilling lives in business, education, and the arts.

It is our intention to keep this tradition alive by providing a sound education combined with high moral values.

Grade Level: 7-12.

Student Gender: Boys & Girls.

Enrollment: 163 boys, 132 girls, 92 boarders, 203 day.

Accredited by: SACS

Faculty: Classes are led by 42 faculty members, 62% of whom hold advanced degrees. Teachers at Webb are deeply committed to seeing students succeed. They are here to challenge their students, to push them to try harder. Because many live on campus, they're available to students long after the school day ends. The faculty here love what they do, and it shows. With a majority holding advanced degrees, they bring expertise, talent, and energy to the classroom. But teachers at Webb are so much more than just teachers. What sets Webb apart is the relationships between students and faculty both inside and outside the classroom. Most, if not all, of the faculty are actively involved in campus life. They're coaches and advisors. They're mentors and trip leaders. They're people you get to know and who get to know you. They're friends.

Tuition: Tuition and Boarding for 2003-2004 is $27,250.

Class Size: 12 students, with a student-to-faculty ratio of 7:1.

Curriculum: The Webb School curriculum includes;

English: I, II, III, and IV (Honors sections in III and IV), AP English IV, Journalism, Creative Writing, Shakespeare.

Mathematics: Algebra I, Geometry, Algebra II (Honors sections at each level), College Algebra and Trigonometry, Precalculus, AP Calculus AB & BC, AP Statistics.

History: World Cultures, Western Civilization, U.S. History, AP U.S. History, AP European History, American Government, U.S. History Since 1945, World Religions, World History, Political Theory, Economics.

Science: Biology, Chemistry, Physics (Honors sections at each level), AP Chemistry, AP Physics, Anatomy and Physiology, Forestry, Freshwater Biology, Psychology.

Foreign Languages: French I, II, III*, IV-AP, and V-AP; Spanish I, II, III*, IV, IV-AP, and V-AP; German I, II, and III; Latin I, II, and III*. (Levels III and higher are considered Honors sections.)

Ethics.

Fine Arts: Studio Art, Painting, Pottery, Speech, Drama, Advanced Acting, Choir, Hitchcock's Films.

Technology: Computer Literacy, Computer Applications, Advanced

Computer.

Fitness: Health, Physical Education, Wilderness Skills.

ESL (English as a Second Language): History; Science; ESL I, II, and III.

Advanced Placement: The Webb School offers Advanced Placement classes in English Literature, U.S. History, French, Spanish, European History, Chemistry, Physics, Calculus AB & BC, and Statistics. In 2003, 37 students took 80 Advanced Placement Examinations, earning scores of 3 or above on 68% of the tests.

ESL Program: Webb School offers ESL (English as a Second Language) courses in History; Science; ESL I, II, and III.

Average SAT Scores of Graduating Students: Mean SAT Scores: Verbal: 598, Math: 584

College Placement: Recent graduates of Webb School have been acceoted to colleges such as Duke, Emory, George Washington, Georgetown University, Harvard University, Purdue, Rhode Island School of Design, United States Air Force Academy, University of North Carolina Chapel Hill, University of Pennsylvania, University of San Francisco, Vanderbilt, Virginia Military Institute, Wake Forest, Washington & Lee, and William and Mary.

Academic Requirements: English 4 credits, Mathematics 3 credits (Algebra I, Algebra II, and Geometry required), Science 2 credits (Biology required), History 2 credits (Western Civilization and U.S. History required), Foreign Language 2 credits (same language in upper school), Electives from above disciplines 3 credits, Economics 1/2 credit, Computer Literacy 1/2 credit, Fine Arts 1 and 1/2 credits (Speech and Art required), Health/P.E. 1/2 credit, Ethics 1/2 credit.

Sports: Webb is committed to its growing number of student athletes and teams. Seen at the left are photos of Webbies in action on the playing fields and a photo of the new Barton Athletic Complex, opened in September, 2002. The four million-dollar facility houses basketball/volleyball courts, a dance and aerobic studio, a walk around track, weight room with state of the art equipment, team meeting rooms, and locker rooms.

Athletics are an important aspect of Webb because students are encouraged to be involved in our community outside of the classroom. Each year Webb fields very competitive sports teams. However, the most important aspect of the athletic program is not the margin of victory but how we went about the game. Varsity teams at Webb include: Baseball, Softball, Basketball, Swimming, Cross Country, Tennis, Golf, Track, Lacrosse, Volleyball, Soccer, Baseball, and Softball.

Extracurricular Activities: Each weekend various trips are offered for our boarding students and any of our day students that want to come along too. Trips range from: Different sporting events (Titans and Predators games), Concerts, White water rafting, Movie and mall trips, Paintball, Bowling, and Nashville dinner trips.

Academic and athletic activities include Outerlimits, Skeet, Webb Players (drama), Physical Training, Aerobics, Interact (community service), Tennis, Fly-Fishing, Bowling, Painting, Newspaper, Yearbook, Choir Class Officers, Ecology Club, Fly Fishing Club, FOCUS (Christian Athletic club), French Club, Honor Council, Interact (service club), Latin Club, Literary magazine, National Honor Society, Quiz Bowl, SCUBA Club, Skeet Club, Son Will Society (admissions), Spanish Club, Student Council, The Oracle (student newspaper), The Sawney (yearbook), The Webb Players, Thespian Society, Young Democrats, and Young Republicans.

Campus: Situated on a 150-acre campus in middle Tennessee, Webb is just 50 miles southeast of Nashville. Our size, close knit community, and picturesque surroundings make Webb an ideal place to learn and grow.

The Webb campus facilities are a mixture of original and modern buildings, laid out across 150 acres of beautiful farmland in the middle-Tennessee hills. With many significant buildings completed within the last fifteen years, the campus is fully equipped as a state-of-the-art center of secondary education, and provides many amentities for the school's boarding and day students. The facilities encourage an open environment for Webb's students to congregate, socialize and learn from their teachers and from one another. The William Bond Library, completed in 1993, houses over 25,000 volumes and is open to the students until 9:30 nightly.

Cooper-Ferris, one of the girls' dormitories, houses up to twenty 10th through 12th grade girls. The "Big Room" is the main humanities building on campus. It also houses our academic and college counseling offices. Our student center is a place to relax in between classes, use the school store, or hang out with friends. The Junior Room is the oldest building on campus. Built in 1886, the Junior Room served as the original classroom building for Webb at its present location. This structure now serves as a museum and is one of three buildings on campus listed on the national register of historic places.

Dormitories: The residential program at Webb offers students wonderful opportunities to join a closely knitted community of approximately 100 students and adults on campus. Getting students involved in dorm life is crucial to making them feel at home. From family dinners on Monday nights to bowling on the weekends, activities within each dorm and between the dorms create a strong sense of community. Both girls' dorms and the older boys' dorm have suitemate designs (two rooms share a bathroom), and the 7th-9th grade boys' dorm has hall baths. Each dorm has faculty members who support students in the dorm throughout the week. Each dorm has at least one commons room that provides students with a computer and internet access, has a TV, VCR, and snack machines. All students are allowed to have telephones and computers in their room. Each dorm has kitchen and laundry facilities for the students.

Nearest International Airport: Nashville International Airport, Tennessee.

The Webb Schools

Location: Claremont, California (U.S. West Coast, Southern California)

1175 West Baseline Road, Claremont, CA 91711
Phone: 909-482-5214; Fax: 909-621-4582
Website: www.webb.org; Email: lmarshall@webb.org

Mr. Leo Marshall, Director of Admission and Financial Aid
Phone: 909-482-5214; Fax: 909-621-4582
Email: lmarshall@webb.org

Mission Statement: The mission of Webb School of California and Vivian Webb School is to provide a superior academic, athletic, and residential experience within the unique context of a coordinate school structure. The Webb Schools offer the full benefit of living and learning in a diverse and supportive community. The principles and traditions of honor and leadership upon which the schools were founded are reinforced through a climate of mutual trust, responsible and caring behavior, service to the school and the community, support of personal development and self-worth, and a strong appreciation of the common good.

Admission Requirements for International Students: Webb considers students who are not U.S. citizens and whose parents' primary address is outside the United States to be international students. Webb reserves the right to determine a student's residence status.

All students applying to The Webb Schools must take the SSAT (Secondary School Admission Test). Webb does not accept TOEFL or SLEP test scores in place of the SSAT. Webb does not admit students midterm nor for their senior year. English proficiency is crucial for successful study at The Webb Schools. The school does not offer a formal program in English as a second language. Candidates must have a minimum of three years' study at a school where English is the primary language used for all instruction. International students are required to submit all official grade reports from the previous three years in school including the first term of the admission year. When the school records are in a language other than English, students must also submit certified translations of their records in addition to the original report. An interview and campus visit is required for all students applying to Webb. Interviews and tours are conducted Tuesday through Friday. Please call the Admission Office at (909) 482.5214 to schedule a visit or email us at admissions@webb.org. Candidates who do not meet the minimum qualification requirements listed above will not be interviewed.

International students must have a family contact or an adult family member who is known to the student in the continental United States who will be responsible for the student during vacations or in the event of an emergency or illness.

Grade Level: Boarding Grades: 9-12 (Day: 9-12)

Student Gender: Boys & Girls.

Enrollment: 367 students, 197 boys, 170 girls, 241 boarders, 126 day.

International Students: Current students come from 12 countries including Belize, China, East Timor, Hong Kong, Indonesia, Korea, Nigeria, Saudi Arabia, South Africa, South Korea, Taiwan, and Thailand.

Accredited by: WASC

Head of School: Susan A. Nelson

Faculty: The Webb Schools have a faculty of 53 instructors, 40 of whom hold advanced degrees, and 38 reside on campus.

Tuition: Tuition and Boarding for 2003-2004 is $23,605.

Class Size: 15 students with a Student/Faculty ratio of 7:1.

Curriculum: The Webb School curriculum includes Algebra, American history, American literature, art, biology, calculus, chemistry, chorus, computer math, computer science, discrete math, drama, English, English literature, environmental science, European history, fine arts, French, geometry, government/civics, history, leadership skills, literature, museum science, music, orchestra, paleontology, physical education, physical science, physics, poetry, pre-calculus, SAT preparation, science, social studies, Spanish, speech, technology, theater, trigonometry, world history, writing, and yearbook.

Advanced Placement: Advanced Placement courses are offered in Art History, Biology, Calculus, Chemistry, Composition, Economics, English Language, Composition and Literature, Modern European History, French Language and Literature, Music Theory, Physics, Spanish Literature and Language, Studio Art, U. S. History and World History.

ESL Program: The Webb School does not offer an ESL program.

Average SAT Scores of Graduating Students: Mean SAT verbal: 620, mean SAT math: 690, mean combined SAT: 1310. 73% scored over 600 on SAT verbal, 87% scored over 600 on SAT math, 81% scored over 1200 on combined SAT.

College Placement: Recent graduates of The Webb Schools were accepted at colleges such as Harvard University; Johns Hopkins University; Northwestern University; Stanford University; University of California, Berkeley; University of Pennsylvania. .

Academic Requirements: Our graduation requirements follow the admission requirements for the University of California system. All students are expected to graduate with 4 years in every core subject.

Sports: We believe that students who develop an interest in sports, teamwork and the outdoors when they are young live healthier, more satisfying lives. Webb has extensive athletic facilities including: Les Perry Gymnasium, which includes basketball and volleyball courts, wrestling facilities, a weight room, trainer's facilities, locker and equipment rooms and three outdoor basketball courts; the Sutro Aquatics Center, a 25-yard pool used for both competition (water polo, swimming and diving) and recreation; Chandler Field for varsity soccer and baseball; six tennis courts; a football field; running track. Additional facilities include a J.V. baseball diamond, a softball diamond, a cross country course and two more soccer fields.

Opportunity for athletic competition for boys and girls is broad. The schools field 40 teams, in 13 sports, competing in over 450 contests each year. Both schools are members of the Prep League of the California Interscholastic Federation. Teams recently qualifying for CIF post season competition include football, girls cross-country, boys and girls tennis, boys water polo, wrestling, boys soccer, girls basketball, baseball and softball. Individual students have also participated in post season competition in track and field, swimming and diving.

Extracurricular Activities: At The Webb Schools, there are over 20 different clubs. Each one is run by students with a faculty advisor. Extracurricular activities include Amnesty International, Art Club, Astronomy, Billiards, Christian Club, Climbing Club, Culinary Club, Debate Club, French Club, Future Business, Gaming, Golf Club, International, Jazz/Music, Key Club, KWEB, Model United Nations, Outside the Box, Photography, Raquetball, Sage, Ski/Snowboarding, Surf Club, Technology, Tennis Club, Triathlon, W.E.A.P., Weight-lifting, and the El Espejo Yearbook.

Weekend activities include pro sports such as Major league baseball (Dodgers and Angels), NBA basketball (Lakers and Clippers), NHL hockey (Mighty Ducks and Kings), Soccer (Galaxy), USC and UCLA Sports. Outdoors activities including Hiking, rock climbing, horse-back riding and camping trips throughout Southern California, surfing, skiing snowboarding, kayaking, ice skating and roller skating. Amusement Parks such as Disneyland, Magic Mountain, Universal Studios, Raging Waters, Knott's Berry Farm. Campus events such as concerts, fairs and festivals, on-campus dances. Golf trips to Marshall Canyon and Claremont. Museum Trips to Norton Simon Museum, Getty Center, Huntington Library and Gardens, LA County Museum of Art, Museum of Natural History (IMAX Theater), Museum of Tolerance, Petersen Automotive Museum, Museum of Contemporary Art, La Brea Tar Pits . Shopping and hanging out at Claremont Village, Ontario Mills , Santa Monica Promenade, Universal City Walk, Montclair Plaza, South Coast Plaza, Cabazon Outlets, Westwood, Rodeo Drive and Old Town Pasadena . Theater performances such as Phantom of the Opera, Rent, Chicago, Titanic, Fosse and Riverdance.

Campus: The Webb Schools are located 25 minutes east of Pasadena, one hour from Los Angeles. Three educational entities providing a rigorous academic and supportive residential experience, as well as a superior college preparatory curriculum for grades 9-12. The Webb Schools offer unique opportunities of single gender education within a co-educational environment. The campus is located in the foothills of the Southern California's San Gabriel Mountains in the city of Claremont. Webb School of California Founded in 1922 by Thompson Webb, the school attracts outstanding boys. Vivian Webb School was founded in 1981 to offer the same superior educational opportunities for girls. The Raymond M. Alf Museum of Paleontology, the only accredited paleontology museum located on a secondary school campus in North America and serving an integral part of the schools curriculum.

Dormitories: The Webb Schools offer our boarding students an idyllic campus environment, significant residential experiences, safety and a "home-away-from-home" habitat to enrich both their bodies and minds while living on campus. With nearly 70% of the students living on campus, The Webb Schools' success is attributed to an amiable family atmosphere, which invites students to partici- pate in school meals, social events, after-school programs and weekend outings. Students can count on comfortable dorms with common rooms,   kitchenette, and laundry facilities. Faculty and senior students supervise the dorms. There are sign-in and sign-out procedures and an enforced "lights out" for freshmen and sopho- mores.

Nearest International Airport: Ontario International Airport , Ontario, CA; Los Angeles International Airport; John Wayne International Airport, Orange County.

Nearby Lodgings: Sheraton Ontario Airport, 909-937-8000; Marriott Ontario Airport, 909-975.5000; Doubletree Ontario Airport, 909-937-0900.

Wilbraham & Monson Academy

Location: Willbraham, Massachusetts (U.S. East Coast, New England)

423 Main Street, Wilbraham, MA 01095
Phone: 413-596-6811; Fax: 413-599-1749
Website: WMAcademy.org; Email: admissions@wmanet.org

Mr. Christopher Moore, Director of Admission and Financial Aid
Phone: 413-596-6811 ext. 109; Fax: 413-599-1749
Email: cmoore@wmanet.org

Mission Statement: Wilbraham & Monson Academy is an independent coeducational college preparatory middle and upper school for boarding and day students. Students and teachers from throughout the United States and around the world live and learn in a caring and supportive community, enriched by its 200-year heritage of inclusion.

Our primary goals are to promote broad intellectual development, good physical health, personal accountability, mutual respect, and commitment to service. Each student is encouraged to meet the highest standards of intellectual and personal responsibility in preparation for the challenges of higher education and for success as a contributing participant in an interdependent world.

Wilbraham & Monson Academy's goal is to instill in our diverse community self-awareness, mutual respect, and personal responsibility. We prepare our students to accept the challenges of higher education and to be concerned and contributing participants in the world community. We cultivate pride and excellence through a commitment to the following Seven Tenets:

Professional development - Faculty and staff take responsibility for their growth and development by becoming proficient in implementing the school program.

Communication curriculum - Community members develop and apply the skills necessary for effective speaking, writing and listening in every aspect of school life.

Collaborative approach - Community members utilize cooperative and group methods as essential elements of the teaching and learning process.

In-depth program - Our program promotes rigor and intellectual curiosity by emphasizing skills and understanding rather than superficial coverage of content.

Service - Service to others, in organized programs or spontaneous actions, is integral to our community and the development of our social responsibility.

Technology - The community embraces the appropriate use of technology in communication, educational research and administration.

Assessment - Community members take responsibility for the on-going evaluation of individual practices and programs in order to ensure quality and growth.

Grade Level: 9-12.

Student Gender: Boys & Girls.

Enrollment: 351 students, 210 boys, 141 girls, 141 boarders, 210 day.

Accredited by: NEASC

Head of School: Rodney LaBrecque, B.A., M.A., Ph.D. candidate Clark University, Joseph Klingenstein Fellow, Teachers College, Columbia University.

Faculty: Wilbraham-Monson has a faculty of 47 instructors, 25 of whom hold advanced degrees. 80 percent of the faculty members live on campus and act as dorm supervisors and student advisors.

Tuition: Tuition and Boarding for 2003-2004 is $30,950.

Class Size: 12 -16 students, with a student-teacher ratio of 8:1.

Curriculum: Classes at Wilbraham & Monson are small and interactive. Our standards are high yet, we understand that each of you learns in your own way. As teachers, we strive to help you find the tools and the knowledge to enable you to achieve a sense of personal accomplishment. Our approachable faculty help create an environment in which students become well prepared not only for the challenge of higher education, but for life. In partnership with their parents and teachers, students graduate from Wilbraham & Monson Academy with the knowledge, critical thinking skills, and moral framework needed to confront a rapidly changing world and to thrive in it.

Advanced Placement: Advance Placement courses are offered in English, Calculus, United States History, European History, Chemistry, Environmental Science, French, Spanish, Latin, and Music Theory.

ESL Program: When students from other countries and cultures come to the United States, everything is different. A new language, new food, new customs, faces, and places make being a new student even more challenging. At Wilbraham & Monson Academy, however, we know how to help international students feel comfortable in their new home. They come from some 14 countries in Central and South America, Asia, and Europe, and they are welcomed into an environment of inclusion where special events and programs bring international students together, acclimate them into American life, and, most importantly, help them become active and valued members of the WMA community.

At the beginning of the school year, new international students come to Wilbraham & Monson Academy a week early to take part in the International Student Orientation Program. This program entails placement testing in English and math, social activities and events to help students get to know each other and WMA, and an off-campus trip to help students learn about the surrounding area.

Everyone in the WMA community is happy to help international students feel like they belong. The dining service, for example, provides ethnic foods in the dining hall. American roommates become excellent sources of information as well as trusted friends. During Worldfest Week each fall, the Academy celebrates the cultures of the many countries represented by WMA students. A spring trip to Boston introduces international students to the history of a nearby major city. During school vacations, WMA finds host families who welcome international students into their homes for the holidays. International students themselves, those who are not new to the school, produce a handbook with helpful information about school rules, where to go with questions - even common slang expressions - for new international students.

International students are also actively involved in leadership at the Academy. Some students are selected to be prefects, working with dorm parents in the dormitories. Others serve as peer counselors, providing support and encouragement for fellow students. Gold Key, the student organization which works with prospective students and families who visit the campus, attracts many international students. Both formally and informally, international students contribute to the WMA community.

College Placement: Recent graduates of Wilbraham-Monson have been accepted to Bates, Boston College, Bowdoin, Cornell, Fordham, George Washington, Mount Holyoke, Smith, and Trinity.

Academic Requirements: The Academy requires 54 credits for graduation (each full year course is worth 3 credits). Departmental requirements include: 12 credits in English, 9 credits in mathematics including Algebra I, Algebra II, and Geometry, 6 credits in history and social studies including US History, 6 credits in laboratory science including Biology and either Chemistry or Physics, 3 additional credits in either history or science, 6 credits in languages with 2 years of the same language, 5 credits in the Fine and Performing Arts including art and music, 1 credit in Computer Science and demonstrated proficiency in keyboarding.

Sports: Wilbraham-Monson offers varsity programs in baseball, basketball, cross-country, football, golf, lacrosse, riflery, skiing, soccer, softball, swimming, tennis, track and field, volleyball, water polo, and wrestling. Greenhalgh Athletic Center features three basketball/volleyball courts, a fitness center, and Cowdrey Memorial Pool. Outdoor athletic facilities include a football field and practice field, 6 soccer fields, 2 baseball diamonds, a softball field, and 9 tennis courts.

Extracurricular Activities: At the Academy, there is no shortage of extracurricular activities to keep students busy. If they have an interest in writing, we have the weekly student newspaper The Bell, our yearbook The Hill, and our two literary magazines The Rubicon and The Tempest. Community Service allows a student to work in the greater Wilbraham and Springfield communities at nursing homes, day care centers, and soup kitchens as well as working on campus to help the Wilbraham & Monson community. Other activities include Academy Players, Tech Theater, Student Video Organization, and the Intern Program.

Each weekend, the Student Activities Office provides various trips and events for the student body. In addition to the regularly scheduled athletic events on Saturday, we plan school dances, trips to the mall, trips to Boston and New York, coffee houses, trips to the movies, on-campus movies, and trips to various highlights in the area. Lists of the weekend activities are posted outside the Student Activities Office as well as on e-mail and on the Academy Web site. Students sign up for weekend activities beginning Wednesday afternoon at the Student Activities Office in the campus center. Many events and trips take place because of student interest; their suggestions are always welcome and encouraged.

Campus: The Academy is in the center of the town of Wilbraham, located in south-central Massachusetts, seven miles east of Springfield. It occupies 300 acres of what was formerly rich farmland and wooded hillsides. The town itself, incorporated in 1763, is essentially rural, and many residents commute to nearby Springfield and to Hartford, Connecticut. Among the ten area colleges are Smith, Amherst, Hampshire, Springfield, Mount Holyoke and the University of Massachusetts. Students and faculty members take advantage of the cultural events held on those campuses.

There are 5 main academic buildings. The Old Academy has classrooms for English and foreign languages, Fisk Hall contains the school theater and classrooms for mathematics and history. Binney Fine Arts Center houses the art department and includes studios for visual arts, a photography studio, and an art gallery. The Pratt Room in Rich Hall serves music classes. The Mattern Science Center has both classrooms and science laboratories. Gill Memorial Library features 20,000 volumes.

Dormitories: Living away from home is a big step in the life of a student. Many experience it for the first time when they enter college. For high school students who attend boarding school, the experience can be the most significant of their lives. The friendships they make among the students and adults in the residential community frequently last a lifetime. At Wilbraham & Monson Academy, our residential life program is designed to foster a sense of security for students away from home for the first time while guiding them in good decision-making skills. The dorm parents and prefects work hard to make our students feel comfortable in their home away from home. On the weekends there are always on- and off-campus activities to appeal to a variety of tastes, and there is coed visitation under guidelines created by students and dorm staff. There are special social and educational activities in the dormitories like Dorm Olympics and Spa Night. Because nearly 20% of our population are international students, the valuable opportunity of getting to know someone of another culture is a very real one. Many of our students visit friends from the Academy all over the world.

The Academy has 3 dormitories with both single and double rooms, and 5 faculty buildings located on Main Street. Some faculty members and their families live in the dormitories as well. Meals are served in the Lak Dining Hall and there is a snack bar in the campus center. Benton House is the health center, with 3 registered nurses, and a medical doctor on call.

Nearest International Airport: Logan International Airport, Boston.

The Williston Northampton School

Location: Easthampton, Massachusetts (U.S. East Coast, New England)

19 Payson Avenue, Easthampton, MA 01027
Phone: 413-529-3241; Fax: 413-527-9494
Website: www.williston.com; Email: admission@williston.com

Ms. Ann Pickrell, Director of Admission
Phone: 413-529-3241; Fax: 413-527-9494
Email: admission@williston.com

Mission Statement: The Williston Northampton School aspires to be a vigorous community of learners and teachers seeking together the ability and courage for lifelong intellectual and moral growth. We believe the foundation for college success and global citizenry is centered in the art of instruction and in the excitement and adventure of discovery.

Our school is structured to create an environment of academic rigor. Our traditional curriculum and interactive classrooms challenge us to think skeptically, to grasp complexity, and to originate, test, and communicate ideas with skill and self-confidence.

To explore life's inclusiveness, we welcome a diversity of personalities, talent, and experience onto our campus. Our mutual respect and caring allow us to address differences as we live, work, and belong together.

Believing that we are wholly educated only when the mind, body, and artistic spirit are equally exercised, we celebrate the expression of our creative natures through music, dance, drama, and the fine arts. We are invested in the discipline and the exhilaration of athletic competition and the friendships derived through teamwork.

Above all in our community we honor character and our individual quests for integrity, accomplishment, and purpose.

Admission Requirements for International Students: English as a Second Language students who succeed at Williston Northampton have been good students in their first language and active participants in school activities in their home countries. Traditionally, they have been considered storong and proficient in th study of English in theiru home schools TOEFL scores of about 425-450 are typically the minimum a student needs to be successful in Williston Northampton's college preparatory curriculum.

Grade Level: 9-12.

Student Gender: Boys & Girls.

Enrollment: 240 boys, 220 girls, 280 boarders, 180 day.

International Students:students come from 22 different countries.

Accredited by: NEASC

Head of School: Brian R. Wright, B.A. Occidental College,M. A. and Ph.D. Politics, Princeton University.

Faculty: There are 114 faculty members, 69 of whom have advanced degrees. 30 faculty members reside on campus. Faculty members also act as student advisors.

Tuition: Tuition and Boarding for 2003-2004 is $22,000.

Average Class Size: 12 students.

Curriculum: When Samuel Williston founded this school in 1841, most people agreed on the definition of a good education, but in an age of rapid technological change and interdependent global economies, no single body of knowledge can define a "good educa-tion" for all. Today, at Williston, we look to the best of the past for guidance as we evaluate what of the present is both worthy and likely to be of lasting value. By reading Euripides in translation, studying and performing Shakespearean drama, and learning about the arts of the Renaissance, Williston students confront age-old questions about human nature and the elements and standards of beauty. Our students still study geometry, but they manipulate math-ematical models on the computer screen and enter questions into graphing calculators. In science classes they spend less time washing glassware and more time analyzing data gathered by means of tech-nology. While methods of teaching writing have changed, Williston requires a great deal of writing practice, and all classes emphasize mastery of language, clarity of thought and academic integrity. Our curriculum is designed to help young men and women develop thinking and writing skills and the capacity to grapple with intellectually complex problems throughout a lifetime. One of the hallmarks of a Williston education is the development of habits of mind and intellectual integrity that gives our graduates confidence in their ability to learn and to contribute to the common good throughout a lifetime.

Advanced Placement: Advance Placement courses are available in U.S. History, Calculus, Chemistry, Biology, French, Spanish, and Latin.

ESL Program: Williston offers two levels of ESL: Intermediate English as a Second Language First course: First level intermediate ESL is designed to improve overall command of the English language with emphasis on verbal fluency and reading and writing skills, especially as they pertain to academic work. The study of grammar is a major component of the course in order to build a good foundation for the work in the second level of intermediate ESL.

Advanced English as a Second Language Second course: Students who have successfully completed the first course in ESL or who demonstrate enough verbal proficiency and knowledge of English grammar to do the work enroll in this course.

Improving specific reading skills, learning and using effectively a process approach to composition over a variety of rhetorical modes, speaking formally and informally, and studying grammar with an eye toward success on the TOEFL are the major components of this course. Academic skills, such as writing the research paper and note taking from lectures, are also emphasized.

College Placement: Recent graduates of Williston have been accepted to Babson, Boston College, Boston University, Brown, Cornell, Dickinson, Hamilton, Hobart and William Smith, Ithaca, Lafayette, Lehigh, Middlebury, Rollins, Skidmore, St. Michael's, Trinity, Vanderbilt, Wesleyan, and the Universities of Denver,

Massachusetts Amherst and Dartmouth, and New Hampshire.

Academic Requirements: In order to receive a Williston Northampton diploma, a student must complete 19 academic credits in grades 9 through 12. A full-year course receives 1 credit and a semester course 1/2 credit. The 19 credits must include: English Language and Literature 4 credits.

Each student must be enrolled in an English course during every semester of attendance at Williston Northampton. Mathematics 3 credits. This must include Algebra I, Geometry, and Algebra II; most students take a fourth year. Science 2 credits. One science credit must include chemistry or biology and one credit must be taken at the 11th- or 12th-grade level; many colleges require a third year of science. Foreign Language 2 sequential credits. The student must complete at least two credits in one language; most students take at least a third year. History/Social Sciences 2 credits. One credit must be taken in U.S. History; many colleges require a third year. It is expected that three- and four-year students take Global Studies in the 9th or 10th grade. Religious and Philosophical Studies 1/2 credit. Two-, three-, and four-year students must complete 1/2 credit. One-year seniors are strongly encourage to complete a semester course. Fine Arts 1 credit. Two-, three-, and four-year students must complete one credit. Students are urged to select from offerings both in these studio and performances courses, as well as in the humanities courses.

Sports: Athletics at Williston are an integral part of our education and community. Our school has always taken great pride in its ability to be both highly competitive and inclusive. For the serious athlete, Williston's outstanding facilities, excellent coaching staff, and strong commitment to its competitive program provide a wonderful opportunity for students to compete at the highest levels of New England prep school sports.

For those students less inclined to compete at this level, the diversity and breadth of our program's offerings provide a wide range of opportunities to participate on a lower level team or to enjoy a recreational instructional experience. Girls interscholastic teams include cross-country, field hockey, soccer, and volleyball in the fall;

basketball, ice hockey, skiing, squash, swimming and diving, and wrestling in the winter; and golf, lacrosse, softball, tennis, track, and water polo in the spring. Boys interscholastic teams include cross-country, football, soccer, or water polo; basketball, ice hockey, skiing, squash, swimming and diving, or wrestling; and baseball, golf, lacrosse, tennis, or track. Horseback riding, modern, fitness training, aerobics, and volleyball are also offered.

Williston's athletic facilities include an athletic center with 2 basketball courts, a six-lane pool, 5 squash courts, a weight room, fitness center, wrestling room, a dance studio, an indoor skating rink, 15 tennis courts, a running track, 30 acres of playing fields, and a cross-country course, and several nearby golf courses.

Extracurricular Activities: At the beginning of the school year an activity fair allows students to see all the extracurricular offerings at once and to talk to the advisors for each organization. Environmental activists, creative writers, graphic designers, musicians and more find like-minded people and this creates an atmosphre of productive involvement. Our most successful students are those who get involved in the life of the school and the surrounding community. Activities include Amnesty International, Arete (senior tutors), As Schools Match Wits Team, Bridge Club, Caterwaulers, Chamber Music, French Club, Gay/Straight Alliance, Gold Key, Janus (literary magazine), Jazz Band, Log (Year Book), Peer Educators, S.A.D.D., Student Council, Ultimate Frisbee, Widdigers, Williston Outing Club, Theater Ensemble, and the Willistonian (student newspaper).

The surrounding area offers hiking, climbing, biking, and skiing opportunities. The cities of Northampton and Springfield, Massachusetts, and Hartford, Connecticut, along with five nearby colleges provide opportunities for cultural events, museums, libraries, and theater performances. Students take off-campus trips for college and professional sports, films, concerts, plays, and skiing. On-campus activities include dances, coffeehouse entertainment, talent shows, lectures, and films.

Campus: Williston is located 85 miles west of Boston, and 150 miles north of New York, on 100 acres in the Pioneer Valley, surrounded by the University of Massachusetts, and the colleges of Smith, Mount Holyoke, Hampshire, and Amherst. The school's academic facilities feature 38 buildings, including the Headmaster's home, the administration buildings, the dining hall, six dormitories Reed Campus Center, the Science Building, the Technology and Student Publications Center, the theater, the Schoolhouse, the library, the chapel, and the Middle School building.

Dormitories: Williston has 6 dormitories that accommodate up to 50 students, 5 residence houses that accommodate up to 12 students, and several faculty homes. Each dormitory is staffed by resident faculty supervisors, and, all dorm rooms are networked to the campus server.

Nearest International Airport: Logan International Airport, Boston.

Nearby Lodgings: Country Inn and Suites, 413-533-2100; Best Western Northampton, 413-586-1500; Hotel Northampton, 413-584-3100; The Inn at Northampton, 413-586-1211; Holiday Inn, 413-534-3311; Hilton Garden Inn, 413-886-8000.

The Winchendon School

Location: Winchendon, Massachusetts (U.S. East Coast, New England)

172 Ash Street, Winchendon, MA 01475
Phone: 978-297-1223; Fax: 978-297-0911
Website: www.winchendon.org; Email: admissions@winchendon.org

Mr. Richard Plank, Director of Admission
Phone: 978-297-4476; Fax: 978-297-0911
Email: admissions@winchendon.org

Mission Statement: The Winchendon philosophy is that most young people can succeed when surrounded by an atmosphere of caring attention to their individual needs. To that end, the school offers academic programs that are closely tailored to each student's strengths and weaknesses in a traditional environment designed to encourage moral and spiritual growth. Small classes, a personalized approach, and flexible guidance and support systems are intended to stimulate an interest in learning and to teach students that they themselves are the most valuable contributors to their own education.

Admission Requirements for International Students: There are no particular testing requirements. We can work with students with all levels of English proficiency – beginning, intermediate and advanced. After we receive the completed application, we send an Enrollment Contract. When we receive the signed Enrollment Contract, we send the I-20.

Grade Level: 8-12 + Postgraduate.

Student Gender: Boys & Girls.

Enrollment: 200 students, 155 boys, 45 girls, 185 boarders, 15 day.

International Students: 45, from 18 different countries including: Australia, Canada, China, Germany, Great Britain, Hong Kong, Japan, Macau, Mexico, Poland, South Africa, South Korea, Switzerland, Taiwan, and Thailand.

Accredited by: NEASC

Head of School: J. William LaBelle, University of Massachusetts (B.S. 1958; M.S. 1968), Massachusetts State College (M.Ed. 1967).

Faculty: Winchendon has 32 full-time faculty and administrators who teach. Of these many live at the school with their families. Faculty members hold baccalaureate and advanced degrees from Allegheny, Assumption, Bates, Boston University, Brown, Colby, Colgate, College of the Holy Cross, Dartmouth, Franklin and Marshall, Hamilton, Harvard, Merrimac, Penn State, Union, and the Universities of California (Berkeley), Massachusetts, New Hampshire, and Vermont. The school infirmary is staffed by 2 full-time nurses, and other staff members are certified in first aid and athletics training. A school physician is on call. Hospitals and emergency rooms are nearby. The faculty is active in all aspects of student life. Many faculty members live in the dormitories with the students, while others monitor evening study halls and work on weekend faculty teams. All members of the faculty are available on a daily basis during Conference Period to provide "extra help" to any student who seeks it.

The Administrative Team of the school includes the Headmaster, the Academic Dean, the Director of External Affairs, the Dean of the Faculty, the Director of Admissions, the Director of Athletics and the Dean of Students. Collectively, these administrators bring a wealth of experience in independent education to the school. The faculty is in written communication with all parents once each week during the academic year. They also serve as advisors to the students enrolled at the school.

Tuition: Tuition and Boarding for 2004-2005 is $32,250.

Class Size: 6 students, with a student/teacher ratio of 5:1.

Curriculum: The Winchendon approach to education is based on highly personalized attention to each student. An academic schedule is created for each student, based on test scores, previous grades, and teacher recommendations. Placement in courses is determined by student need rather than grade level; most students take five courses per term. Faculty-supervised study halls are held in the evening, with an additional conference period scheduled daily to allow for individual consultation between teachers and students. To help students monitor their progress, grade slips are issued daily in all classes and are reviewed with dorm parents during the evening study period. Parents are also sent grades and comments once a week by their child's teachers. Winchendon offers remediation in mathematics, writing, and reading to help students with specific learning disabilities.

Advanced Placement: English, Calculus I & II, Biology, U. S. History, Physics, Economics.

ESL Program: Winchendon offers English as a Second Language, focusing on reading, writing, and oral communications at beginning, intermediate, and advanced levels. Courses in other disciplines and preparation for the Test of English as a Foreign Language are designed to help international students strengthen academic skills and assist their adjustment to American life and customs.

Average SAT Scores of Graduating Students: Verbal 500, Math 570.

College Placement: Recent graduates of Winchendon have been accepted to Bentley, Boston University, Butler, Clark, Clarkson, Colby, Connecticut College, Curry, George Washington, Gettysburg, Hamilton, Harvard, Hobart, Hofstra, Johnson & Wales, Northeastern, Notre Dame, Parsons School of Design, Providence, RIT, Rutgers, Seton Hall, St. Lawrence, St. John's, Syracuse, Temple, Tufts, West Point, Wheaton, Worcester Polytechnic, and the Universities of Maine, Massachusetts, New Hampshire, and Vermont.

Academic Requirements: To graduate, students must successfully complete four years of English, four of mathematics, three of social science (including United States History), and two years of science. The study of a foreign language is encouraged, but not required. Among the required and elective courses offered are English I - IV, English as a Foreign Language; Latin I - III, French I - IV, Spanish I - IV, History, Political Science, American Culture, Psychology, Economics; Algebra II, Trigonometry, Calculus; Physics, Advanced

Biology, Chemistry; Music Appreciation; Art History, Graphic Arts, Photography; and Computer Programming, Word Processing, and Typing.

Sports: Because Winchendon believes that a carefully crafted athletic program can complement and enhance students' growth in other areas, participation in athletic activities is required for each season. Varsity Athletics include volleyball, soccer, basketball, lacrosse, ice hockey, wrestling, baseball; and co-educational golf, tennis, cross-country running, snowboarding, and skiing. Both boys and girls participate in intramural and recreational athletics.

Extracurricular Activities: Students publish a yearbook, newspaper, and literary magazine. They may also join special-interest groups such as the Photography and Outing clubs. Performing arts activities in instrumental and choral music, theater, and dance are also offered. School-sponsored weekend trips to Boston and Worcester allow students access to the cultural and recreational resources there. Closer to home, the school's location in the foothills of the Monadnock Mountains provides excellent nearby skiing and ice skating. Other local entertainment includes movies, bowling, and activities at colleges in the area. With parental permission, students may spend the weekend off campus.

Campus: Winchendon's 236 acres include such outdoor facilities as a swimming pool; tennis courts; an 18-hole golf course; cross-country ski trails; and baseball, lacrosse, and soccer fields. The Winchendon School Country Club is a golf course open to students, faculty, Winchendon residents and guests. It is a Donald Ross designed course (1926) that has received wonderful reviews in newspapers and athletic publications. It winds through the beautiful New England countryside and offers challenges to all who play the sport. The school recently completed a $4 million dollar renovation and construction project which has provided enhanced facilities for student life. The school is situated on a hill overlooking the Town of Winchendon and with a spectacular view of the "most climbed mountain in the world", Mount Monadnock.

Three academic buildings house science laboratories, a 10,000-volume library, and classrooms specially designed for the school's small classes. Ford Hall contains administrative offices, classrooms, a dormitory, the infirmary, and the dining hall.

Other facilities include an art building, a performing arts building, seven dormitories, a gymnasium, a student union, faculty residences, a golf pro shop with locker rooms, and the headmaster's residence.

The Winchendon School has made a large investment in technology. The school is dedicated to being in the forefront of computer capability within the northeast independent school world. The most recent improvement to this system was the introduction of totally wireless technology throughout the campus. In addition, all new computers were ordered and delivered for the Computer Center at the school, including machines with excellent graphing capability, in March of 2001.

Dormitories: Ford Hall, which was once a resort hotel, contains administrative offices, student lounges, a dining hall, faculty apartments, and student dorm rooms. Merrell Hall is a boys' dormitory, which features a student lounge and two faculty apartments. Student rooms are available in both singles and doubles.

Nearest International Airport: Logan International Airport, Boston.

Nearby Lodgings: Colonial Bed and Breakfast Hotel, 978-630-2500; Royal Plaza Hotel, 978- 342-7100; Wachusett Village Inn, 978-874-5351.

Schools by Region

East Coast New England

Avon Old Farms
Bement
Cambridge
Canterbury
Chapel Hill
Cheshire
Emma Willard
Fay
Gould
Governor Dummer
Gow
Greenwood
Hackley
High Mowing
Hillside
Houghton
Indian Mountain
Kents Hill
Kildonan
Lawrence
Linden Hill
Maine Central
Marianapolis
Marvelwood
Middlesex
Millbrook
Miss Hall's
Miss Porter's
Oakwood Friends

Perkiomen
Phillips Andover
St. Andrews
St. Johnsbury
Stoneleigh-Burnham
Storm King
Tabor
Washington Academy
Wilbraham & Monson
Williston
Winchendon

East Coast Mid-Atlantic

Asheville
Ben Lippen
Chatham
Christ School
Episcopal High
Foxcroft
Hargrave
Madeira
St. Timothy's
Virginia Episcopal

Central

Brehm
Chaminade
Crested Butte
Grand River
La Lumiere
Maur Hill
Southwestern
Wasatch Academy

Southern

Indian Springs
Rabun Gap
St. Stanislaus
Vanguard
Webb

West Coast

Cate
Dunn
Happy Valley
Idyllwild
Northwest
Oak Grove
Ojai Valley
Stevenson
Subiaco
Thatcher
Webb Schools

Schools by Gender

Co-Educational

Asheville
Bement
Ben Lippen
Brehm
Buxton
Cambridge
Canterbury
Cate
Chapel Hill
Cheshire
Crested Butte
Dunn
Episcopal High
Fay
Gould
Governor Dummer
Hackley
Happy Valley
Hargrave
High Mowing
Houghton
Idyllwild
Indian Mountain
Indian Springs
Kents Hill
Kildonan
La Lumiere
Lawrence
Maine Central

Marianapolis
Marvelwood
Maur Hill
Middlesex
Millbrook
Northwest
Oak Grove
Oakwood Friends
Ojai Valley
Perkiomen
Phillips Andover
Rabun Gap
Southwestern
St. Andrews
St. Johnsbury
Stevenson
Storm King
Tabor
Thatcher
Vanguard
Virginia Episcopal
Wasatch Academy
Washington Academy
Webb
Webb Schools
Wilbraham & Monson
Williston
Winchendon

Boys Only

Avon Old Farms
Chaminade
Christ School
Gow

Grand River
Greenwood
Hillside
Linden Hill
St. Stanislaus
Subiaco

Girls Only

Chatham
Emma Willard
Foxcroft
Madeira
Miss Hall's
Miss Porter's
St. Timothy's
Stoneleigh-Burnham

Schools by Grade Level

High School

Asheville
Avon Old Farms
Ben Lippen
Buxton
Cambridge
Canterbury
Cate
Chapel Hill
Chatham
Cheshire
Crested Butte
Dunn
Emma Willard
Episcopal High
Foxcroft
Gould
Governor Dummer
Grand River
Hackley
Happy Valley
High Mowing
Houghton
Indian Springs
Kents Hill
La Lumiere
Lawrence
Madeira
Maine Central
Marianapolis
Marvelwood